THE AFRICAN AMERICAN MALE, WRITING, AND DIFFERENCE

THE AFRICAN AMERICAN MALE, WRITING, AND DIFFERENCE

A Polycentric Approach to African American Literature, Criticism, and History

W. LAWRENCE HOGUE

STATE UNIVERSITY OF NEW YORK PRESS

Published by
STATE UNIVERSITY OF NEW YORK PRESS
ALBANY

For information, address
State University of New York Press
90 State Street, Suite 700, Albany, NY 12207

Production, Laurie Searl
Marketing, Fran Keneston

Library of Congress Cataloging-in-Publication Data

Hogue, W. Lawrence, (date)
  The African American male, writing and difference : a polycentric
approach to African American literature, criticism, and history /
W. Lawrence Hogue.
    p. cm.
  Includes bibliographical references and index.
  ISBN 0-7914-5693-5 (alk. paper)—ISBN 0-7914-5694-3 (pbk. : alk. paper)
    1. American literature—African American authors—History and criticism.
2. American literature—Male authors—History and criticism.   3. African
American men—Intellectual life.   4. Difference (Psychology) in literature.
5. African American men in literature.   I. Title.

PS153.N5 H59 2003
810.9'9286'08996073—dc21   2002075873

10   9   8   7   6   5   4   3   2   1

To the memory and Spirit of my sister,
Lola Hogue Thomas

CONTENTS

PREFACE

The narrative of the African American sociopolitical mission of racial uplift and its subsequent mainstream American support are dominant in the lives of African Americans, especially the middle class. The narrative advocates certain mainstream values such as middle-class respectability, the Enlightenment idea of progress, the Protestant work ethic, a certain purity in values, patriarchal political culture, and patriarchal gender conventions. In striving for these values and ideas, the black middle class hopes to show how African Americans can practice these values and thereby prove to white people their worthiness of respect and social equality. According to the racial uplift mission, when one African American proves that he can speak and dress, be intelligent, and show intelligence, culture, and education in ways sanctioned and respected by the dominant society, he brings honor, respectability, and pride to the race. The writing of one's autobiography is the best way that a successful African American can demonstrate his achievements. The hope is that white people will accept him.

At this stage in my life and career, I am told by the racial uplift narrative that I should write my memoir. I have graduate degrees from some of the United States' most prestigious universities. I have published two major critical texts, and I am a tenured, full professor at an urban Research 1 university. Because I am successful, argues the narrative of racial uplift, I should tell my story to show how I succeeded and to prove to white Americans, again, how another African American has become successful by their standards and criteria. Then, hopefully, they will accept/validate me and eventually all African Americans as worthy of social equality.

But writing my memoir seems inapproporiate for me for a number of reasons. First, I am still very young, and my life and career still feel as though they are on the ascent. Second, by my own philosophical and cultural standards, my life is rather uneventful. I have taken a rather traditional approach to life, only taking risks and pushing boundaries within the accepted norms. But third and more important, in the last ten years I have developed some serious issues with the racial uplift narrative, especially its objective of constructing a monolithic representation of African America, thereby repressing and subordinating African America's polyvalent nature. I have profound problems with the narrative's inability or refusal to engage issues of class and difference within African American communities. It covers over the African American as the Same as the middle class white American norm.

IX

Therefore, rather than write another black autobiography, one of the staples of the canon of African American literature, that chronicles yet another African American's particular successes and achievements, and therefore, reinforces the status quo, I have decided to break with tradition and the narrative of racial uplift and write a critical book discussing the white/black binary and how the African American middle class and the sociopolitical mission of racial uplift have colonized African American life, literature, criticism, and history. I want to present a more inclusive representation of African America. In *The African American Male, Writing, and Difference*, I use African American male writers of the twentieth century to explore the issues of class, gender, devalued otherness, victimization, and difference, and to celebrate the polyvalent nature of African American literature, criticism, and history.

Until recently, but still quite prevalent today, mainstream American social reality was/is defined by the white/black binary of signification that defines whites as normative and superior, and that represents blacks as inferior, as a victim, as devalued Other, or, more recently, as the Same. The narrative of the sociopolitical mission of racial uplift reinforces this binary system and the representation of the African American as a victim. To reconfigure the African American as a non-victim, as a subject with agency who is different but equal, I examine historically from whence this binary comes. My research led me to the European Renaissance and to the rise of European colonialism, modernity, and capital. Then, I deconstruct/disrupt the binary.

Using postcolonial theory, I examine the manifestation of the white/black binary on African American literature, criticism, and history. I scrutinize closely the mission of racial uplift, particularly its literary arm, the canon of African American literature, and its version of American/African American history, showing how this mission actually reproduces the white/black binary in the canon of African American literature, African American history, and African American inferiority/victimization. *The African American Male* shows how, prior to the 1970s, African American literary scholars praised and sanctioned those literary texts that could generate or reinforce the values of the racial uplift narrative and ignored and repressed those African American literary traditions, genres, and texts that did not.

Delineating how mainstream African American political and educational institutions, apparatuses, and organizations such as the National Urban League, the National Association for the Advancement of Colored People (NAACP), the National Council of Negro Women, and black newspapers focus *only* on racial oppression and the achievements and successes of middle-class blacks, the book exposes how this racial uplift narrative and mainstream American society assume that other/different non-middle-class, non-Christian, non-Freudian, and/or non-Protestant-work-ethic blacks—who could be Voodoo practitioners, hobos, blues men, jazz men, the African American subaltern, existentialists, or postmodernists—have no value culturally, socially, intellectually, or otherwise.

Taking a polycentric approach, *The African American Male* examines how, in assuming that African America constitutes a monolithic group, the middle class fails to engage the issues of class, otherization, victimization, and difference within African American communities, literature, criticism, and history. In defining African America cosmologically, religiously, and culturally in terms of the Same, the black middle class covers over its differences—thereby ignoring the fact that other African American lifestyles, traditions, and theoretical concepts of life and existence have their own logic and distinction.

In deconstructing the racial uplift narrative, in exposing how it is reinforced by the mainstream American society, and in using the concept of polycentrism to discuss the different African American traditions and theoretical concepts of life *equally*, I present a vision of African American life, literature, criticism, and history that displays their hybridity, heterogeneity, and variety. Polycentrically selecting those African American male literary texts that draw on non-normative African American and normative American and Western belief systems and theoretical concepts of life and history, the book deconstructs and de-territorializes the white/black binary that defines the African American as Other than reason and reconstitutes and re-territorializes those social, historical, and literary spaces where African American differences are privileged, where the positionality/representation of the African American is changed from Other-as-object, and thus as less, to Other-as-subject, where he as Other is equal but different. I use the polyvalent nature of African American literature, criticism, and history as a way of showing the limitations of a singular, totalized approach to this literature, criticism, and history.

The research and writing of this book have benefited from many sources. First, I want to thank the Office of the President at the University of Houston for a President's Research and Scholarship Fund Award (PRSF) for the 1992-1993 academic year and the Office of Sponsored Programs at the University of Houston for a Limited Grant in Aid (LGIA) Award for the Summer of 1996, both of which allowed me to hire a research assistant.

Second, I want to thank Frances Gonzales and Margaret Dunn, who worked diligently through the Interlibrary Loan Department at the Anderson Library at the University of Houston to procure for me articles and books not carried by the library. I also want to thank two very smart and capable research assistants: Mark Damon Puckett, who served as my research assistant during the 1992-1993 academic year, for being thorough and meticulous in his research and for being as enthusiastic about this project as I was; and Shelly Withrow, who was my research assistant during the summer of 1996, for her wonderful organizational skills and her devotion to the project. I want to thank Professors Jerrilyn McGregor and Darryl Dickson-Carr and the English Department Colloquium at Florida State University who allowed me the first opportunity to present publicly the ideas for this book. I also want to thank members of the English departments at the Universities of Oregon and Georgia for early critical responses to the ideas of the book.

I want to thank the African American Studies Program and its Directors (Professors Linda Reed and Janis Hutchinson) at the University of Houston for providing financial support for editing and obtaining permissions. Thank you to my colleague Ann Christensen who loaned me her ear and expertise when I began asking questions about the *other* European Renaissance. I particularly want to thank Quetzil Castañeda, a dear friend, who is always available to give me the anthropological approach/angle on an issue or subject. I want to thank Polly Kock for an excellent job in editing the manuscript at an early stage, and Sabrina Hassumani, a former student and dear friend, who read the manuscript and offered invaluable comments and suggestions. I want to thank my everyday social and/or intellectual friends—Anthony Harris, Claudette Clay, Clarence Hulett, Annette Murrell, Jane Davis, A. Yemisi Jimoh, Doctor Raj, Richard Hobson, William Taylor, Dibas Chandra, Victor Clark, and Patricia Hill— whom I talk to frequently and sometimes infrequently on the telephone, at dinner, or during visits, for giving me the freedom to talk openly about my ideas, and for listening (and talking back to me) as I worked through the ideas in this book. They have all come to accept the fact that when we talk we inevitably get around to talking about ideas and my current research. Although all of these institutions and individuals made wonderful contributions to this book, I take total responsibility for the outcome. Lastly, I want to note the ease, comfort, and joy I had in working with James Peltz, editor-in-chief, Laurie Searl, Senior Production Editor, and Fran Keneston, Director of Marketing, of SUNY.

Finally, much of this book was written between 1996 and 2000, years when one of my older sisters, Lola Hogue Thomas, was struggling/fighting and eventually succumbing to cancer. Lola, who worshipped and celebrated life, was one of my first instructors of life. She was daring, complex, contradictory, beautiful, adventurous, a risk taker, and very much an individual. She also had a wonderful entrepreneurial spirit. Refusing ever to view herself as a victim or with self pity, in our telephone conversations and visits, she deflected conversations about her illness and remained affirmative and open about life. Until the end, she was engaged intellectually with me about ideas and constantly inquired about the completion of the book. Her life was and is an inspiration for what I want to write and how I want to conduct the affairs of my life. It is to her that I dedicate this book.

June 2002
Houston, Texas

ACKNOWLEDGMENTS

The author and publisher gratefully acknowledge permission to use the following materials:

From *Dirty Bird Blues*, by Clarence Major. Copyright 1996 by Mercury House. Reprinted by permission of the publisher.

From *Absolutely Nothing to Get Alarmed About*, by Charles Wright. Copyright 1993 by Charles Wright. Reprinted by permission of HarperCollins Publishers, Inc.

From *The Autobiography of an Ex-Coloured Man*, by James Weldon Johnson. Copyright 1927 by Alfred A. Knopf, Inc. and renewed 1955 by Carl Van Vichten. Reprinted by permission of Alfred A. Knopf, a division of Random House, Inc.

From *A Different Drummer*, by William Melvin Kelley. Copyright 1959, 1962 by William Melvin Kelley. Reprinted by permission of Doubleday, a division of Random House, Inc.

From *A Different Drummer*, by William Melvin Kelley. Copyright 1962 by William Melvin Kelley. Reprinted by permission of William Morris Agency, Inc., on behalf of the author. (U.K. rights)

From *Howard Street*, by Nathan Heard. Copyright 1968 by Nathan Heard. Reprinted by permission of Amok Books.

From *B-Boy Blues*, by James Earl Hardy. Copyright 1994 by James Earl Hardy. Reprinted by permission of James Earl Hardy and Alyson Publications, Inc.

From *Almost Midnight*, by Don Belton. Copyright 1986 by William Morrow. Reprinted by permission of Don Belton.

An earlier version of chapter 5 was published in *CLA Journal* 44.1 (Sept. 2000): 1–42. Published by the College Language Association.

An earlier version of chapter 6 was published in *MELUS* 26.4 (Winter 2001): 113–145. Published by the Society for the Study of the Multi-Ethnic Literature of the United States.

CHAPTER ONE

INTRODUCTION

APPROACHING AFRICAN AMERICAN LIFE, HISTORY, LITERATURE, AND CRITICISM POLYCENTRICALLY

In the United States, the African American is constituted in a white/black binary of signification that defines whites as normative and superior and that represents blacks as victim, as inferior, as devalued Other, or, since the 1960s, as the Same as whites. This binary, which can be traced to the European Renaissance, is reproduced and reinforced not only by mainstream American society but also by the African American sociopolitical mission of racial uplift and its literary and historical extensions: the canon of African American literature and the classic African American historical emancipatory narrative. Elite/middle-class Christian African Americans have always been at the helm of this mission. They believe that it is their responsibility to socialize and educate all African Americans to be the Same as the dominant white society, thereby making them worthy of acceptance by whites. What mainstream America and the African American mission of racial uplift advocate is social equality: they want African Americans to have the same freedom as white Americans. But what do they mean by social equality? Equal access to goods and services? Equal opportunities for all Americans? The acceptance of all Americans and African Americans in their own diversity and complexities? The acceptance of differences? Since mainstream America, the African American sociopolitical mission, and the classic historical narrative all focus on social parity and not on cultural diversity and tolerance of African American differences, one has to assume that social equality means making the African American the Same as some normative American

1

ideal. Thus, the primary function of the mission is to protest those societal forces and institutions that prevent the African American from achieving equality.

But in their move to protest racism and to refute the negative image of the African American constructed by the binary and in their emphasis on defining the African American in terms of some idealized American norm, African Americans intent on racial uplift have established a hierarchy within African America, thereby reducing African American differences to a singular formation. Establishing a binary of self and others—where the elite/middle-class African American is the center/norm—elite/middle-class African Americans fail to engage and appreciate African American differences, the rich cultural diversity and approaches to life that comprise American/African American life. Here, I am talking not only about elite/middle-class Christian African Americans but also about jazz/blues African Americans, Voodoo African Americans, existentialist African Americans, postmodern African Americans, working-class African Americans, subaltern African Americans, modern African Americans, and urban swinging African Americans. Within the white/black binary and the sociopolitical mission of racial uplift, the African American is represented only in terms of his or her experience of racism. All other identities are excluded. The binary, however, until recently, was never questioned.

There are at least two implications in not asking fundamental questions about the unequal white/black binary system. First, asking for social equality in a binary system that structurally defines and represents the African American as inferior, as victim, as devalued Other, or as the Same entraps African American critics and historians inside that system. Second, to simply ask for social equality, to aim simply for a change in the distribution of power, leaving intact the power structure itself (the unequal white/black binary system), is to define the African American within the values and conventions of that binary. It is to resubject the African American to this unequal system and to continue the representation of the African American either as the devalued Other (victim) or as the Same (the white male norm). My concern in this book is to challenge the forms and nature of the white/black binary system, to challenge the contemporary play of powers and power relations. These challenges become prerequisites for moving toward a genuine modification/representation of the African American in literature, history, and criticism. My objective is to eschew the binary and to speak equally of African American differences, to examine and discuss African Americans in terms of their own distinctions and traditions, to engage the polyvalent nature of African American literature, history, and criticism. But, theoretically, how does one speak a language and present a narrative or vision that belies the white/black binary, disputing the African American sociopolitical mission of racial uplift, the classic African American historical emancipatory narrative, and the canon of African American literature with all their exclusions and systematized hierarchies? How does one speak equally of differences?

To arrive at a language and a theoretical concept that can envision differences, I turn to the idea of polycentrism, the principle of advocating the existence of independent centers of power within a singular political, cultural, or economic system. What I see in those constructions of Western, American, and African American literature, history, and criticism that eschew systematized hierarchies, that resist the framing of American/African American life around the unequal white/black binary, and that allow for racial and cultural differences is a more relational and radical approach. Polycentrism, states Walter Laqueur in *Polycentrism*, is a term that was coined by Palmiro Togliatti, who led the Italian Communist Party from 1927 until his death in August 1964 (2). After Joseph Stalin's death, according to Laqueur, polycentrism was used to describe the growth of independence among states and parties within the Communist/Socialist camp, and the emergence of one real and several potential rival centers to the Soviet Union (2). Polycentrism was used a second time by the internationally renowned Marxist economist Samir Amin. In *Empire of Chaos*, Amin takes the concept of polycentrism and applies it to the international world capitalist economy after World War II. In *Delinking*, Amin argues that the new globalization, which happened after World War II, with Japan and China emerging as economic powerhouses, set in motion the disintegration of auto-centered economies of the West (32).

What is common to these uses of polycentrism is a situation in which differences cannot be accommodated adequately in a hierarchical system that privileges a center with a subordinated periphery. Through repression and violence, differences in these instances are denied their logic and validity. The spread of Communism and the great objective differences in the methods and conditions of other countries made a centralized, homogeneous concept of Communism ineffective and repressive. The logic of events and the very dynamic of Communist parties and states propelled them in different directions. Likewise, Amin thinks that the national, auto-centered economic system, which was concentrated in Europe and the United States, cannot account for developing capitalistic economies in the rest of the world. Therefore, the world must become more polycentric to account for these other developing capitalistic economies. Polycentrism gives Laqueur and Amin the language, categories, and vision to talk about differences without getting into the issues of hierarchy, value, center/periphery, and superiority/inferiority. It gives them the concepts to discuss systems that are different but equal within a common framework or ground.

I want to use the concept of 'polycentrism' to envision an American/African American literature, criticism, and history that possess differences, but I do not want to get into the issue of privileging certain definitions, values, and tastes over others. Most, if not all, African Americans have racism, Otherization, and devaluation in common. But—due to class, skin color, geographical location, education, and other sets of conditions—they experience them differently, and they consequently develop/devise different methods, communities, and cosmologies, or have different sets of conditions, for defining and representing their social reality. Polycentrism gives me the theoretical basis to discuss and engage these different African American communities and traditions. It allows me to envision/construct a reading of American/African American life in which relations have many dynamic cultural, historical, critical, and literary locations, many possible vantage points, rather than a center/norm and peripheries.

Polycentrism has less to do with canons, artifacts, and representations than with the communities "behind" the canons and artifacts, which are much more diverse than the canons indicate. A polycentric approach concerns the dispersing of power, the empowering of the disempowered, and the reconfiguration of subordinating institutions, texts, traditions, and discourses. It assumes changes, not just in images but in power relations. A polycentric approach, according to Ella Shohat and Robert Stam, thinks and imagines "from the margins," seeing minoritarian and repressed spaces, traditions, and communities, as well as marginalized groups within minoritarian communities, not as "interest groups" to be "added on" to a preexisting "nucleus, but rather as active, generative participants at the very core of a shared, conflictual" history (48). A polycentric approach to American/African American history and literature engages critically the entire notion of a white or black center/canon. It challenges the construction of a canon of African American literature that privileges select African American texts and ignores or marginalizes others.

In this sense, a polycentric approach reconceptualizes American/African American literature, criticism, and history by focusing on the power relations between and among the different cultural communities and movements. It links together minoritarian—or once repressed and subordinated traditions, canons, and theoretical concepts—with sanctioned traditions and canons within both America and African America, challenging the hierarchies that make some literary texts, concepts of history, or ways of life "minor" and others "major" and "normative." A polycentric approach allows me to subject the "mutual relations" between the various traditions within America and African America to the "varying imperatives of their own internal development and to chart the 'reciprocal adjustment'" among all American/African American communities (*Delinking* xii).

Of course, a polycentric approach to American/African American literature calls into question our concept of literature: it requires us to reconfigure it. In *Marxism and Literature*, Raymond Williams argues that in its modern form the concept of "literature" did not emerge earlier than the eighteenth century and was not fully developed until the nineteenth century, despite the fact that the conditions for its emergence had been developing since the Renaissance (46). According to Williams, the word *itself* came into English use only in the fourteenth century, following French and Latin precedents. The idea of "literature" was often "close to the sense of modern literacy, which was not in the language until the late nineteenth century" (47). As a new category, the concept of literature first shifted "from 'learning' to 'taste' or 'sensibility' as a criterion defining literary qualities; second, [there was] an increasing specialization of literature to 'creative' or 'imaginative' works; third, [there was] a development of the concept of 'tradition' within national terms, resulting in the more effective definition of 'a national literature'" (48). Today, American literature, including African American literature, operates as a "national literature." It is usually defined as the canonical genres of writing.

But, as John Guillory argues forcefully in *Cultural Capital*, this concept of 'literature' privileges the "cultural capital of the old bourgeoisie, a form of capital increasingly marginal to the social function of the present educational system" (x). America has evolved into a diverse, heterogeneous population with the power/cultural capital to demand different notions of literature and different aesthetic values. The presence of this diverse population shows the limitations of the traditional concept of literature. From this perspective, the issue of "canonicity" seems less important than the historical crisis of literature, since it is this crisis—the long-term decline in the cultural capital of literature—that has given rise to the canon debate (x). Guillory argues that it is the institution—the school or university—that is the "historical site of evaluative acts" and that "subordinates specific values expressed in works to the social functions and institutional aims of the school itself. It is only when presented as *canonical*, as the cultural capital of the school, that individual literary works can be made to serve the school's social function of regulating access to these forms of capital" (269).

But out of the canon debate there also emerges the question of aesthetic value, something that Marxist and black aesthetic critics, despite their professed political engagement and radicalism, have failed to engage. Until this debate, the universality of aesthetic perception was restricted to certain hegemonic individuals and social groups. Within mainstream American and African American criticisms, those groups or individuals with power and cultural capital determined the community's aesthetic perception and values. They also determined which literary texts would receive cultural capital, which would stay in print, and which would be "made to serve the school's social function of regulating access to. . . . forms of capital." The critique of the canon enabled a "privileged perspective upon the entire discourse of value, and it was thus the means by which that discourse. . . . could be opened to an antifoundational or relativist reorientation. The new relativist discourse of value could then be turned against the historical discourse of aesthetics, removing once and for all its axiological props" (Guillory 272).

Rejecting the universality of aesthetic value and arguing for a relativist, politically useful aesthetic, Tony Bennett writes:

> The political utility of discourses of value, operating via the construction of an ideal of personality to which broadly based social aspirations can be articulated, is unquestionable. There is, however, no reason to suppose that such discourses must be hitched up to the sphere of universality in order to secure their effectivity. To the contrary, given the configuration of today's political struggles, it is highly unlikely that an ideal of personality might be forged that would be equal service in the multiple, intersecting but, equally, non-coincident foci of struggle constituted by black, gay, feminist, socialist and, in some contexts, national liberation politics. In particular conjunctures, to be sure, an ideal of personality may be forged which serves to integrate—but always temporarily—such forces

into a provisional unity. But, this is not the basis for a generalizable and universalisable (sic) cultural politics. (44)

Given the presence of emergent racial, cultural, class, social, gender, and sexual groups and individuals who protest their exclusion from a hegemonic American "ideal of personality" and thereby simultaneously advocate their own individual aesthetic tastes, a universal aesthetics proves impossible.

The critique of aesthetics always assumes what Guillory calls a concept of value grounded in the notion of a "valuing community" or communities. But the "valuing community" can also reinstate a kind of "local subjective universality" (277), especially if it assumes that it has homogeneous experiences, beliefs, or values. White male advocates of New Criticism before their rise to hegemony in the 1940s, African American racial uplift critics, Alain Locke's New Negro critics, American feminist critics, black aesthetic critics, queer theorists, Mexican American cultural nationalist critics, and Marxist critics question and actively oppose the claims of "necessity" and "naturalness" made for the conditions and perspectives of the dominant society, "pointing out the existence of other conditions, namely those relevant to their lives, and other perspectives, namely their own" (B. H. Smith 181). But these marginal critics also adhere to concepts of value grounded in the notion of a valuing community. All reinscribe a kind of universality in their aesthetic values. Like the dominant society, they repress differences within their valuing communities. "When someone or some group of people insist(s) on the *objective* necessity or propriety of their own social, political, or moral judgments and actions, and deny the *contingency* of the conditions and perspectives from which those judgments and actions proceed," argues Barbara Herrnstein Smith in *Contingencies of Value*, "it must be—and always is—a move to assign dominant status to the *particular* conditions and perspectives that happen to be relevant to or favored by that person, group, or class; it must be—and always is—simultaneously a move to deny the existence and relevancy, and to suppress the claims, of *other* conditions and perspectives" (181).

As Smith points out, there are certain purely conventional "norms and standards (like units of measurement, or safety standards)" that are functionally "unconditional and universal" and may thus be called "contingently absolute" or "contingently objective" (182). But as far as culture is concerned, Smith argues that "a community is never totally homogeneous, that its boundaries and borders are never altogether self-evident, that we cannot assume in advance that certain differences among its members are negligible or irrelevant, and that the conditions that produced the relative unconditionality, local universality, and contingent objectivity are themselves neither fixed forever nor totally stable now" (182). Smith rejects the notion of community as the epistemological ground of value.

Of course, the problem here is that it is impossible to conceive of a valuing community or an identity community without recourse to local universalization of its values. Individuals from such communities—the European and American communities I discuss in chapter 2, the African American community

I discuss in chapters 3 and 4, the gay community I discuss in chapter 9, and some of the various individual writers discussed in the other chapters who represent various American/African American valuing communities and traditions—once they constitute these communities socially, politically, and aesthetically, seldom refrain from policing differences within them. They want to define their community's difference from other communities; therefore, they project their concept of 'social identity' into an ideal of homogeneity. Echoing and reinforcing this same sentiment, Fawzia Afzal-Khan in *Cultural Imperialism and the Indo-English Novel* argues that "the writer, by unconsciously (or, often consciously) attempting to validate himself and his group in the face of what he perceives as an antagonistic other, ends up confining himself to the limited, and limiting, economic and sociopolitical interests of its class or group" (2).

But if we accept, as Smith argues, that "*each of us* is a member of many, shifting communities, each of which establishes, for *each* of its members, multiple social identities, multiple principles of identification with other people, and accordingly, a collage or grab-bag of allegiances, beliefs, and sets of motives" (168), then we are forced to question, accept provisionally, or perhaps even abandon our traditional notion of community. "The grounding of value in discrete communities," argues Guillory, "inaugurates a contradictory practice which moves back and forth between making separatist and universalist claims" (279). But just as no individual writer is unequivocally the member of only one community, neither is any cultural object the bearer of the values of only one community.

Of course, as I argue against a homogeneous American/African American community and a universal aesthetic, my aim is not to abandon aesthetics and values completely. "The dismissal of aesthetics, as the discourse of 'universal' value believed to suppress differences," argues Guillory, "has thus had the paradoxical effect of removing the basis for apprehending the work of art as the objectification not of subjects or communities but of the relations between subjects, or the relations between groups" (282). The value of a cultural object can least of all be expressed as having effect "solely within the limits of particular valuing communities" (282). Smith writes:

> [A] verbal judgment of "*the* value" of some entity—for example, an art work, a work of literature, or any other kind of object, event, text, or utterance—cannot be a judgment of any independently determined or, as we say, "objective" property of that entity. As we have seen, however, what it can be . . . is a judgment of that entity's *contingent* value: that is, the speaker's observation or estimation of the entity will figure in the economy of some limited population of subjects under some limited set of conditions. (94)

Individual critics, observers, or writers thus construct the community.

An individual observer who defines the African American community according to the aims and politics of the African American sociopolitical mission of racial uplift will value a literary text according to how it figures in the limited, elite/middle-class Christian set of conditions. He or she will not define an

African American existentialist, blues, or swing text as figuring in that community's economy and, therefore, will not impute it with any value or cultural capital. Of course, the crucial questions are: Does this individual observer define his or her values/aesthetics universally? Contingently? Does he or she realize that these values/aesthetics are restricted to a "limited population of subjects" under some "limited set of conditions"? Because the African American community is not homogeneous ("its borders and boundaries are not altogether self-evident") and because African Americans have multiple social identities, the same individual observer, or another individual observer from a different segment of the community, can equally adopt, or have a different social identity and so find value in an existentialist, blues, or swing literary text, or respond to these features in a racial uplift canonical text. In this instance, value no longer has a "socially determined function" but "the potential infinity of individual uses" (Guillory 295). For example, Ishmael Reed's *Mumbo Jumbo*, depending on which sector of the African American community is observing, can be defined as a Voodoo, a jazz, a detective, or a postmodern text. Because individuals from the same or different segments of the African American community can construct and grant value to that community differently, a text can belong to several communities. All values are contingent and their price/worth is determined by the market's cultural capital. With this nonfoundational and relativist approach to valuing cultural objects or literary texts, I can impute cultural capital to texts from all the various traditions in African American literature. Taking a polycentric approach to the literature, I can speak of different African American texts as having contingent value, without getting into the issue of hierarchy, superiority, and inferiority.

Finally, the crisis in the traditional concept of literature, which has been accompanied by a change in cultural capital as other African American communities demand other types of literatures or expressive forms, allows us to engage different African American aesthetics and cultural imaginaries. Given the demand for African American readings—not only in the traditional novel but also in autobiography, romance, detective fiction, mysteries, science fiction, popular fiction, experimental fiction, poetry, and the essay—we have to devise a definition of literature that will incorporate, engage, and assess all of these African American expressive forms equally.

This issue of differences also plagues African American history. How does one speak of differences within the classic African American historical emancipatory narrative? Michel Foucault in *The Archaeology of Knowledge* provides a language and theoretical concepts for discussing American/African American history polycentrically:

> For many years now historians have preferred to turn their attention to long periods, as if, beneath the shifts and changes of political events, they were trying to reveal the stable, almost indestructible system of checks and balances, the irreversible processes, the constant readjustments, the underlying tendencies

that gather force, and are then suddenly reversed after centuries of continuity, the movements of accumulations and slow saturation, the great silent, motionless bases that traditional history has covered with a thick layer of events. (3)

These historians are looking for links that can be made between disparate events, for how a causal succession can be established between them, and for the continuity or overall significance these links possess. In short, these historians are looking to "define a totality" (3).

But Foucault supersedes this traditional approach to history, which asks for links, causality, and totality, with a general approach to history, which asks "questions of another type: Which strata should be isolated from others? What types of series should be established? What criteria of periodization should be adopted for each of them? What system of relations (hierarchy, dominance, stratification, universal determination, circular causality) may be established? And in what large-scale chronological table may distinct series of events be determined?" There is something dispersed, decentered, and polycentric about Foucault's notion of general history. Extending this polycentric approach to other disciplines such as literature, science, and philosophy, Foucault wants not to define the totality in these disciplines but to "detect the incidence of interruptions" (4).

In taking a polycentric approach to American/African American literature and history in this book, I eschew historical narratives and an African American literary canon whose focus/center is on racial oppression exclusively, and so challenge the African American sociopolitical mission of racial uplift, that is, the journey of the African American from the colonized subaltern to the values and definitions of mainstream society. I destabilize and, therefore, place into flux the two halves of the white/black binary, thereby unleashing American/African American differences. The relative term *Other* is the obverse of *normal*. Thus, normalizing the *Other* must come through an essential rupture of the white/black binary and other hierarchical hierarchized systems.

In this book, I approach American/African American history and literature by focusing on the various literatures, critical practices, lifestyles, aesthetic forms, cultural imaginaries, and theoretical definitions of life within a range of American/African American communities. And I do not position the once marginal communities and traditions as "interest groups" to be added on to a "preexisting nucleus" (Shohat and Stam 48). This means examining the history and literature of subaltern African Americans, of jazz/blues artists, and Voodoo practitioners, none of which are particularly Christian or middle class. A polycentric approach also allows me to include an examination of African American radical individualism, existentialism, postmodernism, and urban survivalism, which are a part of African American life that is different from mainstream norms and conventions and cannot be engaged, examined, and discussed adequately and positively in the white/black binary or within the historical narrative that posits a quest for social equality.

I turn to Charles Wright's *The Messenger,* to the early novels of John Wideman, and to Robert Boles's *Curling* and *The People One Knows* to discern how the extreme subjectivity of their existentialism renders obsolete such master narratives as the mission of racial uplift. I examine the novels of Robert Deane Pharr and Cyrus Colter, and Nathan Heard's *Howard Street,* which are nonhumanistic, non-middle class, non-Protestant work ethic, and non-Freudian, and examine how they explore survivalism as a theoretical system that challenges through its very existence the positioning of the African American within Enlightenment moral codes. I turn to William Melvin Kelley's *A Different Drummer,* which explores how the instinctive Thoreauvian concept of 'radical individualism' disrupts the notion of a unified African American valuing community and posits a social space where the African American exists as a non-victim. I examine Clarence Major's blues novel, *Dirty Bird Blues,* which constructs a representation of the African American as affirmative, existential, individual, vibrant and different. I turn to James Earl Hardy's *B-Boy Blues* to discuss sexual fluidity as a way of disrupting the heterosexual/homosexual regime that defines sexuality in the West. Finally, I turn to Don Belton's *Almost Midnight,* which uses Voodoo as a different theoretical conception to define African American life and history. I engage all of these different African American texts without the need to exclude or repress any as "negligible or irrelevant" or to establish a hierarchy among them.

Finally, I want to explain why I focus only on African American male writers. First, since the 1970s, emerging feminist criticism and women's studies have created the scholarly space for most previously excluded African American women writers to gain validation and critical attention. Although the 1960s movement and African American studies gave validation and critical attention to certain canonical texts by both men and women, there is no social or literary movement to garner critical attention for existential, Voodoo, blues, and urban subaltern literary texts by African American male writers. They are simply neglected. Second, as a variety of critics and historians have emphasized, black masculinity has occupied a particularly problematic place in American literature and culture. The very essence of racism in the United States required the bestilization or animalization of the African American male, which led both American and African American authors such as Frederick Douglass, William Wells Brown, Harriet Beecher Stowe, Charles Chesnutt, Paul Laurence Dunbar, James Weldon Johnson, Jean Toomer, and others to treat African American men as pacific or passive, to define them according to the definitions and values of the middle-class American norm, or to depict them in some other romantic guise. But, many African American male writers found alternative ways to represent and to examine black masculinity—though their portrayals have often been misread or ignored. Although there are some black women texts that could be configured into my overall theme of African American differences, I want to focus on the various ways African American male writers represent and examine black masculinity. Third, and more important, I want to explore the condition of possibility for an African American male—or any individual who has been defined historically as devalued Other—in the West, despite every effort to define him as devalued Other, to define himself as a subject with agency. Finally, despite the fact the I focus on African American male writers, I employ throughout this book, to use the words of bell hooks, "a feminist analysis that will address the issue of how to construct a life-sustaining black masculinity that does not have its roots in patriarchal phallocentrism" (*black looks,* 111).

HISTORY, THE WHITE/BLACK BINARY, AND THE CONSTRUCTION OF THE AFRICAN AMERICAN AS OTHER

In chapter 1, I discussed the African American as being constituted within an unequal white/black binary system. In this binary system, which is reinforced by the cultural, social, political, and economic institutions and apparatuses of the United States and Western civilization, the African American is represented *only* in terms of his experience of racism. To be represented as a victim of racial oppression is to be defined exclusively and negatively by someone else's discourse. For the African American, racial oppression/victimization becomes the site of a beginning, an origin, and the events of African American history and culture are defined in terms of this beginning. In short, the African American is represented as the passive object of a white middle class that is the maker of history. As a consequence, other African American representations, identities, and experiences that do not fit into this white/black binary are ignored. These exclusions forestall social and cultural heterogeneity, or a polycentric approach to American/African American social reality, in favor of a single paradigmatic perspective in which white, middle-class America is seen as the unique source of meaning, as the U.S. center of gravity, and as the ontological "reality" for the rest of the country. Also, these exclusions further signify, within the context of the Neolithic revolution of the twelfth and thirteenth centuries, a polycentric representation of the world where the civilizations of Asia, Africa, and the Americas stand as pillars of world history in their own right.

The staying power of this white/black binary of signification rests, in no small part, on the fact that it has been rearticulated in a dense cultural network of normative definitions, including binaries such as nation/tribe, middle

13

class/poor, knowledge/ignorance, colonizer/colonized, culture/folklore, Christian/heathen, and suburban/inner city. In other words, the middle-class white norm, along with the representation of the African American as devalued Other, is woven into the core cultural premises and understandings of the U.S. society.

Whence did this white/black binary come? How has it manifested itself historically? How can we disrupt it? All literature dates this particular binary to the birth of modernity in 1492 and to the European Renaissance. As Enrique Dussel argues in *The Invention of the Americas*, whereas modernity "gestated in the free, creative medieval European cities, it came to birth in Europe's confrontation with the Other" (10). The rise of capitalism and colonial Europe and the Renaissance's qualitative break with the earlier history of humanity began when Europeans became conscious of the idea that their conquest of the world was a possible objective. From that they developed a sense of absolute superiority, even if the actual submission of other peoples to Europe had not yet taken place. By conquering, controlling, and violating the Other, Europe soon defined itself as discoverer, conquistador, and colonizer of alterity (12). The so-called voyages of "discovery" inaugurated modernity, catalyzing a new epoch of European colonial expansion that culminated in its domination of the globe. For many revisionist historians, 1492 installed the mechanism of systematic advantage that favored Europe against its African and Asian rivals.

If we look at the world before 1492 from what Ella Shohat and Robert Stam in *Unthinking Eurocentrism* call a polycentric rather than a Eurocentric perspective, it did not contain a single hegemonic power (8). According to Janet L. Abu-Lughod in *Before European Hegemony*, between 1250 and 1350, an international trade economy developed that stretched from northwestern Europe to China, including India and parts of Africa, in which all states and empires were basically equal in terms of economic and social development. This international trade had its roots in the much earlier Neolithic revolution, which saw the birth of agriculture and cities (8). This revolution, according to Dussel and contrary to Georg Hegel's proposal, began primarily in the West, "first in Mesopotamia and later in Egypt, and then surged forward toward the East, usually with few contacts between civilizations" (75). The Neolithic revolution spread eastward to the Indus Valley (today Pakistan), to China's Yellow River Valley, to the Pacific Ocean region, and finally into Mesoamerica, home of the Mayan and Aztec civilizations, and the southern Andes, where the Incas resided (75). This means that prior to 1492, progress toward modernization and capitalism that was taking place in parts of Europe was also taking place in parts of Asia, the Americas, and Africa: whatever happened economically and socially in Europe also happened in the Eastern hemisphere.

Europe's dominance after 1492 resulted not from any internal immanent forces or from an inherent superiority of mind, culture, or environment, or because Europe was more progressive, venturesome, and achievement oriented. Rather, its rise was fueled by the riches and spoils obtained in the conquest and colonial exploitation of America and later of Africa and Asia (Blaut 51), particularly as Asian and African proto-capitalist centers began to decline. What Europe did have was opportunity. It had a locational advantage in the broad sense of accessibility. If the Western hemisphere or the Americas had been more accessible to South Asian Indian centers than to European centers, then very likely India would have become the home of capitalism, the site of bourgeoisie revolution, and the ruler (colonizer) of the world (181).

The leap across the Atlantic in 1492 was certainly one of the great adventures of human history. Iberian ports had the clear advantage over Asian or African mercantile-maritime centers.[1] Sofala, which was the southernmost major seaport in East Africa of that period, is roughly three thousand miles farther away from an American landfall than are the Canary Islands (Christopher Columbus's jumping-off point) and five thousand miles away from any coast densely populated enough to present possibilities for trade or plunder. The distance from China to America's northwest coast was even greater, and greater still to the rich societies of Mexico (Blaut 182). Overall, in the late fifteenth century, it is far more probable that an Iberian ship would have effected a passage to America than an African or Asian ship. Is this rise to capitalistic world hegemony environmental determinism? asks Blaut. If the choices were between an environmentalistic explanation and one that claimed the intrinsic superiority of one group over all others, he answers, we would certainly settle for environmentalism (182–83).

With the "discovery" of America in 1492, the New World became significant in both the rise of Europe and the rise of capitalism. Immediately, the colonizing process began and explosively advanced, involving the destruction of American civilizations and states, the plunder of precious metals, the exploitation of labor, the otherizing of the indigenous Americans, and the occupation of American lands. Within a few decades after 1492, the rate of growth and change had expedited dramatically, and Europe entered a period of rapid metamorphosis.

The colonial enterprise in the sixteenth century produced capital in a number of ways: the mining of gold and silver; plantation agriculture; trade with Asia in spices, cloth, and so on, and the establishment of a variety of productive and commercial enterprises in the Americas. Other ways were slavery and piracy. Accumulation from all these sources was so massive that it fueled a major transformation in Europe: the rise to power of the bourgeoisie and the immense efflorescence of preindustrial capitalism (Blaut 189). But it was not until several centuries later that the new globalized system incorporating the Americas, Africa, and Asia yielded its full return and catapulted Europe to world hegemony.

If the white/black binary of signification dates to modernity in 1492, to Europe's confrontation with the Other or the non-European, what was the mind-set that European explorers, colonialists, adventurers, and missionaries took to Africa, Asia, and the Americas? What caused them to view non-Europeans as different and therefore less? There are historical, cultural, and religious factors leading to the "Europeanization" and "Christianization" of Europe that may explain why.

In the early Middle Ages, Europe was a dispersed, heterogeneous collection of sects who spoke different languages, practiced different religions, and possessed varied economic and cultural systems and beliefs. According to John Hale in *The Civilization of Europe in the Renaissance*, the period of European history from around 1450 to about 1620 has come to be called the "long sixteenth century." It was the first age in which the words "Europe" and "European" acquired a widely understood significance (xix). The Christianization of Europe was an integral part of the Europeanization of Europe. The two comprised the cultural homogenization of Europe, an effort to constitute homogeneous linguistic, national, and religious communities by spreading one particular culture through conquest and influence. According to Robert Bartlett in *The Making of Europe*, it had its core in one part of the continent, namely, France, Germany west of the Elbe, and North Italy, regions that had a common history as part of Charlemagne's Franklin empire. Thus, the cultural homogenization of Europe was, in part, a function of the Frankish military hegemony. It was from this part of Western Europe that expansionary expeditions were launched in all directions, and by 1300 these wars had created a ring of conquest states on the peripheries of Latin Christendom (269). These conquest states gave the new Europeans their formative experience of the Other. For example, when Anglo-Norman invaders settled in Ireland, or Germans in Pomerania, they defined the people of Ireland and Pomerania as devalued Others, as uncultured savages, and proceeded to reproduce social and economic units similar to those in their homelands.

Thus, even before Europeans encountered the non-Europeans, they already had the experience of dealing with an Other: the internal European Other. As Peter Mason points out in *Deconstructing America*, "Europe had its own internal other, and this it could project onto the New World outside the confines of Europe" (41). In Europe during the Middle Ages and the Renaissance, images of the wild man and wild woman, the fool, the beggar, the peasant, and the witch, along with Jews, Gypsies, Huguenots, Muslims, the Irish, the Scots, and the Welsh, served to locate Self to Other for the upper-middle-class European. This means that both European peasants and exotic, non-European Gypsies "could serve as the internal negative self-definition of the European upper classes" (44). The encounter with the internal Other thus served as the "point of articulation of the demands of the European unifying *logos* with the external projection of European fantasies, fears and desires" (41). But when using their experience and knowledge of the internal Other to later define/classify the non-European, the European proto-capitalist class did not identify the non-European with European culture in general, but with that of its subaltern classes, or the European Other. By fixing the status of the Other, the non-European, at the lowest echelons of European society, upper-middle-class Europeans established within their hierarchical classifying system their attitudes toward the non-Europeans.

Furthermore, in terms of the cultural/religious homogenization of Europe, Europe was emerging as a site of Christian nations. When Enea Sylvio Piccolomini was made Pope (Pius II) in 1458, he became an instrumental figure in plac-

[handwritten margin note: colonization w/ in Europe]

ing the idea of a Christian community in consonance with a geographical area: Europe. For him, Europe not only would become more and more identified with the West as opposed to the East, which was occupied by the Islamic world, but would also create a distinction between Western and Eastern Christians.

Until the Christianization of Europe, Christendom had always been a flexible concept. It had flowed outward to include the Byzantine Christians in Anatolia, the Coptic Christians in North Africa, and even the community of Christians supposedly founded by the apostle Thomas in southern India (J. Hale 5). However, the Reformation in the 1520s, a split that divided non-Orthodox Christianity into Catholic and Protestant zones, each calling for rethinking Christian belief, behavior, and observance, is the best evidence that a new, less-flexible Christianity was emerging in Europe. —*which ends up in America westernize*

In northern and eastern Europe, the conversion to Christianity can be seen as one aspect of a wider reorientation or, more precisely, an "Occidentation," a shift toward the ways and norms of Romano–Germanic civilization as it had developed in the territories of the former Carolingian empire. It began when pagan West Slavs were incorporated into Catholic Christendom in the twelfth century, after which the arrival of writing, towns, and money formed part of a larger social and cultural transformation in which Christianization was almost inseparable from Europeanization. Evidence of this shift lies in the changes in people's names. A circulation of new names through the system, linked to the names of saints, began usually as a result of conquest (Bartlett 274). What was happening in Europe during this time was that through conquest, colonization, and cultural transformation Europe was becoming a geographical place that could be identified as homogeneous.[2] A triumphal regime of truth and power, one that overrides its internal contradictions by repressing and subordinating its internal Others, was emerging. Europe was developing an identity.

In addition, other homogenizing and universalizing forces were put into motion during the European Middle Ages. The minting of silver coins started to spread slowly across Europe. The charter, a formal written document, was also spreading through Europe. By the sixteenth century, according to John Hale, the physical nature of Europe could be assessed. It was during this period that the continent itself was given a securely map-based frame of reference, a set of images that established its identity in pictorial terms. A new mathematical interest in cartographical projections that could take account of the curvature of the earth and more accurately assess degrees of latitude enabled Europeans to imagine the geographical space in which they lived (15). All over Europe, maps became part of the mental furniture of educated men. The spread of documentation into the continental peripheries coincided with a vast increase in the quality of written records in the central, post-Carolingian parts of Europe. This movement has been characterized as the "shift from sacred script to practical literacy" (Bartlett 285).

Europeanization/Christianization meant not only the spread of certain elements of linguistic and religious culture or the dissemination of new artifacts of power but also the development of new institutional agencies of cultural change. The university was one of the most powerful instruments of cultural homogeneity to arise in the High Middle Ages. According to Bartlett, France and Italy were easily predominant both in the numbers of universities and in the fact that each possessed one of the outstanding academic centers of the Middle Ages: Paris for arts and theology and Bologna for law. England also had universities such as Oxford and Cambridge in the thirteenth century. In the thirteenth and early fourteenth centuries, anyone outside this academic triangle—anyone from Germany, Scandinavia, eastern Europe or the Celtic countries—who wished for a formal higher education had to travel to France, Italy, or England. They had to travel, for example, from Dublin to Oxford, from Norway to Paris, and from Bavaria to Bologna (288). These universities produced the educated elite for Europe. By 1300, the nonmilitary elite of the Latin West was being shaped by a standard educational experience.

By the time of the Renaissance, European educators and intellectuals had also rediscovered their Greek ancestry. The Renaissance humanists/educators, argues Paul Kristeller, were actively involved in making the sources of ancient philosophy and science available to their contemporaries by discovering, copying, and editing classical Latin texts, by translating Greek texts into Latin, and by discussing and interpreting them in their commentaries (42). By the time of François Rabelais, argues John Hale, educated men and women throughout Europe had come into repossession of Greek civilization. Plato, Aristotle, Virgil, Cicero, Ovid, and others were read "not merely with admiration for their knowledge or their particular expertise, but as models from whom to learn about statecraft, the waging of war, the creation of works of art and the more important art of bearing up under adversity: this impact made the study of the ancient world into a cultural force" (190). By the early sixteenth century, the influence of classical scholarship, and its popularization through translations and paraphrased texs, had acquired a critical mass, which produced unstoppable chain reactions. There was hardly a branch of inquiry—from jurisprudence to mathematics, military science to the arts—that was unaltered by the stimulus of a relevant text, artifact, or record of historical experience (191).

In addition to the Europeanization and Christianization of Europe, and along with a standard educational experience allowing Europeans to establish an identity that defined the non-European as Other, European languages themselves began to code the non-European as Other. European languages, particularly English, had a negative representation of black as a color even before Englishmen encountered the Africans. The Spanish and Portuguese had been in contact with North Africa for centuries and had actually been invaded and subjected by a people both darker and more highly civilized than themselves. But the English lacked that experience, and "blackness" carried meaning long before it was found that men could bear its stamp. According to Winthrop Jordan in *White over Black,* the word *black* for the English was "the symbol of baseness and evil, a sign to men of danger and repulsion. Black bore a primitive association with excrement and dirt, or with unknown dangers of the right. The color black bore not only its own meaning but the conception of its absolute opposite. It was inseparably paired with white." White and black as a binary connoted purity and filthiness, virginity and sin, virtue and baseness, beauty and ugliness, beneficence and evil (7).

But the descriptions of *dark* and *light*, argues Kim F. Hall in *Things of Darkness*, became more than being opposing poles of Elizabethan beauty, symbols of baseness and evil, or markers of moral categories. In the "early modern period," light and dark became "the conduit through which the English began to formulate the notion of 'self' and 'other' so well known in Anglo-American racial discourses" (2). Hall dates the association of dark as Christian death and sin with the African as Other to the moment when England moved from geographic isolation into military and mercantile contest with other countries. The moment set the stage for the longer process by which "preexisting literary tropes of blackness profoundly interacted with the fast-changing economic relations of white Europeans and their darker 'others' during the Renaissance" (4).

Accepting Jordan's argument that the traditional association of blackness in Christian symbolism was with death and mourning, sin and evil, Hall argues that with this awareness of white and black, the English culture:

> recognized the possibilities of this language for the representation and categorization of perceived physical differences. Thus traditional terms of aesthetic discrimination and Christian dogma become infused with ideas of Africa and African servitude, making it impossible to separate 'racial' signifiers of blackness from traditional iconography. (4)

Finally, in defining the non-European as Other, European Renaissance travelers to Asia, the Americas, and Africa also had a different conception of historical time than many non-Europeans, and they defined the non-European within that conception of time. In *Time and the Other*, Johannes Fabian discusses time— as it was prefigured in the Christian tradition, then transformed in the Age of Enlightenment, where it was secularized and naturalized—and the emerging Other, the non-European. "Universal time," argues Fabian, "was probably established concretely and politically in the Renaissance in response to both classical philosophy and to the cognitive challenges presented by the age of discoveries opening up in the wake of the earth's circumnavigation" (3). In the Judeo-Christian tradition, time is conceived as the medium of a sacred history. It is evolutionary. It is thought of as a sequence of specific events that befall a chosen people. Much has been said about the linear character, the idea of progress and development, and the notion of duration that is characteristic of that conception of time, as opposed to a non-Judeo-Christian cyclical view of time, which includes the histories and cultures that are the Others of Western discourse.

According to Peter Burke in *The Renaissance Sense of the Past*, European medieval man's definition of historical time lacked a sense of anachronism, an awareness of evidence, and an interest in causation. It lacked a sense of the "differentness" of the past. Medieval man defined the past in terms of the present, and he projected himself "back on to the men of the past" (1–6). But, Renaissance humanism, according to Denise Albanese, "saw the emergence of what can be called historical consciousness, which is . . . a consciousness that the past was different from the present, and that certain consequences follow from that position" (30). Whereas European medieval societies might have had the same or a similar historical time as societies in Asia and Africa, European Renaissance society's conception of historical time was clearly different.

As a consequence of the European Renaissance's different definition of historical time, and given the fact that it had the power to define history in its own image, the potential for the creation of hierarchies among different societies and cultures was eminent. Fabian writes:

> It [Western's] notion of time promoted a scheme in terms of which not only past cultures, but all living societies were irrevocably placed on a temporal slope, a stream of time—some upstream, others downstream. Civilization, evolution, development, acculturation, modernization . . . are all terms whose conceptual content derived . . . from evolutionary Time. (17)

In hierarchizing the world, in promoting a time schema where "all living societies were irrevocably placed on a temporal slope," European explorers and colonialists during the Renaissance and later denied coevality. They converted differences between cultures into successive stages in the Western history of humanity. They interpreted differences in conceptual frameworks as different stages in linear (Western) historical time, in such a way that non-evolutionary time was equivalent to being less civilized, or "back in time." In the Judeo-Christian cosmology of the West, chronology (and duration) provides a basis for scientific historiography in the sense that it provides a single absolute yardstick by means of which all different "histories" can be synchronized and correlated. For example, in a naturalization of time that defined temporal relations as exclusive and expansive, argues Fabian, "the savage is *not yet* ready for civilization" (26). Non-European societies were defined not as Other and different and equal, or as Other with their own distinctions, but as of the oldest world of all, that of the pre-civilized state of all mankind: unselfconscious, spontaneous, and peaceful. Western expansion and civilization in the sixteenth century, states Walter Mignolo in *The Darker Side of the Renaissance*, coincided with a radical transformation of the concept of time that impinged on the concept of history and created the necessary condition to place different cultures and conceptual frameworks in Africa, Asia, and the Americas somewhere on a temporal scale that had their point of arrival in the present sixteenth-century Christian European civilization (327–28).

Thus, when European explorers, missionaries, colonialists, and adventurers, who belonged economically, culturally, religiously, and educationally to the emerging homogenizing Europe of the Renaissance, traveled to the Americas, Africa, and Asia, the binaries of European/non-European, linear/cyclical (view of time), white/black, civilized/primitive, self/Other, colonizer/colonized, and Christian/pagan were very much a part of their regimes of power and knowledge, their normalized constructions of the world or reality. Most of those who left Europe in the sixteenth century for other worlds, argues Anthony Pagden in *European Encounters with the New World*, regardless of their objectives, left with a pattern of European conceptual expectations, which they used to impose meaning on the world (10–11). When faced with the task of classifying and assimilating the non-European, Europe was caught up in a double movement. On the one hand, it could fall back on traditional representations in order to accommodate the new. Using the parameters/criteria of those traditional representations, the self of Europe could reduce and assimilate the Other, the non-European, that it encountered outside Europe. Anything that fell through its conceptual "grid" was relegated to the "marvelous" or the "wondrous." On the other hand, once the marvelous was given precise shape it had somehow to be fitted back into the grid, to be given a place in the scale of European normative expectations (10–11).

Also, when European explorers and colonialists encountered/confronted the non-European Other, conquest and colonization were already a part of European cultures: the European explorers who sailed to the coasts of the Americas, Asia, and Africa in the fifteenth and sixteenth centuries came from a society that was already colonized. Thus, Europe—the initiator of one of the world's most extensive processes of conquest, colonization, and cultural transformation—was also the product of those forces. Of course, I do not want to argue that there is something unique or essential to European colonization. Ethnocentrism, or the belief that one's own ethnic/racial group is superior to others, has been around for a long time. In addition to Greece and Rome, non-European empires and states throughout history have practiced conquest and colonization. Colonialism per se preexisted latter-day European colonialism, having already been practiced by the Aztecs, the Incas, Mali, Ghana, Songhai, the Muslim Empire, and Japan.[3]

All of these non-European empires that practiced forms of colonialism were heterogeneous and diverse. They dominated and controlled their conquests, comprising many different kinds of people who spoke different kinds of languages and who practiced different kinds of cultures. Hybridity can be understood, argues Renato Rosaldo in his foreword to Nestor Garcia Canclini's *Hybrid Cultures*, "as the ongoing condition of all human cultures, which contain no zones of purity because they undergo continuous processes of transculturation" (xv). Discussing hybridity within the powerful kingdoms of Ghana, Mali, and Songhai, Robert July writes:

> The geography of the Sudan favored absorption and adaptation, for its easy lines of communication made it a natural meeting place where ideas, institutions, and blood strains could touch, fuse, and strengthen one another. Some-

> how, the fusion of local and exotic strains terminated in a hybrid more char-
> acteristically Sudan than otherwise. For example, virtually every one of the
> medieval savanna kingdoms possessed traditions involving immigration of rul-
> ing dynasties from north and east, but these rulers soon became absorbed and
> black kings held the reins of government during the apogee of such powerful
> states as Ghana, Mali, and Songhai. The bulk of the savanna population was
> the product of racial intermixture, and it was commonplace for villages of
> completely different tribal and cultural entities to co-exist peaceably. (69)

Thus, conquest and colonization are common to human history. And in all these conquests and annexations, the colonizers looked upon their own cultures as privileged.[4] Thus, European colonization in Asia, Africa, and the Americas was not a new phenomenon in human history.

What was different was that Europe's conquest of non-Europeans hap-pened at a time when Europe was able to reorganize the world system and place itself at the center of world history over and against a periphery. What was new in classical European colonialism was what Shohat and Stam call "its planetary reach, its affiliation with global institutional power, and its imperative mode," its attempted submission of the world to a single "universal" regime of truth and power (15). As Emmanuel Wallerstein in *Modern World System* has convincingly argued, the "modern" world system that emerged in the centuries following the sixteenth century gradually became organized hierarchically according to differ-ent modes of production (capitalist, semifeudal, and precapitalist) that were roughly coterminous with a specific geographic distribution: a capitalist core hegemon located in northwestern Europe, an agrarian semi-periphery concen-trated in eastern and southern Europe, and a larger periphery located every-where else (qtd. in Abu-Lughod 364).

Classical European colonialism effectively dominated world history from the sixteen century to the mid-nineteenth century. From the late nineteenth century to the middle of the twentieth century, imperialism—a form of colo-nialism—held sway. Imperialism endured roughly from 1870 to 1914, when conquest of territory gave way to a systematic search for markets and an expan-sionist exporting of capital, including, in an extended sense, First World inter-ventionist politics in the post-independence era (Shohat and Stam 15). Within classical European colonialism, the African/African American came to belong to the Other, to the non-European, to alterity.

The white/black binary, including the representation of the African as in-ferior and the "inferiority" of Africa, was an ideological invention of classical European colonialism. The advent of colonialism accordingly inspired a retroac-tive rewriting of African history, especially its relation to classical Greek civiliza-tion. A naturalized Eurocentric construction of the world demanded the eradication of the significance of Nubia for Egypt's formation, of Egypt in the development of Greek civilization, of Africa for imperial Rome, and, more pointedly, of Islam's influence on Europe's economic, political, and intellectual history (Robinson 4). History was recast to conform to colonialist norms, in the name of an eternal "West" unique since its moment of conception.[5]

The capture and transportation of Africans to the Americas occurred within classical European colonialism. The whole process was a part of the rise of capitalism in the Americas: manpower was needed for the slave-based plantation system, which was an integral part of modernity. It "involved heavy capitalization, complex business organization, advanced industrial technology (milling, rum manufacture, transport)" (Shohat and Stam 78). This means that the social, cultural, and economic position of the African within American colonialism had always already been established, despite the debate among American slave historians such as Oscar and Mary Handlin, Carl N. Degler, Winthrop D. Jordan, Eric Williams, and others about the origin of racism in the United States.

If, on the one hand, the European colonial discourse asserted that the colonizers and the colonized were fixed, unchanging identities, then the repetition of this assertion, on the other hand, meant that that discourse must constantly reconstitute and refigure this fixity. As the colonial experience of Africans shifted to the internal colonialism of Africans/African Americans, the colonial discourse split between proclaiming the unchangeability of colonial subjects and acknowledging their changing character as it was forced to reform and reconstitute the African/African American subjects.

Internal colonialism, like classical European colonialism, is characterized by a structured relationship of domination and subordination. Historically, colonialism has served the interests of merchants, industrialists, and would-be landowners, or of the state that ultimately safeguards the interests of the dominant classes. Internal colonialism is no exception. In the United States, this internal colonialism, this structured relationship of white domination and black subordination, has constructed what I call the "white/black binary of signification." "Internal colonialism," argues Mario Barrera, "is a form of colonialism in which the dominant and subordinate population are intermingled, so that there is no geographically distinct 'metropolis' separate from the 'colony'" (194). This definition is similar to that employed by Pablo Gonzalez Casanova, who says "internal colonialism corresponds to a structure of social relations based on domination and exploitation among culturally heterogeneous, distinct groups" (33). Therefore, I am using internal colonialism to describe a relationship in which an ethnic and/or racial group is subjected to systematic structural discrimination within a single society.

The white/black binary, or the system of structured racial discrimination that forms the essence of the internal colonial relationship, exists first in the economic realm, but it extends into political institutions, educational systems, social practices, and all forms of social structures. The persistence of the white/black binary of signification in the United States is the result of this historic relationship, which continues to operate today, rearticulated in a dense cultural network of normative definition and binaries. The other important factor in perpetuating this binary is racism, both by leading to individual acts of discrimination and by providing support for the structural aspects of discrimination. Racism is largely a product of what Robert Blauner in *Racial Oppression in America* calls racial ideologies that were developed to justify structural discrimination (21).

As a part of the colonial experience, the enslaved African was the colonized in the internal colonialism that comprised slavery in the United States. It was only later that the African American became the oppressed person in a structured ensemble of social, economic, and institutional practices and discourses. Slavery has existed in many forms from before the dawn of recorded history through to the contemporary period. There is probably no group of people, Orlando Patterson in *Slavery and Social Death* writes, "whose ancestors were not at one time slaves or slaveholders" (vii). But before classical European colonialism, slavery in the Mediterranean and in Africa tended to amount to little more than domestic servitude. (Actually, during its early years, slavery in the United States was something of domestic servitude.) Absorbed in extended-family structures, the slave could accede to family rights, marry into the owner's family, and even inherit the owner's wealth (Davidson 19). My concern here is not to idealize African forms of slavery or to argue that slavery in Africa was not the product of hierarchical regimes of truth and power, nor to deny the complicity of the African elite in the slave trade; instead, my concern is to mark a qualitative historical difference between slavery in Africa and slavery in the United States, especially after the eighteenth century. It is only with colonialism and capitalism that slavery became modern and industrialized, tied to a mode of economic production and to a systematic ideology of racial superiority.

In *White over Black*, Winthrop Jordan indicates that the white/black binary was present at the beginning of American colonialism. He argues that the first Africans who came to the United States in 1691 came as indentured servants. But from the beginning, the Africans were "set apart from white men by the word *Negroes*" (73). The earliest census reports listed Africans separately from the English. They were "sold" to the English, yet so were other Englishmen without that separate classification. Thus, according to Jordan, prior to 1660, Africans and African Americans in Virginia and Maryland were held in bondage and contempt worse than that inflicted on the European American indentured servants. On the other hand, there is much evidence to show that in those early decades *Negro* was not simply another word for slave. Still, Jordan is forced to concede that until at least 1640, "there simply is not enough evidence to indicate with any certainty whether Negroes were treated like white servants or not" (73).

But the American colonialists, who were mostly English, *did* belong to the European colonial regime of truth and power that defined the African as Other, as being a cannibal, a pagan, a savage, a highly sexed being, and a non-Christian (heathen), therefore, different and inferior. They were aware of the systematized hierarchization within classical European colonialism. To define the Africans as savage or pagan was to define them in a conceptual framework in which they were less civilized, which is the equivalent of being "back in time." "The link between paganism and darkness, carried over from English exploitation of

Africa," Kim Hall paraphrases Jordan, "is practically inseparable from the construction of racial difference as an otherness; this connection is in turn fed by the
traditional Christian associations with white and black" (103). As in the discourse of classical European colonialism in which non-Europeans were denied
their history and cultures and belief systems, under internal colonialism in the
United States, Africans and African Americans were detribalized.[6] Colonial
American authorities made it a matter of policy to frustrate enslaved Africans by
segregating those of the same language or other affinity groups from each other.
There was an assault on the tribal affinities, customs, laws, and institutions of the
Africans. Family ties were destroyed and Christianity was forced on them.

The American colonialists went to great lengths to distinguish themselves
from the colonized, enslaved Africans. During the first half of the seventeenth
century, they referred to themselves most often as "Christians," which was not
purely religious in meaning. It meant civilized rather than barbarous, English
rather than un-English, white rather than black (Jordan 83). By the second
half of the seventeenth century, as some enslaved African Americans became
Christians and began to appropriate the Englishman's language, dress, and
manners, the term *white*, as a way of making a distinction between the races,
became predominant (85).

According to Theodore W. Allen in *The Invention of the White Race*, the
white/black binary of signification, and/or a system of structured racial discrimination, was solidified in the various economic, social, legal, and educational institutions and apparatuses in the United States by the mid-seventeenth
century, following an exponential increase in the number of enslaved Africans
and African Americans in the colonies (21). Racial theories were developed to
justify the exploitation of enslaved Africans.[7] These theories came about in large
part because they were useful in justifying classical European colonialism and the
neocolonial and internal colonial relationships that grew out of it. "The importance of Negro slavery in generating race theories in this country," argues
Thomas Gossett in *Race: The History of an Idea in America*, "can hardly be overes-
timated, but it must be remembered that there was a minimum of theory at the
time the institution [of slavery] was established" (29).

Simultaneously, in the seventeenth century in the United States, a system
of racial privileges for the propertyless "whites" was deliberately instituted in
order to align them with the plantation owners and against the enslaved African
Americans. Since they were not slaveowners, the propertyless whites, or European Americans, did not derive any direct economic benefits from the establishment of slavery. But they were allowed to prosper and were accorded "social,
psychological, and political advantages" because they were "white." From this
moment hence, emigrant populations from "multiracial" Europe who came to
the United States were, by constitutional fiat, incorporated as the "white race"
(Allen 21–22).[8]

This invention of the white race, argues Allen, was not the result of genetic
evolution. Rather, it was a political act (22). Race resides not in nature/biology

but in politics and culture. Thus, the economic and social prosperity and stability of white Americans, even working-class white Americans, is based on an exclusion—or, conversely, on the admission of this group to the privileged status that permits full participation in American life. As for the Africans, African Americans, and Native Americans, Anglo American internal colonialism reduced them to an undifferentiated social status, one beneath that of any member of the invented white race. In this undifferentiated social status, they were objectified—defined as inferior, as victim, or as devalued Other.

In the eighteenth century in the United States, racial ideologies continued to be solidified. Gunner Myrdal in *An American Dilemma* notes that "when the Negro was first enslaved, his subjugation was not justified in terms of his biological inferiority" (84). The origins of a systematic racial ideology in the United States can be traced to the need of pro-slavery interests to respond to criticism based on the "universal rights of man," criticisms that mounted as revolutionary agitation developed in the late eighteenth century. These racial ideologies did not gain strength until three decades before the Civil War, when criticism of slavery became even more vehement.

> In the precarious ideological situation—where the South wanted to defend a political and civic institution of inequality which showed increasingly great prospects for new land exploitation and commercial profit, but where they also wanted to retain the democratic creed of the nation—*the race doctrine of biological inequality between whites and Negroes offered the most convenient solution.* (87–88)

Of course, throughout slavery in the United States, enslaved Africans, Native Americans, and African Americans resisted slavery, a fact that was downplayed by American colonialists and Eurocentric history.[9]

After the Civil War, and especially during post-Reconstruction when southern whites with the assistance of the northern government moved to disenfranchise African Americans, ideologies of racial inferiority survived and were intensified as a means of justifying the continued exploitation of the African American population. Myrdal also argues that the ideologies became more prevalent in the North as a way of justifying the national compromise arrived at in the 1870s that allowed the South to continue its legal oppression of, and structural discrimination of, African Americans (88).

The culture of segregation, which defined American social reality in the South from Reconstruction to World War II, was a structured ensemble of social and institutional practices and discourses. It perpetuated ideologies of racial inferiority or the white/black binary of signification. "Central to the meaning of whiteness," writes Grace Elizabeth Hale about this culture and period in *Making Whiteness*, "is a broad, collective American silence. The denial of white as a racial identity, the denial that whiteness has a history, allows the quiet, the blankness, to stand as the norm" (xi). Segregation was America's "broadest twentieth-century enactment of the difference between blacks and whites" (xi). Segregation, as a metaphor and a law, depended on a myth of absolute racial difference. Through laws and localized conventions, whites controlled both the geographical and representational mobility in the South of African Americans, who were clearly defined as inferior because they occupied "inferior spaces like Jim Crow cars, often literally marked as colored, and across the nation because they appeared at fairs, in advertisements, and in movies as visibly inferior characters" (8).

In addition, the South provided white southerners and America with the cultural artifacts and myths to reconstruct the foundation of racial difference, or the white/black binary. "Stories of the Old South, the Civil War, and Reconstruction permeated the popular fiction. . . . They became the origin narratives that [legitimated] segregation as the only possible southern future" (44). Between 1890 and 1910, leading magazines and newspapers defined African Americans as ignorant, lazy, improvident, clownish, irresponsible, childish, and criminal. Social Darwinists declared that if blacks did not survive, it was because they were not "the fittest" and that no law promulgated by the state could change "the natural order of things." As W. E. B. DuBois points out in "The Negro in Literature and Art," published in 1913, "everything touching the Negro is banned by magazines and publishers unless it takes the form of caricature or bitter attack, or is so thoroughly innocuous as to have no literary flavor" (91).

This culture of segregation was grounded and supported in the South because elite/southern whites had economic and political autonomy. During this period, African Americans were treated as if they were inferior. But they were inferior because, within the culture of segregation, they were excluded from the franchise, the jury, and political officeholding. They were inferior because they attended inferior schools and held inferior jobs. They were perhaps most politically inferior because they "sat in inferior waiting rooms, used inferior restrooms, sat in inferior cars or seats, or just stood. African Americans were inferior because they . . . watched movies from inferior balconies . . . , dined at blocked-off, racially marked, and inferior tables" (Hale 284–85). And for southern African Americans to violate these rituals, to refuse to play the role of the inferior, devalued Other that white southerners continually assigned them, was to invite the "threat of violent retribution that the spectacle of lynching periodically and very publically staged" (285).

Thus, at the end of the nineteenth century and during the first quarter of the twentieth century, urban industrial society, with its poverty, disease, mortality, corruption, immorality, and crime became more visible. And as African Americans migrated from the rural areas to towns and cities in the South and North, sensationalized journalistic accounts of crime, vice, and vagrancy associated black migration with racial morbidity. During this period between 1890 and 1920, according to Kevin K. Gaines in *Uplifting the Race*, racial ideologies reemerged, advocating the biological inferiority of the African American. Eugenics, genetics, and heredity served as a secular rearticulation of the Calvinist notions of original sin and predestination. "While environment is a powerful factor in producing marked modifications of hereditary tendencies," claimed one expert, ". . . the influence of heritage has still greater power in the formation of character" (qtd. in Gaines 80).

Between the mid-1950s and the late 1960s, the Civil Rights movement challenged the southern culture of segregation by staging mass actions such as large marches/protests at Montgomery, Birmingham, Albany, and Selma, where African Americans violated their role of the inferior Other as defined by the existing racial social order. African Americans, led by aspiring middle-class and elite, educated African Americans, wanted social and economic equality and political representation. They wanted to become the Same as the middle-class Christian white norm. These mass actions compelled the federal government to enforce the Reconstruction amendments at last. The Civil Rights Act of 1964 outlawed segregation in all arenas of southern public and commercial life, and across the region the signs "For Colored" and "For White" were removed. In the 1960s, Congress enacted laws banning racial discrimination in housing, education, and employment. These laws provided more economic and educational opportunities for African Americans. Then the Voting Rights Act of 1965 placed voting registration in the hands of federal authorities, and African Americans finally had access to the ballot (Hale 293–94). By the 1980s, these laws had assisted in the creation of a large black middle class. In short, civil rights legislation legally made accessible to many middle-class African Americans the institutions and practices of mainstream American society.

Yet even after the 1970s, many neighborhoods and schools and almost all churches remained segregated, and in isolated small towns throughout the South, the public performance of segregation continued without the laws or the signs. But the South was no longer distinct in its regional racial order, no better and no worse than the rest of an often-racist and often-segregated United States (294).

By the late 1970s, the southern culture of segregation and its various legal and social institutions and practices that perpetuated the idea of black inferiority no longer existed. This does not mean that today the white, middle-class American norm still does not depend on the subjection or Otherization of the African American. It simply means that the white/black binary, or order, in America is no longer maintained around the positioning of the African American as excluded or biologically inferior. This stereotype was contested/resisted not only by African Americans but also by liberal, mainstream Americans. Since the 1970s, the African American has been, to use the words of Hal Foster in *Recodings*, "recouped, processed in [his] very difference through the order of recognition, or simply reduced to the same" (166). The enforcement of civil rights laws made it possible for the African American to become the Same as whites: legally, blacks were now equal to whites. Yet, this legal equality, and/or blacks' aspiration to be the Same as whites, did not disrupt the white/black binary; it did not transform the representation of the African American as devalued Other, or address African American differences and America's heterogeneity.

Labels and categories such as *black, African American, Native American, European, white, colonizer,* and *colonized,* which had been used from the beginning to define/represent the American and the African American, are slippery. They do not represent "zones of purity." Despite the fact that American colonialists went to great lengths to distinguish themselves from the colonized, enslaved Africans/African Americans and Native Americans, there was intermingling racially, socially, and culturally in the South from the sixteenth through the twentieth centuries. For the past four hundred years, underneath social and legal categories of segregation and staged racial difference, there was a hybrid American society that was the product of an intermingling among all of America's citizens. "Even before Africans arrived in this hemisphere," writes Ishmael Reed, "there was a mixing between European males and African women. This mixing began in the slave ports where the Africans were prepared for shipment to this hemisphere" (74).

From very early on, long before the Civil War was fought and the African Americans were freed, the African Americans and Native Americans "had begun to exact a subtle but very powerful influence on the Anglo-Saxon majority culture by their very presence" (Cook 51). The rape of black and Native American women during slavery and legal segregation and, later, legal interracial marriages have intermingled and continue to intermingle the bloods not only of Europeans and the descendants of enslaved Africans but also of Native Americans, Asian Americans, and Hispanics with both European American and African Americans. In *Black Indians,* William Loren Katz discusses how Native Americans and Africans/African Americans merged by choice, invitation, and love. "The number of Afro-Americans with an Indian ancestor," Katz contends, "was once estimated at about one third of the total." Today just about every African American family tree has a Native American branch (2).

Culturally, many American musical forms are hybrid. They, too, do not comprise a zone of purity. The great African American musical forms—the blues and jazz—are the product of American/European, Asian, and African American instruments and musical traditions. The African American blues musician was an "agent of change, working continually from as early as the eighteenth century on the music that he heard around him, shaping and reshaping it, giving it back to the culture as something ever more distinct" (Cook 51). Southern country music is influenced by the blues thematically and musically. Black musicians, composers, and singers as diverse as Duke Ellington, Ethel Waters, and James P. Johnson drew from European, black folk, and black and white popular traditions (Hale 38). Two of John Coltrane's influences were Bismilla Khan, who played a double reed Indian instrument called *shenai,* and great sitarist Ravi Shankar, after whom Coltrane named his son. Randy Weston has infused some of his jazz compositions with traditional South Asian instruments. Fred Ho, the Chinese American baritone saxophonist, leads the Afro Asian Music Ensemble; and jazz pianist Vijay Iyer, a solo artist who records and performs with jazz saxophonist Steve Coleman, cites

Thelonious Monk, Duke Ellington, John Coltrane, and James Brown as his heroes (Kim 41–42).

Linguistically, the southern drawl did not have its beginnings in Europe, but in the South where southern whites lived in close proximity with blacks. For the past four hundred years, America has been a place where different peoples of different races with different gods and different languages have intermingled and intermixed, creating a genuinely hybrid American society. Assessing American society and culture, and the inability of labels and categories to repress and deny American heterogeneity and hybridity, Ralph Ellison writes: "Whatever the efficiency of segregation as a socio-political arrangement, it has been far from absolute at the level of *culture*. Southern whites cannot walk, talk, sing, conceive of laws or justice, think of sex, love, the family or freedom without responding to the presence of Negroes" (116).

Of course, in the United States, migration, urban expansion, and the commodification of culture have intensified the processes of transculturation. But, as Canclini points out about these processes:

> [I]n the exchange of traditional symbols with international communications circuits, culture, industries, and migration, questions about identity and the national, the defense of sovereignty, and the unequal appropriation of knowledge and art do not disappear. . . . They are placed in a different register, one that is multifocal and more tolerant, and the autonomy of each culture is rethought— sometimes—with smaller fundamentalist risks. Nevertheless, the chauvinist critiques of "those from the center" sometimes engender violent conflicts. (240–41)

Thus, in the midst of America's intermingling, "questions about identity and the national . . . do not disappear."

In addition, within the category "African America," there are differences. There are many African American communities, lifestyles, and theoretical definitions of life based in such traditions as jazz/blues, Voodoo, the African American subaltern existence, middle-class, Christian, and the working-class African American life. These different African American lifestyles and communities, which do not generate the image of the African American as victim, as inferior, or as the Same, are dependent on mutual relations between individuals and groups. Thus, they destabilize the white/black binary's representation of the African American.

Although, the Civil Rights movement was successful in overturning the southern culture of segregation and in marginalizing a distinctly southern and American whiteness, the movement did not succeed in transforming America. It did not succeed in disrupting the white/black binary of signification that defines white as normative and superior and that represents black as inferior, as victim, or as devalued Other. It did not evoke in the United States an "integration, [a] true equality, a mutual respect for the shifting play of difference and commonality among all Americans" (Hale 294) despite the fact that hybridity, or that shifting play of difference and commonality among all Americans, was/is very visible behind the labels and laws and categories. "It is not possible," argues Michel de Certeau, "for a minority movement merely to confine itself to a political demand. It also has to change the culture" (*Culture* 78). The Civil Rights movement in the United States, in confining itself to "political demand," did not produce successfully "the condition of possibility for a new [American] culture" (78). It did not represent American culture differently. It did not change the cultural paradigm and, therefore, change the perception of the African American. It only asked that the African American be the Same.

The white/black binary with its racial ideologies has been embodied in the history, culture, and beliefs of the American and European past since the Renaissance. The present generation of Americans has no conception of the exact context in which racial ideologies originate and are thus transformed into broad-based racial prejudice, even among people, particularly poor and working-class whites and African Americans whose interests are not served by it. Discussing institutionalized racism in *Caste, Class, and Race*, Oliver Cox writes:

> In our description of the uses of race prejudice . . . we are likely to give the impression that race prejudice was always "manufactured" in full awareness by individuals or groups of entrepreneurs. This, however, is not quite the case. Race prejudice, from its inception, became part of the social heritage, and as such both exploiters and exploited for the most part are born heirs to it. It is possible that most of those who propagate and defend race prejudice are not conscious of its fundamental motivation. (333n)

Thus, structured racial discrimination, or the white/black binary of signification, in becoming a part of the economic, cultural, educational, and social apparatuses and institutions in the United States, becomes naturalized. From slavery to Reconstruction to the Jim Crow legal segregation era to the Civil Rights movement to the present, this white/black binary of signification maintained its fixed, unchanging identities by constantly reconstituting and refiguring this fixity.

Even after the Civil Rights movement successfully fought to pass laws that banned discrimination, structural racism, the white/black binary continued to be reconstituted and refigured in American educational, housing, and employment practices and discourses. Structural racial discrimination persists not only for subaltern and working-class African Americans but also for elite/middle-class African Americans who are often confined to a largely or entirely African American clientele in their small businesses or independent professional practices. Occupational stratification also appears to be an important factor for African Americans who manage to make it into the professional-managerial class. African American professionals who work in bureaucracies are often hired to deal only with an African American clientele, much as African American white-collar workers have historically been employed. Most firms have an African American manager in a senior position. But currently no more than a handful of black executives head operating divisions. Most common are positions in charge of community relations, corporate diversity, and market development, the last usually referring to promoting products among black customers (Hillard-Jones 151).

African American faculty in mainstream American colleges and universities are often deemed employable primarily in ethnic studies programs and departments, which are usually run on soft money and are not considered a permanent central aspect of the university. The percentage of African American tenured faculty is down since the 1980s, whereas the percentage of untenured African American faculty has increased. In part, these patterns reflect the existence of structural discrimination at lower levels of the public education system, that few African Americans reach the university level, but they also reflect certain institutionalized practices at the university and professional levels.

In situation after situation, Ellis Cose in *The Rage of a Privileged Class* presents the anger of those African Americans who have entered the highest echelons of America's professional managerial class. They are bureau chiefs at the *New York Times*, law partners in prestigious law firms, professors at high-ranking universities, and generals in the U.S. army. Yet they are angry because they are still represented by mainstream society as being inferior and Other. They are still *marked* as an outsider and a stranger. Despite the passage of civil rights laws that gave African Americans access to better jobs, housing, and education and despite the rise of a large African American middle class, being black in America today is still a negative in American society. Systematized hierarchies still exist. The white/black binary has again been reconstituted. "America is filled with attitudes, assumptions, stereotypes, and behaviors that make it virtually impossible for blacks to believe that the nation is serious about its promise of equality— even . . . for those who have been blessed with material success" (5). Discussing this same issue, Ellen Willis writes:

> At its deepest and most intractable level, it [racism] is the displacement onto skin color of powerful wishes and fears about class, sex, and violence—the "dark" underside of a hierarchical and repressive culture despite the decline of both the racial caste system and the Victorian morality with which it was closely linked. The black–white polarity is still charged with meaning. While it is no longer intellectually respectable or socially acceptable for whites to proclaim racial mythology as fact . . . , unconscious associations live on. (49–50)

The fact that there are elite/upper-middle-class African Americans who are still defined as being a victim, as being inferior, or as being a devalued Other by both white and black Americans shows that economic inequality, which is a prevalent issue in the United States, is not the sole reason for the continuation of the white/black binary. America has never had an educational or cultural transformation in which whiteness as a construct, rather than a metaphysical certainty, with all its subsequent privileges, has been exposed, fractured, or undermined, where the "unconscious associations" of racial mythology are engaged and challenged. It has never produced a hegemonic narrative or national culture about an "integration, [a] true equality, a mutual respect for the shifting play of difference and commonality among all Americans" (Hale 294) to show all Americans a different concept of social reality. And elite/middle-class African Americans leaders and organizations perpetuate the white/black binary by continuing to perform public variations of their role as victim, as inferior, and as devalued Other, or, at best, by becoming the Same as the dominant white society. By ignoring American hybrid culture, by repressing African American differences, mainstream Americans and aspiring middle-class and elite/middle-class African Americans reinforce the single paradigmatic perspective in which white, middle-class Christian Americans are the norm and blacks are the Other. You change/transform a culture by changing the hegemonic cultural narrative. Even with most efforts at multiculturalism, I see attempts to achieve difference by assimilating racial and religious minorities who espouse the same values as the hegemonic American cultural narrative but very few attempts to change the hegemonic cultural narrative to accept not only different racial and religious minorities but also different belief systems and definitions of life.

CHAPTER THREE

THE WHITE/BLACK BINARY AND THE AFRICAN AMERICAN SOCIOPOLITICAL MISSION OF RACIAL UPLIFT

In the previous chapter, I discussed at length how the African American in the United States is constituted in a white/black binary of signification that represents white as normative and superior and that defines black as either inferior, as devalued Other, or as the Same. I also traced the beginning of this binary to modernity, the European Renaissance, classical European colonialism, and internal American colonialism, showing how it had been articulated and rearticulated in a network of normative definitions and binaries. The two halves of a binary belong together because they have something in common, because they have a symbiotic relationship. Since power lies mostly with the white half of this particular binary, I explore in this chapter how the African American has responded historically to and interpreted his negative representation as the devalued Other. I will focus initially on the so-called African American sociopolitical mission of racial uplift, including the African American literary canon and the classic historical narrative of emancipation, and I will show how this sociopolitical mission excludes and represses the polyvalent nature in African American literature, criticism, and history. Then, I will give a polycentric reading of African American literature, history, and criticism since the 1960s, which is the best way to disrupt the white/black binary.

From the abolitionist movement to the Reconstruction and post-Reconstruction eras to the various mainstream organizations and movements of Frederick Douglass, David Walker, Maria Stewart, W. E. B. DuBois, and Booker T. Washington; from the Afro-American League, the Equal Rights League, the National Council of Negro Women, and the National Association for the Advancement of Colored People (NAACP) to the Civil Rights and Black Power movements of the 1950s and 1960s, the response of African Americans as a

35

group posed a deadly challenge to black freedom. The purpose of these various organizations and movements was to seek freedom for the African American by challenging structured racial discrimination legally, socially, educationally, and politically; by refuting the racist devaluation invested in the African American by the colonizer; by reacting to the negative, dehumanizing portrait imposed by the colonizer; and by adopting and embracing the values of the colonizer: "The ideology of a governing class is adopted in large measure by the governed classes. . . . The first ambition of the colonized is to become equal to that splendid model [of the colonizer] and to resemble him to the point of disappearing in him" (Memmi 120).

This strategy of assimilating the values of mainstream white society and of tearing away from the darker subaltern self is at the core of the African American mission of racial uplift, which began during slavery and which was advocated by elite/middle-class and aspiring middle-class African Americans. Its ultimate objective was equality and social advancement: to adopt the values of, and to become the Same as, the dominant American society. The desired mainstream values included education, self-help, a patriarchal political culture and patriarchal gender conventions, Christianity, the bourgeois nuclear family, the Enlightenment idea of progress, and a bourgeois morality. (Of course, this one-dimensional, male-dominated mythology of who the African American is did not represent all that she is or could be.) Racial uplift was offered as a form of cultural politics in the hope that unsympathetic whites would eventually relent and recognize the humanity of African Americans. Thus, the ideology of racial uplift became the dominant way that elite/middle-class African Americans moved to achieve what John Guillory in *Cultural Capital* calls "symbolic or cultural capital," which includes the knowledge and values necessary to receive the economic, social, and political rewards of the dominant American society (viii–xi). Of course, as Guillory also points out, "the distribution of cultural capital . . . reproduces the structure of social relations, a structure of complex and ramifying inequality" (6).

A sense of racial uplift as liberation theology began during slavery and flourished after emancipation and during the democratic reforms of Reconstruction. Since then, it has been kept alive by generations of aspiring middle-class and elite/middle-class African Americans, along with the liberal and leftist sectors of the American population. During slavery and the abolitionist movement, racial uplift described the passage of African Americans from slavery to freedom. Advocates of racial uplift presented a broad vision of collective social aspiration, advancement, and struggle. Racial uplift signified both the process of group struggle and its object: freedom. It was a part of the antislavery efforts made by both African Americans and the network of antebellum institutions for group liberation established within free black communities.

Racial uplift as liberation theology stressed the importance of group education and based black claims for suffrage, leadership, and jury service on a natural rights argument. The black church was prominent in championing this perspective through education, moralizing, and antislavery activities. White and black abolitionists affirmed the Enlightenment ideals of inalienable rights and human progress by insisting on freedom, not merely as a reward for up-right cultural behavior but also in the spirit of the Declaration of Independence. The objective was to refute the dominant society's myth of slave docility and black depravity.

Many of these objectives, along with the broad vision of racial uplift, flourished during the rise of freedmen's schools and education during Reconstruction, and the emphasis on education continues to today. Among elite/middle-class and aspiring middle-class African Americans, there is no disputing the value of education. Before the assault on Reconstruction and the rise of Booker T. Washington, black educators and intellectuals such as R. R. Wright, Anna J. Cooper, Ida B. Wells, and others studied under the classical liberal New England curriculum and then transplanted it into southern black elementary, normal, and collegiate institutions. Such an education was basically assimilationist. Students trained in the schools established by the freedmen's aid societies generally imbibed the missionary, service-oriented ideals of their liberal New England teachers. Mainstream, middle-class, Christian values were promoted and deemed crucial for economic success and citizenship. What emerged in the United States among African American political leaders, intellectuals, writers, and educators during the periods of slavery, Reconstruction, and post-Reconstruction was identity politics, with the African American sociopolitical mission as its motor.[1]

It was only after the assault on Reconstruction progress by southern whites that elite/middle-class African Americans made racial uplift the basis for an elite racialized identity, claiming black improvement through class stratification as progress. With the rise of Jim Crow laws and repressive social practices in the late nineteenth century, the concept of racial uplift departed from the liberation theology model of the emancipation era. Dominant discourses on race at that time were fraught with a biological determinism that naturalized and promoted a regime of power and knowledge that defined the African American as inferior, as lazy and sexually promiscuous, and as less intelligent than whites. As Kevin K. Gaines points out in *Uplifting the Race*, these theories of heredity and biological determinism "clashed with the environmentalism of [elite/middle-class] African American's uplift's call for home training" (81). Strongly influenced by the racial assumptions of elite whites, elite/middle-class African American reformers in turn "reinforced dominant racial assumptions and theories" (81): barraged with sexual and racial stereotypes, African American leaders campaigned for moral authority, Victorian mores, and respectability. For them, the family and conformity to patriarchal family ideals became crucial signifiers of respectability.

Furthermore, with the advent of Jim Crow laws, the self-help component of racial uplift increasingly bore the stamp of evolutionary racial theories that contrasted the civilization of elite/middle-class African Americans with the moral degradation of subaltern African America. A racial hierarchy was soon established. By devising a form of cultural politics, elite/middle-class African Americans believed that they were replacing the racist notion of fixed biological/racial differences with an evolutionary view of cultural assimilation, measured primarily by the status of the family and the degree of civilization. Cultural differences, then, rather than biological notions of racial inferiority, were considered more salient in explaining the lower social status of subaltern African Americans. Furthermore, an elite/middle-class African American consciousness—stressing racial solidarity and self-help and uniting blacks across class lines—promised a more legitimate basis for social differentiation than color. This shift to bourgeois evolutionism not only obscured the social inequities resulting from racial and class subordination but also marked a retreat from the earlier unconditional claim made by black and white abolitionists for emancipation, citizenship, and education based on Christian and Enlightenment ethics.

This post-Reconstruction definition of racial uplift was fraught with tensions and contradictions. Whereas most elite/middle-class African American educators advocated assimilation into the values of the dominant white society—disappearing into the "splendid model" of the colonizer—cultural nationalist leaders and writers such as Alexander Crummell, Henry McNeal Turner, William Hooper Councill, John Edward Bruce, Sutton Griggs, Martin Delany (*The Condition of the Colored People*), Walter F. Walker, Chief Alfred C. Sam, and T. Thomas Fortune, and later Marcus Garvey, Carter G. Woodson (*The Miseducation of the Negro*), Claude McKay, Zora Neale Hurston, Langston Hughes, Jean Toomer, and others equated black progress and humanity with territorial nation building, civilization, Afrocentric education and cultural models, black folk culture, and patriarchal authority.[2]

More fissures appeared when, giving in to the pressures of unreconstructed southern whites, Booker T. Washington began to advocate an industrial education for African Americans. The rise of Washington and the form of ideological education he came to embody, which was shaped by the views of southern whites who feared that any kind of education, however minimal, would instill in African Americans a desire for social equality, clashed with the assimilationist vision of education. To appease southern whites, as well as northern philanthropists and industrialists, the ideological thrust of the industrial education espoused by Washington effectively opposed blacks' involvement in politics, situated the black labor force at the bottom of the southern economy, and acquiesced in the separation of the races (Gaines 34). Washington's Tuskegee Institute in Alabama, founded in 1891, emphasized manual training, sought to exalt the dignity of labor, taught a curriculum of only rudimentary education, and was intended to produce common schoolteachers who would inculcate habits of industry, thrift, and morality in southern black farmers and their families. Washington's industrial education was advertised as a missionary program of uplift. In his popular 1901 autobiography, *Up from Slavery*, Washington appropriated the spirit of evangelical reform in a manner that eclipsed the Radical Republican tradition. He also appropriated racial uplift ideology, transforming the freedmen's education into his program of industrial training. But his was a more conservative version of uplift, shaped by the political climate and antiblack sentiments of the time. "Industrial education," argues Gaines, "would produce the class distinctions necessary for the tutelage and uplift of a race of thrifty agricultural toilers who had little use for organized labor or political activity" (34).

By the turn of the century, some elite/middle-class African American intellectuals and educators, including W. E. B. DuBois and Ida B. Wells, would rise to challenge Washington and his industrial education. In 1887, Wells castigated blacks for retreating from principles of full equality. By taking segregated excursions and accepting segregated public facilities, she argued, blacks gave whites further justification for drawing ever more rigid social barriers (cited in Gaines 35). In 1906, DuBois shocked a gathering at the Hampton Institute, whose brain child was industrial education, by calling Washington's Tuskegee Institute the center of "education heresy" in its pursuit of a "false distinction" between industrial and higher education (35).

But, despite the tensions, contradictions, and fissures, all of the previously mentioned strains of racial uplift—from DuBois to Crummell to Washington—were conventionally defined as male dominant. This patriarchal definition of racial uplift created gender tensions: antagonizing black women leaders of the late nineteenth century. Beginning with their national mobilization in the 1890s and the creation of the National Association of Colored Women (NACW) to the 1935 founding of the National Council of Negro Women, black women would form over time a vital network that laid the institutional foundation for most of their social reform, community uplift, and self-improvement work. The motto of the NACW clubs, "Lifting as We Climb," captures the myriad dimensions of their movement (Hine 60–61). It was during the early 1890s, however, that middle-class black women journalists, intellectuals, novelists, and reformers first began contributing their own visions of racial uplift, calling for women's leadership as vital to racial progress in views that clashed with the male-dominated vision of racial progress within a patriarchal political culture.

Despite their many differences, all movements of racial uplift believed universally in education. The debate was over precisely what kind of mainstream education would be made available to blacks. And despite their many points of disagreement, all proponents of racial uplift—from Washington to DuBois to Wells to Crummell to Frances Harper—were elite/middle-class African Americans of similar education and Christian belief. More important, they all believed in the values of Western civilization, having adopted the ideology of the colonizer, the dominant white society.

But their passion for the colonizer's values had a negative side. They had to crush African American differences, particularly subaltern African America's cultures and belief systems. They believed in a racial hierarchy that assumed the black masses of subaltern African America were inferior to elite/middle-class African Americans culturally, materially, and socially. Regardless of how sympathetic they were toward subaltern African Americans, educated elite/middle-class African Americans could not imagine that subaltern African Americans—illiterate peasants and farmworkers, urban workers, blues journeymen, Voodoo practitioners, hobos, and others who constituted the black majority—were different but also equal.[3] Instead, they projected their own values and customs onto subaltern African America, defining it in the name of racial uplift and racial solidarity as the possessions of the Same to be conquered, colonized, modernized, and civilized. Subaltern African America, as Other, was thus constituted as part of the Same.

In the twentieth century, racial identity politics continued to define African American life in terms of social equality. The NAACP and its organ, *The Crisis*, and the National Urban League and its organ, *Opportunity*, along with about two hundred African American newspapers such as the *Chicago Defender*, the *Pittsburgh Courier*, the *Cleveland Call and Post*, the *California Eagle*, the *Los Angeles Sentinel*, the *New York Amsterdam News American*, the *Negro World*, the *Afro-American* (Baltimore), the *Atlanta World*, the *Norfolk* (Virginia) *Journal and Guide*, the *Richmond* (Virginia) *Planet*, and the *Tampa Times* continued to foster the idea of a unitary African American identity. New and old leaders, educators, and newspaper editors such as W. E. B. DuBois, Charles Johnson, James Weldon Johnson, Robert S. Abbott, Joseph and Charlotte Bass, Charles Alexander, Eloise Bibb Thompson, Noah Thompson, John H. Johnson, and others (many of whom were also leaders of community-based African American organizations)[4] continued politically to organize African Americans around important but narrowly defined grievances and goals. The dominant agenda of the national black press was building community, exposing racism and denigrating racist images, and winning civil rights and full equality for the African American.[5] Racial uplift ideology was basically inseparable from African American identity politics.

As I discussed in chapter 2, the Civil Rights movement, which reached its height and effectiveness in the 1950s and 1960s, continued the fight successfully by tearing down social and legal barriers that had denied African Americans access to the social, economic, and educational rights and privileges as other Americans. In 1954, *Brown vs. The Board of Education* outlawed separate but equal education of the United States. In the 1960s, Congress passed a series of laws outlawing discrimination in employment and housing. In 1965, Congress passed the Voting Rights Act giving African Americans the franchise. By the 1980s, these laws, along with affirmative action, had assisted in the creation of a large black middle class. In short, they made legally accessible to African Americans the institutions and practices of mainstream American society. But as I also discussed in chapter 2, the issue of the white/black binary remained very much alive, and subaltern, middle-class, and upper-middle-class African Americans today continue to be Otherized, defined as inferior, as victim, or as devalued Other.

As in the post-Reconstruction era and the first half of the twentieth century, in the 1960s, the racial uplift ideology was fraught with tension and conflict. Whereas the NAACP, the National Urban League, and Martin Luther King and the Southern Christian Leadership Conference (SCLC) still advocated some form of assimilation into the values and conventions of mainstream American society, the Black Power movement—with such leaders as H. Rap Brown, Stokley Carmichael, Bobby Seale, Huey P. Newton, and others—the Cultural Nationalist movement—with such leaders as Ron Karenga, Amiri Baraka, Haki Madhubuti, and others—and the Black Muslims—including early on Malcolm X—again, equated black progress and humanity with nation building, Afrocentric education and cultural models, and patriarchal authority. Although these movements and individuals were effective in bringing empowerment, pride, and a redefinition of self, they were still caught up in many of the patriarchal, sexist, homophobic, and classist attitudes, definitions, values, and concepts of mainstream American society.

Later in this chapter, I will enter into a discussion about disrupting this white/black binary. But first I want to discuss how the canon of African American literature and several classic African American historical narratives also reproduce racial uplift ideology and racial identity politics, thereby entrapping the African American in the binary. More important, I want to demonstrate how the canon, despite its various reformulations and reinventions, and these classic historical narratives repress African American differences—the most potent weapon in disrupting the white/black binary, with its naturalization of whiteness and its representation of the African American as Other. But I want to discuss this canon and these historical narratives polycentrically, showing how after the 1960s, this historical canon and these narratives became increasingly one of many dynamic cultural, historical, and critical locations, one of many possible vantage points, rather than centers/norms.

Charles Altieri's chapter in *Canons* assesses canon formation. "Literary canons," he argues, "are an institutional form for exposing people to a range of idealized attitudes"; they "preserve rich, complex contrastive frameworks, which create . . . a cultural grammar for interpreting experience" (46, 51). Canons establish "models of wisdom" (51). They are essentially strategic constructs by which societies or communities maintain their own interests: the canon allows control over both the texts a culture takes seriously and the methods of interpretation that establish the meaning of "serious" (42).

The canon of African American literature as the literary and critical extension of the African American sociopolitical agenda of racial uplift creates a "cultural grammar for interpreting [the African American] experience" (Altieri 51). It has gone through several stages of invention, reconfiguration, and reinvention since the early twentieth century at the hands of both American and African American critics.[6] But expanding and reinventing the canon along the lines of similarity is a problematic practice because while the canon grows, what it says does not change. John Guillory states that "literary culture has aspired to canonical consensus. . . . Very simply, canonical authors are made to *agree* with one another" ("Ideology" 350). He suggests that new works are included by critics only to the degree that they can be read as duplicating what is already canonized (350).

Although earlier American and African American critics such as Benjamin Brawley, Alain Locke, Nick Aaron Ford, Sterling Brown, J. Saunders Redding, Vernon Loggins, Carl Milton Hughes, Hugh M. Gloster, and Robert Bone invented and reconfigured the canon of African American literature, my examination begins with the reinvention of the African American canon in the 1970s and 1980s. This reinvention came with the rise of African American studies programs and departments, the institutionalization of African American literature, and the publication of certain canon-forming critical texts such as George Kent's *blackness and the adventure of western culture*, Sherley Anne Williams's *Give Birth to Brightness*, Houston A. Baker Jr.'s *Long Black Song* and *Singers of Daybreak*, Robert Stepto's *From Behind the Veil*, Michael G. Cooke's *Afro-American Literature in the Twentieth Century*, Henry Louis Gates Jr.'s *Figures in Black, The Signifying Monkey*, and *"Race," Writing, and Difference*, and Valerie Smith's *Self-Discovery and Authority in Afro-American Narrative*.

These critical texts organized African American literature into a canon that privileged certain classical (mostly male) African American texts and subordinated and repressed others.[7] This reinvented canon viewed African American literature in terms of the experience of racial oppression and defined it according to the journey of the African American from the subaltern to the values and definitions of mainstream, middle-class, Christian American society. Their university positions enabled elite/middle-class African American literary critics to make these cultural and aesthetic identifications by giving them access to the cultural capital, the means of literary and cultural production, formerly restricted to white scholars. With their cultural capital, mainstream African American critics then reproduced "a structure of complex and ramifying inequality" (Guillory, *Cultural Capital* 6). They established a "model of wisdom" (Altieri 51) by deciding which African American texts would be taken seriously.

When theorizing about or canonizing African American literature, all the critics I mentioned, with the exception of Cooke, focus on approximately ten (mostly male) classical African American authors and/or texts. These include Frederick Douglass's *Narrative*, Booker T. Washington's *Up from Slavery*, W. E. B. DuBois's *The Souls of Black Folk*, the poetry of Paul Laurence Dunbar, James Weldon Johnson's *The Autobiography of an Ex-Coloured Man*, Jean Toomer's *Cane*, Richard Wright's *Black Boy* and *Native Son*, the poetry of Gwendolyn Brooks, Ralph Ellison's *Invisible Man*, Chester Himes's *If He Hollers Let Him Go*, John A. Williams's *The Man Who Cried I Am*, and sometimes Zora Neale Hurston's *Their Eyes Were Watching God* and Toni Morrison's *Song of Solomon*. According to Altieri, canonical works are examples of the "forms of imagination considered valuable in a culture" (51). He defines canons as playing a more conservatorial role, providing a way for a society or community to maintain itself. The canonical African American texts I have listed are read to protest racial oppression and the inferior status of the African American, and to advocate a construction/representation of the African American that gives him or her social, cultural, and intellectual equality within the unequal white/black binary system. Qualifying Altieri's statement, these canonical texts provide forms of African American imagination considered valuable by elite/middle-class African Americans in African American culture. They provide the values, artistic models, and definitions of social reality necessary to maintain a particular representation of the African American community, and in most instances, these values, models, and definitions are the same as those of mainstream American society.

The African American critics who would reinvent the canon of African American literature in the 1970s and 1980s reacted overtly to pre-1960s constructions by both white and black critics that devalued African American literature or read it sociologically rather than aesthetically. But in their reconfiguration of African American literature and in their repositioning of certain African American texts, these later critics reinscribed the canonical economy—that is, the means by which the canon organizes, regulates, and reproduces itself. In fact, they produced a more narrowly constructed canon, which excludes even more African American texts than the pre-1960s constructions. Ultimately, as I have already noted, they would identify seven or eight classical (usually male) African American texts and focus on them almost exclusively.[8] As with most canon formation, these texts were selected, argues Guillory, because they had been or could be judged "not only as expressions of approved social or moral [or political] values, but also for their specifically 'aesthetic' value" (*Cultural Capital* 270).

According to these later African American critics, particularly Baker, Stepto, Gates, and Smith, the tradition of combining art with racial progress, of linking the "acquisition of literacy to the process of liberation" (Smith 2), and of adopting the theme of the journey from the African American subaltern/Other to the values and definitions of mainstream American society began with the slave autobiographers. This advocacy, they argue, was kept up in the work of Phyllis Wheatley, John Marrant, Olaudah Equiano, George Moses Horton, Linda Brent, and Frederick Douglass, and it continued with the turn of the century and into the first half of the twentieth century through the fiction and poetry of Paul Laurence Dunbar, W. E. B. DuBois, James Weldon Johnson, Jean Toomer, Countee Cullen, Claude McKay, Richard Wright, Ann Petry, Chester Himes, Ralph Ellison, Gwendolyn Brooks, and others. These writers' texts protest the inferior status and the devalued representation of African Americans in the American norm and ask for social equality for them. They generally invite a portrait of the African American as a victim. This journey by certain African American writers to the normative values of the colonizer or to assimilation into mainstream white society, characterized so poignantly by Gates, provided the foundation for the reconfigured and reinvented 1970s/1980s canon of African American literature.

But at a time when African Americans were experiencing a literary renaissance, these critics, in setting and enforcing borders, paradoxically narrowed the definition of African American literature. They policed the differences within African American literary texts in order to affirm both a hegemonic, aesthetic ideology and the ideology of the African American sociopolitical mission of racial uplift. Despite the fact that the 1970s was a period of renaissance in African American fiction, the African American texts that were privileged to receive scholarly attention were few. Novels such as Ann Petry's *The Street*, Chester Himes's *If He Hollers Let Him Go*, Nathan Heard's *Howard Street*, William Melvin Kelley's *A Different Drummer*, Willard Motley's *Knock on Any Door*, John O. Killens's *And Then We Heard the Thunder*, Charles Wright's *The Messenger*, John A. Williams's *The Man Who Cried I Am,* and others that were popular and successful critically before the reinvention of the canon were lost from the literary histories of African American literature owing to a reconfiguration of cultural capital and a strict narrowing of attention to a few select texts. Many novels that were published after the 1970s but did not meet the aesthetic, political, and ideological criteria of the reinvented canon were also excluded, repressed, marginalized, or simply ignored.

The reinventors of the 1970s/1980s canon of African American literature began "historicizing and theorizing at a point where [they] have eliminated from view, in advance, works that might, should they remain in view, challenge [their] histories and theories" and canons (Neilsen 10). They have eliminated the differences in African American literature. In the histories and theories of Baker, Gates, Stepto, Smith, and others, texts by African American women writers from Frances Harper to Alice Walker to Terry McMillan were ignored, as were the rural/urban/subaltern texts of George Wylie Henderson, Claude McKay, Arna Bontemps, Rudolph Fisher, Nathan Heard, Robert Deane Pharr, Vern E. Smith, Clarence L. Cooper Jr., and others. There was a total elimination of the blues/jazz-centered texts and stories of George Wylie Henderson, Wallace Thurman, Evan Hunter, John Clellon Holmes, Clarence Major, August Wilson, Walter Mosley, Jane Phillips, Gayl Jones, Michael Ondaatje, Albert Murray, William Melvin Kelley, Arthur Flowers, Toni Cade Bambara, Kristin Hunter, John Edgar Wideman, Xam Wilson Cartier, Herbert Simmons, James Alan McPherson, LeRoi Jones, John A. Williams, John McCluskey, Rafi Zabor, and others.

There were other exclusions. The African American existentialist texts of Charles Wright, Cyrus Colter, Richard Wright, John Edgar Wideman, William Demby, Bill Gunn, Henry Van Dyke, Robert Boles, and others were missing, as were Voodoo-centered African American texts such as Charles Chesnutt's *The Conjure Woman*, Rudolph Fisher's *The Conjure Man Dies*, Ishmael Reed's *Mumbo Jumbo*, Steve Cannon's *Groove, Bang and Jive Around*, Don Belton's *Almost Midnight*, Gloria Naylor's *Mama Day*, Jewell Parker Rhodes's *Voodoo Dreams*, Mary Monroe's *The Upper Room*, Rainelle Burton's *The Root Worker*, Darius James's *Negrophobia*, Carl Hancock Rux's *Pagan Operetta*, and Gayl Jones's *Healing*. There was no mention of the African American detective/mystery/science fiction texts of Chester Himes, Octavia Butler, Samuel Delany, Walter Mosley, Stephen Barnes, Valeria Wilson Wesley, Dolores Komo, Eleanor Taylor Bland, Nikki Baker, and Barbara Neely. There was a total elimination of the Omni-American tradition, which defines the African American culturally rather than racially, in such texts as James Alan McPherson's *Elbow Room*; Reginald McKnight's *Moustapha's Eclipse*, *The Kind of Light That Shines on Texas,* and *White Boys;* and Leon Forrest's *There Is a Tree More Ancient than Eden, The Bloodworth Orphans,* and *Divine Days.* And the emerging tradition in experimental/postmodern African American fiction that begins with Charles Wright (*The Wig*), early Ishmael Reed *(Yellow Back Radio Broke Down* and *Mumbo Jumbo*), Clarence Major (*No, All-Night Visitors, Emergency Exit, Reflex and Bone Structure*), Richard Perry (*Montgomery's Children*), the later John Edgar Wideman (*Philadelphia Fire* and *Reuben*), and that culminates with Percival Everett (*Glyph* and *Erasure*) and Colson Whitehead (*The Intuitionist*) was also ignored.

Finally, the reinvented canon excluded those texts that are either race neutral or are written by white authors about black characters and vice versa. This long list includes Harriet Beecher Stowe's *Uncle Tom's Cabin*, Paul Laurence Dunbar's *Uncalled*, Emma Dunham Kelley's *Medga* and *Four Girls at Cottage City*, Sinclair Lewis's *Kingsblood Royal*, George W. Cable's *The Grandissimes*, William Dean Howells's *An Imperative Duty*, Mark Twain's *The Adventures of Huckleberry Finn* and *The Tragedy of Pudd'nhead Wilson*, T. S. Strinbling's *Birthright*, Clement Wood's *Nigger*, H. A. Shand's *White and Black*, Dorothy Scarborough's *In the Land of Cotton*, Eugene O'Neill's *Emperor Jones* and *All God's Chillum Got Wings*, e. e. cummings's *The Enormous Room*, Waldo Frank's *Holiday*, Carl Van Vechten's *Nigger Heaven*, Sherwood Anderson's *Dark Laughter*, Julia Peterkin's *Scarlet Sister Mary*, William Attaway's *Let Me Breathe Thunder*, Chester Himes's *Cast the First Stone*, Richard Wright's *Savage Holiday*, William Melvin Kelley's *Dem*, William Faulkner's *Light in August,* James Baldwin's *Giovanni's Room*, Zora Neale Hurston's *Seraph on the Suwanee*, Willard Motley's *Knock on Any Door*, Ann Petry's *Country Place*, Carl R. Offord's *The Naked Fear*, and Susan Straight's *Aguaboogie, I Been in Sorrow's Kitchen, Blacker Than a Thousand Midnights*, and *the getting place.*

In eliminating these American and African American texts and traditions from among the texts to be considered, let alone from the canon, these African American critics, to use the words of Aldon Nielsen, end "by offering readers an anemic and inadequate account of both the history and nature of American literature in general and of African African literature in particular" (4). Guillory in *Cultural Capital* argues that exclusion from a literary canon should be defined as exclusion from the means of literary and cultural production (15). The eliminations and exclusions by the 1970s/1980s reinventors of the canon of African American literature effectively denied cultural capital to ninety percent of African American literature. These 1970s/1980s reinventors assumed that these eliminations, these differences, were "negligible or irrelevant," and that the conditions that produced the "relative unconditionality, local universality, and contingent objectivity are themselves" stable (B. Smith 182).

But simultaneous with the 1970s/1980s reinvented African American canon that charted the journey of the African American from the subaltern to the values of the American mainstream were other critical sites/locations that began giving validity, critical attention, and cultural capital to some of these excluded and repressed texts and traditions. There was the Black Aesthetic critical practice, the literary and critical arm of Black Cultural Nationalism, which devised its own canon of African American literature. It became a different dynamic cultural, critical, and literary site/location for representing African American literature. In the 1960s, Black Cultural Nationalism produced a black literary and critical community by establishing institutions and apparatuses such as publishing houses (Broadside Press, Lotus Press, Third World Press, Free Black, and Black River Writers), journals and magazines (*Freedomways, Black World, Black Books Bulletin, Soul-book, Journal of Negro Poetry, Amnistad, Umbra,* the *Journal of Black Studies,* and so forth), and educational institutions such as the Institute of Positive Education in Chicago and Spirit House in Newark, New Jersey.

The Black Aesthetic discourse, like Black Cultural Nationalism, was preoccupied with producing positive black images of the African American. The Black Aesthetic, as Deborah McDowell suggests, emphasizes "a 'positive' black self, always already unified, coherent, stable, and known" ("Boundaries" 57). Critics such as the early LeRoi Jones/Amiri Baraka, Don L. Lee/Haki Madhubuti, Addison Gayle, Stephen Henderson, Hoyt Fuller, Ron Karenga, Larry Neale, and others established through the previously mentioned institutions and journals a critical discourse that privileged those critics and literary texts that reinforced the Cultural Nationalist ideology. In *The Black Aesthetic*, Addison Gayle collects essays from Langston Hughes's "The Negro Artist and the Racial Mountain," published in 1926 to Julian Mayfield's "You Touch My Black Aesthetic and I'll Touch Yours," published in 1971. Gayle's objective is to advocate and generate poems, plays, and novels that transform "an American Negro into an African-American or black man. The Black Aesthetic, then, as conceived by this writer, is a corrective—a means of helping black people out of the polluted mainstream of Americanism" (xxii).

In his critical text, *The Way of the New World*, Gayle determines the worth and value of African American texts and poetry from William Wells Brown's *Clotel or The President's Daughter* to Ernest J. Gaines's *The Autobiography of Miss Jane Pittman* using a Black Aesthetic criteria. Gayle praises those texts—such as Sutton Griggs's *Imperium in Imperio*, Martin Delany's *Blake*, Charles Chesnutt's *The Marrow of Tradition*, Claude McKay's *Banana Bottom* and *Home to Harlem*, John O'Killens's *And Then We Heard the Thunder*, Ernest J. Gaines's *Bloodline* and *Miss Jane Pittman*, John A. Williams's *The Man Who Cried I Am* and *Captain Blackman*, William Melvin Kelley's *A Different Drummer*, and the poetry of Gwendolyn Brooks, Langston Hughes, Sonia Sanchez, Askia Toure, Haki Madhubuti, and Johari Amini—that situate their fiction and poetry within African American folk culture. He identifies them as works that "attempt to recreate legends of the past, create symbols, images, and metaphors anew," and that present "courageous men and women who set examples for blacks yet unborn, by stealing away from slavery, murdering masters and overseers, and committing untold acts of rebellion against the slave system" (xii).

Certainly, unlike the 1970s/1980s reinventors of the canon of African American literature, the Black Aesthetic critics intend to disrupt the white/black binary of signification by challenging the representation of the African American as inferior, as victim. But in their desire for closure, mastery, and totality, they end up reproducing a canon of African American literature that is as exclusionary and as hierarchical as the canons designed by mainstream American critics and the 1970s/1980s African American reinventors. While initiating a radical redefinition of black literature, the Black Aesthetic discourse, to use the words of Madhu Dubey, "consolidated around the sign of race, [and] discouraged any literary exploration of gender and other [African American] dif-

ferences that might complicate a unitary conception of the black experience"
(1). It eventually precluded "any exploration of the differences and contradictions that destablizes a monolithic conception of black identity" (3). Like the
1970s/1980s reinventors, Black Aesthetic critics repress African American differences as negligible or irrelevant. But unlike the 1970s/1980s reinventors,
Black Aesthetic critics were not imputed with cultural capital by the dominant
society's educational institutions. They did not hold prestigious professorships in
the English departments at Yale, Stanford, Harvard, Princeton, and Penn.

But before this 1970s/1980s reinvented canon and the Black Aesthetic discourse were able to solidify themselves completely, however, other African
American critics, particularly African American women and feminist critics,
began to deconstruct them, to expose their limitations and their exclusionary
acts. Critical works by Mary Helen Washington, Barbara Christian, Hazel Carby,
Deborah McDowell, Cheryl Wall, Thadious M. Davis, Frances Smith Foster,
Hortense Spillers, Michael Awkward, Karla Holloway, and Ann duCille
emerged to remind the makers of the decidedly patriarchal African American
canons that they had excluded the literature and the experiences of African
American women. Writing in the preface to *Black Women Novelists*, Barbara
Christian explains that she had been a "student of Afro-American literature and
read much of it, [but] knew little about black women, their history, or their literature" (ix). In writing *Black Women Novelists*, Christian hoped to give credibility and visibility to ignored and excluded black women writers. In her seminal
anthologies, Mary Helen Washington also attempted to remedy the dearth of
critical attention given to black women writers. Writing in the introduction to
Black-Eyed Susans, Washington attributes the "misconceptions and confusions
surrounding the woman" to the treatment of the black women writer: like all
black writers, "black women have never been as well known as Ellison, Wright,
Baldwin, or Baraka, not to mention white American authors" (ix). And in her
introduction to *Invented Lives*, Washington interrogates the notion of an African
American tradition that excludes black women writers. For Washington, tradition is a "word that has so often been used to exclude or misrepresent women.
It is always something of a shock to see black women, sharing equally . . . in the
labor and strife of black people, expunged from the text when that history becomes shaped into what we call tradition" (xvii). Deborah E. McDowell singles
out one of the reinventors of the 1970s/1980s canon of African American literature, Robert Stepto, for his exclusion of black women from the African
American tradition ("New Directions" 6).

In *Black Women Novelists and the Nationalist Aesthetic*, Madhu Dubey gives an
exhaustive history of how the Black Aesthetic discourse excluded black women
writers. "Its race-centered aesthetic hindered a just appreciation of the works of
black women novelists" (1). Dubey examines how Deborah McDowell in
"Boundaries: Or Distant Relations and Close Kin," Mae Henderson in "Speaking in Tongues," Anne duCille's *The Coupling Convention*, Hortense Spillers, and
Karla Holloway not only expose the exclusionary nature of the Black Aesthetic

discourse, but also advocate differences among black women writers. "Emphasizing the multiple orders of difference that constituted the black feminine subject," the black woman theorists seek "to resist the totalizing moves of other discourse on the subject" (3). The critical studies of black women literature by black women, feminist critics, and others show the limitations of this 1970s/1980s reinvented canon and the Black Aesthetic critical practice. Thus, after the 1970s, African American women and feminist critics became another cultural, literary, and gender site/location for representing African American literature. They gave validity, critical attention, and cultural/literary capital to another excluded tradition in African American literature.

There are other critics whose theories of African American literature are uninformed by the racial uplift narrrative and the journey from the subaltern to the mainstream, the woman/feminist tradition, or Black Cultural Nationalism. They focus on other repressed and/or excluded literary traditions in African American literature. Houston A. Baker Jr., in *Blues, Ideology, and Afro-American Literature* devises a blues vernacular theory of African American literature. But he undercuts his effort by limiting his examinations of the blues as a literary technique to such canonical texts as Ralph Ellison's *Invisible Man*, Zora Neale Hurston's *Their Eyes Were Watching God*, Richard Wright's *Black Boy*, and Paul Laurence Dunbar's *The Sport of the Gods*, totally ignoring and repressing such blues-centered texts as George Wylie Henderson's *Jule*, Langston Hughes's *Not Without Laughter*, Kristin Hunter's *God Bless the Child*, Albert Murray's *Train Whistle Guitar*, Baldwin's "Sonny's Blues," Jane Phillips's *MoJo Hand*, and Gayl Jones's *Corregidora*. Yemisi Jimoh's *Spiritual, Blues, and Jazz People in African American Fiction: Living in Paradox* also selects and reads African American literature according to a blues/jazz paradigm. Unlike Baker's *Blues, Ideology, and Afro-American Literature*, Professor Jimoh does engage some non-canonical texts such as Thurman's *The Blacker The Berry*, Larsen's *Quicksand*, Hughes's *Not Without Laughter*, Petry's *The Street*, and Baldwin's "Sonny's Blues." The blues tradition in African American literature is emphasized.

Since the 1990s there has emerged other single studies that focus on African American texts and literary traditions that are excluded from the 1970s/1980s reinvented canon, the Black Aesthetic canons, the aforementioned blues canon, and the emergent black feminist canon. Claudia Tate in *Psychoanalysis and Black Novels* uses Freudian/Lacanian psychoanalysis to examine some excluded African American texts such as Emma Dunham Kelley's *Megda*, W. E. B. DuBois's *Dark Princess*, Richard Wright's *Savage Holiday*, Nella Larsen's *Quicksand*, and Zora Neale Hurston's *Seraph on the Suwanee*. In realizing that canonical black novels have been defined by their focus on racial oppression and that other African American texts such as the ones she discusses violate "the conventions of racial protest writing" (7), Tate signifies differences in African American literature. Likewise, Aldon Lynn Nielsen in *Black Chants*, in acknowledging and discussing innovative, experimental, and postmodern African American poets excluded from the canonical Black Arts movements of the 1960s, signifies differences in African American poetry. Professor Darryl Dickson-Carr's *African American Satire: The Sacredly Profane Novel*, a full-length study of African American satire, engages texts such as George Schuyler's *Black No More*; Rudolph Fisher's *The Walls of Jericho;* Ishmael Reed's *The Terrible Twos, Reckless Eyeballing*, and *The Terrible Threes*; John O. Killens's *The Cotillion*; Cecil Brown's *The Life and Loves of Mr. Jiveass Nigger*, Paul Beatty's *The White Boy Shuffle*; and Darius James's *Negrophobia* that are excluded from other canons. Dickson-Carr constructs a satirical literary tradition in African American literature.

The *Blues Detective: A Study of African American Detective Fiction* by Stephen F. Soitos engages the repressed tradition of African American detective fiction in Pauline Hopkins's *Hagar's Daughter*, John Edward Bruce's *The Black Sleuth*; Rudolph Fisher's *The Conjure Man Dies: A Mystery Tale of Dark Harlem* and "John Archer's Nose"; Chester Himes's *For Love of Imabelle, The Real Cool Killers, The Crazy Kill, The Big Gold Dream, All Shot Up, Cotton Comes to Harlem, Run, Man Run, The Heat's On, Blind Man with a Pistol*, and *Plan B*; Ishmael Reed's *Mumbo Jumbo*; and Clarence Major's *Reflex and Bone Structure*. Madhu Dubey's *Signs and Cities: Black Literary Postmodernism* engages such contemporary postmodern or postmodernly influenced writers as James Edgar Wideman (*Reuben* and *Philadelphia Fire*), Toni Morrison (*Jazz* and *Song of Solomon*), Gloria Naylor (*Mama Day*), Ishmael Reed (*Mumbo Jumbo*), Octavia Butler (*Parable of the Sower*), Sapphire (*Push*), Samuel Delany (*Stars in My Pocket Like Grains of Sand*), and Colson Whitehead (*The Intuitionist*). What is emerging is a polycentric reading of African American literature, allowing us to talk about differences within that literature.

Finally, beginning in the late 1980s and culminating in the 1990s as Shelley Fisher Fishkin documents, there are numerous publications—Aldon Lynn Neilson's *Reading Race*, Dana Nelson's *The Word in Black and White*, Sterling Stuckey's *Going Through the Storm*, Eric Sundquist's *To Wake the Nations*, Eric Lott's *Love and Theft*, Rafar Zafar's *We Wear the Mask*, Henry Wonham's *Criticism and the Color Line*, and Toni Morrison's *Playing in the Dark*—that bring to the forefront of American scholarship the interrelatedness of "blackness" and "whiteness," the role that race plays in shaping American literature, and the impact that African American "presence has had on the structure of the work, the linguistic practice, and fictional enterprise in which it is engaged" (254). Because of the historical resistance to white/black interracial relationships, Fishkin holds up interracial relationships as a sign of racial progress and, consequently, as the representation of race in the United States.

These are excellent scholarly works that open up new avenues of race discussion in the United States because they allow for the discussion of racial-neutral American/African American texts, as I discussed previously, that have been excluded. But from the works that I have read, and especially the way that Fishkin's article represents these works, there is no evidence that they construct an image of the African American that is anything but Other or the Same as the normative white society. At best, they show that whiteness and blackness are not essential categories. They embed white within blackness and black within whiteness, but they totally ignore other racial, sexual, and ethnic cultural identities such as Asian Americans, Hispanics, Native Americans, and gays. Because Fishkin is preoccupied with creating an assimilationist space, she ignores/represses racism, white privilege, and history. Despite Fishkin's argument that these critics are innovative and are on the cutting edge, they really embody an old tradition in America. It is the tradition of Sameness. Also, Fishkin's assimilationist discourse is reductionist. It does not address the issue of African American differences. Since both the black and the white categories have differences, which African American representation embeds which white American representation?

But, Fishkin does not, to use the words of Timothy Powell, "reconstruct [white and black] cultural identity in the midst of a *multiplicity* of cultures, in a theoretical matrix where there are no centers and margins" (5). She does not propose a "new critical paradigm that will help scholars to theorize the fluidity, multiplicity, and intricate contradictions that characterize all forms of cultural identity" and finally, she does not produce critical sites that "will allow for the theorization of difference and conflict as well as commonality and community" (2). Instead, she offers black/white embedding as the be-all and end-all. For Fishkin, everything hinges on the white/black encounter.[9]

Although none of these emerging cultural, literary, and critical sites/locations individually engage African American differences and the diverse traditions within the literature, together they challenge the construction of a canon of African American literature that privileges select African American texts and traditions and ignores and marginalizes others. They also allow for a polycentric representation of African American literature, in which different African American traditions can be examined equally in terms of their own distinctions and in which relations have many dynamic cultural, historical, critical, and literary locations, many possible vantage points. In this polycentric approach to African American critical practices, the once hegemonic racial uplift canon/tradition is repositioned at a point at which it becomes one of many representations/organizations of African American literature.

But defining the African American in the terms, conventions, and values of mainstream society is not restricted only to literary critics. Classic African American history texts such as John Hope Franklin's *From Slavery to Freedom* and Lerone Bennett Jr.'s, *Before the Mayflower* also construct African American history according to this middle-class Christian journey from the space of the Other, and/or the subaltern, to the American mainstream. After the 1980s, there emerged other constructions of African American history that challenged this paradigmatic approach and, thereby, made a polycentric approach to African American history possible. But, this classic historical narrative is still very dominant. In the preface to *From Slavery to Freedom*, Franklin writes:

> I have made a conscious effort to write the history of the Negro in America with due regard for the forces at work which have affected his development. . . . While I have sought to interpret critically the forces and personalities that

have shaped the history of the Negro in the United States, I have attempted
to avoid a subjective and unscientific treatment of the subject. (xi–xii)

Likewise, in the preface to *Before the Mayflower*, Bennett writes:

> This book . . . deals with the trials and triumphs of a group of Americans. . . .
> This is a history of "the other Americans" and how they came to North Amer-
> ica and what happened to them when they got here. . . . The story begins in
> Africa . . . and ends with the Second Reconstruction which Martin Luther
> King, Jr., and the "sit-in" generation . . . fashion[ed] in the North and South.
> The story deals with the rise and growth of slavery and segregation and the
> continuing efforts of the Negro American to answer the question of the Jewish
> poet of captivity: "How shall we sing the Lord's song in a strange land?'" (vii)

Franklin's and Bennett's historical narratives desire to produce totalities of
knowledge: Franklin attempts to "avoid a subjective and unscientific treatment"
of African American history and Bennett states that he has written a "full history
of the Negro." Their histories assume a stable subject—the African American—
whose deeds are ordered into a coherent whole by the stable text—History. As
with most Western historians, Franklin's and Bennett's approach is anthropocentric, teleological, and causal with pretensions to universality, reality, and truth.
It assigns a deed to every doer and seeks the right reason for the taking place of
any event. Franklin and Bennett in their histories also proceed with a chronological reconstruction overly obedient to the fiction of a linearity of time, which
admits to having no gaps or errors in a good, whole, coherent narrative of the
movement of the African American transcendental consciousness through various epochs that has a distinct closure. Universal and evolutionary time is used
to organize the unconnected American and African American events into a coherent, meaningful narrative that tracks the progress from blacks' primitive origins to their place within the European Enlightenment. The future is utopian
(one in which rationality blooms in full).

Historiography, or the writing of traditional total history, assumes that totalities can be gleaned from a scrutiny of details. Traditional total history works
from the assumption that history itself consists of congeries of lived stories, individual and collective, and that the principal task of historians is to uncover these
stories and retell the narrative. It also believes that history can explain what happened in the past by providing a precise and accurate reconstruction of the
events reported in surviving documents. But at any time in the writing of history, Michel de Certeau maintains in *The Writing of History*, only a limited number of representations can be made (44). Hayden White in *Metahistory* begins by
denaturalizing the concept of 'history.' He historicizes it (from the eighteenth
century onward) and shows that no history is complete, existing instead as a collection of discursive formations and not a unitary discourse (xi). In that context,
and as was the case for the African American sociopolitical mission of racial uplift, Franklin's and Bennett's historical narratives are not complete histories. Not

only do they focus on a limited number of representations or discursive formations, their narratives also incorporate and reinforce broadly mainstream American social, intellectual, and cultural norms and conventions such as Enlightenment ideas, middle-class respectability, the Protestant work ethic, the patriarchy, and Christian values.

In these exhaustive, thorough, and brilliant traditional histories, Franklin and Bennett use the hegemonic, Western emancipatory narrative that is one of the overarching philosophies of history—like the Enlightenment story of the gradual but steady progress of reason and freedom, Hegel's dialectic of Spirit coming to know itself, and Karl Marx's drama of the forward march of human productive capacities via class conflict culminating in proletarian revolution—to construct African American history. According to Edward Said in *Culture and Imperialism*, historical "narratives of emancipation and enlightenment in their strongest form [are] also narratives of *integration* not separation, the stories of people who [are] excluded from the main group but who [are] now fighting for a place in it" (xxvi). Franklin and Bennett focus on the struggles and aspirations of elite/middle-class and aspiring middle-class African Americans who have been excluded from the dominant American society but who are striving to achieve equality and on the dominant white society's resistance to that struggle for equality. In constructing their coherent, meaningful narratives, Franklin and Bennett, in their chronological reconstruction, examine the African past, the period before institutionalized slavery, the slave trade, slavery, the changes in African American history that came with the Abolitionist movement and the abolishment of slavery followed by the Civil War and the Reconstruction period and the gains elite/middle-class and aspiring middle-class African Americans later made in education and politics. They scrutinize the rise of Jim Crow laws and the disenfranchisement of the African American in the nineteenth century and the efforts of various African American movements and leaders of the late nineteenth century, such as W. E. B. DuBois, Booker T. Washington, and others, to resist those laws and to uplift the race. Then they focus on the struggles of the NAACP, the National Urban League, other organizations and movements, and elite/middle-class and aspiring middle-class African Americans to build a black community and to achieve rights in the area of jobs, education, and franchisement. Finally, through an examination of the Civil Rights movement, its leaders, and their long struggle to use the courts to pass and enforce laws banning discrimination in education, employment, and housing, Franklin and Bennett signify progress in the integration of the African American into American society.

Within these emancipatory historical African American narratives, it is individuals such as Harriet Tubman, Sojourner Truth, Frederick Douglass, Nat Turner, Booker T. Washington, W. E. B. DuBois, Roy Wilkins, A. Phillip Randolph, Mary McLeod Bethune, Rosa Parks, and Martin Luther King Jr., who show courage and who risk their lives to establish viable black institutions while tearing down racist and discriminatory barriers that prevented African Americans from having access to jobs, the vote, housing, and education. Certainly, through their long struggles these individuals accomplished an incredible feat in American history, and we should forever honor and cherish them. But Franklin's and Bennett's emancipatory narratives, in their move to chart the progress of the African American to full social equality, embracing the values and definitions of the dominant American society, leave out much African American history. They reduce the plurality and heterogeneity of American/African American history to a set of apprehensible units that can be ordered. In short, they exclude the polyvalent nature of African American history.

In their most obvious omission, Franklin's and Bennett's studies subordinate or exclude almost completely the history and the experiences of African American women.[10] They also exclude the history of those blues/subaltern African Americans who did not have the options of education or aspiring to the American dream, whose existence was almost completely beyond the pale of middle-class Christian life. In *The Negro Family in the United States*, E. Franklin Frazier describes these roving men and homeless women, the journeymen and hobos:

> Among the million Negroes who deserted the rural communities of the South, there were thousands of men and women who cut themselves loose from family and friends and sought work and adventure as solitary wanderers from place to place. In the 1920s and 1930s, this mobile group of isolated men and women constituted between seven and twelve percent of the African American population. (210)

When many of these wanderers sang, they sang the blues, which was defined by its existence on society's margins. According to James H. Cone in *The Spirituals and the Blues*, the blues probably emerged in the late nineteenth century, but the cosmology, the values, and the attitudes that comprise the blues have "roots stretching back into slavery days and even to Africa" (109). The blues is related to the "*functional* character of West African music. And this is one of the essential ingredients of black music which distinguishes it from [other] Western music and connects it with its African heritage" (109): lying at the core of daily life, the blues tells us about the feeling and thinking of certain non-middle-class, non-Christian black people.

Historically, the blues has been condemned by both the sociopolitical mission of racial uplift and the elite/middle-class Christian African American leadership. Many black church people call the blues "devil songs." It is shunned by the black middle class. Cosmologically, the blues express conditions associated with the "burden of freedom." However, freedom in the blues is not simply the "existential freedom" defined by modern Western philosophy or the promise of eternal peace in the promised land offered by Christianity. For the blues, freedom took on historical specificity. It meant that simple alternatives became momentous options. It meant getting married, drinking gin, and accepting and proceeding with the fact that life is fraught with frustration and contradiction—and expressing these experiences in song. Being non-Christian, non-Enlightenment driven, and non-middle class, the blues lifestyle presents a problem for African American historians such as Franklin and Bennett who are middle class and Christian, who write their histories according to those narratives, and who believe in the Western notion/concept of the gradual but steady progress of reason and freedom. Therefore, they excluded the blues people/subaltern African Americans from their narratives.

Likewise, the history of the lives and struggles of those African Americans who live by the tenets of Voodoo is also excluded and repressed in the emancipatory historical narratives of Franklin and Bennett. Voodoo came from mostly West Africa to the Americas via the slave trade. Enslaved Africans brought with them various forms of religions, and Voodoo was derived from them. In successive decades and centuries, the arrival of additional Africans into slavery in the United States reinvigorated Voodoo and other African customs. Lorenzo Dow Turner, an African linguist, found over four thousand words of West African origin in the Gullah dialect of the blacks of the South Carolina and Georgia coasts (Finn 108). Dances, songs, and passwords were ways to keep Voodoo and these African religions and customs alive.

Voodoo is derived from the word *Vo* (to inspire fear) of the Ewe-speaking peoples, meaning a god—one who inspires fear. *Vodu* is not the name of a particular deity but is applied by the African to any god (Puckett 177). During the one hundred years that slavery held the African American in bondage, the colonialist could deprive him of his culture, language, personhood, wife, child, and the fruits of his toil. But "there was one thing of which he could not deprive him—his faith in fetich charms (Voodoo). Not only did this religion of the fetich endure under slavery—it grew" (Finn 16).

The Vodu religion, with its adoration of the snake god, was also carried to Haiti by enslaved Africans from Dahomey: thousands of Africans from these serpent-worshiping tribes were sold into slavery and carried across the Atlantic. In Haiti, the religion became an aspect of the resistance that the enslaved Africans marshaled against their oppressive situation. The Haitian nationalists later claimed that Voodoo's influence had been all-important on the men who won independence for their country (Metraux 41). The revolt by the enslaved Africans against the white French planter class began in Santo Domingo in 1791 and lasted for thirteen years before the rebels succeeded in founding the independent black Republic of Haiti in 1804. Thousands of French fled the island, taking with them as many enslaved Africans as they could. Thousands of Santo Domingan free people of color left, too. Many of these refugees sought shelter in Cuba. But when Napoleon invaded Spain in 1809, they were forced by Spanish Cuba to leave, and some ten thousand of these refugees found their way to New Orleans. Their impact on the city and its environs was considerable. The black refugees, both free and enslaved, had been steeped in the knowledge and practice of Voodoo, and they had a great respect for its rites and traditions. When the Santo Domingan refugees began holding their Voodoo rites in New Orleans, New Orleans blacks joined them in their rituals and practices (Haskins

58). By the end of the eighteenth century, Voodoo was firmly entrenched. It extended through the entire slave population and among the free blacks as well (Finn 110).

Although Voodoo was eventually outlawed in New Orleans, it continued to be practiced secretly under the cloak of Catholicism. But by the end of the nineteenth century, with the death of Marie Laveau and the rise of a powerful, middle-class, Christian African America whose goal it was to enter the American mainstream, Voodoo had been repressed and abandoned, although certain Voodoo magical practices remained incorporated in the black Baptist Church and the black Catholic Church throughout North America. The sole survivors of this repression of Voodoo were the root doctors who continued to set up shop and to "divine the future, concoct medicine, work spells, give advice and make charms to ward off evil and to bring good luck" (Finn 123). In 1885, it was estimated that in Atlanta more than one hundred old men and women practiced Voodoo as a profession, telling fortunes, locating lost and stolen goods, furnishing love potions, and casting spells on people. Such incantatory beliefs were found in the northern states as well, in cities such as Philadelphia, Pittsburgh, and New York (Puckett 196). Remnants of Voodoo in the form of spells, "tricks," conjuration, and witchcraft of all kinds still persist today. With a continued migration of blacks from Haiti and an upsurge in migration of blacks from West Africa to the United States, Voodoo has had a resurgence in the United States. Advocates of Voodoo contend that in the United States, today, "there are some 1.5 million adherents of Voodoo." The main centers are New Orleans, Chicago, Philadelphia, and Brooklyn (J. Jones 1).

In its most potent form, Voodoo is eclectic and non-moral: "The African gods are not concerned with moral practices. With them the same spirit can be persuaded to work indifferently good or evil, while in our moral religion, it is impossible to conceive of God being called upon deliberately to take a direct hand in dastardly enterprise" (Puckett 175). In Voodoo, the same power can be used to different ends, for good and evil, in the same way that fire may be used for warmth and protection or for burning down a neighbor's house. Whereas European logocentrism defines meaning in terms of binaries such as good and evil, Voodoo believes that good and evil are but two sides of the same coin. Given this salient feature, along with the fact that Voodoo advocates heterogeneity and diversity, it would be very difficult for Franklin and Bennett to incorporate that culture/religion into their emancipatory historical narratives about the journey of the African American to the Christian, logocentric, middle-class values and definitions of the dominant American society.

The classic emancipatory African American narratives of Franklin and Bennett also historically ignore members of the vast African American working class who did not belong to either working-class organizations that strove for middle-class respectability or to black political movements and organizations that strove for social parity with whites. In *Race Rebels,* Robin D. G. Kelley "begins to recover and explore aspects of black working-class life and politics [and culture] that have been relegated to the margins" by mainstream African American historical narratives (4). Kelley writes of African American working-class "secular spaces of leisure and pleasure" and the "rich expressive culture" or "commercialized leisure" that included "the entire body of folklore, jokes, and various other oral texts" (44). These "secular spaces" accommodated such cultural behavior as spending time in gin joints, wild dancing, gambling, gum chewing, loud talking, wearing gaudy colors in clothing, and patronizing the nickelodeon, blues, and jazz: "In darkened rooms ranging in size from huge halls to tiny dens, black workers of both sexes shook and twisted their overworked bodies, drank, talked, engaged in sexual play, and—in spite of occasional fights—reinforced their sense of community" (46).

These secular spaces were places where black patrons socialized with people who had a shared knowledge of these cultural behaviors. They were often spaces that allowed for freer sexual expression, particularly for women, whose sexuality was often circumscribed by employers, family members, the law, and the church. These secular spaces—particularly dance halls, blues clubs, and house parties—were also places of employment for some segments of the African American working class. Besides waitresses, barmaids, coat checkers, and assorted service workers, we also must consider the experiences of a wide range of "sex workers" and escorts. Some dance halls employed young women to dance with unescorted men for a small fee, and sexual liaisons and companionships could be purchased by men. The men and women involved in the trafficking of female bodies made their living selling women's sexuality (48).

This "rich, expressive culture" or "commercialized leisure" of the African American working class represents at least a partial rejection of the dominant American Christian ideology, of the African American church's strict moral codes and rules for public behavior, and of the moralizing of the African American middle class. In addition, it was "frequently in conflict with formal working-class institutions" (44). When you consider the needs of employers and the power of the Protestant work ethic in American culture, the behaviors and folkways of the secular spaces of the African American working class could be seen as undermining labor discipline. Franklin's and Bennett's emancipatory historical narratives ignore such African American secular, social, and cultural spaces; they were too preoccupied with privileging the public utterances of the African American elite/middle-class leadership and black political movements that were embarrassed by working-class culture.

Also, Franklin and Bennett in their respective narratives repress the African American subaltern—which includes the poor, the working poor, and the outlaw, among others. Gunnar Myrdal in *Challenge to Affluence* predicted that rising unemployment in the United States might "trap an under-class of unemployed and gradually unemployable and underemployed persons and families at the bottom of society" (qtd. in Lemann 281). Remnants of a subaltern/urban sector of the African American poor had appeared in southern and northern urban centers as early as the late nineteenth and early twentieth centuries. The African

American subaltern today includes marginalized black male youth and young adults who are unemployed and no longer aspire to the American middle class, single mothers on welfare, unskilled workers, poor farmers, low-wage service sector workers, slum dwellers, and riffraff—many of whom break the law daily, sell drugs, disrupt the social decorum and behavior, disrespect middle-class African American civil rights leaders, taunt the police, and engage in petty crimes. Going to jail has become an integral part of many of their lives. Although some poor African Americans make efforts to have their interests addressed and voices heard by organizing and becoming involved in black administrations in American cities, in most instances, their interests are not addressed and their voices go unheard. Other poor/subaltern African Americans become socially isolated from, and indifferent toward, mainstream political institutions and black social movements.

In discussing the sexual and social mores of the "lower-class" African Americans of Bronzeville in Chicago in the 1920s and 1930s, St. Clair Drake and Horace R. Cayton in *Black Metropolis* examine "hustling women" who promiscuously "'turn tricks' for money," professional women "who cater to white men and high-status Negroes" (596). Prostitution at that time, along with bootlegging, freak shows, reefer dens, and pads, comprised the underworld in the urban black community, not only in Chicago but in all major cities in the United States from New York to Los Angeles. Discussing the "underworld" in Harlem during the 1920s, James Weldon Johnson in *Black Manhattan* writes: "And Harlem has, too, its underworld, its world of pimps and prostitutes, of gamblers and thieves, of illicit liquor, of red sins and dark crimes" (169). The primary institutions of the underworld were the tougher taverns, the reefer pads, the gambling dens, the liquor joints, and the call-houses and buffet-flats where professional prostitutes catered to the trade in an organized fashion. It was a protected business: "Money passes, but in a very guarded fashion, and usually it is small change—to the cop on the beat or to the minor ward politicians" (Drake and Cayton 610).

The prominent Christian African American sociologist William Julius Wilson in *The Truly Disadvantaged* also defines the visible emergence of the urban poor in the 1960s as an "underclass." Characterizing the urban poor in terms of black crime, drug addiction, out-of-wedlock births, teenage pregnancy, female-headed families, and welfare dependency—in the process positing the middle-class Christian American as the norm—Wilson cannot represent the subaltern/urban poor as having any value or culture (20–21). Therefore, using pathological language, he defines them as deviants, as Other than reason. But the moment you define subaltern African Americans culturally rather than economically and sociologically, the pathology becomes irrelevant: Wilson clearly is using the cultural criteria of middle-class Christian America to define, assess, and cover over the African American subaltern, which is simply culturally different. Poor people have their own cultures, and in the midst of the most oppressive situations, people and individuals learn, to use the words of Ralph

Ellison, "[their] own insights into the human condition, [their] own strategies of survival. There is a fullness, even a richness here; and here *despite* the realities of politics, economic and social oppression. Because it is human life" (112). Since the great mass of peasants and urban dwellers constitute almost eighty percent of the world's population, it would be ludicrous and offensive to call them pathological because they do not conform to some middle-class Christian norm. Essentially, a culture is a way of life. In this sense, every individual is a cultured individual. Peasants and the urban poor, whether in rural India or on the south side of Chicago, have their own language, customs, eating habits, religious beliefs, gestures, notions of common sense, attitudes toward sex, concepts of beauty and justice, and responses to pleasure and pain. They have their own structures and rationales, their own material cultures, economic lives, social relations, interpersonal relations, and psychologies that are different from, and as complex as, middle-class American life.

The African American poor/subaltern, working poor, and outlaw element all practice a survivalist culture that is at odds with the values not only of middle-class and aspiring middle-class African Americans, but also the dominant white society. Furthermore, the reality of the lives of the African American poor/subaltern, the working poor, and the outlaw element exists, in many instances, outside the African American middle class's protest of racism and its struggle for racial uplift and middle-class respectability. Therefore, this reality is repressed, excluded, or subordinated in Franklin's and Bennett's works.

Writing in the introduction to *In the Life*, Joseph Beam states that homosexual African Americans:

> have always existed in the African-American community. [They] have been ministers, hairdressers, entertainers, sales clerks, civil rights activists, teachers, playwrights, trash collectors, dancers, government officials, choir masters, and dishwashers. You name it; we've done it—more often with scant recognition. We have mediated family disputes, cared for and reared siblings, and housed our sick. We have performed many and varied important roles within our community. . . . [But homosexual African Americans] are the poor relations, the proverbial black sheep, without a history, a literature, a religion, or a community. (16, 17)

The classic emancipatory historical narratives of Franklin's *From Slavery to Freedom* and Bennett's *Before the Mayflower* repress and exclude the history of even those homosexual African Americans who were very visible among the middle-class, working-class, and subaltern African American populations in the urban centers of the nineteenth and twentieth centuries. To document historically the presence of homosexual African Americans within urban black communities, one has to resort to other sources such as biographies, social histories, interviews, and essays.

In America's urban centers from the 1870s through the 1930s, there emerged a class of people who practiced homosexuality. Case histories compiled by doctors, vice commission investigations into the underworld of American urban centers, newspaper accounts of the scandalous and the bizzare, and, more rarely, personal correspondence and diaries, all document a wide variety of homosexual lives. The group included letter carriers and business executives, department store clerks and professors, factory operatives, civil service employees, ministers, engineers, students, cooks, hobos, and the idle rich. Both men and women, blacks and whites, immigrants and the native born comprised these accounts (D'Emilio 11–12). However, as Jonathan Katz points out in "The Invention of Heterosexuality," same-sex experiences of intimacy in nineteenth-century America were not the same phenomena as what we mean by "gay" experience today (10). Thus, documentation becomes more difficult because of the absence of a defined category of homosexuality in American popular culture until the twentieth century.

The earliest documentations of homosexual African Americans are drag balls. Charles H. Hughes discusses the 1893:

> annual convocation of negro men called drag dance. . . . These men are lasciviously dressed in womanly attire, short sleeves, low-necked dresses and the usual ballroom decorations and ornaments of women, feathered and ribboned headdresses, garters, frills, flowers, ruffles, etc. and deport themselves as women. . . . [The members of this convocation are] cooks, barbers, waiters and other employees of Washington families, some even higher in the social scale—some being employed as subordinates in the Government departments. (42–43)

Similar annual balls existed in Harlem in New York City and in St. Louis at the turn of the century (49).

A homosexual subculture that was uniquely African American in substance began to take shape in New York's Harlem from at least the early 1900s. Throughout the 1920s and the Harlem Renaissance period, black lesbians and gay men were meeting each other on street corners and socializing in cabarets, literary gatherings, private parties, buffet-flats (after-hours spots that were usually in someone's apartment), speakeasies (where gays were usually forced to hide their preferences and to blend in with the heterosexual patrons), rent parties, and church on Sundays. They created a language, a social structure, and a complex network of institutions. In discussing who attended the rent parties in Harlem in the 1920s, David Levering Lewis in *When Harlem Was in Vogue* includes black lesbians, adding that rent parties began anytime after midnight, "howling and stomping sometimes well into dawn in a miasma of smoke, booze, collard greens, and hot music" (107).

Finally, many of the writers, intellectuals, and artists of the Harlem Renaissance were homosexual, bisexual, or otherwise sexually unorthodox (Garber 318, 326). In his biography of Bayard Rustin, an openly homosexual activist and civil rights leader, Jarvis Anderson states that when Rustin moved to Harlem in 1937, he "found himself drawn to an elite society of homosexuals, most of them residing in the well-to-do neighborhood called Sugar Hill" (156). The home of

Hall Johnson, leader of the famous Hall Johnson Choir, was a gathering place for musicians, people in the arts, and "if you happened to be gay or lesbian," states Rustin, "then you were there too" (qtd. in Anderson 157). Also, in the 1930s, homosexual African Americans attended dances such as the Good Times Club and the Unity Club socials, where they socialized with friends. "These dances have been a fixture in gay life in Harlem for forty or fifty years" (Haweswood 83).

This African American homosexual subculture existed as well in Detroit, Pittsburgh, Washington, DC, New Orleans, Atlanta, and Los Angeles in the 1920s and 1930s. In *Lush Life*, a biography of Billy Strayhorn, David Hajdu identifies a homosexual community in Pittsburgh: "There was a quiet, insular gay social scene in Pittsburgh in the 1930s . . . most of the gay socializing took place at private homes where there were parties . . . [or] private clubs on Liberty Street" (33). Homosexual black artists and performers attended these house parties. In *Rage to Survive*, Etta James, in describing Central Avenue in Los Angeles in the 1930s and 1940s, which was the center of black life, mentions Professor Hines and other African American homosexuals who were visible in the church choir, in the bars, and on the streets (18, 23, 116).

In *The Gay Metropolis*, Charles Kaiser documents the presence of homosexuals in New York in the 1940s and 1950s. In the 1940s, he argues, wealthy homosexuals congregated at the old Metropolitan Opera House on Broadway just below Times Square. Homosexual men also assembled in elegant men's bars such as the Oak Room in the Plaza and, most famously, at the Astor, on Seventh Avenue at 45th Street (14). Kaiser also documents a thriving hustler scene on the streets surrounding Times Square in the 1950s and early 1960s. In the Village in the 1950s, the more conventional gay bars included Mary's Main Street, the Eight Street Bar, and the Old Colony (107). Homosexual African Americans patronized these bars.

In discussing homosexual African Americans in Harlem, Kaiser mentions the Harlem annual drag ball at the Fun Makers Social Club, which was a hit in 1944. And for other places in Harlem that homosexual African American New Yorkers frequented, Kaiser names Luckey's Rendezvous and the Mount Morris Baths on upper Madison Avenue. Hajdu describes Billy Strayhorn in the 1940s moving "in a circle of like-hearted spirits, most (though not all) black and gay" (71). On many nights after visiting the Cafe Society, Strayhorn "would lead whoever still had life to [the] piano joint," Luckey's Rendezvous, which was located at St. Nicholas Avenue and 149th Street (72). In *Urban Blues*, Charles Keil alludes to "a surprising number of lower-class Negro men and women" in Chicago during the mid-twentieth century who were "ambisexual, homo- or hetero- according to circumstances," noting a high tolerance of sexual deviancy in some Chicago blues bars (28).

Discussing homosexual African America in the 1940s and 1950s, Samuel R. Delany, the noted African American author, confirms that homosexual African Americans in Harlem went to existing bars, baths, and the halls of the

YMCA on 135th Street to meet other homosexuals (qtd. in Beam 187). Delany discusses their frequenting the bars—mentioned by Kaiser—around Times Square. Also, in discussing the life of Bruce Nugent, a Harlem Renaissance poet, short-story writer, and openly homosexual artist, Charles Michael Smith speaks of the African American bohemian/homosexual population in Harlem who frequented "gay bars" and "gay places" (216).

Yet, the history of these homosexual African Americans is excluded not only from the classic African American historical narratives such as Franklin's *From Slavery to Freedom* and Bennett's *Before the Mayflower,* but also from Frazier's sociological books such as *The Black Bourgeoisie* and *The Negro Family in the United States,* Nathan Huggins's *Harlem Renaissance,* W. E. B. DuBois's *Philadelphia Negro,* Roi Ottley's *New World A-Coming: Inside Black America,* Kenneth Clark's *Dark Ghetto,* Gilbert Osofsky's *Harlem: The Making of a Ghetto,* James Weldon Johnson's *Black Manhattan,* Claude McKay's *Harlem: Negro Metropolis,* St. Claire Drake's and Horace R. Cayton's *The Black Metropolis,* Darlene Clark Hine's *Black Women in America: An Historical Encyclopedia,* and David Levering Lewis's *When Harlem Was in Vogue.* There is obviously something about homosexuality or sexual difference that is antithetical and threatening to Christianity, to middle-class respectability, and to heterosexuality—challenging values and definitions that inform elite/middle-class African American issues and concerns, including those of Franklin and Bennett.

Barbara Smith in *The Truth That Never Hurts* attributes this historical silence to homophobia and heterosexism. But she thinks that:

> there is also the reality that Black history has often served extrahistorical purposes. . . . Black history's underlying agenda frequently has been to demonstrate that African Americans are full human beings who deserve to be treated like Americans, like citizens. . . . The theme of uplift, of social validation, and of prioritizing subject matter that is a "credit to the race" have burdened and sometimes biased Black historical projects. (89).

Jewelle Gomez attributes this silence to the black middle class:

> which might be said to be "passing" in their emulation of white values and culture [and] didn't want anyone around who would call attention to differences—perhaps fearful of the demonization of black sexuality during slavery and the Jim Crow era. . . . The importance of assimilation for many in the black middle class made being openly queer increasingly difficult in the black community. (33).

Thus, we can discern how the protest against racism and the journey to the values and definitions of mainstream American society pervade all aspects of the construction of African American life, including sexuality.

Like the 1970s/1980s reinventors of the African American canon, Franklin and Bennett protest the structural racism that prevents African Americans from enjoying all of the social, educational, and economic privileges of the dominant American society. Of course, the protest is sincere and the effort heroic. As Ishmael Reed makes clear in an interview with Mark Johnson: "It was the [African American] middle-class orators, and writers, and craftsmen, and businessmen, [who were] petitioning, and speaking out and doing the hard intellectual detailed work . . . to improve the conditions of Black people in this country" (57). But Franklin, Bennett, and other American/African American historians, who assume the necessity of identity politics or who assume that the African American community is homogeneous, police differences within the American/African American community because they want to establish their unified distinction from other communities.

Obviously, the authors of the classic African American emancipatory historical narratives do not consider the histories of subaltern African American, the African American working class, blues people, homosexual African Americans, and Voodoo practitioners to be appropriately historical. This exclusion is a clear example of how the subaltern cannot speak. Therefore, like the reinventors of the 1970s/1980s African American canon, these historians leave intact the white/black binary of signification. In their "move to become equal to that splendid model [of the colonizer] and to resemble him to the point of disappearing in him" (Memmi 120), they crush differences in African American history and culture. They ignore the polyvalent nature of African American history.

But since the mid-1980s, some African American historians and social critics, particularly women, have begun to expose the limitations of the traditional historical narratives of Franklin and Bennett. They have begun to construct African American history from other, different cultural and historical sites and locations. Paula Giddings in *When and Where I Enter* describes it as "a mission to tell a story largely untold. For despite the range and significance of our history, we have been perceived as token women in black texts and as token blacks in feminist ones" (5). Darlene Clark Hine discusses the "reclamation of the history of black women in the early 1980s" (60). Giddings's study and Hine's *When the Truth Is Told, Black Women in White*, and *Black Women in America: An Historical Encyclopedia* add black women to the histories already established by Franklin, Bennett, and others. But, there is something terribly middle class, and therefore exclusionary, about both Giddings's and Hine's histories. Like Franklin and Bennett, they take a logocentric, linear approach to history as they chronicle the struggles and triumphs of elite/middle-class black women. Neither Giddings nor Hine deals extensively with differences within black women's history, including rural and urban subaltern black women who are not Christian and who have devised other theoretical definitions of life that are antithetical to a middle-class, Protestant work ethic, Freudian, and Christian worldview. They repress the history of African American lesbians, sexual workers, and subaltern black women. Jacqueline Jones in *The Dispossessed: American Underclass from the Civil War to the Present* identifies another site/location, the American underclass, to represent the American/African American. Social and literary critics such as bell hooks in *Yearning, black looks,* and *Outlaw Culture,* Angela Davis in *Blues Legacies and Black Feminism,* and Hazel Carby in *Race Men* also add black women to the African American narrative.

Likewise, Kelley, in showing the limitations of Franklin's and Bennett's narratives, constructs a working-class site to represent African American history. He does an exhaustive and erudite study of the black working class, exploring forms of resistance that are different from those of the middle class. But in not dealing with African American differences, he tends to define black workers in terms of conventional modes of resistance. For example, he challenges Wilson's notion that the black poor or the black "underclass" is "socially isolated from and indifferent toward political institutions" because he defines resistance only through organized institution (99). When he discusses Birmingham's untouchables, he does not completely define them as the reason of the Other. He can only define them in terms of the middle-class narrative of the quest for social equality. But the indifference to political institution characteristic of Birmingham's untouchables is *also* a form of resistance. Ultimately, Kelley reproduces the same meta narrative of the struggle for full equality into mainstream American society that defines/covers over even the history of the subaltern African American.

Although I have delineated various repressed and excluded American/African American historical traditions or theoretical concepts of life, these traditions and concepts, along with elite/middle-class traditions and concepts, in most instances, do not exist as separate entities. They are integrated. They intermingle. They have mutual relations. They are "active, generative participants at the very core of a shared, conflictual" American/African American history (Shohat and Stam 48). They make a polyvalent African American history. Kelley discusses working-class African Americans using conjure or "hoodoo" as a strategy of resistance, retaliation, or defense in their daily lives (43). Voodoo also intermingled with Christianity. As one Mississippi ex-slave admitted, "Folks back then were religious and superstitious. They believed in divinities and ghosts as well as in signs and hoodooing. 'Our religion and superstition was all mixed up'" (qtd. in Spencer 13).

The blues repertoire is also saturated with songs attesting to the bluesman's credence given to Voodoo. To certain bluesmen, Voodoo conjures the supernatural forces they need to overcome the obstacles in their path; bluesmen who believe in Voodoo think of themselves as privileged beings in league with mighty spirits (Finn 145). For example, in his "Louisiana Blues," the great blues singer Muddy Waters tells of heading to the Voodoo capital to get his luck with the ladies fixed up: "I goin' down to New Orleans/Get me a *mojo* hand;/I'm gonna show all you good-lookin' women/Just how to treat yo' man." John Lee Williamson in "Hoodoo, Hoodoo" also speaks of the need to go to New Orleans to procure a "mojo hand" from a Voodoo practitioner for the purpose of conjuration. Perhaps the best known of all Voodoo blues songs is Willie Dixon's "Hootchie Cootchie Man" in which the Voodoo man's fate and kit are described (Finn 150).

Showing further the intermingling of the various repressed and excluded American/African American social, sexual, cultural, and historical traditions, the blues songs, particularly by female blues singers, are saturated with references to sexual fluidity. "There's two things got me puzzled, there's two things I don't understand," moans blues great Bessie Smith, "That's a mannish-acting woman and a lisping, swishing, womanish-acting man." In "Sissy Blues," Ma Rainey complains of her husband's infidelity with a homosexual named "Miss Kate." Ma Rainey's "Prove It on Me Blues" speaks directly to the issue of lesbianism. In it, she admits to her preference for male attire and female companionship, yet dares her audience to "prove it" on her. Lucille Bogan, in her "B. D. Woman Blues," warns that "B. D. [bulldagger] women sure is rough; they drink up many a whiskey and they sure can strut their stuff." In "Sissy Man Blues," a traditional blues tune recorded by numerous male blues singers over the years, the singer demands that "if you can't bring me a woman, bring me a sissy man." George Hanna's "Freakish Blues," recorded in 1931, is even more explicit about sexual fluidity. The blues/subaltern African American cultures accept sexuality, including homosexual behavior and identities, as a normal part of life (Garber 320, 326). Likewise, if you had examined the bars in the working-class neighborhoods and in the underworld in African American communities of major U.S. cities beginning in the 1920s, you would have found blues fans and musicians, homosexual and heterosexual African Americans, subaltern African Americans, Voodoo practitioners, white American patrons, and middle-class African Americans intermingling and coexisting in the same social and cultural spaces.

In making salient the various repressed and excluded histories, traditions, images, and theoretical conceptions of life, I am approaching African American history polycentrically. I am deconstructing the privileging of traditional American and African American history and questioning its pretension to truth, reality, and coherence. I am returning a polyvalent nature to American/African American history. I am recognizing that there is always a social play of discourses even at moments when a single discourse appears to have asserted its dominance. The presence of repressed and excluded histories, along with a visible African American women's history and experience, allows the contradictory coexistence of different African American modes in one social and cultural present. This coexistence makes it impossible for any one cultural, social, or literary movement or canon to present itself as a total system. I am also contesting and decoding the oppressive quality of the assertion of the mainstream African American mission of racial uplift as the only narrative to define African American reality. I am rejecting a universal, evolutionary conception of time, an anthropocentric, teleological, and causal concept of history, and the idea of the future as utopia. Instead, I am pointing to different ways of constructing "reality" and of making sense of essentially incoherent, isolated, unconnected moments. Lastly, I am restoring to African American history, literature, criticism, and life the conflictual hybridity of productive modes and sign systems that are currently written out of the causal history of traditional African American life (Foster 178).

Using the critical and theoretical tools of poststructuralism, gender theory, postcolonial criticism, race theory, and poststructural feminism, this volume disrupts at the literary and historical levels the white/black binary of signification that not only defines African American life as inferior but also organizes African American history, literature, and critical practices to reaffirm and generate this unequal binary system. Using a polycentric approach, I have already shown how the label "black/African American" is slippery and reductionist, masking African American differences. Next, and for the remainder of this book, I will show not only how various African American identities do not conform to the fixed identity of the lower half of the white/black binary but also how they undermine, expose, and destabilize the unity of the category black/African American and subsequently the systematized hierarchization of the white/black binary. Polycentrically selecting those African American literary texts that draw on non-normative African American and normative American and Western belief systems and theoretical concepts of life and history, the book deconstructs and de-territorializes the white/black binary system and re-territorializes and reconstitutes those social, historical, and literary spaces where African American differences are privileged, where the positionality/representation of the African American is changed from Other-as-object, and thus as less, to Other-as-subject, where he as Other is equal but different. The objective is to produce a representation of the African American (male) in history and literature that is so diverse and heterogeneous as to disrupt the binary's representation. The next chapter investigates James Weldon Johnson's *The Autobiography of an Ex-Coloured Man* to show how it is read to reaffirm the African American sociopolitical mission of racial uplift and how it functions as cultural capital.

CHAPTER FOUR

FINDING FREEDOM IN SAMENESS

JAMES WELDON JOHNSON'S *THE AUTOBIOGRAPHY OF AN EX-COLOURED MAN*

Today, James Weldon Johnson's *The Autobiography of an Ex-Coloured Man* is defined as an archetypal text in the canon of African American literature. The positioning of *The Autobiography* as a pivotal canonical text did not happen in 1912 when it was published anonymously, or in 1927 when it was reissued bearing Johnson's name, but in the 1970s and 1980s with the emergence of African American studies and the rise of mainstream, elite/middle-class African American critics in predominantly white American colleges and universities that brought with them the inevitable need to reinvent the canon of African American literature. Although it was not until the 1970s and 1980s that *The Autobiography* became a pivotal canonical text, it was defined as a seminal and original African American text after its 1927 reissue. It was defined as a text that captured the black experience, that embodied the essence of the African American struggle for racial equality, and that manifested the race problem in the United States. The interesting questions I have about Johnson's *The Autobiography*, questions I will attempt to answer in this chapter, are: As an archetypal, canonical African American text, how is it represented politically and culturally? How does it function aesthetically, socially, and politically? Whose class interest does it serve?[1]

As a pivotal text that draws all African American texts around it, that embodies everything that comes before it, and that signifies everything that comes after it, *The Autobiography* becomes a center, a graspable essence, of African American literature. It allows elite/middle-class Christian African American and mainstream American critics to establish among successive African American literary texts a community of meanings, symbolic links, or an interplay of resemblance and reflection. It becomes the vortex, engaging "the interconnections of [African American] history and conditions with the life history of the individual" (V. Smith 44). As a center by which African American literary texts are defined in terms of their relation to it, *The Autobiography* allows African American critics to master African American literature, to master the African American experience. But this mastery also allows for a reduction in the differences within African American literature and life. It allows for the repression of the polyvalent nature of this literature and life.

I want to examine *The Autobiography*, this pivotal, archetypal text in the 1970s/1980s reinvented canon of African American literature, in terms of the white/black binary of signification that defines white as normative and superior and that represents black as victim, devalued Other, or as the Same. Both as an original and seminal African American text and as the pivotal text in this 1970s/1980s reinvented canon, how did it become the "epitome of the race situation in the United States" (Fauset 38)? How is it a "composite autobiography of the Negro race in the United States in modern times" (Van Vechten xxxiv)? How does *The Autobiography* embody the "key tropes which form the Afro-American tradition" (Stepto 96)? What does *The Autobiography* reveal of "the mind of the Negro" (Collier 365)? How is it an "inclusive survey of racial accomplishments and traits" (Van Vechten xxxiii)? How does the plight of the "tragic mulatto" symbolize/define African American life (Baker, *Singers* 22)? *The Autobiography* interconnects what African American "racial history and conditions with the life of the individual" (V. Smith 44)? How does it construct African American life? What construction of African American life does it privilege? Finally, does it reproduce or disrupt the white/black binary?

The Autobiography is an archetypal African American text because it is informed by and reproduces the ideology of the African American sociopolitical mission of racial uplift and the white/black binary of signification. It defines the journey from the African American subaltern to the middle-class, Christian, Protestant work ethic values, conventions, and definitions of mainstream American society as *the* African American experience and *the* African American literary tradition. In this instance, it embodies the sociopolitical mission of racial uplift—the main tenet of elite/middle-class Christian African Americans. It also protests against mainstream society for not accepting the African American. Finally, *The Autobiography* represses and subordinates the African American subaltern.

Written as an autobiography echoing earlier slave autobiographies, *The Autobiography* is a first-person retrospective narrative of an "ex-coloured man." He is born in Georgia to a prominent, wealthy white man and a light-skinned black woman, who obviously love each other although the social situation will not permit a union. He is raised middle class in Connecticut by his mother with rare visits from his father. Until he is eleven, he is raised as white but is then told that he is black. Later he chooses to pass for white to achieve fully the American dream. He writes his story after he has already passed. In choosing at that point to write his autobiography and to divulge "the great secret of [his] life," the ex-coloured man is "led by the same impulse which forces the un-found-out criminal to take somebody into his confidence, although he knows that the act is likely, even almost certain, to lead to his undoing" (3). But the ex-coloured man, in keeping his secret hidden, also suffers "a vague feeling of unsatisfaction, of regret, of almost remorse, from which [he is] seeking relief" (3).

Because his physical appearance is not identifiably black, the ex-coloured man's earlier years are spent thinking that he is white. His mother never tells him differently, and she is "careful about [his] associates" (7). Until he is nine years old, he has no "playmates." He knows a "few boys" from church but he formed "no close friendships with any of them" (10). At the predominantly white school he attends, his white classmates and friends assume that he is white. The ex-coloured man internalizes the values and cognitive styles of mainstream white society: "Within a few days [of beginning school] I had made one staunch friend and was on fairly good terms with most of the boys" (10).

In thinking that he is white, the ex-coloured man enjoys the social power of being in the majority all the time, of being routinely connected psychologically to a whole spectrum of normative institutions. His whiteness gives him security and privilege. At school, he is confident and has "wit and quickness"; he is "a perfect little aristocrat . . . about as popular as it is good for a boy to be" (16). As a white schoolboy, he embraces Western culture and values with abandon. He reads the Bible, and his heroes are King David, Samson, and Robert the Bruce. He also reads "a weekly paper which was then very popular for [middle-class American] boys" (26). "I read white books," writes Franz Fanon, "and little by little I take into myself the prejudices, the myths, the folklore that have come to me from Europe" (191–92). Although he learns to play Negro folk music from his mother, the ex-coloured man is trained very early in European classical music. He plays Chopin for his father on one of his rare visits. At a recital, he plays in a duet of Beethoven's "Sonata Pathetique."

But in assuming that he is white, the ex-coloured man also internalizes the white/black binary of signification, a regime of power and knowledge that defines white as normative and superior and that represents black as devalued Other, as inferior, or as victim. By assuming the position of a white in this binary, he defines his black classmates as Other, invisible, and inferior, as abstractions, as a black mass that does not possess the same humanity, ego, or complex human consciousness as he and his white classmates. Literally, he refers to them as "the others." He has "no particular like or dislike for these black and brown boys and girls; in fact, with the exception of 'Shiny,' they had occupied very little of [his] thought" (23). Shiny, who is considered the "best speller, the best reader, the best penman—in a word, the best scholar—in the class . . . was in some way looked down upon" (14). With Johnson playing off, and reversing, the minstrel show description, the ex-coloured man innocently and disparagingly calls Shiny "Shiny Face" because "his face was as black as night, but shone as though it were polished" (14). He continues in this observation: "The other black boys and girls were still more looked down upon. Some of the [white] boys often spoke of them as 'niggers' " (14). The ex-coloured man eventually joins the white boys in taunting the black boys, calling them "nigger," and when his mother scolds him for using the word, he recounts, "I hang my head in shame, not because she had convinced me that I had done wrong, but because I was hurt by the first sharp word she had ever given me" (15). Indifferently, he notices and participates in the racism of his white classmates.

But on the memorable day when the white principal enters his classroom and asks "all of the white scholars to stand for a moment," and he stands but is asked to "sit down . . . and rise with the others" (16), leading his white classmates to exclaim, "Oh, you're a nigger, too" (16), the ex-coloured man moves psychologically and socially from the privileged white half of the white/black binary to the marginal, negative lower half of the binary, and he is devastated. In this moment, we witness how race is not biologically determined but is a culturally and politically invented category—a designation coined for the sake of grouping and separating people along lines of presumed differences. For one moment, the ex-coloured man thinks he is white. In another moment, he is presumed to be different and, therefore, is defined as black.

The ex-coloured man defines this moment as "one of the tragedies of life" (20). He knows that according to the definitions of his society, to be a "nigger" is to be Other, something ugly and bad, and he regrets becoming a "nigger." So, he rushes home and asks his mother, "Mother, tell me, am I a nigger?" (17). Speaking the language of the white/black binary, where she is defined as the devalued Other but aspires to the values of the dominant white society, the mother informs the ex-coloured man that he is "as good as anybody . . . your father is one of the greatest men in the country—the best blood of the South is in you" (18). Reflecting later on this incident, he observes that "when the blow fell, I had a very strong aversion to being classed with them [blacks]" (23). What the ex-coloured man (and his mother) does not question, at that moment or even later (and I will discuss whether even Johnson questions this construction), is the representation of the African American as devalued Other. Instead, the ex-coloured man tries to regain his previous social status and to become the Same as the norm, the upper half of the binary. He strives "to become equal to that splendid model [of the middle-class, white American] and to resemble him to the point of disappearing in him" (Memmi 120). He states: "And so I have often lived through that hour, that day, that week, in which was wrought the miracle of my transition from one world into another; for I did indeed pass into another world" (*The Autobiography* 20–21).

What I want to argue in the remainder of this chapter is first that the ex-coloured man spends the rest of his colored life trying to reassimilate back into Sameness, into the upper half of the white/black binary, into the values and definitions of the privileged white regime of power and truth. Second, I want to argue that in this attempt to reassimilate back into this regime the ex-coloured man *and* Johnson, wishing to uplift the race by showing how African Americans can practice the values of the dominant society and thereby prove to white people their worthiness of respect and social equality, establish a hierarchy within African America that privileges those African Americans who approximate or come closer to the mainstream norm and that rejects and crushes subaltern African American life—life that is different, that exists outside the lines of mobility that extend into mainstream American life.

In analyzing his experience of that memorable day and in executing his racial uplift mission, the ex-coloured man essentializes his experiences.[2] He makes the aspirations of the elite/middle-class Christian African American those of every African American. The "I" of these light-skinned African Americans generically becomes the eye/I of the race. The ex-coloured man identifies his own elite/middle-class values with the values of the race, with the conviction that African America is monolithic:

> And this is the dwarfing, warping, distorting influence which operates *upon each and every coloured man in the United States.* He is forced to take his outlook on all things, not from the view point of a citizen, or a man, or even a human being, but from the view point of a *coloured* man. It is wonderful to me that the race has progressed so broadly as it has, since most of its thought and all of its activity must run through the narrow neck of this one funnel." (21; emphasis added)

In this essentialist move, the ex-coloured man reduces African Americans to a singular formation, in which African American life is defined in terms of racial oppression exclusively and in which African American differences and heterogeneity are repressed and excluded. The ex-coloured man, like other elite/middle-class, Christian African Americans who believe in racial uplift, develops and makes "natural" a system of thinking in which differences within African America are maintained largely through a persistent habit of hierarchical placement. In this reduction, we have an example both of the typical operation of exclusion through which totalization takes place and of the way in which the Other—in this case, African American differences or those non-elite/middle-class African Americans—is constituted as the Same.

As a result of the classroom incident, the ex-coloured man changes. He looks at his mother "critically for the first time" and sees that her skin is brown, that her hair is not as soft as his, and that "she did differ in some way from the other ladies who came to the house" (18). Because he is now constructed as black, he comes to define himself as a victim, a devalued Other. He becomes "reserved . . . [and] suspicious," grows "constantly more and more afraid of laying [himself] open to some injury to [his] feelings or [his] pride," and "frequently [sees] or fancie[s] some slight where, [he is] sure, none [is] intended" (22). His "friends and teachers [are] . . . more considerate of [him]," and "it [is] against this very attitude in particular that [his] sensitiveness revolted" (22). Some of his white classmates have "evidently received instructions at home on the matter [of his being colored], and more than once they displayed their knowledge in word and action" (23). "Red" is the only friend "who does not so wound [him]" (22). He learns what it is like to be defined as a "nigger" from the manner in which the "other coloured children in school" are treated; he discovers "what their status was, and now [knows] that theirs [is his]" (23).

Because he becomes alienated from his white classmates and because he absolutely refuses to associate with his black classmates, he becomes solitary. He becomes a searcher. His forced loneliness causes him to "find company in books, and greater pleasure in music" (24). During this period, he turns again to the Bible, where his heroes are King David and Samson, and to Robert the Bruce. After reading the Bible, the ex-coloured man reads *Pilgrim's Progress*; Peter Parley's *History of the United States*; and Jacob and Wilhem Grimm's *Household Stories, Tales of a Grandfather* (a bound volume of an old English publication), and a little volume called *Familiar Science and Somebody's Natural Theology*.

But the older he grows, the more he thinks about the question of his and his mother's position in society, and about what their "exact relation to the world in general" is (40). During this period in his life, the ex-coloured man is very much a modern figure: he is alienated and fragmented, and he lacks historical continuity and social identification. But his later reading of Harriet Beecher Stowe's *Uncle Tom's Cabin* gives him a framework or meta narrative within which to conceptualize his life. It gives him the "first perspective of the life [he] was entering" (41). Although Stowe's book has "been the subject of much unfavorable criticism" because Uncle Tom is too good, the ex-coloured man believes that "there were lots of old Negroes as foolishly good as he; the proof of which is that they knowingly stayed and worked the plantations that furnished sinews for the army which was fighting to keep them enslaved" (41). He concludes that the text is "a fair and truthful panorama of slavery," adding that it "opened my eyes as to who and what I was and what my country considered me; in fact, it gave me my bearing. . . . One of the greatest benefits I derived from reading the book was that I could afterwards talk frankly with my mother on all the questions which had been vaguely troubling my mind" (42). The conversations between the two kindle a strong desire for him to see the South, his parents' homeland.

Forced into the position of the colonized, or the lower half of the white/black binary where all the images and representations of him and the race are negative, how does the ex-coloured man cope? According to Memmi, the colonized seeks freedom by rejecting self and race as they are defined by the colonizer, and by embracing and assimilating the colonizer's values. "By this step, which actually presupposes admiration for the colonizer, one can infer approval of colonization," or the white/black binary (121).

Seeking freedom, the ex-coloured man crushes and destroys self and race as they are constructed by the colonizer. According to Memmi, the "crushing of the colonized is included among the colonizer's values" (121); "rejection of self and love of another are common to all candidates for assimilation" (121). In his move to be the Same as whites, to assimilate their values and their world, the ex-coloured man, as a member of an elite/middle-class, Christian, colonized African America, accents those qualities and virtues that make the African American equal and acceptable to whites, thereby refuting the myth of African American inferiority. According to the racial uplift mission, when one African American proves that he or she can speak and dress, be intelligent, and show intelligence, culture, and education in the ways sanctioned and respected by the dominant society, he or she brings honor, respectability, and pride to the race. At the grammar school graduation, Shiny is the principal speaker and the ex-coloured man interprets this as serving the race well:

> But the real enthusiasm was aroused by "Shiny." He was the principal speaker of the day, and well did he measure up to the honour. He made a striking picture, that thin little black boy standing on the platform, dressed in clothes that did not fit him any too well, . . . I think that solitary little black figure standing there felt that for the particular time and place he bore the weight and responsibility of his race; that for him to fail meant general defeat; but he won, and nobly. . . . But the effect upon me of "Shiny's" speech was double; . . . *I felt leap within me pride that I was coloured; and I began to form wild dreams of bringing glory and honour to the Negro race.* For days I could talk of nothing else with my mother except my ambitions to be a great man, a great coloured man, to reflect credit on the race and gain fame for myself. (44–46, emphasis added)

It is important to note that the ex-coloured man feels pride in being "coloured" because Shiny has performed at a "high standard of excellence" as defined by the white audience.

He thinks of other colored men "who have been chosen as orators in our leading universities, of others who have played on the varsity football and baseball teams, of coloured speakers who have addressed great white audiences" and "in each case where the efforts have reached any high standard of excellence they have been followed by the same phenomenon of enthusiasm" (45). He believes these black men are "stirred by the same emotions which actuated 'Shiny' on the day of graduation" because they believe that the Anglo Saxon ascribes to "fair play" and so will accept them and deem them worthy (45). And in his "ambitions to be a great man, a great coloured man," the ex-coloured man will perform at a similar high standard of excellence as defined by mainstream white society and will expect other African Americans to do likewise.

In high school, the ex-coloured man "continued [his] study of the piano, the pipe organ, and the theory of music" (46). He also becomes more focused on those elite/middle-class Christian African Americans who have achieved a high standard of excellence, or who have embraced the values of the dominant white society. He reads "with studious interest everything [he] could find relating to coloured men who had gained prominence" (46). His heroes change from King

David and Robert the Bruce to people such as Frederick Douglass. When he learns that the noted French author Alexandre Dumas is a colored man, he rereads *Monte Cristo* and *The Three Guardsmen* "with magnified pleasure" (46).

After high school and the death of his mother, when he travels to Atlanta and later to Jacksonville, Florida, the ex-coloured man focuses on, and identifies with, what W. E. B. DuBois calls the African American *talented tenth*—the best of the race who takes responsibility for bringing the entire race up to "civilized" standards. On his first day in the auditorium at Atlanta University, the ex-coloured man cannot help noticing that

> many of the girls, particularly those of the delicate brown shades, and with black eyes and wavy dark hair, were decidedly pretty. Among the boys many of the blackest were fine specimens of young manhood, tall, straight, and muscular, with magnificent heads; these were the kind of boys who developed into the patriarchal "uncles" of the old slave regime. (62)

In Jacksonville, through his music teaching and the church, he becomes "acquainted with the best class of coloured people. . . . This [is] really [his] entrance into the race" (74). They are DuBois's talented tenth, "the advanced element of the coloured race. . . . They are the ones among the blacks who carry the entire weight of the race question . . . and [he believes that] the only thing which at times sustains them is that they know that they are in the right" (81). "Advanced" here means closer to the values of the white middle-class norm. Those who successfully imitate whites are "independent workmen and tradesmen, and . . . the well-to-do and educated coloured people. . . . [They] have acquired . . . money, education, and [European] culture" (78–79, 80–81).

Although the ex-coloured man is "a hail fellow well met with all of the workmen at the factory," his norm was "the professional and well-to-do class," and asserts that even though he takes an occasional drink and is "a bit wild," he never does "anything disgraceful, or . . . anything to forfeit [his] claim to respectability" (84). When the cigar factory burns down, the ex-coloured man is about to marry a young schoolteacher, raise a family, and live respectably and permanently among the elite/middle-class Christian African Americans in Jacksonville. He is keen on becoming the Same as middle-class America.

Even in New York, where the ex-coloured man becomes associated with the bohemian world, he still defines the middle class as the norm. The ideal novel for the ex-coloured man is a "novel dealing with coloured people who lived in respectable homes and amidst a fair degree of European culture and who naturally acted 'just like white folks' " (168). But the narrator admits that this portrait would be taken by the larger society in a "comic-opera sense," realizing that the American "public is loath to give him [the African American] up in his old character [, to view him as devalued Other]; they even conspire to make him a failure in serious work, in order to force him back into comedy" (168). (Interestingly, he assumes that he has only two choices: accept being inferior or become the Same as whites.) He refers to the world of the gambling house and the "Club" as this "gas light life," this "lower world" (115). It is a world that possesses greater social integration, but also a world where a "score of bright, intelligent young fellows who had come up to the great city with high hopes and ambition . . . had fallen under the spell of this under life" (113). For the ex-coloured man, it is a world not of freedom but one that "enervated and deadened one's moral sense," a world that he in retrospect looks back upon "with a shudder when [he thought] what would have been had [he] not escaped it" (113). Therefore, during his stay in New York, he regrets that he "did not become acquainted with a single respectable [African American] family. [He] knew that there were several coloured men worth a hundred or so thousand dollars each, and some families who proudly dated their free ancestry back a half-dozen generations" (114).

Just as the ex-coloured man embraces the middle-class norm, he also moves to separate himself from the African American subaltern by defining it in negative, stereotypical terms. Discussing the subaltern in an interview with Donna Landry and Gerald MacLean in *The Spivak Reader*, Spivak defines the subaltern as "the space that is cut off from the lines of mobility in a colonized country. You have the foreign elite and the indigenous elite. Below that you will have the vectors of upward, downward, sideward, [and] backward mobility" (288). For Spivak, the subaltern is "more than just strategic exclusion. . . . It is not something like 'going in search of the primitive'. . . . It is just a space of difference" (288–89, 293).

When the ex-coloured man arrives in Atlanta and encounters the African American poor/subaltern, he is repulsed:

> [In Atlanta] I caught my first sight of coloured people in large numbers. . . .
> They filled the shops and thronged the sidewalks and lived on the curb. I asked
> my companion if all the coloured people in Atlanta lived in this street. He said
> they did not and assured me that the ones I saw were of the lower class. I felt
> relieved, in spite of the size of the lower class. The unkempt appearance, the
> shambling, slouching gait and loud talk and laughter of these people aroused in
> me a feeling of almost repulsion." (55–56)

Later, in Jacksonville, not only does the ex-coloured man move to distance himself from subaltern African America, but he attempts to crush it. In his reconstruction of blacks in Jacksonville, the ex-coloured man speaks for the race. He argues that "the coloured people may be said to be roughly divided into three classes, not so much in respect to their relations with whites" (76). Describing the subaltern African American—the desperate class—the ex-coloured man states:

> There are those constituting what might be called the desperate class—the men
> who work in the lumber and turpentine camps, the ex-convicts, the bar-room
> loafers are all in this class. These men conform to the requirements of civilization

much as a trained lion with low muttered growls goes through his stunts under the crack of the trainer's whip. They cherish a sullen hatred for all white men, and they value life as cheap. . . . Happily, this class represents the black people of the South far below their normal physical and moral condition. (76–77)

Then he proceeds to castigate them for not being the Same as he and other elite/middle-class Christian African Americans.

Much later in the text, when the ex-coloured man decides to leave Europe and return to the South, he moves into the interior of rural Georgia and has his "first real experience among rural coloured people," describing the subaltern African American as a "happy-go-lucky, laughing, shuffling, banjo-picking being" who really is "an obstacle in the way of the thoughtful and progressive element of the race" (168). In this representation of subaltern African America, the intellectual, middle-class ex-coloured man identifies his own values with the values of the race and, thus, covers over and represents subaltern African America as the Same.

Likewise, the doctor that the ex-coloured man meets on the returning ship establishes a hierarchy within African America with elite/middle-class African America as the norm. He refers to those African Americans who are different, who do not strive for the white, middle-class, Christian norm as, "those lazy, loafing, good-for-nothing darkies; they're not worth digging graves for" (155). For the doctor, these subaltern African Americans must be crushed because:

they are the ones who create impressions of the race for the casual observer. . . . But they ought not to represent the race. We [elite/middle-class Christian African Americans] are the race, and the race ought to be judged by us, not by them. Every race and every nation should be judged by the best it has been able to produce, not by the worst. (155–56)

Here, the best and worst are determined by how close African Americans approximate the values, education, and culture of a Eurocentric America. The practice of saving and speaking for the Other, the African American masses, is often born from a desire for mastery, to privilege oneself as the one who more correctly understands the truth about another's situation. That elite/middle-class Christian African Americans such as the ex-coloured man and the doctor speak for the African American subaltern becomes a form of erasure and reinscription. But neither acknowledges the fact that he is speaking from his own class position and is expressing his own class interest.

But what happens to the colonized—in this stance, to the elite/middle-class Christian African American who has crushed/destroyed/impoverished his or her "true" self, the African American differences, by choosing to achieve freedom through assimilating the values of the dominant white society—when he or she is rejected by the colonizer—in this instance, the dominant white society? This predicament of the elite/middle-class, colonized African American who wants to leave his or her group for another, desiring assimilation and being refused it by the colonizer, is exemplified in several instances in Johnson's text. It is manifested in the conversation on the street in Jacksonville between the ex-coloured man and the young professional who has just returned home from college. The young African American professional recounts passing on the street a young white man whom he grew up with, "played, hunted, and fished" with, someone whom he, as a child, had "even eaten and slept" with. But when he returns to Jacksonville as an educated professional, as someone who has acquired mainstream education, values, and culture, the young white man "barely speaks" (80). The young African American professional analyzes the white man's rejection of him thusly:

> I think that the white people somehow feel that coloured people who have education and money, who wear good clothes and live in comfortable houses, are "putting on airs," that they [black people] do these things for the sole purpose of "spiting the white folks," or are . . . going through a sort of monkey-like imitation. (80)

Of course, there is a paradox in the young professional's situation. On the one hand, whites, or the colonizers, consider themselves to be the norm/superior. Therefore, the colonizer or the white man, writes Fanon, wants the colonized to "bring [him]self as quickly as possible into step with the white world" (98). On the other hand, the black/colonized also serves as a marker for the identification of the white/colonizer. To be white is not to be black. The African American as Other is structurally necessary, for he defines the limits of mainstream American society—what is (a)social, (ab)normal, and (sub)cultural. In short, the American white norm is produced around the positioning of the African American as Other. Therefore, the colonized/African American cannot ever be assimilated into the white/black binary as the Same. "It is the colonized who is the first to desire assimilation, and it is the colonizer who refuses it to him" (Memmi 125). Thus, the young Jacksonville African American professional is left wanting—waiting for white people to accept and validate him.

This paradox/contradiction of wanting to assimilate but constantly being rejected is further exemplified in the ex-coloured man's stay in New York and Paris. In the two bohemian spaces—the Club in New York City and Paris—where the social barriers between blacks and whites are blurred and elite/middle-class Christian African Americans can be on a social par with whites, blacks are not able to assimilate completely into the dominant white society. They are not able to disrupt the white/black binary and how it defines reality for the races. The Club in New York City is "well known to both white and coloured people of certain classes. A great deal of money was spent [there], so many of the patrons were men who earned large sums" (105). It is a gathering place for "coloured Bohemians and sports. Here the great prize-fighters were wont to come, the famous jockeys, the noted minstrels, whose names and faces were familiar on every bill-board in the country" (105).

The Club is also one of the few places where whites and elite/middle-class blacks can mingle socially. But it, too, has its social barriers and hierarchies. At the Club, the "one or two parties of white people" who came nightly are "out sight-seeing, or slumming," whereas another "set of white people who came frequently" is "made up of variety performers and others who delineated 'darky characters'; they [come] to get their imitations first-hand from the Negro entertainers they [see] there" (107). Finally, the Club is patronized by another set of white patrons, composed of women: "They were all good-looking and well dressed, and seemed to be women of some education," and they are always in "company with coloured men" (108). As the example of the widow in the book shows, these upper-middle-class, educated white women are into dating black men. Whites slumming with blacks or using blacks as a source of minstrel imitation and white women dating black men are not signs of genuine social integration between blacks and whites nor a sign of blacks becoming equal to whites. They are signs of whites defining blacks as the exotic Other. The Club is a place where whites can go and be entertained by the Other. "Even in such an apparently liberated, morally fluid, and ideologically liberal space as the bohemian world of New York night clubs," concludes Donald C. Goellnicht, "race remains a mark of hierarchized difference" (26).

In Paris, the ex-coloured man comes closest to being accepted as the Same. According to Goellnicht, the stay in Paris "obviates the need to deal with the color issue, . . . and gives him a false sense of security and freedom" (24). Paris "impressed [him] as the perfect and perfectly beautiful city," becoming his "charmed spot" (128). In Paris, the ex-coloured man's relationship with the millionaire changes. His patron/benefactor buys him the same kind of clothes that he himself wears, and he treats him as an equal. For the first two weeks, they are together almost constantly, seeing the sights. During the day, they take in the places of interest, and at night they attend the theaters and cafés. Alone, the ex-coloured man learns French, attends the opera, and really enjoys moving socially throughout the city. But even in Paris, he fails to escape racial marking or the reminder of an America where he belongs to the lower half of the white/black binary. A friend from Luxemburg, who is a great admirer of the United States, asks him: "Did they really burn a man alive in the United States?" (136).

The ex-coloured man is further reminded of racial hierarchized differences when he encounters his father and sister in Paris one night at the opera *Faust*:

> the desolate loneliness of [his] position became clear to [him. He] knew that
> [he] could not speak, but [he] would have given a part of [his] life to touch her
> hand with [his] and call her "sister." . . . [He] walked aimlessly about for an
> hour or so, [his] feelings divided between a desire to weep and a desire to curse.
> (134–135)

In the first situation, "the narrator flees from the situation," and in the second, "he evades the issue, feeling embarrassed at being American rather than expressing outrage at being part of a group victimized by American racism" (Goell-nicht 24). Therefore, the ex-coloured man's personal past and his country's past disrupt his move to assimilate completely into European culture and society.

But this paradox/contradiction is resolved for the ex-coloured man upon his return to the South and his decision to pass for white. After an extended stay in Europe and feeling that his life has found direction, the ex-coloured man leaves his patron/benefactor with the intention of returning to "the very heart of the South, to live among [his] people, and drink in [their] inspiration firsthand" (142). Having gotten the idea of playing ragtime and "the old slave songs" as if they were classical music from a German musician while in Europe, the ex-coloured man feels that his mission has crystallized (142–43). This will become his contribution to uplifting the race. He "felt stirred by an unselfish desire to voice all the joys and sorrows, the hopes and ambitions, of the American Negro, in classical musical form" (147–48). But he never decides whether the return trip to the South is more a "desire to help those [he] consider[s his] people, [which is racial uplift] or more a desire to distinguish [him]self, [which is opportunism]" (147).

Upon his return to the South, however, the ex-coloured man never lives "among the people." He is never able to gather ragtime and other African American folk music and turn them into classical music—which is really appropriating subaltern African American musical and cultural forms into mainstream/Western forms. When he witnesses the lynching of a black man, and the "smell of burnt flesh—human flesh—[is] in [his] nostrils" (187), he walks a

> short distance away [and sits] down in order to clear [his] dazed mind. A great
> wave of humiliation and shame [sweeps] over [him]. Shame that [he] belong[s]
> to a race that could be so dealt with; and shame for [his] country, that it, the
> great example of democracy to the world, should be the only civilized, if not
> the only state on earth, where a human being would be burned alive. (187–88)

He is ashamed "at being identified with a people that could with impunity be treated worse than animals" (191). Therefore, he decides to pass for white so life for him and his children will be much easier. Actually, in this decision, he has taken the advice of his patron, which is to make himself as "happy as possible, and try to make those happy whose lives come in touch with" his (146).

Although the ex-coloured man accepts the ease and comfort with which he finally lives his life, he has remorse and regret for the way he achieves that ease and comfort. He has achieved it as an individual, abandoning the plight of the race and the whole mission of racial uplift. As Memmi argues: "few of the colonized almost succeeded in disappearing into the colonizer group. It is clear . . . that a collective drama will never be settled through individual solutions. The individual disappears in his lineage and the group drama goes on" (126–27).

The ex-coloured man, in choosing to assimilate, to pass, is able to disappear "into the colonizer group." But in passing, in achieving the American dream, the ex-coloured man is not happy because he, having once adopted the racial uplift ideology in which his individual 'I' becomes the 'eye' of the race, is still tied psychologically to the black race, and the race's drama, or its struggle for equality, goes on. Of course, this explains his "vague feeling of unsatisfaction, of regret, of almost remorse, from which [he is] seeking relief" (3). His individual assimilation has not proven to be a solution for African America. It has not uplifted the entire race.

The respectful way to achieve comfort and equality, to attain the American dream—and this becomes the message *The Autobiography* offers the talented tenth and African American readers aspiring to the talented tenth—is to struggle against the barriers that prevent all African Americans from participating fully in the institutions of the American society and from embracing fully the values of mainstream American society. After passing, the ex-coloured man comes to admire people like Shiny and other black professionals. But who are these men the ex-coloured man admires and respects? What are their values and aspirations? How are they different from him? Are they passing? What are Johnson's attitudes toward them in contrast to his attitude toward the ex-coloured man? And are they successful in becoming the Same as the dominant white society?

Shiny stands out as an exemplar race man when he delivers the grammar school graduation speech. In high school, he and Red visit the ex-coloured man's house "quite often of evenings," where they talk over their "plans and prospects for the future" (48). Because he has an uncle in Amherst, Massachusetts, Shiny plans to attend Amherst College and live with his uncle. Years later, the ex-coloured man runs into one of Shiny's former students and learns that Shiny is a professor at one of the southern black colleges where he works among the people. He has become an intelligent black person who is "too much in earnest over the race question," trying to make a "race-over" and taking responsibility for bringing the entire race up to the "civilized" standards (211).

Later that summer, after the ex-coloured man has decided to pass, he and his female companion encounter Shiny on the streets in New York City. Shiny is "spending his vacation north, with the intention of doing four or six weeks' work in one of the summer schools; he was also going to take a bride back with him in the fall" (203). From the description of this encounter, we learn that Shiny has taken on the values of the dominant society: he has accepted the values of "nobility, intelligence, strength, articulateness, virtue, rationality, courage, self-control, . . . and physical attractiveness as defined in white Western terms" (Yarborough 168). Unlike the time when he gave the graduation speech in ill-fitting "clothes, he is today a refined black man." He is the embodiment of mainstream success. "The polish of his language and the unpedantic manner in which he revealed his culture greatly impressed her [the ex-coloured man's white female companion]" (203). In fact, Shiny's appearance aroused such an interest in her that even afterward, when he changes the subject of the conversation, she "revert[s] several times to the subject of 'Shiny'" (203). The "Shiny" incident gives the ex-coloured man encouragement and the confidence to cast the die of his fate, for Shiny represents the black man in such a way as to refute white people's notion of black inferiority, and he is working to uplift the race.

Likewise, the doctor that the ex-coloured man encounters on the ship is another intelligent elite/middle-class African American he respects and admires. He, too, is a man "defined in white Western terms," described as a "tall, broad-shouldered, almost gigantic, coloured man. His dark-brown face [is] clean-shaven; he [is] well-dressed and [bears] a decidedly distinguished air" (149). The doctor, who believes in the African American sociopolitical mission of racial up-lift, is also working for the betterment of the race. He believes that once the black man equals the white man according to what the white man defines as "civilization," the white man will accept him. He advises the ex-coloured man:

> the Negro is progressing, and that disproves all the arguments in the world that he is incapable of progress. I was born in slavery, and at emancipation was set adrift a ragged, penniless bit of humanity. I have seen the Negro in every grade, and I know what I am talking about. Our detractors point to the increase of crime as evidence against us; certainly we have progressed in crime as in other things; what less could be expected? And yet, in this respect, *we are far from the point which has been reached by the more highly civilized white race.* (151–52, emphasis added)

The assumption is that when African Americans have reached the same level as the "highly civilized white race," they will have achieved success and freedom, and racism will disappear. The doctor and the ex-coloured man, along with Shiny, possess the same values. Both want to "pass." Both belong to the African American talented tenth, and both feel it their responsibility to speak for the race, to uplift the race. As Robert Fleming points out:

> the narrator . . . [and] his high opinion of the doctor is determined by the many similarities between the two men. Like the protagonist, the doctor can discuss the "Negro question" in objective, detached terms. . . . Also like the protagonist, the doctor deplores the fact that some classes of black people are not so cultivated as he, and in some ways he can sympathize with Southern [white] attitudes. (93)

But Shiny, the doctor, the young Jacksonville African American professional, along with other elite/middle-class Christian African Americans whose mission it is to uplift the race, run into the same paradox as the ex-coloured man. They seek freedom by becoming the Same as the mainstream norm, which rejects them. They are people who have acquired European education and culture, who live in comfortable homes, and who dress according to the norm's standard of success. Their language/speech is polished, and they have unpedantic manners. And their mission is both to assimilate into the American norm and to bring all African Americans to their level of education and (European) culture: they want all African Americans to become the middle-class, Christian, white American norm.

But Shiny, the doctor, the young Jacksonville African American professional, and other elite/middle-class Christian African Americans all fail to understand, as I have discussed, that they will be rejected inevitably by the dominant white society because blacks serve as a marker for the identification of whites. They do not understand that the American white norm is produced around the positioning of the African American as Other. The problem, as the ex-coloured man defines it, is more than just "the mental attitude of whites," which can be changed more easily than the actual condition of blacks, instead, the "burden of the [racial] question is . . . that they [whites] are unwilling to open certain doors of opportunity and to accord certain treatment to ten million aspiring, educated and property-acquiring [coloured] people" (166). But a "mental attitude" is produced by actual conditions, and here, the actual condition of elite/middle-class blacks is a world where whites are defined as normative and superior, and blacks are constructed as devalued Other, as inferior, or as victim. To change the mental attitudes and the actual conditions means that whites, to again use Memmi's terms, "would have to put an end to themselves" (127), or that blacks would have to refuse their Otherized role in the white/black binary. The colonized/African American "can never succeed in becoming identified" with the colonizer/Euro-American, "nor even in copying his role correctly. . . . Everything is mobilized so that the colonized cannot cross the doorstep" (124-125). Because whites and blacks exist under conditions of colonization in the West where whites define themselves against blacks, "assimilation and colonization [the white/black binary] are contradictory" (127).

The crucial questions are: Where is Johnson on the issue of assimilation? Passing? What does he think about the journey to the values of the dominant society? Is he and the project of *The Autobiography* caught in the same paradox/ contradiction as the ex-coloured man and other elite/middle-class African American characters? What is his relationship to his nameless narrator? Critics are divided on this last question. Many argue that the ex-coloured man is an unreliable narrator and that Johnson takes an ironic tone toward him; others say that Johnson is in ideological agreement with his narrator. Joseph Skerrett summarizes this division:

> James Weldon Johnson's only novel, *The Autobiography* . . . , has divided its readers over the years into two distinct camps. One group, which includes Sterling Brown, Hugh Gloster, David Littlejohn, Stephen Bronz, and Nathan Huggins, feels that Johnson's narrator and his opinions are a direct reflection of their author. The other group, whose membership includes Robert Bone, Edward Margolies, Eugenia Collier, Robert Fleming, and Marvin Garrett, argues that Johnson's treatment of his narrator is essentially ironic. (540)

Let us examine those critics who define Johnson's treatment of his narrator as "essentially ironic." Fleming argues that when the ex-coloured man interrupts the movement of the narrative to generalize about the various stratifications and classifications of black life, he adopts an ironic tone. Fleming defines these moments of "objective analyses" as the ex-coloured man's viewing his "race in detached sociological terms because he never feels a part of it" (91). Goellnicht argues that when the ex-coloured man describes subaltern or lower-class African Americans in negative terms, he is choosing "to adopt the gaze of white society" (20). Bone in *The Negro Novel in America* states that the ex-coloured man "avoids self-pity . . . through an attitude of ironic detachment" (48). Marvin P. Garrett argues that "the narrator's recollections represent the key to the novel's narrative design, becoming the primary means by which Johnson directs irony at his narrator" (5). Garrett further argues that Johnson in *The Autobiography* achieves ironic effect or duplicity of meaning by using the early recollections as a device that reveals the fallibility of the narrator: "Extreme sensitivity to pain and excessive concern with security and self-protection are the most prominent patterns in the narrator's earliest recollections" (7). Garrett characterizes the protagonist's duplicity, especially in how he behaves toward other students, as hypocrisy.

First, these assessments of the narrator as being ironic can be true, and Johnson can still agree with his narrator on larger political and social issues, especially since these critics do not examine how irony affects the narrator's relationship to such issues in the text. The ex-coloured man does have "extreme sensitivity to and excessive concern with security and self protection" (Garrett 7). In describing subaltern African Americans, the ex-coloured man does adopt "the gaze of white society" (Goellnicht 20), and he views his race "in detached sociological terms because he never feels a part of it" (Fleming 91). But isn't this detachment from negative, disparaging representations of subaltern African America an integral part of the elite/middle-class Christian African American's racial uplift ideology, of which Johnson is a part? In adopting the values of the dominant white society and in distancing himself from the subaltern African American, wouldn't the elite/middle-class Christian African American also adopt the "gaze of white society" (Goellnicht 20)? Like the ex-coloured man, the doctor also discusses the "Negro question" in objective, detached terms (Fleming 93).

Furthermore, isn't this negative representation of the subaltern African American a part of the elite/middle-class Christian African American's effort to make racial uplift the basis for a racialized elite identity claiming black improvement through class stratification as race progress? Also, isn't this device of the elite/middle-class narrator's disrupting his narrative and speaking objectively and generally about African America in the tradition of the slave autobiographers such as Frederick Douglass in *Narrative* and W. E. B. DuBois in *The Souls of Black Folk*? As Gates points out in *"Race," Writing, and Difference*, their "descriptive 'eye' [is] put into service as a literary form to posit both the individual 'I' of the black author as well as the collective 'I' of the race" (11). According to the ideology of the talented tenth and the African American sociopolitical mission of racial uplift, it is the individual's responsibility to uplift the race, to prove black humanity, and to make all members of the race worthy of white acceptance. When the ex-coloured man and the doctor give their "objective analyses," are they not simply trying to convince their white reading audience to accept blacks, particularly middle-class Christian blacks, as worthy of being treated humanly?

To explain Johnson's complex relationship with his narrator, Skerrett turns to Johnson's life and argues that in *The Autobiography*, Johnson is trying to incorporate the complex relationship between himself and his old friend D, a talented, confident, and intelligent black American who was in skin color, hair texture, and facial features indistinguishable from a white man (551). In the spring of 1909—if not earlier—D chose to sell his heritage: he married his Jewish fiancée and began to "pass." Johnson had difficulties with D's decision and, according to Skerrett, Johnson used *The Autobiography* to work out his ambivalent feelings (558).

Johnson's relationship with his narrator can also be explained in terms of his own political and social views, which show him in agreement with his narrator. Johnson was very much a part of the elite/middle-class Christian African American talented tenth, and he espoused many of its views. Eugene Levy has shown that, given "the consistency between Johnson's views as expressed in *The Autobiography* and those expressed elsewhere" (qtd. in O'Sullivan 60–61), he would hardly have been using his main character's opinions in *The Autobiography* to make him ironic. Moreover, in a letter to George Towns, Johnson himself suggests that he had tried to avoid a negative impression of his protagonist:

> The form of the story was for a long time a problem to me, but I finally decided that a direct, almost naive, narrative style would best suit the purpose of the book. It was my objective to put before the reader certain facts without having him feel that the narrator himself was prejudiced. I feel that I have fairly well succeeded. (qtd. in O'Sullivan 61).

In addition, Levy points out that Johnson, in his writings, repeatedly urged his fellow blacks "to take pride in their racial identity. . . . Since he considered himself above all a man of letters, Johnson frequently pointed out that the American Negro's artistic contributions to American culture, particularly in music, provide ample justification for pride in being Negro" (357). But Johnson also accepted the values and tastes of mainstream society. In the lyrics he wrote for vaudeville acts on Broadway in New York, Johnson became a commercial success "by refining and universalizing the lyrics" and by "altering the lusty coon song[s] and making [them] palatable to white, middle-class audiences" (364). In 1905, when he was asked to write an article on contemporary black music, "Johnson gave his highest praise to those colored composers and performers whose music was least identifiably Negro" (365). Johnson believed that the acceptance of black music and musicians by the white American public not only demonstrated the ability of the race but also encouraged race pride. Yet coupled with this belief:

> was his lack of contact with lower-class Negro culture and its music, as well as his firm commitment to accepted American values, musical and otherwise. . . . He wanted to maintain the racial identity of Negro music and at the same time "refine" and "elevate" it, thus bringing it into conformity with acceptable middle-class musical and moral standards. (366)

But more important, Johnson defined as one of his major responsibilities what Lynn Adelman calls "the cause of the Negro . . . or the Negro struggle" (137, 138). Although Johnson served in the foreign service from 1906 to 1913, "his ambition to be a leader and a spokesman had only been in abeyance" (138). In 1914, he moved to New York where he became head of the editorial staff of the *New York Age*, the oldest black newspaper in New York. His editorship of the *Age* propelled him to the forefront of African American leadership. Johnson realized that the myth of African American inferiority was often a coverup for complex emotional forces and that the first step toward equality was to disprove the notion of black inferiority. Thus, he "advocated a two-pronged approach of seeking to awaken the Negro and to enlighten the white" (138). In his daily column called "Views and Reviews," he "passionately defended the Negro and the Negro's ability. No important Negro activity missed his attention. He praised Negro artists and performers. . . . He also berated the Negro for not helping himself" (139). In 1916, he assumed the newly created position of field secretary for the NAACP, and from 1920 to 1930, he was the executive secretary of the NAACP. Commitment to the African American struggle and to uplifting the race was essential to Johnson's political and social agenda.

Therefore, when the ex-coloured man in *The Autobiography of an Ex-Coloured Man* defines spirituals and ragtime as "lower forms of art" and expresses his desire to elevate them to a classical musical form, there is no irony. Johnson himself is speaking. When the ex-coloured man holds up African American music to show the African American's contribution to America and, therefore, to prove the African American worthy of social equality, there is no ideological difference between Johnson and his narrator. When the ex-coloured man expresses a desire to gather up the Negro folk materials, which affirm the cultural value of his race, and to preserve and publish them, he is doing exactly what Johnson did in *The Book of American Negro Spirituals* and *God's Trombones*. When the ex-coloured man praises Shiny's graduation speech, is he not echoing what Johnson does as editor of *Age* when he "praised Negro artists and performers."

The ex-coloured man is a DuBoisian talented tenth African American. When he makes various observations on the race question, especially in terms of convincing middle-class whites to accept those African Americans who have become the Same as they, he is not an unreliable narrator. He is espousing Johnson's political views. Also, when the ex-coloured man and the doctor speak disparagingly of or "berate" subaltern African Americans because they will not work hard to become the Same as the middle-class norm, they do not differ in their views from Johnson. The ex-coloured man's attitudes on black pride, race, and class are consistent with Johnson's views on these issues. Finally, when the ex-coloured man strives for the American dream, Johnson does not criticize him. Johnson believed in the American dream and had a "firm commitment to accepted American values" (Levy 366). The pertinent question then becomes, does Johnson embrace his nameless narrator completely? Does he agree with everything his ex-coloured man does? Is there ever a moment when Johnson parts company with his narrator?

I want to argue that the narrator's crime, and the moment when Johnson seemingly either distances himself from the narrator or develops an ironic stance toward him, is not when the narrator chooses to pass, but when he rejects his heritage and the African American struggle for social equality. In the final paragraph of *The Autobiography*, the narrator writes:

> My love for my children makes me glad that I am what I am and keeps me from desiring to be otherwise; and yet, when I sometimes open a little box in which I still keep my fast yellowing manuscripts, the only tangible remnants of a vanished dream, a dead ambition, a sacrificed talent, I cannot repress the thought that, after all, I have chosen the lesser part, that I have sold my birthright for a mess of pottage. (211)

Johnson in *The Autobiography* does not criticize the ex-coloured man for achieving freedom and comfort through assimilating, through acquiring the values and the American dream of the dominant white society. He does not condemn him for doing well financially and living the secure and comfortable life he has so desired. If we examine the ambitions and class aspirations of the other elite/middle-class characters in the text, Johnson does not critique their material possession or their quest/aspiration for the American dream. The doctor, Shiny, and other elite/middle-class African Americans in *The Autobiography* embrace American values of nice clothes, big houses, and "refined" European manners and behavior, and Johnson does not criticize or abandon them.

Rather, Johnson criticizes the ex-coloured man for the way he achieves the dream, for abandoning the race's struggle for equality. He criticizes him because he is "unfitted for the practical struggles of life" (46) and because he refuses to "carry the entire weight of the race question." Johnson criticizes his narrator not because his love for his children has caused him to pass but because he is failing to make "history and a race" (211), because he is failing to take responsibility for bringing the entire race up to the "civilized" standards, because his dream has "vanished," because his "ambition" is "dead," because he has "sacrificed" his "talent," and because he is not taking part in a work so glorious, that his musical manuscripts, which are still in his little box, are lost as a black contribution to American culture.

The ex-coloured man, like Shiny, the young Jacksonville African American professional, and the doctor, is never able to resolve the paradox of wanting all African Americans to be assimilated into a white/black binary system in which assimilation is impossible because whites refuse to accept blacks as Same and equal. Although the ex-coloured man and the doctor talk about uplifting the race, they never engage the issue of class, which is an integral component of the white/black binary. They never discuss the capitalist economic system that structures subaltern African America. Discussing the refusal of elite/middle-class African American intellectuals to engage the issue of class, bell hooks explains:

> Class difference is an aspect of black identity that is often overlooked. It is not just white people who refuse to acknowledge different class status among blacks; many of us want to ignore class. . . . The connectedness of capitalism and the perpetuation of racist exploitation makes class a subject privileged blacks seek to avoid. . . . [Elite/middle-class blacks] emphasize racism as a system of domination without drawing attention to class. . . . It is in their class interests to emphasize the way racism inhibits their progress. ("black on" 166)

Although the ex-coloured man, Shiny, the doctor, and other elite/middle-class Christian African Americans advocate and struggle "for social equality between the races," they in actuality are motivated, argues bell hooks, by a desire "to gain access to middle-class incomes and lifestyles" (163).

The ex-coloured man, Shiny, the young Jacksonville African American professional, and the doctor seek equal treatment within the social framework that whites have already established and nothing else. They are happily willing to conform to this system if it will only give them social equality with whites. Thus, their racial uplift agenda focuses not on African American differences or on disrupting the white/black binary but on the limited goal of equality. But if the ex-coloured man, Shiny, the doctor, and other elite/middle-class blacks want not to just reform the system but to transform it, to change it fundamentally, thereby changing the position of the African American within the binary, they would have to advocate blowing up the white/black binary. And until that happens, the white/black binary will continue to exist, and blacks will continue to be defined as "Other," as "victim," or as "inferior."

Furthermore, in seeking equal treatment within the existing social framework and their willingness to conform to this system if it would only give them social equality with whites (males), the ex-coloured man, Shiny, the doctor, and other elite/middle-class black males are also seeking the patriarchy. The fact that the ex-coloured man masks his feelings and sacrifices for the well-being of his family, that he wants to be the head of his household, a provider, makes him, what bell hooks in *black looks* calls "the fulfillment of the patriarchal masculine ideal" (88). The fact that Shiny aspires to and takes on the values of the Western notion of manhood and the doctor is defined in white Western terms mean they want ready-made patriarchal identities.

To end the white/black binary (to put it bluntly), whites would have to put an end to themselves, or blacks would have to refuse to participate any longer in the binary. In *The Autobiography*, neither whites nor blacks move to disrupt the binary. Thus, we see how Johnson's *The Autobiography*, in its inability to move beyond the white/black binary, actually ends up reproducing it. It gives us elite/middle-class characters in the ex-coloured man, Shiny, the doctor, the young Jacksonville African American professional, characters who can define

freedom only by rejecting African American differences and by aspiring to become the Same as the white norm, which rejects them. They are caught in an
impasse. In this sense, they define themselves as victims. Because these characters (and the project of *The Autobiography*) do not offer different ways to seek and
achieve freedom, they can only protest their blocked attempts to become the
Same, attempts that ultimately affirm the middle-class white norm. Thus, in *The
Autobiography*, the white/black binary of signification remains in place.

The racial uplift ideology that informs *The Autobiography* entraps African
Americans in the values, conventions, and definitions of mainstream American
society. This ideology and the world it constructs also become a mirror for
mainstream society, whose tryanny it critiques. Lastly, the ideology is as exclusivist, as limited, provincial, and discriminatory in its suppressions and repressions as the dominant American discourse. The brunt of its repression is focused
on African American differences and subaltern African America, as well as other
individuals whose experiences and interests are not represented in the dominant
racial uplift identity constructions. Thus, in *The Autobiography*, we can discern
the kind of repressive construction of African American life that is taking place.
We can become aware of the kind of African American literary tradition that
privileges it. We can identify which "Negro mind" is being privileged. We can
detect which "life of the American Negro" is being documented. We can discern why until recently the center of African American existence was manifested in the mulatto. We can recognize the kind of reading of African
Americans that is being privileged. Finally, we can detect what is left out of, or
is repressed and subordinated in, *The Autobiography* and racial uplift ideology. We
see what readings are not privileged, what is not there, and what questions that
cannot be asked.

In accepting and embracing uncritically the values of the dominant, Eurocentric American society, the ex-coloured man, Shiny, the doctor, the young
Jacksonville African American professional, other elite/middle-class Christian
African Americans, and the whole project of *The Autobiography of an Ex-
Coloured Man* reject subaltern African America—which could include blues,
swing, and Voodoo African Americans—because it does not meet the high standards of excellence established by middle-class American society. For the
elite/middle-class Christian African American, African America has its own internal Other. Images of subaltern African America are all products of a process
of exclusion: the unkempt appearance, the shambling, slouching gait, and the
loud talk and laughter are aspects of African America that the elite/middle-class
Christian African American cannot tolerate.

The unkempt, shambling, loud-talking African American subaltern serves as,
to use the words of Peter Mason in *Deconstructing America*, "the internal negative
self-definition" of the elite/middle-class Christian African American (44). What is
made clear for such African Americans is that the Other, the African American
subaltern, is not the self. What they refuse to acknowledge is that the African
American "Others are egos too" (Todorov 11), that there is a reason of the Other.

Although the ex-coloured man understands that the ability to laugh heartily is part of the salvation of the African American, he cannot imagine that on "the street . . . which consisted chiefly of low bars, cheap dry-goods and notion stores, barber shops, and fish and bread restaurants," these black people have egos, too, that they possess a culture and belief system that are different but equal to Western European culture. He cannot believe that these subaltern African Americans' conventions of talking and laughing "without restraint" belong simply to a different cultural system (56). Therefore, he Otherizes them and covers them over as the Same.

Despite the fact that at some level they know that subaltern African America is the source of most of African American culture, art, and creativity, Johnson and other elite/middle-class Christian African Americans cannot believe that the subaltern is different but equal. Yet, they use subaltern African American contributions to American society to refute the myth of black inferiority. The ex-coloured man states:

> It is my opinion that the coloured people of this country have done four things which refute the oft-advanced theory that they are an absolutely inferior race, which demonstrate that they have originality and artistic conception, and, what is more, the power of creating that which can influence and appeal universally. The first two of these are the Uncle Remus stories, collected by Joel Chandler Harris, and the Jubilee songs. . . . The other two are ragtime music and the cake-walk. (87)

But these four major contributions that African Americans have made to Western civilization have their origin in subaltern African America. The ex-coloured man first saw the cakewalk not at one of the black professional class's events but at a public ball in Jacksonville. The cakewalk in its "original form" belonged to subaltern African Americans, after which professional, middle-class "coloured performers on the theatrical stage developed" it "into the prancing movements now known all over the world" (86–87).

Ragtime "originated in the questionable resorts about Memphis and St. Louis by Negro piano-players who knew no more of the theory of music than they did of the theory of the universe, but were guided by natural musical instinct and talent" (99). Yet the ex-coloured man, who defines these subaltern artifacts as "lower forms of art," will take credit for these subaltern artifacts. In this appropriation of subaltern African American artifacts, the reader sees how Johnson and other elite/middle-class Christian African Americans need subaltern African Americans in the construction of their text and in their desire to prove to the dominant white society that elite/middle-class blacks are worthy of acceptance, but they cannot acknowledge that need.

A tradition in African American literature—from Phyllis Wheatley to Frederick Douglass's narrator in *The Narrative* to W. E. B. DuBois's narrator in *The Souls of Black Folk* to James Weldon Johnson's ex-coloured man to Jean Toomer's narrator in *Cane* to Dr. William Miller in Charles Chesnutt's *The Marrow of Tradition*, who is hopeful for a time of racial understanding, to Booker T. Washington's narrator in *Up from Slavery*, to Ann Petry's Lutie Johnson in *The Street* to Richard Wright's narrator in *Black Boy* to Gwendolyn Brooks's Maud Martha in *Maud Martha* and to Lorraine Hansberry's Walter Lee Younger in *Raisin in the Sun*—presents texts about the journey from subaltern African America to the values and conventions of mainstream American society as a way of seeking freedom. All are caught up in this paradox and in the limitations of assimilation. They all reproduce mainstream American values and the representation of the African American as victim, as inferior, or as devalued Other.

But what happens when some elite/middle-class and other African Americans know or become aware that assimilation and colonization (the white/black binary) are contradictory? They revolt. "Revolt is the only way out of the colonial situation," argues Memmi, "and the colonized realizes it sooner or later. His condition is absolute and cries for an absolute solution; a break and not a compromise. He has been torn away from his past and cut off from his future, his traditions are dying and he loses the hope of acquiring a new culture" (128). At this point, the elite/middle-class African American abandons assimilation.

There are some literary traditions and a body of African American literary texts that present protagonists and heroines who realize that they have been "torn away from [their] past and cut off from [their] future" (Memmi 128). Therefore, they abandon assimilation, refuse the colonizer, and revolt. One thinks immediately of Jake in Claude McKay's *Home to Harlem*, Janie in Zora Neale Hurston's *Their Eyes Were Watching God*, Augie in Arna Bontemps's *God Sends Sunday*, Tucker Caliban in William Melvin Kelley's *A Different Drummer*, Ishmael Reed's *Mumbo Jumbo*, Hip in Nathan Heard's *Howard Street*, Charles Stevenson in Charles Wright's *The Messenger*, Manfred Banks in Clarence Major's *Dirty Bird Blues*, Daddy Poole in Don Belton's *Almost Midnight*, Avey Johnson in Paule Marshall's *Praisesong for the Widow*, and Milkman Dead in Toni Morrison's *Song of Solomon*. These are African American texts and literary traditions that simply present different representations of African American life.

In presenting African American differences and other sites for constructing African American literature and in representing non-normative African American and normative Western belief systems and theoretical conceptions of life and history, these other texts and traditions deconstruct and de-territorialize the white/black binary system, and then re-territorialize and reconstitute social, historical, and literary spaces in which African American differences are privileged, in which the polyvalent nature of African American literature and life is acknowledged.

Johnson in *The Autobiography*, along with other texts in the 1970s/1980s reinvented canon, never revolts. He, along with elite/middle-class African American critics, remains locked in the white/black binary in which his text continues to be pivotal to defining not only African American literary texts from the past but also those in the future. In remaining as the pivotal text, Johnson's

The Autobiography, and the closed system it belongs to, will continue to repre-sent/construct the African American not in terms of his differences but in terms of his Sameness to the mainstream American society.

The "survival" and "endurance" of *The Autobiography* and its achievement of high canonical status are "the product," to use the words of Barbara Herrn-stein Smith:

> neither of the objectivity . . . [and] conspiratorial force of establishment insti-tutions nor of the continuous appreciation of the timeless virtues of a fixed ob-ject by succeeding generations of isolated readers, but, rather, of a series of continuous interactions among a variably constituted object, emergent condi-tions, and mechanisms of cultural selection and transmission. (47)

The Autobiography performs "certain desired/able functions" quite well for elite/middle-class Christian African Americans, and does so by virtue of certain of its "properties" as they have been specifically constituted—framed, fore-grounded, and configured—by those same elite/middle-class, Christian African Americans under "certain conditions and in accord with particular needs, inter-ests, and resources" (47). *The Autobiography* has been constituted in this way be-cause the critics

> who do the constituting are themselves similar, not only or simply in being human creatures . . . but in occupying a particular universe that may be, for them, in many respects recurrent or relatively continuous and stable, and/or in inheriting from one another, through mechanisms of cultural transmission, certain ways of interacting with [the text]. (48)

Because *The Autobiography* performs certain desired/able functions at a given time both of elite/middle-class Christian African Americans and of main-stream Americans, it is not only "better protected from physical deterioration," but is "more frequently used or widely exhibited and . . . more frequently read or recited, copied or reprinted, translated, imitated, cited, commented upon, and . . . in short, culturally re-produced" (48). But in an increasingly polycen-tric reading of African American literature, *The Autobiography*, along with the racial uplift mission, is repositioned where it looses its centered position and be-comes one of many traditions in African American literature.

In subsequent chapters, I will explore and explicate African American male writers (and literary traditions) who go outside the narrative of racial uplift ide-ology, outside the psychological, social, sexual, and cultural norms and conven-tions that define the African American (male) as inferior, as victim, as devalued Other, or as the Same. They are *resisting* the white/black binary. These writers give us characters whose experiences, lives, and theoretical concepts of life and history are different from the ones sanctioned by the dominant American soci-ety, the African American sociopolitical agenda, and the canon of African American literature. I will write about these subordinated and repressed texts

without experiencing at the same time their status as cultural capital. This volume accents those characters, images, and theoretical conceptions of life that
cannot be defined by the categories of the white/black binary. The book shows
how these marginalized writers produce the model, the potential social space,
for the African American male to free himself from the white/black binary past,
which does not allow for any other axes of power relations.

CHAPTER FIVE

DISRUPTING THE WHITE/BLACK BINARY

WILLIAM MELVIN KELLEY'S
A DIFFERENT DRUMMER

William Melvin Kelley's *A Different Drummer* disrupts/challenges the white/ black binary of signification and Western rationalism. As a consequence, its revolutionary zeal—its disruption of the white/black binary and its reconfiguration of the African American—puts it outside the aesthetic expectations, the political and literary ideologies, and the conventions of mainstream American critics and of the 1970s/1980s reinventors of the African American literary canon— many of whom define African American literature within the mainstream American institutionalized literary norm. They also define African American life within the white/black binary. *A Different Drummer* was excluded from discussion in the canon-forming critical texts of George Kent's *blackness and the adventure of western culture*, Houston Baker Jr.'s *Singers of Daybreak* and *Long Black Song*, Robert Stepto's *From Behind the Veil*, Henry Louis Gates Jr.'s *Figures in Black* and *The Signifying Monkey,* and Valerie Smith's *Self-Discovery and Authority in Afro-American Narrative*.

Most critics and reviewers either reject *A Different Drummer* outright, or they define it within the conventions of the American/African American tradition. Frank H. Lyell, a close observer of Deep South mores and a member of the English faculty at the University of Texas at the time Kelley wrote, panned *A Different Drummer* in the influential *New York Times Book Review*. Lyell deemed Kelley's novel to be history, sociology, and/or political science, but not art. He represents *A Different Drummer* as a "highly impossible fantasy on racial tensions in the Deep South," and asking for historical accuracy, he thinks Tucker:

is too obvious, not to say dubious, a symbol of the Southern Negro's lot; and the main events following the destruction of his farm are too oversimplified to be convincing. . . . The author merely announces that similar migrations are taking place everywhere else in the state. Strangest and most glaring omission of all, his vision includes nothing whatsoever about their result. (25)

Requiring *A Different Drummer* to meet his political resolution to the race problem, Lyell states: "His [Kelley's] novel, which recommends an unreasonable and impossible uprooting of the Negro's past, could only increase, rather than diminish, racial misunderstanding if it were taken seriously" (26).

A Different Drummer has since appeared in some of the subsequent surveys of African American literature. But in most of these surveys, it is defined within existing American and African American traditions and conventions. Addison Gayle in *The Way of the New World* thinks that "Kelley is both a mythologist and historian, and the search for the historical importance of the black migration has taken him back to the latter half of the nineteenth century, to the exploits of old Pap Singleton, the slave's Moses, leading men, women, and children from south to west" (302). Gayle criticizes *A Different Drummer,* unnecessarily I think, for having flaws:

The major flaw . . . lay in Kelley's unwillingness to experiment with the form of the novel, to fashion a distinct vehicle. He has gone to Faulkner's *As I Lay Dying* for a model, and, as a result, *A Different Drummer* borders on structural chaos. Kelley's characters, like those of Faulkner, comment upon the action of the novel and each other through a series of autobiographical portraits. Kelley attempts innovations, however, within this format. Some chapters are straight narrative; in others, stream of consciousness is used to delineate character; in addition, the experiences of David Willson are told through use of a diary format. In attempting to merge these disparate elements into a complete unit, the novel is rendered fragmentary. (304–05)

Other American and African American critics in surveys also define Kelley's *A Different Drummer* within institutionalized traditions and conventions. Bernard Bell in *The Afro-American Novel and Its Tradition* argues that Kelley has become "one of the most talented and innovative postmodern fabulators" (25). In Kelley's four novels, including *A Different Drummer*, Bell states that

we see his inventive genius at work exploring the Afro-American oral tradition and the complexity of interracial and intraracial color, sexual, and class relationships. From *A Different Drummer* to *Dunfords Travels Everywheres* Kelley interweaves the histories of the Dunford and Bedlow families and their heritage as Afro-Americans from Africa and the South. (296)

To define Kelley's novel solely within the institutionalized conventions and traditions is to ignore its innovation and originality.

But unlike Lyell, other mainstream critics and reviewers recognized *A Different Drummer* as art. More important, they noted its originality and innovation as a new kind of African American text. The reviewer for the *Library Journal* writes: "This provocative first novel deals with the crisis in a Southern state when all of the Negroes suddenly depart. . . . [T]his is a good novel with much to say in a style generally excellent" ("Reviews" 2157). The reviewer for *Kirkus* echoes this assessment of Kelley's novel: "Not a flawless novel, his is nevertheless a stunning work and one which explores all kinds of Negroes, from Oxford derived to Uncle Tom survived. It is an Odyssey of the Negro gone full circle, back again to the stature of the African" ("Fiction" 340). Jean Carey Bond of *Freedomway* represents *A Different Drummer* as "an imposing first novel of quiet power and originality. . . . Rich in social comment and artistic facility, this is a laudable first effort" (503, 504). Reviewing *A Different Drummer* in *Phylon*, James W. Byrd writes: "This volume is a bargain; its covers contain a superb short story and an intriguing novel" (99). Finally, W. G. Rogers in the *New York Herald Tribune Book Review* refers to *A Different Drummer* as:

> this remarkable first novel. For all Mr. Kelley is a novice novelist, he has hit on an unbeatable idea and couldn't have worked it out more smartly. But this is infinitely more than smart. It's as timely as today's page one. It is radical, idealistic, and wonderfully fresh—people, action, thought, love, brutality and hate, all in the right proportions. (4)

Although these mainstream reviewers and critics recognize the freshness, innovation, originality, and radicalism of *A Different Drummer*, their reviews are too short to expound and explore the various ways Kelley's text breaks with existing American and African American conventions and stereotypes. They do not have sufficient space to discuss how Kelley's text rewrites and refigures Shakespeare's Caliban, how there have been historically many African American characters who, like Caliban, had the instinct to rebel, but only Kelley found a way to envision a new kind of African American, a different future outside Western/American colonialism and the white/black binary. In this chapter, I will read Kelley's *A Different Drummer* in terms of its innovation, originality, postcoloniality, and radicalism. I want to discuss how it disrupts the white/black binary.

When William Melvin Kelley's *A Different Dummer* was published in 1962, the United States was in the early stages of a social, economic, and cultural transformation/revolution. One of the agents of this revolution, the fermenting Civil Rights movement, presented the opportunity for African Americans and other disenchanted and repressed groups—people of color, women, and sexual liberators—to challenge and disturb the various binaries that legitimated a Eurocentric regime of power and truth, one that defines Europeans/whites (males) as superior and normative, and one that represents African Americans/blacks, women, and other people of color as inferior, as victim, as Same, or as devalued Other. Kelley's *A Different Drummer* coincides with and is informed by this fermenting movement.

But Kelley's *A Different Drummer* also disrupts and reconstitutes historically and generally the European colonial regime that began with the birth of capital and modernity and with Europe thinking itself the center of the world while Latin America, Africa, and Asia existed as the periphery. More specifically, *A Different Drummer* begins with colonial America, which was a part of classical European colonialism and the transportation of Africans into American slavery. In this European colonial regime, the world was envisioned from a single, privileged point, mapped in a cartography that centralized and augmented Europe while literally belittling, demonizing, and Otherizing Africa, Asia, and Latin America. This Eurocentric construction of the world bifurcated the world into "the West and the Rest." It constituted other cultures, worlds, and persons as objects. Africans were denied as Others and were obliged, subsumed, alienated, and incorporated into the dominating totality like a thing. Within the framework of European colonialism, African societies that had their own cultures, histories, and complex religious and belief systems were represented as the Other than reason, as barbarians, savages, and cannibals who were to be "civilized" by the Europeans.

Thus, the arrival of the enslaved African in the United States, where he had already been constructed/represented in this European colonial regime as Other, is where Kelley begins *A Different Drummer*. But Kelley moves to rewrite, reconstitute, and refigure the positionality, or the fixity, of the African and the African American within the regime of European colonialism and the unequal white/black binary of signification. As an intervention with, or a reinscription and disruption of, the European colonial regime, Kelley's *A Different Drummer* uses Henry David Thoreau's concept of radical individualism, transforms Caliban (whose name forms an anagram of cannibal) in Shakespeare's *The Tempest*, and shows the limitations of the white/black binary of signification in order to offer a social space for both whites and blacks outside this binary, which is at the foundation of the construction of social reality in the West.

In Shakespeare's *The Tempest*, Caliban tells Prospero, "You taught me language, and my profit on't/Is, I know how to curse. The red plague rid you/For learning me your language" (1.2. 356–67). Caliban accepts uncritically the master's value system as superior. His plot to murder Prospero to gain power and superiority relative to his existing position as devalued Other mimics the slave master's need to define the self relative to what the binary constructs as an evil Other. Caliban simply exchanges masters (Prospero for Antonio) and realizes in the end that he is still a slave, stating, "I'll be wise hereafter,/And seek for grace. What a thrice-double ass/Was I to take this drunkard for a god/And worship this dull fool!" (5.1. 295–98). Caliban remains confined to an asymmetrical allegory in which one character is historically fleshed out, whereas the other is a countercultural token of innate black wisdom and sensuality. But Kelley in *A Different Drummer* reconstitutes and refigures Caliban, turning him into a postcolonial figure. Tucker Caliban sheds his current servitude—which had been the condition of his great-grandfather and grandfather who operated within the white/black, colonizer/colonized regime—and in the process of discovering his essential, precolonial self or heritage, he signifies the African and disrupts/destroys the Prospero-like reign over the Caliban family.

Just as in the European colonial regime and the white/black binary of signification in the United States, where Africans and African Americans are represented as Other, Kelley in *A Different Drummer* textualizes this Otherization by having the history of the Other, the colonized, told by the colonizer. The various white narrators or colonizers in *A Different Drummer* tell their narratives in their own voice or serve as focal figures from whose point of view the chapters radiate. How they relate their stories depends "greatly upon the degree to which his/her life is/was linked to Tucker's" (Beards 25). "Tucker," argues Charles E. Davis, "is always viewed from the outside, from the perspective of individuals whose cultural heritage [and language] makes it difficult, sometimes impossible, to understand the implications of either Tucker's acts or the exodus they precipitate" (5). The reader can know Tucker only as he relates to, or figures into, these narrators' subjective experiences. Yet, Kelley is able to subvert their narratives to show their exclusions and limitations, and to signify the Other that the African and the Calibans represent. And with information from the various narrators/narratives, the reader is able to put together a strategic, or provisional, representation of Tucker Caliban as a defiant and *resisting* Other.

To begin my discussion of Kelley's textualization of the Otherization of the African and the Calibans in *A Different Drummer*, I want to summarize Tucker Caliban's action in *A Different Drummer*. The setting of the text is a mythical state, "an East South Central state in the Deep South, bounded on the north by Tennessee, east by Alabama, west by Mississippi" (3). On a Thursday in June 1957, Tucker Caliban—descendant of the African who had been captured and eventually murdered by General Dewey Willson—with Sutton looking on spreads salt on his land, kills his cow and horse, splinters a tree, destroys the grandfather clock that had been brought over with the African, burns down his house, takes his pregnant wife and child, and leaves town, thus provoking the exodus of all blacks throughout the state. Tucker Caliban never explains his actions. Why Tucker commits such actions and the reason for the exodus of blacks from Sutton become a source of speculation/interpretation for the various white narrators as they attempt to provide cause and motive.

Though *A Different Drummer* ostensibly concerns the exodus of all blacks, the only black characters to receive any development are those associated with the Willsons. Defining the world of *A Different Drummer* in colonial American terms, middle-class whites—including the Willsons—are the colonizers, and middle-class blacks such as the Calibans are the "indigenous elite." (The text basically ignores subaltern African America.) Both exist in the binary, but the indigenous elite African Americans seek freedom by rejecting their African and African American differences and by embracing the values of the Willsons, the colonizers. As blacks and whites in the South are symbiotic halves of a binary, so, too, are the Calibans and the Willsons. This is recognized several times. In discussing her outsider status in Sutton, Camille Willson, who is married to David Willson, remarks that "even the Calibans were Willsons because they had been with the family so long" (146). Dewey Willson notices at the funeral of John Caliban that "the Calibans weren't very popular among their own people, that their devotion to us and our love for them had separated them from other Negroes, so that there weren't a great many people who would want to call them friend" (122).

Also, we learn that the Calibans have established a pattern of not only being owned by the Willsons but culturally and socially imitating the Willsons. The Caliban men serve as chauffeurs to the Willsons and internalize many of the Willsons' values and conventions, which extends to wearing the Willsons' hand-me-down clothes. Dewey Willson narrates:

> The first picture of John [Caliban] is when he is a boy, about fourteen, in front of a brand-new buggy. He is wearing a white starched shirt, which bulges rigidly because his chest is thrust way out. If you don't know better, you'd think he owns the buggy, but he doesn't. It belongs to the General. (118)

The language of the white/black, colonizer/colonized binaries that privilege whites and denigrate blacks is evident from the beginning. The European contact with the African is continually mediated by representations. Indeed, contact itself, argues Stephen Greenblatt, "is very often contact between representatives bearing representations" (119). There are forces of domination, constriction, and repression at work in representational practices. In the first chapter of *A Different Drummer*, after all the blacks have left Sutton, some of the white male population meet on the porch of the Thomason Grocery Company, trying "for the thousandth time in three days to discover how it ever began in the first place" (6). The narrator, Mister Harper, retells the tale of DeWitt Willson and the African. He tells us of Tucker Caliban's genealogy, which is linked to that of the Willsons. He tells of how the general's father bought Tucker's great-great-grandfather fresh from a slave boat in New Marsails. He offers a long account of the African's superhuman strength, and his escape, pursuit, and violent death. But Mister Harper can only use his Western Christian language to define the African.

Kelley goes to great lengths to show the limitations of Mister Harper's language/narrative. Even before Mister Harper begins to retell his story of the African's "blood," there is an authorial comment, making relative any attempt to unravel the enigma of the exodus: "They [the men] could not know it all, but what they did know might give them some part of an answer" (6–7). Furthermore, Mister Harper's narrative is considered suspect. He begins his narrative with a disclaimer: "Like I said, nobody's claiming this story is all truth" (9). And when Mister Harper recounts the dialogue between the slave ship's captain and the auctioneer, he explains, "You understand, they spoke different in them days, so I can't be certain exactly what they said, but I reckon it was something like: 'How do. How was the trip?'" (10).

European culture/American language has an image of the African American. When the European/American sees the black man, argues Franz Fanon in *Black Skin, White Masks*, he sees "biology, penis, strong, athletic, potent, boxer, savage, animal, devil, sin" (166). Operating out of the Eurocentric colonial regime of power and truth, Mister Harper certainly reproduces the prevailing European image of the African American. He constructs the African as devalued Other, as savage with enormous strength, by representing the African in animal terms: "out of the bottom of the ship, way off in some dark place, came this roar, louder'n a cornered bear or maybe two bears mating. It was so loud the sides of the boat bulged out" (13). He also represents the African as having enormous physical strength: "God damn—if he ain't pulled his chain outen the wall of the boat" (13). The African emerges from the boat, his shoulders:

> so broad he had to climb those stairs sideways; then his body began, and long after it should-a stopped it was still coming. Then he was full out, skin-naked except for a rag around his parts, standing at least two heads taller than any man on the deck. He was black and glistened like the captain's grease-spot wound. His head was as large as one of them kettles you see in a cannibal movie and looked as heavy. (13–14)

The African is objectified into Otherness, his size symbolizing a threat to the se-cure identity of the white male ego. Yet the African, as the phobic object, is also contained by the chains. Thus, Mister Harper is made safe in his identification. In reiterating the terms of colonial fantasy, Mister Harper's descriptions of the African serve the expectations of European desire, but they say nothing directly about the African's wants and desires.

In addition, Mister Harper and DeWitt Willson are struck by the African's difference. His unclothed state, his language, his customs—"He was African and likely spoke the gibberish them Africans use" (16), "DeWitt tripped over the pile of stones the African'd been talking to" (24), and "He had a cloth over his head and set up in front of him was a pile of stones, which he seemed to be a mumbling at" (21)—place the African beyond the pale of European civiliza-tion. The African differences within the West's secularized, evolutionary frame-work of time used by Mister Harper make him "back in time," before civilization. The African's "unknown quantities," his "language and custom," make him appear so foreign to Mister Harper and DeWitt Willson that they can believe that he does not "belong to the same species as [their] own" (Todorov 3). In starting from differences, which "immediately translate into terms of superiority and inferiority" (Todorov 42), Mister Harper and DeWitt Willson can deny the African's humanity.

Mister Harper, in telling the story of the African, also uses Christian mythology to construct the African. To Mister Harper, the African is a black Christ. He has a band of followers that numbers twelve or so and he is betrayed by his own black Judas, the auctioneer's Negro who offers to lead DeWitt to the

African. As Charles Adams points out, "through the successive retelling over several generations, the story has acquired the status of myth" (27). But now it is a myth that complements and reinforces culturally and ideologically the white community of Sutton.

Around the African's cultural practices, an absolute blockage occurs for Mister Harper. These cultural practices by the African—ones that are not part of the European repertoire—allow Mister Harper and other Europeans to justify the enslavement of the African. They allow them to reduce the African to property that is to be bought and sold. In representing the African as Other, and therefore different and less, Mister Harper denies "the existence of a human substance truly other, something capable of being not merely an imperfect state of oneself" (Todorov 43). He denies the complex history, culture, system of belief, and rituals that the African's language and the pile of stones represent.

DeWitt Willson, as told by Mister Harper, is responsible for the attempted conquest, domestication, and colonization of the African and the subsequent conquest and colonization of the Calibans. When DeWitt first sees the African, he wants to own him: "some folks . . . heard him saying slowly to himself over and over again: 'I'll own him. He'll work for me. I'll break him. I have to break him' " (14). He sees the African as "the most magnificent piece of property any man'd ever want to own" (15). Once during his monthlong search for and unsuccessful attempt to capture the African, DeWitt wakes from a nightmare, exclaiming, "I'm worth a thousand too! I am!" (19). DeWitt's self-worth is tied up in conquering and domesticating the African.

The African threatens Dewitt Willson's racial and sexual identity, as indicated by several images. Described as resembling a Christmas tree and as a maypole—both symbols of masculine sexuality—the African proceeds to decapitate the auctioneer in a classic image of castration. After escaping to the woods and successfully evading captivity, the African, "dressed in African clothes of bright colors" and armed "with a spear and a shield," attacks DeWitt's home, "bearing down on the house like he was a train and it was a tunnel and he was going right through" (19). Afterward, he crosses "the back lawn to the slave quarters, where he free[s] every last one of DeWitt's Negroes and le[ads] them off into the dark of the woods before DeWitt could even set down his glass and get up out of his chair" (19). The African is affirming his own individuality and identity as the leader of a people and is flatly refusing to accept the inferior role and status of a victim, or a devalued Other, in the plantation system (Nadeau 14). Therefore, to maintain his identity as a white man, as a colonizer, and to challenge his "feeling of impotence or sexual inferiority," DeWitt has to conquer and to break the African.

When DeWitt Willson and the African finally meet up with one another, it is initially less a meeting of the master and the servant, or the colonizer and the colonized, than a meeting of equals, a meeting of two subjects who are equal but different:

They stared at each other, not like they was (sic) trying to stare each other down, more like they was (sic) discussing something without using words. And finally it seemed like they came to an agreement because the African bowed slightly like a fighter bows at the beginning of a match, and DeWitt Willson raised his rifle, . . . and shot him. (23–24)

As a product of the Eurocentric regime of power and truth that cannot accept the Other as different but equal, but only as different and less, DeWitt kills the African when he refuses to be colonized. "It is ideologically inconceivable," argues Wlad Godzich in the foreword to Michel de Certeau's *Heterologies*, "that there should exist an otherness of the same ontological status as the same, without there being immediately mounted an effort at its appropriation" or demise (xii). The African refuses to accept the terms of DeWitt Willson. He would rather accept death than the inhuman bondage of slavery or the position of Other.

However, in capturing the African's baby, DeWitt begins the process of colonizing the African's successive generations. The African's baby is named Caliban, "after the General read Shakespeare's *The Tempest*" (25). Caliban becomes a Christian because conversion to Christianity was one of the ways the colonizers covered over the Other and represented him as the Same. He is named First after he has a family and "there were more than just one Caliban" (25). He has a son named John Caliban and a grandson named Tucker Caliban. "For Christian imperialism," argues Greenblatt, "there can be only one order of truth, an order whose universality paradoxically enables the strategy of exclusion I have called blockage: the belief that 'all men are brothers'. . . is quickly transformed into the belief that 'only my brothers are men' " (139). To be considered human and brothers, the Calibans must become the Same as the Willsons.

In subsequent narratives, the white narrators, such as Mister Harper, and particularly the Willsons, continue to accept the white/black binary, representing the Calibans as the Same but different and therefore less. Dymphna Willson covers over Bethrah as the Same by noticing the "light gray summer suit with a plain white blouse and the cutest pair of black shoes" that Bethrah is wearing when she comes to interview for the maid job (95). Dymphna also pays attention to the fact that Bethrah did not "look like a maid" and that "she hardly looked like she was colored, except maybe her nose" (95). Bethrah also speaks the same language as Dymphna. They can talk about courtship and men, and Bethrah, who has had two years of college, is intelligent enough to discuss current issues and ideas with Dewey. But Dymphna also sees Bethrah as different and less. One advantage of having Bethrah for a friend is that "she was colored and there wouldn't be any competition between us as far as boys were concerned" (97). Also, very much aware of the white/black binary and hers and Bethrah's positions in it, Dymphna feels it "strange asking her [Bethrah's] opinion when she was colored" (100), assuming that to be colored is to be less than to be white.

Dewey Willson III also defines the Calibans as the Same but different and, therefore, less. He thinks that Tucker is a very good friend. Dewey cries when

John Caliban dies, and he attends the funeral as family. When he goes away to college up North, Dewey asks Tucker to write to him, and he does. When he returns home after his first year of college, he is disappointed "at not seeing Tucker and Bethrah anywhere on the platform" (85). Yet, as a product of the white/black binary, he also defines the Calibans as different and less. When John dies and Dewey goes with Tucker and Missus Caliban to retrieve the body, he feels "strange riding with so many Negroes, even though they were [his] friends" (120). Also, in Missus Caliban's presence he almost refers to dead John Caliban as a nigger but catches himself: "this old nig—" (120). The whole idea of the Calibans being both a part and not a part of Dewey, on the one hand, provokes "an uneasy perception of the [Calibans'] otherness," and, on the other hand, "becomes a blocking agent that continually prevents" Dewey from defining the Calibans as brothers (Greenblatt 25).

Finally, David Willson also accepts the white/black binary of signification. When young David leaves the South to attend college in Cambridge, he notices that "when a negro sits next to [him]," he finds himself "distracted from what [he] was reading, or from looking out of the window because [he is] not used to being that close to a negro in public" (55). Later, he joins with Bennett Bradshaw, an African American, to "get away from the old patterns" and "discover . . . some ideas, some principles that, in four years, [he] can bring back here to help the South up off its behind and into the twentieth century" (155). But even as he and Bradshaw talk about "politics, theories of government, communism versus capitalism, the race problem," and "even with his liberal feelings," David personally remains a white "clubbie" (159). He socializes *only* with whites and he dates southern white women exclusively.

Even when he returns to the South, David continues to accept and live within the white/black binary of signification. Initially, he supports rights for blacks by writing pamphlets such as "The Corrosive Effects of Racial Segregation on Southern Society," which is published in "some communist magazines in New York" (173). But when the crucial test of involvement and commitment arrives—either to take up roots and risk a new life with Bradshaw in Harlem, or to remain secure as a patrician who collects rents from his black tenants in the South—he fails it, falling back on his inherited status as a prominent landowner and practicing a three-century-old tradition of human exploitation (Ingrasci 5).

In addition to defining Tucker and the Calibans as different and, therefore, less, none of the white narrators is able to fully explain Tucker's actions and the subsequent exodus of blacks from Sutton. Watching Tucker destroy his land, the white men look at the other blacks for a motive: "The white men had watched them carefully, looking for something that might help them to understand what they were seeing" (41). Mister Harper attributes Tucker's action to "pure genetics" or the "blood" of the African; according to Mister Harper, Tucker has "something special in his blood just a-laying there sleeping, waiting, and then one day waking up, making Tucker do what he did. Can't be no other reason" (8). But Bobby-Joe does not accept Mister Harper's blood explanation. With Mister

Harper absent from the porch the following evening and with blacks still leaving Sutton in large numbers, Bobby-Joe offers his own explanation for the events:

> Well, all right, so I didn't know yesterday, but you-all heard me when I said I didn't believe that blood business Mister Harper was trying to feed us. I didn't believe that crap, and that's what it was too: crap! How the hell can something what happened a hundred fifty years ago—if it happened at all—how can that have something to do with what happened this week? That ain't nothing but tripe. No sir, it was that northern nigger, that agi . . . agi . . . what they call fellows what come in and stir up trouble. . . . That's right . . . them agi-TAT-ors. He came down here, him in that big black car, and got all the niggers to move off, go somewhere else instead of staying here where they belongs. (192)

Although Mister Stewart describes Tucker as having "gone insane" and "running wild," to Harry Leland, Tucker seems "quiet and thoughtful as if he was doing nothing out of the ordinary" (40). Harry Leland, who watches with the rest as Tucker destroys his farm, cannot explain why Tucker is committing these actions, but he does know that "*craziness ain't driving him. I don't know what IS pushing at him, but it ain't craziness*" (44). Explaining the exodus of the blacks to Mister Leland, Harry states:

> I reckon they [the blacks] all heading for some place where they think they can get on better. . . . I reckon they making what we call in the Army a STRATEGIC WITHDRAWAL. That's when you got thirty men and the other side got thirty thousand and you turn and run saying to yourself, "Shucks, ain't no use in being brave and getting ourselves killed. We'll back up a ways and maybe fight some tomorrow": I reckon them Negroes is backing up all the way. (60)

Harry Leland as interpreter, argues Gladys M. Williams, seems non-interpretative, reluctant to ascribe motives or to entertain psychoanalytic notions (227). And although Tucker tells Mister Leland that he is going, leaving Sutton, because he "lost something," Mister Leland does not understand.

To Dymphna, who "realize[s] [she] knew so much about him," the whole affair is "really mysterious as the **Dickens**" (91). Even though Dymphna can only conclude that "maybe something happened yesterday, but I can't imagine what" (115), her recollections do provide some insight into Tucker's motivations. In a conversation with Dymphna, Bethrah tries to explain why she and Tucker must leave the Willsons: "Maybe those of us who go to school, Dewey, myself, not so much your mother, I guess your father, maybe we lost something Tucker has. It may be we lost faith in ourselves. . . . But Tucker, he just knows what he has to do. He doesn't think about it; he just knows" (114). But Dymphna does not hear or understand Bethrah's explanation. After Bethrah finishes, Dymphna confesses, "[T]hat's all I know about everything: I guess it isn't much" (114).

In Camille's narrative, Tucker's role as a spiritual adviser and teacher is expanded as he becomes the savior of her disintegrating marriage. But she also has no clue as to why Tucker commits the actions he does. Reviewing her courtship and her early happy years of married life to David, as well as the unhappy years spent at Sutton, Camille recalls a scene between her and the nine-year-old Tucker. One night she tells Dewey and Tucker a bedtime story about a princess and a prince that reflects her own marital desperation. Asked by Camille to supply an ending to the story, Tucker thinks the princess should wait. She shouldn't run away. Years later, when Tucker learns that Camille is about to start divorce proceedings against David, he repeats his advice almost verbatim: "I think the princess should wait, Missus Willson. Leastways, now when her waiting is almost over" (150). But even though Camille is aware that Tucker's counsel did indeed save her marriage and even though she realizes that his departure positively affected David's attitude toward her, she is unable to discover the reason for this change. As she acknowledges: "Nothing happened until yesterday. And then I'm not sure anything happened" (150). Finally, Camille Willson "can't really believe he [Tucker] set it [the fire] himself" (92).

Dewey Willson tries "to find some cause, some reason for Tucker doing what he did, like something that had happened to him in the past, that he could brood about, that would get him mad, and the only thing [Dewey] could think about was last summer, when John died" (118). After John Caliban's funeral, when he visits Tucker in the garage, Dewey does not understand what Tucker means when he says, "Not another time. This is the end of it" (124). After Dewey recounts the life of the Calibans and Tucker's behavior at the funeral as well as his subsequent actions, he still does not understand Tucker. He still cannot make a connection between John Caliban's death and what Tucker says to him in the garage. Therefore, Dewey reasons that "this doesn't seem like enough. There's more to a man than the day, and the way he died; there's his whole life, no matter how dull or unimportant, before that" (118). Even after Dewey acknowledges that "an old man dies, whom [he] loved a great deal, and the last thing that he [the old man] sees is the COLORED sign on a segregated bus," and concludes that "this is a little more than ironic," he still decides that there has to be "something else," some other "reason for Tucker to have done all this" (124). Later Bradshaw has to explain to him the significance of Tucker's action.

Finally, the local newspaper's account of Tucker's action is incomplete because "Caliban was not available for comment" (153). The reporter only has the reports of "witnesses," and even they assert that Tucker "walked away without explanation" (153).

But unlike Tucker, Dewey Willson, his sister, Camille, his mother, and his grandfather, along with Mister Harper, think that there is nothing wrong with the world, that it is natural for the African American to be in a servant position, and that the systematic economic/social forces, or the colonialism, that have brought about this world do not exist or are irrelevant. Dewey feels that if he "loved [John Caliban] a great deal" and if he considered himself a friend of Tucker, everything would be fine. Although he, along with Mister Harper, Dymphna, and Camille, would argue that racism is wrong, he would never think that the Calibans wanted anything more in life than to be the Willsons' servants.

But, more important, Dewey, along with Dymphna, Camille, John Caliban, Missus Caliban, and Mister Harper, can never understand that the regime of power and knowledge that sustains order in Sutton, and that privileges whites and demeans blacks, had to be deconstructed/disrupted before Tucker and the Calibans could be seen as human, equal, and different. In not seeing Tucker as human, different, and equal, as Todorov's "human substance truly other, something capable of being not merely an imperfect state of" (43) himself, Dewey and the others cannot acknowledge Tucker as *resisting* the regime of power and knowledge that they have naturalized.

Perhaps it is David Willson and Bennett Bradshaw who come closest to understanding the motives for Tucker's action. Unlike the retrospective reflections of Dewey, Dymphna, and Camille, David's chapter is presented in the form of diary entries that begin when he is a young man attending Harvard. The various entries detail his close relationship with Bennett Bradshaw, his commitment to socialist causes, and his being blacklisted as a journalist, as well as his moving back to Sutton where he collects rents for his father. Chronologically, the entries begin on September 22, 1931, and, for the time being, end on September 22, 1938, the day David starts working for his father. For the next sixteen years, his diary reveals nothing about his life. It is not until October 20, 1954, that he resumes his entries with a newspaper clipping that reports the activities of Bradshaw, who is now a militant church leader. David's next two entries include a record of the death of John Caliban and of the sale of the seven acres of land to Tucker. In the last entry, which opens his section, David realizes that something special has indeed happened. After reading about Tucker in the newspaper, David writes:

> He has freed himself; this has been very important to him. But somehow, he has freed me too. He is only one man, and this, of course, does not make a reality [of] all the things I had dreamed of doing twenty years ago . . . his act of renunciation was the first blow against my twenty misspent years, twenty years I have wasted feeling sorry for myself. Who would have thought such a humble, primitive act could teach something to a so-called educated man like myself? (153)

He is "quite certain he [Tucker] did" set fire to his house (92). In selling Tucker the land, David realizes, he "was doing something [he] had always wanted to do, and also because it was almost like those things [he] wanted to see done twenty years ago" (183). What David understands about Tucker is that "he had realized something was wrong with his life and was trying to set it straight. What each of us wanted so much individually we helped each other to do" (183).

But, more important, David *does* understand that the regime of power and knowledge that has reduced the Calibans/African Americans to the status of victim and devalued Other for three centuries has come to an end with Tucker. After he sells Tucker the land, he goes into his drawer, retrieves the "white stone" given to him by his father, and gives it to Tucker. "It belongs to the Calibans," David's father had said to him, "but they're not ready to have it yet. You give it to them when you think they should have it" (184). In receiving the "white stone," Tucker's eyes cloud. This is the closest David "had ever seen [Tucker] come to tears or, in fact, to any other emotion" (184). The "white stone" represents African history and culture and an African belief system that had been suppressed by DeWitt Willson's colonization and later the Christianization of the Calibans. Although David understands Tucker's individual stand and acknowledges Tucker as human, different, and equal, there is no evidence in the text to lead one to believe that he can envision a new world, that he knows how to live a history and/or a culture outside the West and the white/black binary.

Although Bennett Bradshaw recognizes the significance of Tucker's action at the farm, he would have never thought of doing what Tucker does because he has spent his life operating within the conventions, intellectual paradigms, and theories of Western civilization: "I'd never have imagined such a movement could be started from within, could be started at the grass roots, through spontaneous combustion" (127). Educated with David Willson in Cambridge, Bradshaw wants to change the American system, but he wants to do it within the Western humanistic tradition. He and David meet at a socialist meeting where they share "common aspirations for social betterment, . . . hatred of ignorance, poverty, disease, and misery" (167). Their weapon for bringing about change is socialism and communism. And when the National Society for Colored Affairs gives "him the gate, [and] finding all other gates closed to him," Bradshaw decides "to sneak in by the back door of race relations: religion" (178). Therefore, he organizes the Black Jesuits, who believe in black supremacy and antisemitism, and who have a "doctrine which is a mixture of Mein Kampf, Das Kapital, and the Bible" (179). But in interpreting Tucker's actions at the farm and the subsequent black exodus, Bradshaw realizes that Tucker, "an ignorant southern Negro" (128), is successful at something he has spent his life trying to do: bringing about a revolution in America: "Your Tuckers will get up and say: I can do anything I want; I don't need to wait for someone to GIVE me freedom; I can take it myself. . . . I don't need anyone. I can do whatever I want for myself by myself" (134). Bradshaw also realizes that he needs the Tuckers "to justify his existence" and that the "day is fast coming . . . when people will realize there isn't any need for [him] and people like [him]" (134). Both David and Bradshaw are defined completely by the conventions and values of Western civilization.

To disrupt the white/black binary of signification that has organized life in the southern United States, Kelley creates two characters who violate the binary's process of normalization and so challenge its principle of unity. The characters who exist outside the binary are Tucker Caliban and Mister Leland: their attitudes and visions lie in the space outside. It is a space in which Kelley envisions salvation for both races. The two represent radical differences and, according to Greenblatt, the articulation of "radical differences . . . make[s] renaming, transformation, and appropriation possible" (135). Both Tucker and Mister Leland are the ideal future of the South: Mister Leland for his ability to empathize with the Other and Tucker for his rejection of the role of victim and the position of devalued Other that the binary has forced on him. The two recognize this in each other. Mister Leland does not accept the reasons the whites suggest for what Tucker has done, and it is to Mister Leland that Tucker offers his only explanation: "You young. . . . And you ain't lost nothing, has you" (50). The implication is that if Mister Leland suffered a great loss, he might then understand Tucker's action. Bradshaw later explains Tucker's comment to Mister Leland: "I think that he meant that he had been robbed of something but had never known it because he never even knew he owned what had been taken from him" (68). This description of loss would also accurately describe a loss of innocence, since by definition one does not know one is innocent until one has moved outside of innocence. It is this loss that Mister Leland is heading toward at the end of the book.

Tucker Caliban represents a different theoretical conception of time and space from the southern, liberal humanist, Age of Enlightenment regimes of power and knowledge. He represents the reason of the Other. He has his own logic and distinct subjectivity. With very little formal education, Tucker escapes one of the vehicles that transmit modern, secularized consciousness. He is not weighed down with all the baggage of rationalism, Enlightenment ideas, reason, and notions of progress. He responds more instinctively to life. Bethrah explains to Dymphna:

> [M]aybe those of us who go to school, Dewey, myself, not so much your mother, I guess your father, maybe we lost something Tucker has. It may be we lost a faith in ourselves. When we have to do something, we don't just do it, we THINK about doing it; we think about all the people who say certain things shouldn't be done. And when we're through thinking about it, we end up not doing it at all. But Tucker, he just knows what he has to do. He doesn't think about it; he just knows. (114)

Therefore, when Tucker, at his grandfather's funeral, recognizes the futility of his grandfather's life, he acts. At the funeral, when a eulogizer commends John Caliban for his "sacrifice of hisself to help others," Tucker explodes with "Sacrifice? Is THAT all? Is that really all? Sacrifice be damned!" (123). Later, when Dewey goes to Tucker to express his sorrow for John Caliban's death, Tucker remarks, "Not another time. This is the end of it" (124). Two months after John Caliban's funeral, Tucker buys the farm, "a piece of land at the south-western corner of what had been DeWitt Willson's plantation, on which Tucker's people had worked as slaves and then employees" (124). Then, during the nine months between his grandfather's death and his leaving town, Tucker acts. In addition to buying the farm ["Bethrah said she knew he wasn't just going to become a farmer" (108)], he and Bethrah have one child, and Bethrah becomes pregnant with a second. It is also during this time frame that he refuses to give Bethrah the dollar to rejoin the Society, and she leaves him and later returns. At the end of this nine-month period, he destroys the farm.

When Tucker Caliban puts salt on his land, shoots his cow and horse, splinters the tree and clock, and burns down the house, he seeks freedom from the binary. He is washing "his hands of it." In *Afro-American Literature in the Twentieth Century*, Michael G. Cooke, comparing Tucker Caliban to the Moses-like Joe Starks in Zora Neale Hurston's *Their Eyes Were Watching God*, argues that "Kelley in *A Different Drummer* brings Tucker Caliban, like a Moses, to the stage" where one expects the "founding of a black township" (74–75). But Tucker Caliban knows that the acquisition of material wealth and property and the "founding of a black township," à la Joe Starks, mean becoming the Same as the normative white society. Like Thoreau in *Walden and Civil Disobedience*, he knows that "injustice is part of the necessary friction of the machine of government" (396). Choosing Sameness perpetuates the white/black binary, and he realizes that supporting the white/black regime requires him "to be the agent of injustice to another" (396). Therefore, he breaks the law and lets "his life be a counter friction to stop the machine" (396). But his resistance does not take a traditional, modern form. He does not protest, he does not organize the people, and he does not anoint himself a leader. He does not develop intellectual strategies. Instead, he passively resists. He hears his inner voice and acts.

Tucker wins his freedom from the white/black binary of signification, his enslavement to the Willsons, by relying on inner resources. Freedom beyond the binary is attained through a state of mind, a hopelessly optimistic belief in radical individualism—that faith in oneself will set one free and that the path to salvation/peace lies within. In committing his acts, Tucker "advances confidently in the direction of his dreams" and passes through the "invisible boundary" (Thoreau, *Walden* 116)—the binary—into a space in which self-worth comes from being a radical individualist. The hope is that as a result of his actions more "liberal laws will begin to establish themselves around and within him" (116).

Tucker identifies his plight with the search for "something that was lost." The "something that was lost" is the courage to listen to the inner drummer that will lead the listener down an individual path to freedom, even if that path counters or disrupts normative society. It is the courage, as Harry Leland defines it, to strategically withdraw from an existence that denies humanity for an existence that vindicates it, to reject the societal binary for a radically free individualized and self-actualized space.

Tucker, in buying and destroying the land—the very means of his material southern survival and livelihood—symbolically revenges himself on and renounces servitude. By rescinding his "property and physical possessions which can't be taken," he has an "opportunity for free choice" (Nadeau xx). And in leaving the Willsons and the state, he completes the act of delayed freedom started almost one hundred years earlier with the Emancipation Proclamation.

Also, in buying and destroying the land, Tucker reconnects with the spirit of the African, who was perceived as different but equal. A scene near the end of *A Different Drummer* indicates Tucker's postcolonial status and his refusal to submit to the southern regime's limited, dehumanizing racial stereotyping and points to a new social space. When Tucker makes the offer to buy the "seven acres upon the plantation" from David Willson, and David asks him where he got the money, Tucker says, " 'I saved it. My grandpa left me some.' He was annoyed by the question, did not want to be *fathered*" (181, emphasis added). Later, when David offers to sell him another piece of land, Tucker says, with "the tone of his voice . . . almost irritated, almost angry, 'I don't want that land. Now will you sell me some land on the plantation?' " (182). David then patronizingly and paternalistically snaps, "You shouldn't speak that way, Tucker. It can get you into serious trouble" (182). Reflecting the site of a different social definition and echoing the different but equal encounter between DeWitt and the African, Tucker responds, "We ain't white and black now, Mister Willson. We ain't here for that" (182), recognizing that it is impossible for the black man to have a firm, positive sense that he is a free, individuated human being if he allows himself to be defined by the language of the colonizer. And Tucker's refigured and reconstituted position outside the white/black relations forces David Willson to adjust to this new social space. David responds: "We had come to a very strange kind of agreement. . . . I was doing something I realized I had always wanted to do . . . like those things I wanted to see done twenty years ago. . . . What each of us wanted so much individually we helped each other" (183). Interestingly, this response echoes a social space in which both Tucker and David Wilson "want *equality* without its compelling [them] to accept identity," a space in which they can accept "*difference* without it degenerating into superiority/inferiority" (Todorov 249).

The cycle of unjust enslavement of an equal that begins with the African ends with Tucker. The African and Tucker are the two family members who have the most in common. If the African's size suggests an epic, Tucker's size suggests a parable, for he is a "tiny husband" who looks like "a fourteen-year-old boy" (44). But, his identification with the African is made clear by his disproportionately large head. Just like the African, Tucker has "a huge head" and just as it is said of the African that his eyes made "his head look like a gigantic black skull," Tucker's eyes are described as "great, hard brown eyes, with more in them than should be there" (119). Also like the African, Tucker is fatherless. Tucker and the African are unencumbered by Western rationalism, culture, and ideology. Finally, both occupy a social space in which they are different but equal to their white counterparts. Because the unequal white/black binary cannot comprehend an Otherness of the same ontological space as itself, they exist outside, and, therefore, pose a threat/challenge to, the white/black binary, and Western history and rationality. Although the African's armed insurrection in the late 1700s fails, Tucker successfully leads all the blacks out of the state in a nonviolent exodus in 1957 (Weyl 16).

Furthermore, in his postcolonial state, Tucker does not attempt to recapture selfhood by appropriating the language of the colonizer, thereby losing his interior status and reinscribing himself within Western imperialist discourse. "To speak," writes Fanon, "means to be in a position to use a certain syntax, to grasp the morphology of this or that language, but it means above all to assume a culture, to support the weight of civilization" (17–18). Tucker's silence is neither a sign of submission nor merely a strategy of passive resistance, but a counterstrategy through which the Other, Tucker, preserves and even asserts his alterior, his non-Western, status against assimilation by the West. In his assertion, he interrogates the fixity of dominant power structures and positions. The white narrators attempt to give Tucker voice, but all such attempted violations/representations in *A Different Drummer* are resisted and implicitly judged by Tucker's silence. Silence empowers Tucker as guardian. In fact, it becomes the means through which Tucker resists the language of the white/black binary and of colonialism/imperialism.

With Tucker, Kelley rejects the binary. He rejects the Otherization of people to achieve identity and self-fulfillment as manifested in the various white narrators, including the men on the porch. Kelley also rejects blacks' defining themselves as victim, as inferior, as the Same, and as devalued Other, particularly as manifested in John Caliban and Bradshaw. And perhaps more important, Kelley rejects collective black protest, the historical African American mission to uplift the race, as manifested in Bethrah and the National Society for Colored Affairs, because it does not change the individual or transform society. When Tucker refuses to give Bethrah the dollar to join the Society, which claims to be "working for Tucker's rights and the rights of all colored people," he states: "Ain't nobody working for my rights; I wouldn't let them. . . . Ain't none of my battles being fought in no courts. I'm fighting all of my battles myself. . . . My very own battles . . . all mine, and either I beat them or they beat me. And ain't no piece of cardboard making no difference in how it turns out" (111). Tucker is not fighting with reason, intellect, or violence—features of resistance in the West—for the freedom of all blacks under a racist system. His instinctive approach to life is far removed from the high rhetoric of Bradshaw and race discussion. He identifies his plight with the search for something that is lost.

In *A Different Drummer*, Kelley is arguing that the individual is responsible for dealing with racism, an unfulfilled life, and the denial of his or her humanity and integrity. It is the change in individual lives as a consequence of individual actions that transforms society. Tucker's method of achieving freedom is presented as a contrast to collective protest. (And we can discern Kelley and *A Different Drummer* moving to a different beat in the 1960s. In 1962, as David Bradley points out in his foreword to the 1989 edition of *A Different Drummer*, "blacks were not only protesting, but protesting loudly; speeches and singing were as much a hallmark of mass marches as was marching itself. But Tucker makes no sound—makes not even a public statement" [xxv].) Unlike those of Bradshaw and Bethrah and the National Society for Colored Affairs, Tucker's actions have consequences. His actions spur others to reject the binary and leave Sutton. For Tucker Caliban, the entire act of salting the land and destroying the property comes as naturally as if it were prophesized. This is partly why the other blacks follow him. His exodus is rational and just. As explained by another black leaving Sutton, they are leaving "because it's right to go" (131). Interestingly, Tucker's non-organized action and silence are duplicated in the rest of the black population, who leave individually and who do not speak: "At least ten Negroes were waiting silently, patiently, each hour, as if enclosed in invisible coffins, no longer having the power of communication or even possessing anything to communicate to the world around them, or each other" (57).

But Tucker's actions also affect some of the whites in Sutton. At the end of *A Different Drummer*, David Willson's newfound sense of freedom from guilt is a direct result of Tucker's actions from which David finds new courage and faith. He states:

> I have always felt what I needed and lacked most twenty years ago was courage and faith, and that I had neither. . . . I could always say I did the responsible thing, but that rationale never for an instant convinced me. . . . At times I have vainly (or so I thought) wished someone could have helped me, given me faith in myself and courage to do what I so wanted to do . . . perhaps I DID possess the courage . . . but I despaired of ever finding it. Well, it has now been found, or given, or whatever. (151–52)

Like his son Dewey, who is paralyzed in dreams because of an arresting, inherited southern guilt, David has been paralyzed with the guilt of having turned traitor to the cause of black and southern liberation. By selling Tucker the land and accepting Tucker's subsequent destruction of it, David symbolically acknowledges his cowardly role in maintaining a regime of power and knowledge that defines whites as normative and blacks as inferior. Because of Tucker's actions, David is able to purge his guilt and reclaim his identity as well as his marriage. He finally realizes that his wife is "actually a human being capable of thought, not just a slave or a pet or a southern woman" (185), and he is able to begin to relate to her and their son again.

Mister Leland also exists outside the white/black binary. Although he is born and raised within the rules of the southern regime of power and truth, his parents have moved to inculcate him with values and attitudes that will make him a "passable human being," refusing to allow him to use the word "nigger," saying "you don't call nobody a bad name unless you want to hurt them" (35). They inculcate in their son the belief that "*it must not matter at all how folks look or what they says, just what they does*" (49). They sense that the world will change, and they want Mister Leland to be able to accept that and "get on with all kinds of folks" (35). Even Tucker recognizes that Mister Leland is different. Meeting him sitting on the grocery steps a year before the salting, Tucker buys him a bag of peanuts and says, "Tell your pa I knows what he trying to do with you" (49).

Mister Leland becomes the "ideal future" of the South because of his ability not to Otherize that which is different—in this instance, the African American—but to empathize, to plumb the experiences of the Other through comparison with his own, regardless of skin color. How is Mister Leland able to define the African American as different but equal? Throughout *A Different Drummer*, Kelley uses Mister Leland as an example of how one can use one's individual experiences to normalize, understand, and accept, rather than to Otherize and devalue, differences. Mister Leland uses his own experiences to understand the world. For example, when Tucker says to Mister Leland, "You young, ain't you. . . . And you ain't loss nothing," as an explanation for his destruction of the land and for his leaving, Mister Leland does not at first understand. And in the car ride when Mister Leland tells Bradshaw what happened and recounts what Tucker said to him, and Bradshaw interprets Tucker's statement with "I think he meant that he had been robbed of something but had never known it because he never even knew he owned what had been taken away from him" (68), Mister Leland is puzzled. But a puzzled and intrigued Mister Leland then spends most of the trip back into town trying to find something in his own experience that might help him make sense of Bradshaw's explanation. He finally arrives at a simple but sophisticated understanding of Tucker's action/behavior by imagining a scenario that would be similar in his own experience:

> *If Tucker lost something but didn't know he had it, he couldn't know he lost it. That's silly. You got to know you got something to know you lost it, unless, when you lost it, you go to look for it and find it ain't where you left it, but then if you left it somewhere you must-a knowed that you had it, so that ain't the same thing. Maybe it's like if somebody give you something at night when you're sleeping, but before you find it in the morning, somebody like Walter comes in and sneaks it out, and plays with it in the woods and leaves it there so you won't never find it, and then next day the person what left it for you comes in and says, "Harold, did you find what I left for you?" And you says, "No." And he says, "Well, I left it right in plain sight on the dresser so how come you didn't find it this morning?" And you says, "I don't know." And then you think on it and says, "Walter, he must-a took it before I woke up. I'll go beat the tar out-a him." And Walter says that he left it in the woods and don't know where and so you lost it and never even had it in the first place, but know you lost it all right. Maybe it's like that. (68–69)*

Mister Leland uses an analogy between his own personal experience and Tucker's loss. In giving up his own ego and in drawing in the being and presence of Tucker through an analogy of his own experience, Mister Leland is no longer "Other-ing" Tucker. Rather, he is empathizing with and humanizing Tucker's loss. He is saying "there's no space [Tucker inhabits] that cannot be a space [he] can connect with" (hooks, *Outlaw* 219). He is able to imagine and make himself Other to himself. Thus, he abandons his feeling of superiority and defines Tucker as different but equal.

Mister Leland's *"maybe it's like that"* echoes a remark he makes earlier in the chapter, after constructing a similar analogy to account for another experience/concept outside of his own existence. Sitting on Thomason's porch with his father one Friday afternoon, Mister Leland asks his father about the black exodus from the state. He is especially curious about his father's idea that the blacks are executing a "strategic withdrawal" from Sutton:

> "Don't that make them scaredy cats, Papa?"
>
> "Don't think so. Seems like this time it should take more guts to go, boy."
>
> Mister Leland had nothing more to ask, but to himself wondered about it, munching on the warm, almost bitter apple. How could you have more guts to run than to stay? Perhaps it was like the time Eden MacDonald at school had said his father could beat the tar out of Mister Leland and Mister Leland had answered, "No, my papa can beat the tar out of your'n because my papa ain't scared of nothing or nobody." . . . When Mister Leland came home and asked his father if he would run from a bear when he didn't have a gun, his father had said, "I reckon I would Harold." . . . And when Mister Leland thought about it, it seemed like his father was right, even though he did not like to think of his father running away from a bear or anything else . . . . And perhaps it was the same with the Negroes. (60–61)

Again, through analogy and empathy, Mister Leland comes to understand why the blacks leave town.

In another example, Mister Leland attempts to understand the "lie" he and his father conspire to tell his mother about the visit to Miss Rickett's: *"it was not like a lie at all, really, more like the soldiers in Korea, where Papa fought, looking out for each other because they were all soldiers and had to keep each other alive else the enemy would-a done them harm"* (52). As Adams points out, these analogies "represent imaginative acts, yoking together disparate elements of the world to create patterns for understanding experience. His efforts to comprehend Bennett Bradshaw's and his father's points of view by comparing them to real or fancied events in his own life . . . effectively draw him out of himself" (28). Trying not to create binaries and hierarchies between self and Other and in showing how one can move between the self and other, Mister Leland successfully normalizes and defines Others as different and equal. He invests the Other with agency and subjectivity.

Thus, both Tucker and Mister Leland exist in spaces outside the unequal white/black binary of signification, which stifles and limits the humanity of both halves/oppositions of the binary. That these outside spaces remain socially mostly undefined do not make them any less a solution to the reader or to the characters in the novel, for the presence of the undefined space problematizes, undermines, and exposes the binary space. As representatives of these spaces, Mister Leland and Tucker define/signify new sites of individuation, identity, social definition, and politics that cannot be comprehended by the southern regime of power and knowledge.

At the end of *A Different Drummer*, Mister Leland imagines he hears a welcome home party for Tucker. He could hear men "slapping him [Tucker] on the back, happy to see him again, especially since they thought he had left for good" (204). He imagines running across the "soft, gray earth of the plowed and salted field toward him . . . [and] Tucker would say he had found what he lost" (205). Mister Leland is envisioning a future ideal southern society, one based on the belief in the brotherhood of all men, a belief that all men, even the men on the porch, will be able to give up their need to affirm their identity against a devalued Other and to understand the experience of the Other by abandoning their own egos and drawing "in the being and presence of someone else" (hooks, *Outlaw* 219). Jane Campbell argues that Mister Leland's perceptions in *A Different Drummer's* final scene suggest "that Kelley sees this child as the embodiment of hope for the South, perhaps for all the United States" (117). Presenting his redemptive vision through Mister Leland, Kelley "enunciates the virtue of instinct rather than rationalism" (118).

Of course, in reality Mister Leland hears the noise of the lynching party and the death of Bradshaw, the last black in the state. Tucker will not return, but his leaving is a transformative act for this existing society. And as Mister Leland, Dewey, David Willson, and Dymphna are the state's metaphoric future, there is what Robert Nadeau calls the sense of a "growing consciousness of the immorality of racist views and behavior" (xx).

Whereas Tucker Caliban and Mister Leland exist outside the white/black binary, the men on the porch are victims of it. After the blacks have left Sutton and the state, the men on the porch:

> sat silently, thinking, trying to figure out what all this had to do with each of them, how tomorrow, next week, or next month would be different from yesterday, last week, last month, or all their lives had been up to this time. None was able to think it through. It was like attempting to picture Nothing, something no one had ever considered. None of them had a reference point on which to fix the concept of a Negro-less world. (188)

Kelley continues: "they began to get angry, quietly fighting mad, like a bride left at the church, wanting revenge, but having no one on whom to avenge herself, angered by her own frustration more than anything else. They disguised their loss by maintaining it was no loss at all" (189). Since in the West identity is determined in terms of binary oppositions, the men on the porch, who have always defined themselves as not being black, suddenly have an identity crisis. They do not have an Other by which to define themselves. Writing in *the location of culture*, homi k. bhabba, in discussing identity in terms of self and Other, states: "to exist is to be called into being in relation to an otherness" (44). Therefore, without an Other, the men on the porch become angry and want revenge. Unfortunately, Bradshaw, the last black person in town, comes along and they lynch him.

In this rejection of the unequal white/black regime, of collective social movements, and of the Otherization of human beings, Kelley in *A Different Drummer* deconstructs a social order, along with the European colonial regime of power and knowledge, that denies radical individualism and each person's ability to live life according to his or her own wants and desires, to live according to the dictates of his or her inner voice. And in this deconstruction, Kelley produces a different, postcolonial site/location to represent the African American male. He produces an African American male character who ceases to be a victim or a devalued Other, who has his own distinct subjectivity, who becomes a liberator, and who becomes a model of the ultimate autonomy of the individual regardless of race or other modern social organization.

Also, in rejecting the white/black binary and all the civilization and literature that have been built on it, Kelley is signifying a new, pregnant moment in African American letters, for Tucker Caliban becomes a new phenomenon of African American literary production. Reinforcing this point, Cooke writes:

> The idea of redemption comes as a radical new phenomenon in black literature. Perhaps Tucker Caliban's leading his people out of the house of bondage in Kelley's *A Different Drummer* prefigures it, or at least draws on the same biblical reservoir; but Kelley is only refurbishing the name Caliban, almost casually taking off the curse imposed by Shakespeare in *The Tempest*. (113)

And it is important to realize, argues Campbell in *Mythic Black Fiction*, that for the first time in African American literature the rebellion succeeds: "the whites are completely powerless to retaliate" (116). Describing the emergence of Tucker Caliban as a new kind of African American hero, Arthur P. Davis argues that "Kelley gives us not only a new, bitter, and effective type of protest novel, but also a new type of Negro character as well" (142–43). Echoing this same sentiment, David Bradley in the foreword to the 1989 edition of *A Different Drummer*, states:

> Tucker [is] a new kind of black hero, a transformation of the hero as seen in [Richard] Wright's work or in [Ralph] Ellison's *Invisible Man*, or in any number of other stories and novels written by blacks. Typically, black characters who triumphed had been comedic figures who, using guile and deception, ran away or went underground, but who never went head-on against the forces of oppression. If they did go head-on, they were tragic, fatalistic figures, who ended up dead. But Tucker liberates himself in a perfectly straightforward manner and lives to go on. He not only succeeds but survives. (xxiv)

It is clear that Tucker Caliban in *A Different Drummer* is constituted in a postcolonial position outside the white/black binary. But is he a patriarch? Because he says very little, it is impossible to discern from what he says. We learn from the various narrators that he is smart, strong, and tough. But we are also told that he is tiny. We learn from Bethrah that he made the decision to buy and destroy the land without consulting her. He does not explain anything to her. But Bethrah also informs us that, in line with his Thoreauvian ideas of self-reliance and radical individualism, each individual should fight his/her own battles. Bethrah follows Tucker "not just because she loves him, but because [she] love[s] herself." She continues: "I think maybe, if I do whatever he tells me to do, and don't think about it, well, for a while, I'll be following him and something inside him, but I think maybe someday I'll be following something inside me that I don't even know about yet. He'll teach me to listen to it" (114). Given Thoreau and Tucker's philosophy, Tucker would have to understand and support Bethrah if something inside her causes her to reject her marriage and family. Tucker would have to allow her to hear and act according to her inner voice. In this sense, Tucker does not read like a patriarch.

Kelley's *A Different Drummer* is pivotal because it is the first African American novel that abandons racial uplift's mission of assimilation and revolts. It is the first novel to locate its alternative paradigm in the periphery. Is the first novel that feels free to strip away Western rationalism and the Eurocentric regime of power and knowledge and to seek successfully nonrational, instinctual, heterogeneous American and African American belief systems as alternatives. It echoes and completes Sutton E. Griggs's *Imperium in Imperio* and Bernard Belgrave's proposal in that book to "demand the surrender of Texas and Louisiana to the Imperium. . . . Thus will the Negro have an empire of his own, fertile in soil, capable of sustaining a population of fifty million people" (245), although the plans adopted by the Imperium are revealed to the government. *A Different Drummer* creates a social space for Gabriel Prosser's failed self-assertion in Arna Bontemps' *Black Thunder* to be realized. It creates a social space as well for Ernest Gaines's many heroes—Marcus Payne in *Of Love and Dust* and Jimmy in *The Autobiography of Miss Jane Pittman*—who in their rebellion come up against the hegemonic forces of society and fail to fulfill their dreams. With Tucker, as Campbell points out, the government is "completely powerless to retaliate," and perhaps it has something to do with Tucker's strategy.

But to show this radical individualism, Kelley's *A Different Drummer* had to subordinate or repress other options for ameliorating repressive racial conditions and Otherization in society and other theoretical definitions of life such as the subaltern African American lifestyle, the blues lifestyle, the urban swing lifestyle, the existential lifestyle, thereby concealing its signifying process and naturalizing its own regime of power and knowledge—its message of radical individualism. In *A Different Drummer*, the religious, civil rights, and Marxist narratives of Bennett Bradshaw, David Willson, and Bethrah, or even the racist narrative of the Governor, are rendered ineffective. The African American blues, swing, and Voodoo lifestyles are excluded, thereby repressing the polyvalent nature of African American life. Yet, we know that when these organizations, movements, lifestyles, and regimes of power and knowledge are represented in other contexts in which they take on positive value, we can discern how they are discourses that permit and exclude. To privilege its message of radical individualism, *A Different Drummer* has to represent unfavorably, and therefore subordinate, these movements, lifestyles, and organizations. (Of course, from the middle-class Christian regime of power and knowledge, radical individualism can be criticized as being antisocial.)

I raise these repressed/subordinated options not as a way of discrediting or undermining the text, but as a way of exposing how *A Different Drummer* is the product of discursive practice. In its move to speak a particular discourse, it has to exclude, subordinate, and repress others. I want to expose how *A Different Drummer's* naturalized and privileged position is only a product of the text. But, of course, Kelley, in showing the problematic of representing Tucker Caliban and other African Americans, points to how language distorts and signifies rather than reflects a social reality.

A Different Drummer does not reaffirm the sanctioned "black experience" of the journey from the African American subaltern to the values of mainstream American society. But under changing conditions (after the 1970s) and in competition with new and reissued works, *A Different Drummer* continues to perform some desired/able functions particularly well. Since the 1970s, it has continued to be written about, cited, and recited; it has continued to be visible and available to succeeding generations of American/African American readers, critics, and scholars—particularly those interested in its radical individualism, its postcoloniality, and its radical vision. Thus, it continues to be culturally reproduced.

CHAPTER SIX

EXPOSING LIMITING, RACIALIZED HETEROLOGICAL CRITICAL SITES

AN EXISTENTIAL READING OF CHARLES WRIGHT'S *THE MESSENGER*

Twenty-five years before Farrar, Straus and Company published Charles Wright's *The Messenger*, in 1963, Librairie Gallimard of France published Jean-Paul Sartre's novel, *Nausea*, in 1938, and two years before the publication of Wright's *The Messenger*, Alfred A. Knopf published Walker Percy's *The Moviegoer*, in 1961. In 2003, Sartre's and Percy's novels, unlike Wright's *The Messenger*, are represented as seminal works of existential fiction. On the back cover of the New Direction paperback edition of *Nausea*, the publisher writes: "*La Nausee* . . . is [Sartre's] finest and most significant. It is unquestionably a key novel on the Twentieth Century and a landmark in Existential fiction." In the introduction to *Nausea*, Hayden Carruth gives a summary of the principal themes of existentialism and provides an existential reading of the novel. Sartre's novel is defined as an extension of existential philosophy, as a metaphysical tract, as a dramatic enactment of an existential definition of the human condition.

Likewise, Percy's *The Moviegoer* is also represented and received as a work of existential fiction. The epigraph at the beginning of the novel is a quote from the noted Christian existentialist Søren Kierkegaard's *The Sickness Unto Death*: "the specific character of despair is precisely this: it is unaware of being in despair." In his acceptance speech for the National Book Award for *The Moviegoer*, collected in *Signposts in a Strange Land*, Percy speculates: "It is perhaps not too farfetched to compare it [*The Moviegoer*] in one respect with the science of pathology . . . that the pathology in this case has to do with the loss of individuality and the loss of identity at the very time when words like the 'dignity of the individual' and 'self-realization' are being heard more frequently than ever" (246). Phrases such as the "loss of individuality" and "loss of identity" are two key features of existentialism as defined by Martin Heidegger. Discussing *The Moviegoer* in his review of Percy's *The Thanatos Syndrome*, Sven Birkerts assesses: "His [Percy's] novel, *The Moviegoer*, was a Kierkegaardian meditation on the attainment of authentic selfhood. Its thrust was philosophical, not psychological" (190). Like Sartre's *Nausea*, Percy's *The Moviegoer* is also represented as an extension of an existential philosophy, as a dramatic enactment of Kierkegaard's Christian existentialism.

Wright's *The Messenger* is also an existential novel. Yet, it was not received and has never been represented or defined as an existential novel. The history of the critical reaction to and reception of *The Messenger* is complicated and varied. But it is accurate to say that the text has been represented, interpreted, and defined by the publisher and mainstream American and African American reviewers and critics alike, not as an existential metaphysical tract, or as a dramatic enactment of an existential definition of the human condition in the twentieth century, but, primarily as a vehicle of sociological, political, racial, and cultural commentary or protest.

This reduction of *The Messenger* to racial and social commentary situates it, and the existential African American experience it textualizes, within a white/black binary of signification that defines white as normative and superior and represents the African American as inferior, as Same, as devalued Other, or as victim of racial oppression. Within this white/black binary, which constructs social reality in the United States, skin color or African ancestor is made to represent a set of denigrated experiences, and these experiences are applied to everyone who ever had an African ancestor. When *The Messenger* fails to reproduce the white/black binary, it is ignored and repressed. It is assumed to have no aesthetic value. But *The Messenger*'s otherness, its existentialism, which is ignored and/or repressed by the publisher and its critics and reviewers, is what is most challenging and subversive to the white/black binary. Finally, *The Messenger*'s existentialism offers a countertradition that allows for a refiguring of the African American as a non-victim, as a subject that is different but equal. In this polycentric approach to African American life and literature, *The Messenger* offers another site/location to construct a representation of the African American male.

Like Sartre's *Nausea* and Percy's *The Moviegoer*, Wright's *The Messenger*, in print in 1993 for the first time in fifteen years (but currently again out of print), is considered a classic by the publisher and by some American and African American critics and writers. But it is represented as an African American classic, in which race and racism are the only concerns. The most significant quotes on its first hardback (Farrar, Straus and Company in 1963) and more recent paperback editions (Fawcett in 1965 and HarperPerennial in 1993) represent it as sociology or protest literature. On the front and back covers of the 1963 hard-back edition and the 1965 Fawcett paperback edition of *The Messenger*, the pub-lisher presents a blurb by James Baldwin: "Reads with an urgency which is all the more painful for being, in the main, so quiet and taut. It seems sometimes to be scarcely a book at all, but a happening. *This is New York; this is the way we live here now*" (emphasis added). Also, on the back cover of these same editions, Kay Boyle represents *The Messenger* thusly: "For some time now, a new and ruthlessly honest literature has been emerging from the lonely horror of the junkies and homosexual world of New York. Wright's *The Messenger* is the most recent and in many ways the most moving of these statements from our contemporary lower depths. These depths are not to be ignored. Wright's book . . . is impor-tant as fresh, unencumbered writing and *important as social comment as well*" (em-phasis added). Also, on the first page of *The Messenger*, the publisher quotes a blurb from the The Associated Press: "Wright . . . distills a *bitter social protest* in a minimum of taut words . . . told with slashing effectiveness" (emphasis added). On the back cover of *Absolutely Nothing to Get Alarmed About: The Complete Nov-els of Charles Wright*, published in 1993, the publisher writes: "By turns brutally funny and starkly real, these three classic American novels create a memorable portrait of a young, working class, black intellectual—a man caught between the bohemian elite of Greenwich Village and the dregs of male prostitution and drug abuse." In these blurbs, the entire focus on representing *The Messenger* is one of sociology and social protest. Unlike with Sartre's *Nausea* and Percy's *The Moviegoer*, the issue of existentialism is never mentioned.

First, I want to draw brief sketches of Sartre's *Nausea* and Percy's *The Moviegoer*, making salient their existential features. Second, I want to do an ex-istential reading of Wright's *The Messenger*. Third and finally, I want to discuss the reception of *The Messenger*, examining why it is defined as social commen-tary or protest literature rather than as an existential novel. But, first, the brief sketches. *Nausea* is the diary of Antoine Roquentin, a bachelor of thirty years of age who has an independent income and who, after extensive travels in North Africa and the Far East and Central Europe, retires in the year 1932 to the little town of Bouville-sin Mar to write a biography of an obscure eighteenth-cen-tury nobleman: the Marquis de Rollebon. Although he is a man who has trav-eled widely, Roquentin no longer believes in the possibility of what men call "adventures." He now believes that immediate experience is utterly meaningless. And the novel is largely devoted to an analysis of the essentially nauseous sensa-tion that is provoked in us by our encounter with the absurd world. As he faces the world, Roquentin is overcome with nausea and disgust—simply because things do so stubbornly persist in being there; and the sheer thereness of things, such as the pebble, wounds him deeply because it seems in no way to be related to his own existence and seems, therefore, to oppose his own human reality. As Roquentin moves around Bouville, everywhere the scene of life appears to be nothing but a spectable of absurdity. The middle class holds to its niche in soci-ety, refusing to ask questions about being and existence. The world to which he is condemned appears to be without stability or permanence; and since he finds no evidence of things being governed by any real necessity, he has a sense of it being possible for them to be very nearly anything at all. In short, there is nothing in the world that appears to have any preordained order or form: the world as a whole seems to be characterized by the complete absence of any kind of necessity. Roquentin discovers that the complete absence of necessity in the world means that things are uncertain.

In the end, Roquentin comes to realize that nausea is the result of the refusal to accept things as autonomous objects that exist outside of rational man who sees himself as the center and who cannot imagine nothingness. Rollebon represents the only justification for his existence. But, Roquentin stops writing his book on Rollebon because he realizes that if he cannot hold to his own past how can he hold to the past of someone else. The actual process of living through an experience is quite without any sort of real meaning at all. It is only when we are able to view it, past experience, retrospectively that we can proceed to make it a part of some kind of conceptual order. Roquentin realizes that he has never had adventures. Therefore, he abandons his project. Ultimately, Roquentin comes to understand that existence is necessitated by our essences and that the present is all that exists.

Next, I want to sketch very briefly the plot of Percy's *The Moviegoer* and his main character, Binx Bolling. When the novel opens, Binx is alone and on the search. He has spent the past four years living in Gentilly, a middle-class suburb of New Orleans, working for his uncle's brokerage firm, dating girls, and trying to be a model citizen. He is also trying desperately to escape the search. "And there I have lived ever since, solitary and in wonder, wondering day and night, never a moment without wonder" (39). But, as the novel opens, a dream about the Korean War puts him back on the search.

To be on the search is to not be in despair. To be on the search is to have "immense curiosity" and heightened awareness of the world around him, to feel like a man on a strange island, a castaway. When one is a castaway, he seeks "clues" to the mystery of his existence. When Binx is on the search he is outside of all of society's rituals and metanarratives. He is outside the litigating absolution of the aristocratic southern tradition represented by his aunt Emily because this tradition, this construct, denies him the mystery of his existence. Binx is drawn to others who are exiles and who mirror his alienated, fragmented situation such as the Amazon woman, his father, and Jews. But he is unable to find truth and meaning in an absurd world. Binx, at twenty-nine years of age and just before his thirtieth birthday, concludes that "in the thirty-first year of [his] dark pilgrimage on this earth," he knows "less than [he] knew before, having learned only to recognize merde when [he sees] it" (180). In *The Moviegoer's* epilogue, Percy provides Binx with a religious experience that allows him to be in the world, but not of it. It allows him to be socially responsible.

For the purpose of this chapter and the existential reading of *The Messenger*, I must offer a short and terribly reductive definition of French existentialism. The non-Christian version of existentialism is attributable to Martin Heidegger and Jean-Paul Sartre. In "Existentialism Is a Humanism," which borrows heavily from Martin Heidegger, Sartre posits the idea that man is alone in a godless, absurd universe. Man is thrust into the world with no meaning from an identifiable source. In this atheistic philosophy of Sartre, man has no reality if he unthinkingly follows social laws or conventions:

> Everything is indeed permitted if God does not exist, and man is in consequence forlorn, for he cannot find anything to depend upon either within or outside himself. . . . For if indeed existence precedes essence, one will never be able to explain one's action by reference to a given and specific human nature; in other words, . . . man is free, man is freedom. . . . Thus we have neither behind us, nor before us in a luminous realm of values, any means of justification or excuse. We are left alone, without excuse. That is what I mean when I say that man is condemned to be free. Condemned, because he did not create himself, yet is nevertheless at liberty, and from the moment that he is thrown into this world he is responsible for everything he does. (353)

In this Sartrean existential philosophy, there are no hopes, dreams, expectations, or progress, and no reality except in action. Suffering, anguish, and despair comprise man's loneliness. Suffering is a prerequisite for establishing the self; it is a way out of the nothingness of existence. Man may become what he wishes by the exercise of free will, for man is nothing else but what he makes of himself. In addition, Sartrean existentialists are concerned with man's being; they have the feeling that reason is insufficient to understand the mysteries of the universe. The awareness that anguish is a universal phenomenon and the idea that morality has validity only when there is positive participation are prominent characteristics of Sartrean existentialism.

Bearing in mind the tenets of Sartrean existentialism and bearing in mind the plot summaries of Sartre's *Nausea* and Percy's *The Moviegoer*, I want to present an existential reading and to draw a portrait of the main character of Wright's *The Messenger*. *The Messenger* is written in the episodic-journal format—common to existential novels such as Henry Miller's *Tropic of Cancer* and Sartre's *Nausea*—with a first-person narrator. Wright's protagonist, Charles Stevenson, is a typical existential, Sartrean hero. He is thrust into the world with no meaning from an identifiable source. He finds himself alone in a godless, absurd universe in New York City. He has "neither behind [him], nor before [him] in a luminous realm of values, any means of justification or excuse" (Sartre 353). Therefore, he searches for the why of his existence. For most of the novel, he does not know that he is condemned to be free, that he is to take responsibility for everything he does, and that he may become what he wishes by the exercise of free will.

At the opening of the novel when we encounter Charles Stevenson, he, like Percy's Binx, is twenty-nine years old and he, "who [has] always been alone" and has "developed what others" define as "arrogance for [his] protection," still has not figured out the meaning of life (10). Therefore, in New York, he continues to search and ask questions. Living in his about-to-be demolished five-story walk-up "old midtown brownstone" and constantly being visited by a parade of marginal figures—prostitutes, homosexuals, drag queens, an "aging, ageless co-quette . . . dancing through an army of Puerto Rican gigolos," gypsy kids who are con artists, con women and con men—who are just as lost and lonely as he, Charles drifts in an absurd world. It is a world where people are searching for truth, holding on to social conventions, or are devising their own truths.

From flashbacks we learn that Charles's early searches for meaning and truth cause him to act, to seek answers. They cause him to travel to nearby and distant cities in Kansas, take him through many experiences, many of them sexual. He reads "everything that [he] could lay [his] hand on" (49) in hope of finding meaning, but to no avail. At the age of eight, he left home for the first time. He was headed thirty miles to the next town to visit his great-grandmother. But after walking three miles, a family friend spots him and returns him home. At fourteen years of age, he hitchhiked to Kansas City and St. Louis every weekend. "It alarmed Grandma, but I had to move. What would a fourteen-year-old boy do alone in a city? Well, I walked and walked, met all types of people. I went to movies, museums, the library" (47). These trips also brought him sexual encoun-ters with older men who lured him to their apartments. After a while he grew tired of Sedalia, St. Louis, and Kansas City. The "undiscovered world beckoned and one Sunday night, three months before graduation" from high school, he headed for California, where he "began to move through the subterranean junkie world where there is no day or night but an endless golden dusk if you are 'on' " (50). After getting a girl, Maria, pregnant, Ruby, his cousin, comes to California for him, and he returns home where he "work[s] on and off, hitchhiking back to Kansas City on weekends" (51). At eighteen, he had his first slice of life and wants more. During these early years, Charles was searching for meaning.

As an adult he continues to search. He joined the army for adventure and experience. He looked "forward to the United States Army and Korea with glee; it was to be another adventure, another experience, and when [he] re-ceived [his] draft notice shortly after [his] nineteenth birthday, it was like Christ-mas. [He] looked forward to fighting, perhaps even to dying" (101). He took basic training with an "exuberant spirit." He was excited by the skirmishes of the war, the "steep, dusty hills of Korea, riding in a two-ton truck, and suddenly hearing from far off the explosion of a bomb" (100). But when the action was over, military life for him became "routine, petty. [He] grew bored and difficult." After the war, Charles returns home "with thousands of GIs for whom Korea had been pretty meaningless. It was if they had never left this country" (101). These sojourns and experiences leave him feeling unsatisfied. Discussing the sig-nificance of adventure and experience to the existentialist, Sartre's Antoine Roquentin, in *Nausea,* writes:

> I have never had adventures. Things have happened to me, events, incidents, anything you like. But no adventures. It isn't a question of words; I am begin-

ning to understand. There is something to which I clung more than all the rest—without completely realizing it. . . . I had imagined that at certain times my life could take on a rare and precious quality. . . . I look back and tell my-self . . . I have known great moments, I have had adventures. . . . I have sud-denly learned . . . that I have been lying to myself. (37)

Like Antoine, Charles wants adventure; he wants to know "great moments." He wants his life to take on "a rare and precious quality." But it does not.

Charles Stevenson is what Julia Kristeva calls a "foreigner."

Indifference is the foreigner's shield. Insensitive, aloof, he seems, deep down, beyond the reach of attacks and rejections that he nevertheless experiences with the vulnerability of a Medusa. This is because his being kept apart corresponds to his remaining aloof. . . . Not belonging to any place, any time, any love. A lost origin, the impossibility to take root, a rummaging memory, the present in abeyance. The space of the foreigner is a moving train, a plane in flight, the very transition that precludes stop-ping. As to landmarks, there are none. His time? The time of a resurrection that remembers death and what happened before, but misses the glory of being be-yond: merely the feeling of a reprieve, of having gotten away. (269)

Because he has "always been a travelling lad," after two years in the army and about a year in St. Louis, Charles Stevenson comes to New York City. There, he works as a messenger for a service in Rockefeller Center, a job he does not take seriously. In addition to allowing him to travel throughout the city, the job permits him to meet "with all kinds of people" (69). But he spends much of his time reading Ernest Hemingway, Lawrence Durrell, and other writ-ers—searching for the meaning of life—and listening to jazz. When he does not have money or is laid off from his job, he occasionally scores as a hustler.

Although Charles is a working-class intellectual who lives among the parade of marginal figures or outcasts, he, even if he might think that he is better, does not otherize them. He represents them not as objects but as human subjects. First, he connects with them because, like him, they are fellow travelers. They, too, are lost and lonely. Second, Charles deals with and accepts these outcast in-dividuals where they are. Charles is understanding and compassionate with Mrs. Lee, the aging, ageless coquette, who dances through an army of Puerto Rican gigolos. When she visits, he tells her what she has "come to hear." Although he is not interested, he tries to show interest in Maxine's, the honey-colored seven-year-old, abstract drawing. She loves him because she knows that he is "for real." He plays with her and offers her gifts. Charles considers Claudia, the fabulous Negro drag queen, a friend. He thinks she is "nothing much to speak of as a man, but he makes a winging broad" (36). He is the play father to Lena, a prostitute and a professional thief. She can trust him. When she gets busted, he attends her trial. Charles does not cover over the outcasts and require that they become the Same, that they embrace his beliefs and values. He deals with them on their own terms. But, unlike most of these outcasts or marginal figures, Charles is an existential hero; he is aware of his loneliness. He knows that he is a traveler.

Charles's awareness of this loneliness puts him in possession of himself. It prevents him from seeking freedom through social conventions and laws, from establishing a comfortable niche in conventional society. "Man has no reality if he thinkingly follows social laws or conventions" (Sartre, "Existentialism" 354). He refuses to participate—or is incapable of participating—in the rituals that attend the systems of society. But, he still thinks that there is an answer, one certain "kick" or narrative, that will put his fragmented, alienated world together and unite him into a whole being. Early in the novel, in his apartment in New York City, he assesses his existential predicament: "Here in this semi-dark room, I became frightened. Am I in America? The objects, chairs, tables, sofas are not specifically American. They, this room, have no recognizable country. I have always liked to believe that I am not too far removed from the heart of America. . . . Yet I'm drowning in this green cornfield. . . . This country has split open my head with a golden eagle's beak. Regardless of how I try, the parts won't come together" (4). Charles no longer feels himself "to be a whole, but rather a series of diverse zones, subject to differing constraints, frequently of an irreconcilable sort" (Godzich ix). Charles becomes "frightened" because the reason and logic of language that order the world and his notion of the unified self clash with the absurdity of the world. The "objects, chairs, tables, [and] sofas" stubbornly persist in being there, having their own existence. These objects seem in no way to be related to his own existence and seem, therefore, to oppose his own human reality. At this moment, he becomes nauseous. He is overcome by a sense of how the names/signifiers and the concepts/signifieds that we apply to things have become arbitrary. There is nothing in the world that appears to have any preordained order or form. Here, Charles is experiencing the failure of reason or human-made rational structures.

Initially, for Charles, New York City held excitement. It had a sense of adventure: "[T]here was something that held me powerless. The pace, the variety, the anonymity, the sense of walking on glittering glass eggs, walking in a city like a big-time prostitute with her legs cocked open. A challenging, wondrous city, fit for a wide-eyed country boy" (106). But after five years in New York City, he wonders what he is "doing in this city." He still has not found Meaning and Truth. He still cannot connect the fragments of his life. He has "a rummaging memory." Therefore, he goes "back through the bowels of his memory" to his past, in the hope of finding meaning, "a lost origin." He recounts the death of his mother and the absence of his father. He recalls the "fun" of living with his grandfather and grandmother. But after Charles goes "back through the bowels of memory, back to Missouri" trying to "connect the fragments of [his] life," looking for "beginnings, his past," he realizes that the question of the "Great Why of Everything" had not formed when he was fourteen years old. But more important, although Charles does not find meaning and truth in his past, this rummage informs him that he "began to be aware of something at this time, something perhaps [he] had been born with, and which was never to leave [him]. Loneliness. And this consciousness is here with him now" in New York (26).

Earlier, in a flashback to November, 1958, one year and three months after he arrives in New York, a dream about his grandmother haunted him for days, and his grandmother's most recent letters had not been cheerful. Therefore, he decides to go home. The frame for the recounting of this trip home and his grandmother's eventual death comes as Charles tries to survive the "hot days and nights" of a New York August. He recalls his grandfather's lament, "This world is not my home" and he realizes that he has "nothing to look forward to but [his] own death, which [he does] not fear. But this, this doomed air of the present; what will happen to me before I die? What could possibly happen after all that *has* happened" (110)? When he arrives home to Missouri, he realizes that in coming home he "was on the run, and fatigued, played out. And now [he] want[s] to turn around and flee the town" (112). He realizes that he "had loved in another time when this town had been [his] world." But on this trip home, just before his grandmother's death, he realizes that he "had lost whatever [he] had had in those days, a shy lonely boy, veteran of a small war at twenty-one, who had made the bohemian pilgrimage without finding a roosting place" (112). The past fails to provide him with Meaning.

Also, on this retold trip, Charles encounters a grandmother who is growing old and frail and he rejoices in the "connection" between them. "We were not only connected by blood; we were friends. Whatever had happened to us, whatever thoughts crossed our minds that early November morning could not destroy the love we bore each other" (113). Charles settles in with his grandmother, and for a while, he is at peace. "I read a lot that winter, going to the library three times a week. I tried to avoid the kids I had grown up with. They all worked eight-to-five shifts and were carving out their future[s] in this small-town Negro world. And in this quiet world for the first time in years, I relaxed; I drank very little and did not feel the need for sex. Gone was the fevered air of New York, gone the hipped-up, Freudian complications" (115). As his grandmother, "now permanently bedridden," slowly moves into a second childhood before she dies, Charles awaits her end, "sitting in the rocking chair with a black coffee and a cigarette, rocking peacefully" (116).

But after the death of his grandmother, Charles realizes that "there was nothing to keep [him] in Missouri." Therefore, he returns to New York where he finds himself in a "cluttered, yellowing room on West Forty-ninth Street, in the heart of Manhattan. Here, there, again, and always, the Why of my life, the meanings. Terrible depression as I sit here watching darkness settle in the corners of this room" (116–17). He is still "aware of the loss of something" and he feels the "suffocation of this small room." He is still plagued with the question, "Where did it all begin?"

Charles also recognizes those who are the living dead, and he does not want to become one of them. "Death was [his] father, standing around looking lost, although he didn't live with [them] anymore" (22). The man, Alfonzo, in the New

Jersey couple who gives him a ride, had resigned himself to life in death. "I thought of the expression on the man's face. It was like something terrible had happened to him once long ago that had destroyed his sense of being a man, but it didn't matter much anymore. Whatever it was, resignation has settled in the creases of the pale, puffy face and under the tear-filled, forlorn eyes" (35).

But, Charles also encounters and recognizes fellow travelers. Walking through New York City during an early Sunday morning, Charles notices the streets "saddled with a numb, self-centered despair." He witnesses the "lonely people everywhere. . . . The shameful, envious, eyes-lowered glances at passing couples. You recognize other solitary fellow travellers. Both of you go separate ways, moving with the knowledge of Sunday papers, endless cigarettes . . . and the feeling of having missed out on Saturday night's jackpot prize" (26), or the answer to the ultimate question of existence. He also encounters and recognizes people such as Alice and Maxine who accept life as it is, who "got such a bang out of just living," and the messengers he works with, who "are still very much alive despite their various ailments" (6, 70). He likes some of the people in the "small town" in Missouri because they face their problems "by looking them square in the eye, accepting them as they accepted changes in the weather" (115).

In *The Messenger*, Charles is an intellectual in exile. Discussing the intellectual as exile, Edward W. Said, in *Representations of the Intellectual*, writes: "Exile for the intellectual . . . is restlessness, movement, constantly being unsettled, and unsettling others. You cannot go back to some earlier and perhaps more stable condition of being at home; and, alas, you can never fully arrive, be at one with your new home or situation" (53). For Charles, exile is an experience of "constantly being unsettled." He "cannot go back to some earlier and perhaps more stable condition of being at home." He "can never fully arrive, be at one with" his "new home" in New York or his existential "situation." Exile is the experience of crossing boundaries and charting new territories in defiance of the white/black binary, social conventions and laws, or the standard categories of race, class, and sex. As an exile, Charles becomes a being who has lost his country without thereby acquiring another, who lives in a double exteriority. He has experienced both American and African American cultures from within, and he is neither traditionally/conventionally Black, Indian, nor white. He admits to his mixed heritage: "I am the result of generations of bastard Anglo-Saxon, African, Black Creek, and Choctaw Indian blood" (88). He bends and challenges sexual categories by having sexual relations with both men and women; "I'm rather free sexually" (79). He does not empower only one form of sexuality. And he does not get caught up in the greatest problem of the American male, proving his masculinity. He doesn't have "to lift weights, wear heels with clicks, to assert [his] maleness" (79). He does not have to dominate. In addition, he defies class categories. He is a working-class intellectual/writer who does not embrace material possessions or the Protestant work ethic and who lives among the underclass. He listens to the blues and jazz and reads Hemingway and Durrell. We can say that Charles wants equality without its compelling him to accept identity, that he also wants difference without its degenerating into the superiority/inferiority opposition. Furthermore, we can also discern how Charles, to use the words of Barbara Herrnstein Smith, "is a member of many shifting communities, each of which establishes, for each of its members, multiple social identities, multiple principles of identification with other people" (168).

In addition, there are with the exile what Edward W. Said calls, in *Representations of the Intellectual*, "pleasures of exile, those different arrangements of living and eccentric angles of vision that [the exile] can sometimes afford, which enliven the intellectual's vocation, without perhaps alleviating every last anxiety or feeling of bitter solitude" (59). This means that although he lives in poverty, he gets a pleasure out of his "different arrangements of living," of having the options to become middle class but refusing it for some higher reason, which he thinks has much more value than a sterile middle-class life. Also, as an exile or what Kristeva calls a "foreigner," Charles "feels strengthened by the distance that detaches him from the others as it does from himself and gives him the lofty sense not so much of holding the truth but of making it and himself relative while others fall victim to the ruts of monovalency. For they are perhaps owners of things," but he "tends to think he is the only one to have biography, that is, a life made up of ordeals—neither catastrophes nor adventures . . . , but simply a life in which acts constitute events because they imply choice, surprises, breaks, adaptations, or cunning, but neither routine nor rest" (269). In Charles's eyes those who are not exilers/foreigners/sufferers/fellow travelers "have no life at all: barely do they exist, haughtily or mediocre, but out of the running and thus almost already cadaverized" (268–69).

Although Charles is searching for truth, his awareness, his exile, and his foreignness, as I have mentioned, put him outside the various supernarratives and metanarratives which give meaning to and regulate the behavior of "civilized" man. First, he is beyond the litigating absolution of the Church. At the death of his mother, his grandmother tells him the Christian meaning of death: that death is "a long, long sleep and you did not wake until you got to heaven." But Charles, after looking up at the sky and not getting a confirmation, "did not believe that that was true" (22). Also, when he is preparing to go to Korea and his grandmother prays and then turns to him and informs him that it is his turn to pray, he "turn[s his] head and stare[s] out at the dark night. There [is] nothing out there. Darkness." Therefore, he says nothing. When she reminds him again that it is his turn to pray, Charles "bow[s his] head again and open[s his] mouth. The words would not come. [He] look[s] up at the porch ceiling. It seem[s] as if the ceiling [is] between [him] and God" (102–03). Ultimately, Charles believes that his grandmother, and her religion, is an agent of false solace. She thinks that "if you *believe*, it will be all right" (103). But Charles Stevenson and existentialism know that "the sin is believing, hoping," and he is "too tired, too afraid . . . to commit this sin" (29).

Second, his awareness, foreignness, and exile put him outside the narrative of work, the Labor movement at his job. On May Day and in the midst of the "loyalty and Communist Front celebrations," Charles defines the day as "just another day for this worker." When the "other messengers, especially the elderly men . . . who take their messenger jobs seriously, talk labor," he is "silent." During the stock market crash of 1962, everyone is in a panic. "Everyone is tensely excited." Brokers are "picking their noses." An elevator operator loses four hundred dollars in the drop. A vice president has "moments when his nerves give and he overplays his role" (31). But all Charles wants to do is to "deliver the stuff and go home. The sudden change of fortune has no effect on [him]." He doesn't give a "Goddam dollar" for helping to bring "this historic day [stock crash] to a close" (33).

Charles's awareness, foreignness, and exile also put him beyond/outside other social rituals and conventions. He is outside the "sophisticated scum of New York." He feels strangled "by those millions of feet making it toward Mr. Greenbacks and what it takes to be a 'smaht' New Yorker" (16). He also feels marginal to young African American intellectuals. When he meets them at "liberal white parties and chic black parties," the young Negro intellectuals turn "out in Ivy League garb, usually with a pipe and mustache. Perfect gentlemen: sophisticated Uncle Toms. I certainly don't go for most Negro girls who have gone to a good college. They are usually phony intellectuals" (87).

Finally, Charles Stevenson's awareness, foreignness, and exile put him outside the narrative of middle-class life and respectability. This marginality is shown in two instances. In the first instance, he looks out of his window at a Tiepolo sky above the towering buildings and observes the office workers. "They have found their niche in this world and they are going to make damned sure that you know it and that you will not attempt anything foolish that threatens to destroy their world" (42). Charles thinks that they are "bourgeois right down to their underwear." He watches "the paralysis of mummified Americans waiting for their cars to take them back to suburbia" (43). And although he witnesses some of his people down there participating in the middle-class American dream, he realizes that he does "not belong down there" (42–43). In the second instance, he looks out his fifth-floor window and watches "the young Americans out on the town, healthy, laughing, contented as mother hens. Their faces indistinguishable as blades of grass. Look how happy they are! They are united and one" (58). And although he fantasizes about becoming one of them, despite the fact that he is black and that he thinks that he is "as American as apple pie," he concludes that he "cannot, simply cannot, don a mask and suck the c—— of that sweet, secure bitch, middle-class American life" (58).

There is the one time he decides to search for a job to achieve middle-class respectability. But it proves a failure. (Earlier, he had dreamed of "quitting the messenger service, get[ing] a better job, sav[ing] money, put[ting] a down payment on a house, and marry[ing] Shirley" [10].) He plays "hookey from the messenger service," shaves "very close that morning," glues on his "average, boyish American smile," puts on his "white" face, and applies for "the fifty-seven-dollar-a-week midtown mailroom flunky job" and a "brokerage house trainee"

(59) job. Due to lack of experience, he does not get the mailroom job. But before reporting to personnel at the brokerage house, he observes who he will be working with and gives up halfway through the interview. "If I worked with these slobs, I would be stoned from nine to five, I thought. The average jerk, going along like a cog, questioning nothing, seeking nothing. I've heard tell that these young men are the beefsteak on tomorrow's menu" (59).

Charles's awareness, foreignness, and exile put him outside these narratives and social conventions because the absurdity of these constructs and their ceremonies would diminish him as a man, as an agent of free will. Charles's stance is an existential one, and he is "outside" the absurdities of systems designed to oppress and suppress the last control of the individual under the burden of history and futility—that is, the command of his own naked free will. These constructs will not allow him to accept the mysteries in the world, to ask "the Great Why of everything" (25). Finally, Charles stubbornly resists any metanarrative based on a wishful need to infuse a random and absurd universe with meaning. Charles Stevenson's awareness, exile, foreignness, and "eccentric angles of vision" that put him outside these social conventions and rituals marginalize him from society. They "do not alleviate every last anxiety or feeling of bitter solitude." But they are "pleasures of exile" and they do "enliven [his] intellectual's vocation." His "discomforts," to again use Kristeva's description of the foreigner, "change into a base of resistance, a citadel of life" (qtd. in K. Oliver 270).

As with Roquentin in *Nausea* and Binx in *The Moviegoer*, near the end of *The Messenger*, Charles does some "stocktaking." At twenty-nine years of age, he realizes that he is

> a fairly young man with a tired boyish face, saddled with the knowledge of years and nothing gained, lacking a bird dog's sense of direction most of the time, without point or goal. 'I am the future,' I once wrote in a passionate schoolboy essay. Now...I am not expecting much from this world. Fitzgerald and his green light! I remember his rich, mad dream: 'Tomorrow we will run faster, stretch out our arms farther.' But where will this black boy run? To whom shall he stretch out his arms? . . . At the moment, I need not think of tomorrow. I've come to a decision. I am getting my possessions in order. Tonight there will be an auction in my pad. Everything will be sold, got rid of. And then I'll go away. (127)

But even with the stocktaking, he cannot find meaning.

Finally, at the end of *The Messenger*, Charles has an incredible existential revelation and breakthrough. Throughout the novel, drinking—along with listening to jazz, having sex, and reading—has been one of the ways Charles copes with existence, with the pain, suffering, despair, and frustration of life. "Alcohol is merely a brace for my spine, the fine oil for my reflex" (8–9). He thinks drinking and jazz go hand in hand. "A wonderful tranquilizer. Problems do not get less, but [he] can see them more clearly" (124). As his friends come to his apartment to bid him farewell, Charles has been drinking all day, but it has "done absolutely nothing for [his] head." But he does see himself more clearly. "There was horror in the knowledge that nothing was going to happen to [him], that [he] was stoned on that frightening, cold level where everything is crystal clear. It was like looking at yourself too closely in a magnifying mirror" (130). He becomes existentially aware.

Observing his friends at the party, he recognizes that the party has turned into a microcosm of the world. He realizes that his drunken friends, like the people in conventional society, are searching fruitlessly for the "crazy kick," the meta-narrative that will "still the fear, confusion, [frustration] and the pain of being alive on this early August morning" (131). But Charles has come to accept pain and suffering as being a part of life. He now knows that there is "no such thing as peace of mind and goodness." This knowledge becomes a prerequisite for establishing the self. It is the way out of the nothingness of existence. This revelatory moment allows Charles to analyze his own culture and the world. And he realizes that everyone has acquiesced: Shirley to middle-class respectability, Bruce to the Episcopalian church, Mitch to morality, Claudia to the notion of "a fabulous Negro drag queen," Jim to a desire to "save the world," and Mrs. Lee to a "succession of lovers." They have acquiesced to systems of unexamined/naturalized codes—and unexamined or naturalized codes are self-deceptions. "Self-deception," writes Sartre, "seeks by means of 'not-being-what-one-is' to escape from the in-itself which I am not in the mode of being what one is not" ("Self-Deception" 328). And, in the end, all the systems seem absurd to Charles.

Of course, Charles has already reached the conclusion or has already decided that there are no metanarratives that can allay life's obstacles. Therefore, he has no need to "find a roosting place." During most of *The Messenger*, Charles Stevenson does not "understand" the nature of his search, his exile, his loneliness, in the absurdity that is his life, his actions. The societal results of his action do not equate. "I was searching for something I would tell Ruby. What? she would ask. I don't know, I would say. But I'll know when I find it" (51). It is only at the end of the book that Charles synthesizes and reconciles—by his own standards—his actions with his motives. He attains freedom through scorning the absurd world, through an understanding that his existence is valid although absurd, through the realization that the world is wrought with suffering and pain, that man is nothing but what he makes of himself.

In this moment, Charles realizes that he cannot explain his "actions by reference to a given specific and human nature," that he is free, that he has neither behind him, nor before him "in a luminous realm of values, any means of justification or excuse." He is "left alone, without excuse." Therefore, when Charles recognizes that existence precedes essence, that he simply exists, that he is his "own problem," he is "condemned to be free. Condemned, because he did not create himself, yet is nevertheless at liberty, and from the moment that he is thrown into this world he is responsible for everything he does" (Sartre, "Existentialism" 353). It is this realization, this awareness, this freedom that allow him to assert his independence and accept the "fears, confusion, and the pain of being alive."

Although the power of Wright's *The Messenger* is its existential philosophical countertradition, *The Messenger* does not ignore the presence of racial oppression in its portrait of Charles Stevenson. Interestingly, racial oppression exists
in the world of the text, but Charles does not define himself as a victim of racial
oppression. In the sexual encounters with the men in the Midwest and in New
York City—with Peter, the crew-cut soldier, who watches him at the Step
Down Bar and who invites him for some bizarre racial sex; with the couple in
New Jersey where the husband offers his wife to him; and with Mr. Bennett,
whom he meets in the park, who uses his "large collection of books" to lure
him to his apartment—Charles is represented as a sexual, racial Other. As Other,
he comes to symbolize a racialized, sexual exotica, the object of sexual arousal
and fantasy. (Also, he is represented as the Other when he is walking "through
the concourse of the RCA building, sneezing and reading Lawrence Durrell,
dead drunk from the explosion of his words," and encounters Steven Rockefeller "who doesn't . . . think poor people read" [7].)

In his hometown and in New York City, Charles experiences racism. There
is the racism involved in the confrontation with the small-town Missouri cop
who stops him because he is in a white neighborhood, in his friend's son calling
him a "nigger," in the six-year-old playmate who never came to his birthday
party despite the fact that he went to hers, and in members of the dominant
white society who define him in stereotypical terms. He experiences racism
with Penelope Browne whom he played with as brother and sister, until they
"arrived at the acute age of twelve. Afterward, very polite and formal" (84). He
experiences racism with Bobby who always greeted him with "Neigaaar." He
experiences racial segregation when, "at the local movie, he had to sit in the bal-
cony on hard wooden seats. Downstairs, the seats were upholstered with ma-
roon leatherette" (84). The first time Charles spent a weekend exclusively with
white people, he was fourteen years old. When he arrives late for dinner, he
hears his fifteen-year-old host's uncle, a Missouri state senator, say, "Maybe he
won't come down because we ain't got no watermelon." Finally, at sixteen,
Charles takes a job as a pinboy at Harry O'Malley's Fair Lanes Bowling Alley. In
his presence, he hears a white friend of his boss, Harry O'Malley, say to Harry,
"Hey, Harry, see you have a coon back there" (85). Racism permeates Charles's
life. But, for Charles, this racism becomes one of many obstacles to be overcome: "Wounds [of racism] of my Missouri childhood were no worse than a
sudden, sharp pain" (84). Charles chooses to overcome his obstacles, rather than
be defined as a victim by one of them: racial oppression.

Finally, Wright in *The Messenger* argues that the blues and jazz have the
same or similar philosophical suppositions as existentialism. Like existentialism,
the blues and jazz do not believe in hope and progress and safety, but believe that
life is wrought with pain and suffering and that the objective in life is to confront and acknowledge this pain and suffering. Throughout *The Messenger*,
Wright uses the blues and jazz to reinforce and to reaffirm a life that is condemned to be free, that is outside hopes, dreams, expectations and self-decep-

tion. The blues and jazz require individuals to accept the spectrum of human life—the pain, the suffering, the frustration, and the joy.

In *The Messenger*, Ruby Stonewall embodies the blues. As a blues singer who lives a blues life, Ruby recognizes and accepts the fact that suffering and pain are facts of life. She has lived a hard and difficult one. "She [has] bags under her gunpowder eyes that never seemed to give off any warmth." She is "one mean woman. She [doesn't] give or take nothing from nobody." Her "red mouth always [seems] to be on the verge of a smile that never appeared." Her "baby had the flu and died. Some bitching husband left [her], and [she] got into a mess with a white man in Kansas City" (52). She has been forced to work low-paying jobs. "She couldn't make twenty-five [dollars] a week in a ginmill unless she hustled on the side" (53). When her voice "was shot," she takes a "job in a hotel as a chambermaid" (53). Suffering allows Ruby to establish the self, to find a way out of the nothingness of existence.

Although she experiences racism, she refuses to pity herself, to allow it to define her as a victim. She passes on to Charles this blues definition of life. When Charles does not get a busboy job because of blatant racism and proceeds to pity and feel sorry for himself, Ruby lectures: "You make me sick. You go to that department store and ask to be interviewed and they tell you to wait outside. So you wait and wait and then some white boy comes along and gets the job. And you get hurt and mad as hell. Starting hating the white people again. If you had gotten the job, the white folks would be just fine. Now you're feeling sorry for yourself because you're black. . . . Nobody has the tough luck that us colored people have. And you're too Goddamn miserable feeling sorry for yourself to get up out of the gutter" (54). When Charles responds with the question, "Since when did you hit the big time?" Ruby snaps, "Since I stopped feeling sorry for myself. *Since I learned that there ain't nothing really bad. There ain't nothing that can really hurt you*" (54; emphasis added). Then, Ruby gives Charles blues advice: "I've spent thirty-five years discovering how rotten life is if you waste it on nothing. Never bitter, Sonny. Only people who can't face life and hate themselves are bitter. Maybe I was born black and lost my voice to teach me a lesson" (55). Thus, as a blues woman, Ruby is not bitter or angry at the world; she does not pity herself or represent herself as a victim of any of life's obstacles, especially racial oppression. She is facing life. She is "confronting, acknowledging, and contending with the infernal absurdities and ever-impending frustrations inherent in the nature of all existence" (Murray, *The Omni-Americans* 90). She is accepting the fact that suffering and pain and frustration are not aberrations but facts of life.

Likewise, jazz, "good jazz," which is based on improvisation and spontaneity and which does not exist as essence, tells no lies about a better tomorrow, or deceives us about progress. Writing in *Stomping the Blues*, Albert Murray defines cool and bebop jazz musicians such as Charlie Parker, Louis Armstrong, John Coltrane, Miles Davis, Billie Holiday, Dizzy Gillespie, and Ornette Coleman as "blues-idiom musicians." Describing their attitude toward life, he writes:

What it all represents is an attitude toward the nature of human experience . . . that is both elemental and comprehensive. It is a statement about confronting the complexities inherent in the human situation and about improvising or experimenting or riffing or otherwise playing with . . . such possibilities as are also inherent in the obstacles, the disjunctures, and the jeopardy. It is also a statement about the maintenance of equilibrium despite precarious circumstances and about achieving elegance in the very process of coping with the rudiments of subsistence. (250–51)

Jazz, like the blues, generates, resignifies, and reaffirms existential life in *The Messenger*. Throughout the text, Charles listens to "good jazz." When he lies "under the boardwalk at Coney Island" with Shirley, he listens as the "black radio plays muted jazz." When he has the sexual encounter with Keith, a young executive on Wall Street, for money and afterward he visits San Remo's for "a quick bourbon," he has to hear "The Billie Holiday Story album. Lovely, sad, bitter, Baltimore songbird. Singing a timeless song" (66). When he visits Barry's apartment, he hears "the bedside radio . . . playing early morning jazz" (72). On a visit to the Step Down Bar, Charles plays a "couple of Lady Day sides"—"Yesterday" and "Ain't Nobody's Business If I Do" (77). Visiting Jim and Laura, he turns "on the old, dependable, Zenith AM–FM just in time to catch Lady Day with 'Fine and Mellow' "(124). Finally, listening to his FM radio in his fifth-floor walk-up, he hears "cool jazz."

Constantly listening to jazz, which is spontaneous and open to the mysteries of life, Charles is assisted in defying the status quo, in refusing society's metanarratives, in accepting and "confronting the complexities inherent in the human situation." The jazz music also assists him in being perseverent and resilient and in maintaining equilibrium, despite precarious circumstances. Billie Holiday is obviously a blues/jazz singer who confronts, acknowledges, and contends "with the infernal absurdities and ever-impending frustrations inherent in the nature of all existence." The "timeless song" that Billie Holiday sings is not one of lamentation, protestation, or exaggeration, which prevent what Murray calls "heroic endeavor." It is one of accepting pain and suffering as facts of life, of accepting "the all too obvious fact that human existence is almost always a matter of endeavor . . . a matter of heroic action" (Murray, *Stomping the Blues* 251).

But although the blues and jazz generate and reaffirm existentialism in *The Messenger*, Wright does not present Ruby and the blues as possessing the same power and "universality" as existentialism. Existentialism, unlike the blues, Wright seems to argue in *The Messenger*, has an intellectual, rational dimension. Writing in *The Sprituals and the Blues*, James H. Cone argues that the blues does not deal with large abstract philosophical ideas. It deals with concrete experiences and realities.

Freedom in the blues is not simply the "existential freedom" defined by modern [Western] philosophy. Philosophical existentialism speaks of freedom in the context of absurdity and about the inability to reconcile the 'strangeness of the

world' with one's perception of human existence. But absurdity in the blues is
factual, not conceptual. The blues, while not denying that the world was
strange, described its strangeness in more concrete and vivid terms. (112)

But Charles, the existentialist, is an intellectual who reads; Ruby, the blues
woman, does not. Charles is concerned with larger abstract questions of existence,
and Ruby derives her truth from everyday experiences. There is a clear sense in
the text that Ruby's blues are most effective in African American communities,
whereas Charles, as an existential character, has the scope of the world for his ter-
rain. Yet, the blues and jazz, like existentialism, offer a freedom that is beyond the
absurdities of systems designed to oppress and suppress man's free will.

Using the examples of Sartre's *Nausea* and Percy's *The Moviegoer* as existential novels, Wright's *The Messenger* is also an existential novel. Certainly, by
the earlier definition of existentialism, Charles Stevenson, Antoine Roquentin,
and Binx Bolling are all existential characters. Sartre's Roquentin and Percy's
Binx are ciphers, existential constructs, definitive Others, characters whose ex-
istences precede and define their essences. The same can be said of Charles
Stevenson. In fact, almost everything that applies to Antoine Roquentin and
Binx Bolling, except for the Kierkegaardian religious resolution in the epilogue
of *The Moviegoer*, can also apply to Charles Stevenson. All three find themselves
"alone in a godless universe." They are searching for a truth that will bring
unity and meaning to their fragmented worlds. Despite their vigorous search
for meaning during their years on earth, all have learned that nothing has been
learned from their stay in the world and all must take responsibility for their existence. The awareness of their existence is constantly putting them outside all
social laws and conventions. They also understand that reason is insufficient to
understand the mysteries of the universe, that anguish is a universal phenomenon, and that morality has validity only when there is positive participation. All
three characters resist any false paradigms that will preclude the asking of large
questions about being and existence. Finally, Antoine, Binx, and Charles accept
the world's absurdity and realize that only through the use of free will can they
achieve freedom.

Yet, *Nausea* and *The Moviegoer* are represented as seminal works of existential fiction, and *The Messenger* is represented as social commentary or as a vehicle for racial protest. Percy's *The Moviegoer*, published in 1961, is set in the
pre–civil rights South, where legal and de facto segregation was very much a
part of the social landscape and where African Americans were denied their
basic human and civil rights. *The Moviegoer* does allude distantly to these social
issues. But these issues are not the publisher's, reviewers' and critics' focus in
their interpretations, representations, and reactions to the book. Reviewers and
critics are concerned with *The Moviegoer* as a dramatic enactment of the existential definition of the human condition. Percy in *The Moviegoer* has not been
criticized for misrepresenting the South. Nor has *The Moviegoer* been appropriated to generate or reaffirm a white southern tradition, thereby negating or re-

pressing its existential core. Sartre in *Nausea* has not been held accountable for misrepresenting the social and economic crises in France or the treatment of Jews in France in the 1930s.

Taken together, added up, these facts, existential reading, plot summaries, and quotes point to an extreme irony. A text that is instinctively, intuitively, philosophically, and discursively existential in its concern, nature, and telling is read and interpreted and examined from a different position and with a different set of agendas than existential texts written by white, Western male writers such as Jean-Paul Sartre and Walker Percy. What does the reception of *The Messenger* tell us about the agenda that has defined and represented it? Exactly how has *The Messenger* been received?

The Messenger was ignored by African American reviewers when it was published in 1963. It was reviewed and represented exclusively by mainstream white American reviewers. To some of these white reviewers, the book's worth, artistic and otherwise, hinges principally on its depiction of the effects of racial oppression on the African American, or on the place of the African American in society. This means that, according to these white reviewers, what is considered worthy about African American life and African American literature is their representation of the African American as the victim of racial oppression, in which color is made to represent a set of denigrated experiences. All other aspects, specificities, and dimensions of African American life and existence are considered irrelevant or nonexistent. Of course, portraying the African American as a victim is the most subtle and effective way of disempowering him, of colonizing his image, and of empowering mainstream white America. To be represented as a victim of racial oppression is to be defined exclusively and negatively by somebody else's discourse.

The representation of the African American as victim of racial oppression by mainstream white American reviewers is quite evident. These reviewers use *The Messenger* as a vehicle for racial commentary. They define African America's relationship to white America as a be-all and end-all. Everything hinges on the white/black encounter. Reviewing *The Messenger* in *The Nation*, Robert Kiely chooses to define the protagonist's problem racially: "Mr. Wright's hero is a Negro, and one of the reasons he lives on the fringes of the 'normal' world is that he is forced to do so. . . . The narrator's account of his relationship with his pious grandmother, the humiliation suffered at the hands of Southern police and Army superiors, his pathetic attempts to join the middle class, give point and poignancy to his later dissipation" (550). What is minimized and repressed in Kiely's review are the larger metaphysical questions about being and existence that Charles Stevenson is asking and that are at the core of the book. Furthermore, Wright in *The Messenger* makes it very clear that race is not the main reason why Charles lives on the "fringes" of the "normal" world. He shows other African Americans joining the middle class and the quest for the American dream. Geoffrey A. Wolff, in reviewing Wright's *The Wig*, writes thusly about *The Messenger*: "His first novel, *The Messenger*, worked another side of the street. There the anger, expressed through a raw autobiographical account of his youth with drugs, queers, whores, and Southern police, held some promise. At least it looked as if the author [Wright] needed to write it" (17). And Thomas Curley, in *Commonweal*, overtly represses and ignores all aspects of *The Messenger* and the life of Charles Stevenson that do not deal with two minor black female characters. He writes: "[W]e have two excellent characterizations, those of Ruby Stonewall, the narrator's cousin, and his grandmother. These two women do not merely give substance to a book that is otherwise rather weightless; they also serve to define a place, a small Missouri town which, although the scenes there are few contrasts well with the banal images of New York" (566). Curley ignores *The Messenger's* existentialism because it does not have an "intercourse with temporal reality" for African Americans; it does not leave a "mark upon our memories." To Richard Kluger, in the *New York Herald Tribune,* the only value in *The Messenger* is the racial confrontation between the hometown cop and Charles Stevenson, and he is disappointed that Wright's portrait of racism is not more plentiful, graphic, bitter, and angrier. "And the few incidents the author begins to involve us in—when the hometown cop makes him jog around the station house for an hour just for walking home through a white neighborhood or when the infant son of a white couple supposed to be friendly calls him 'nigger'—are reported so clumsily and fleetingly that we do not feel the impact" (7). Writing in the *New Yorker,* Whitney Balliett focuses on "one horrifying [racial] scene" that helps to "make him what he is" and helps "to make the book the achievement it is" (208).

Other mainstream white reviewers represent *The Messenger* as sociological commentary, as mostly a slice of life, and not as a work of art having artistic merits. To them, its worth hinges on its portrayal of the seamy side of the other urban street. Writing in *The Critic,* Doris Grumbach declares: "Now here is a first novel whose burden of obscenity and lurid situation is so heavy that one is hard put to find any literary, artistic, or aesthetic justification" (83). William Barrett, the reviewer for the *Atlantic Monthly* also defines *The Messenger* sociologically. It is about the "urban underworld . . . the bustle, the sights, sounds, smells of the streets of New York" (121). Writing in *Library Journal,* Milton Byam has this to say: "In its plotless though apparently autobiographical meandering it is concerned with homosexuality, alcoholism, narcotics addiction, and incidentally, Negro-white relationships" (2730). And, Katherine Gauss Jackson, writing in *Harpers,* argues that *The Messenger* inhabits "the desperate shadowy world of New York: lonely misfits who are friends of 'the messenger,' the narrator" (115).

In addition, most mainstream white reviewers criticize *The Messenger* for not being a novel. The reviewer for the *Atlantic Monthly* represents the book not as a novel, but as "a series of vignettes" (121). Curley thinks that Wright in *The Messenger* "really missed any development . . . of a story . . . at all, and [he is] glad to report that he [Wright] didn't quite make it" (567). Byam argues that "it is plotless" (2730). Jackson writes that "the book, like the lives, is made up of episodes and thus as a novel isn't quite successful" (116). All of these mainstream responses to *The Messenger* define it sociologically; none mentions existentialism.

The Messenger seems to exist in the fissure between what Wlad Godzich calls "the conception of the subject as the organizer and sense-maker of lived experience," on the one hand, and "the challenger posed to forms of Western thought by the liberation movements of the past forty years" (viii), on the other. The alienation and fragmentation of an African American self that Charles Wright depicts in *The Messenger* and that, to again quote Godzich, which constitutes "the psychological ground of French existenialism," seem to apply not only to Charles Stevenson but also to Wright's book itself—or rather to the reactions to Wright's book. The book, rather than the character Charles Stevenson as Wright has rendered him, has been shattered into seemingly diverse zones in which it is "subject to differing constraints, frequently of an irreconcilable sort" (ix).

When *The Messenger* enters the domain of African American and American critical practices, it continues to be repressed or misrepresented. First, existential writers and critics such as Walker Percy, Ralph Ellison, Tony Tanner, and others simply ignored *The Messenger* or were blinded by the racial and sociological interpretations imposed on the book. Second, the poststructural and contemporary criticism of Robert Stepto, Houston A. Baker Jr., Henry Louis Gates Jr., Sherley Anne Williams, Phyllis Rauch Klotman, Charles Johnson, Michael G. Cooke, Barbara Christian, Hortense Spillers, Hazel Carby, Michael Awkward, Valerie Smith, and others excludes any discussion/interpretation/representation of the book.

Third, for African American critics such as Addison Gayle and Bernard W. Bell—who belong to the "liberation movements of the past forty years" but whose critical practices do not pose a fundamental "challenge to the forms of Western thought" (Godzich viii)—the book's worth hinges almost exclusively on its representation of the African American as defined by cultural nationalist ideology, or the embodiment of an African American tradition. Both Gayle and Bell ignore what Godzich calls the [African American] "fragmented subject" and the "historical forces" that produced it. In 1975, Gayle, in the concluding chapter of *The Way of the New World*, defines *The Messenger* as being a part of a "surrealistic" movement in African American letters—a movement that does not abandon "the racial artefacts." For Gayle, Wright uses *The Messenger* "to war against symbols, images and metaphors of Blacks handed down from the Euro-American past" (302).

Bernard W. Bell, in *The Afro-American Novel and Its Tradition*, represents Charles Wright and *The Messenger* as being a part of "the profound ironies and blues-like absurdities of the 1960s and 1970s." Wright is, Bell continues, one of those

> contemporary black novelists [who] employs distinctive combinations of fabulation and satire to spread the news of their tragicomic visions of our time. They have not completely lost faith in the power of satire and laughter as therapy for

the ills of the world, but more like [George] Schuyler, and [Wallace] Thurman and [Rudolph] Fisher, they are much more irreverent and scornful of the hypocrisy of Western civilization, Christian orthodoxy, American principles, and black togetherness. (320)

Keith E. Byerman, in *Fingering the Jagged Grain*, interprets *The Messenger* in still another critical tradition. He defines the text as belonging to the tradition of Ishmael Reed and early Imamu Baraka that has "redefined what is possible in black fiction. Following the lead of Ellison, they tend to emphasize the telling more than the tale and have thereby added a new dimension to black writing" (238). Gayle, Bell, and Byerman define Charles Wright and *The Messenger* in terms of three different African American traditions. But they ignore the existential philosophy that is at the core of the book, further shattering the book into more diverse and seemingly irreconcilable zones.

Even among the book's champions, it seems, the problem of Charles Wright as social scientist or protector of "racial artefacts" versus Charles Wright as poetic artist bifurcates any cohesive evaluation. Noel Schraufragel in *The Black American Novel* acknowledges "the influence of such French writers as Sartre and Camus" on Charles Wright and *The Messenger*. Schraufragel admits that Charles Stevenson is portrayed as an existential hero who "merely drift[s] along in a world that seems devoid of meaning" (122). Yet, despite this admission, Schraufragel ultimately defines *The Messenger* not as a dramatic enactment of an existential definition of the human condition but as racial accommodationist fiction: "This nonprotest or accommodationist fiction concentrates basically on the adjustment an individual makes to function in accordance with the standards of white society. This adjustment includes a resignation to the existence of racism and the search for a meaningful identity that will serve as a compensatory stratagem. The individual accommodates himself to the conventions of the dominant culture in order to survive, or because there seems to be no plausible alternative, but at the same time he hopes for a positive change in his life" (121). But this reading of *The Messenger* by Schraufragel is problematic. Schraufragel praises *The Messenger* for its lesser achievements—that it has the influence of Sartre and Camus—however, its preeminent ambition—that it is an existential novel—is subordinated or ignored. In short, an existential evaluation of the book will not conclude that Charles "accommodates himself to the conventions of the dominant culture in order to survive." Rather, it will conclude that Charles comes to understand that he does not need a metanarrative or social conventions to give his life structure and meaning, that he has to take responsibility for his own existence.

Likewise, Jerome Klinkowitz argues that *The Messenger* shatters "the old conventions" and presents "the usual 'search for meaning' theme in a radical new form: imaginative literature, and ultimately fantasy. His [Wright's] impetus for *The Messenger* . . . is the black experience, but only as environment can provide the stimulus to any artist" (123). But, Klinkowitz does not define *The Messenger* as the dramatic enactment of an existential philosophy as his statement "search for meaning" indicates. Rather, he concludes that Charles is seeking "imaginative space, a better world to make than simply the banal American quest" (126). Klinkowitz's conclusion suggests that Charles is rejecting one narrative in the hope of finding another. But an existential reading of the novel and a close examination of the closing scenes in the novel show that Charles is rejecting all narratives.

Finally, David Littlejohn in *Black on White* briefly defines *The Messenger* as an existential text. He writes: "*The Messenger* . . . is set more in James Baldwin's New York, that big brittle loveless town of queens and queers and neurotic lonely nights. . . . What we have is a pure, calm existentially true bit of self-awareness by a very genuine, very sad, very lonely human being. It is a small book . . . but the author's sad honesty is touching and rare" (149). But Littlejohn does not develop an existential reading of *The Messenger*.

Wright's *The Messenger* is an existential novel. But its reviewers and critics, as I have indicated, never fully explain and understand the existential aspect of Charles Stevenson and the novel. The book has been criticized repeatedly by mainstream white reviewers because it fails to deal more extensively with the victimization of the African American by racial oppression. The book is used by American and African American critics to generate or reaffirm African American traditions. And in being represented almost exclusively as racial and social commentary and in reaffirming African American traditions, *The Messenger*'s existential elements get short shrift where they are mentioned at all. Charles Wright and Charles Stevenson and the project of *The Messenger* have yet to be redeemed from a circumscribed and limiting heterological site and then to be placed in another heterological site that has much greater resonance and speaks with more impact to an existential philosophy of the human condition.

Why are existential texts defined by different sets of agendas? We may look again to de Certeau for an explanation. The condition of Other-ness that he seems most preoccupied with in *Heterologies* applies to Wright's *The Messenger* and to Charles Stevenson, to an unexampled and almost oppressive degree. "The disciplinary outlook," argues Godzich, further characterizing de Certeau, "permits each discipline to function as if the problem of fragmentation did not arise since the concepts that it mobilizes [and] the operations it performs are adequate . . . to its object. . . . This may well account for the blindness of the disciplinary perspective to the problem of fragmentation: it is constitutive of that perspective" (ix).

Certainly, Charles Stevenson embodies Godzich's/de Certeau's "conception of the subject as the organizer of sense-maker of lived experience" (Godzich viii). He also represents that "sense of fragmentation" that Godzich/de Certeau argues is "widespread in our culture" (viii). But the disciplines of American and African American critical practices are blind to the problem of fragmentation of the self, particularly the modern, otherized African American self. However, the discipline of American critical practices are not completely blind to the fragmentation of the modern European and American [white] self. They acknowledge in *Nausea* and *The Moviegoer* the "sense of fragmentation" that is "widespread in our culture." In short, to be blunt and no doubt too simplistic, the spirit of existential philosophical countertradition which is "widespread in our culture" and which animates and informs *The Messenger* puts it outside all the critical and aesthetic expectations and preconceptions of its various interpreters, especially since its various interpreters can only define and represent it racially or according to racial oppression.

In representing and interpreting *The Messenger* in strictly racial terms or as the product of racial oppression, is it not possible that the reviewers and critics are asking the wrong questions about it?—demanding too much of it while overlooking and repressing its philosophical and discursive nature? In reading *The Messenger* against narratives of racism, racial oppression, and established African American traditions, critics and reviewers ignore not only other "Western" or modern dimensions to African American life and African American literature, but they also overlook the book's power. The power of *The Messenger* is Charles Wright's ability to articulate the relevant rituals of the black and white cultures and present Charles Stevenson's response to them. These cultural and social rituals/constructs include middle-class respectability (or sanctity), job, home, marriage, Christianity, Communist Front, and finding a bourgeois niche in society. Charles Stevenson's response to these cultural and social contructs speaks of the absence of the preoccupation of rational drive, individualism, curiosity, revolutionary will, self-consciousness, "searching for something," "seeking answers," and "questioning everything," or the contorted versions of the absent preoccupations that Charles encounters in Claudia, Jim, Shirley, Bruce, Peter, Al, and the middle class.

Also, in reading *The Messenger* against racism or racial oppression exclusively, its otherness, its existential philosophical countertradition, is "interpreted," to again use the words of Godzich, "as the realm of the dead, for it is ideologically inconceivable that there should exist an otherness of the same ontological status as the same, without there being immediately mounted an effort at its appropriation" (xiii). In a world, or a critical practice, where African American literature and the African American are defined in a white/black binary of signification as Other, as victim of racial oppression, and, therefore, as less and inferior, it becomes impossible to view them as an otherness of the same ontological status as the dominant white society, as different but equal. It becomes impossible to represent them according to their other class identities, subjectivities, and dimensions. "Ontology," writes Franz Fanon in *Black Skin, White Masks*, "does not permit us to understand the being of the black man. For not only must the black man be black; he must be black in relation to the white man. . . . The black [man] has no ontological resistance in the eyes of the white man" (110).

But in *The Messenger*, Charles Wright does represent the African American according to his other class identities, subjectivities, and dimensions. Wright produces an existential site/location to define African American life. He refigures and reproduces in *The Messenger* a different organization of African American life and experience that challenges and subverts the fixed image of the African American in the white/black binary of signification as being inferior, as being a victim of racial oppression. In making racism one of many obstacles Charles encounters, Wright repositions racism to expose its brutal history but not have it serve as the defining element/character of Charles's identity or being. Charles is more than the representation of a set of denigrating experiences. He is also a modern, fragmented subject of diverse and varied experiences who is asking questions about existence and being. These experiences of Charles constitute a whole series of sites of individuation, identity, social definition, and politics that cannot be comprehended by the white/black regime. In this instance, Charles Wright in *The Messenger* produces a viable model, which speaks to the fragmentation of the modern African American. In this sense, Wright makes speak and gives legitimacy to the African American as the reason of the Other, thereby making the Other a possible site of ontological resistance/insurgency in the white/black binary or regime of power/knowledge. Being existential means defining one's existence and being outside of societal conventions and rituals of society.

Finally, is Charles Stevenson a patriarch? Certainly in rejecting getting a serious job, marrying Shirley, and settling down to middle-class respectability, Charles indicates his rejection of patriarchal identity. But the fact that he does not need to embrace a superficial masculine mask, that he is caring and giving, and that he can engage sexually with both men and women shows that he is choosing an alternative lifestyle, that he is practicing a different form of manhood/masculinity/sexuality.

But, of course, Charles Wright's *The Messenger* and existentialism, as representatives of a regime of power/knowledge, create their own binaries, oppositions, and hierarchies. In *The Messenger*, Wright establishes a binary between existential/blues/jazz life, which it privileges, and middle-class, Christian, Protestant work ethic life, which it represents negatively. In this instance, we can discern how *The Messenger*, especially in borrowing from the blues, jazz, and existential traditions to reproduce itself, integrates, intermingles, and/or shows the mutual relations among different American and African American traditions and theoretical concepts of life. We can also discern how the reader understands the kind of construction of African American life that is taking place in *The Messenger*. We can see the kind of reading of African Americans that is being privileged in *The Messenger*. Finally, we can see what is left out of existentialism and out of *The Messenger*. We see what readings of African American life are not privileged. Thus, we see how all forms of representation are the product of discursive formation and, therefore, are not innocent.

When *The Messenger*, then, is seen in the context of the existential charter, when it is placed in a heterological site that speaks with more impact to an existential philosophy of the human condition, many, if not all, of its perceived weaknesses are explained. Thomas Curley is elaborately praiseful of "two excellent characterizations" in *The Messenger*, but, feels, like Richard Kluger and

Whitney Balliett—who also praise the book for its portrayal of horrifying racial scenes—that the book contains no imagination in the New York scenes. He writes: "Had Mr. Wright confined his scenes to New York, the reader might just as profitably have gone to the movies" (566). Richard Kluger writes: "*The Messenger* fails . . . because Mr. Wright gives us no reason to care about the title character or any of the others. Charles is shiftless, joyless and self-pitying" (7).

Curley and Kluger are identifying the discrepancy between what they define as the moral/sociological and the artistic schemes of the book. The New York scenes have no meaning in a racial/sociological interpretation of the text. They tell us nothing about racism or racial progress. They tell us nothing about the white/black encounter, which has been defined as the cornerstone of race relations in the United States. But this discrepancy does not exist once we understand that Charles's problem is not one of race but one of being, that his morality is outside, other than, a programmatic morality of racial victimization. Once we understand that Wright's depiction of the absurdity of existence is grounded in reality and artistically a metaphorical model of man's cosmological environment ("alone in a godless universe . . . suffering anguish and despair in his loneliness"), we can most fully understand Charles and the absurd scenes in New York City.

In addition, if we define/represent *The Messenger* as an existential text, we can explain the criticism leveled at its episodic-journal-format structure by Katherine Jackson and Thomas Curley, and the text, to use the words of Thomas Curley, just might "make it" as an existential novel. Like Henry Miller's *Tropic of Cancer* and Sartre's *Nausea,* and in the existential pattern, the text is composed of a series of scenes designed to reveal the absurd aspects of life in the crowded city. As with Roquentin in *Nausea,* these scenes are presented as journal entries, as if Charles is recording the incidents as they actually happen. Each entry builds until there is some kind of revelation on the part of the protagonist. And, again, like Sartre in *Nausea,* Wright's main purpose in *The Messenger* is not to weave about Charles a realistic narrative, but rather to explore the absolute revulsion he experiences as he confronts the world's absurdity.

Further, if we take into consideration the existential variants of free will and moral validation, we may understand that Wright's critique and exposure of all "kicks," or metanarratives, including racial ones, become his way of rendering them "false trials." Charles Stevenson has found his redemption by coming to the realization that crazy kicks do not "still the fears, confusion and the pain of being alive." Whether his realization is misguided, repulsive, harmful to the cause of the African American liberation to Black survival or Black unity or to whites's need to define him as a victim or a devalued Other, is irrelevant to an existential reading of *The Messenger.* An existential reading will interpret all of these causes and movements as crazy kicks or false trials, designed to prevent (the African American) man from admitting that life is absurd, that it is full of pain and suffering and confusion, that he must take responsibility for his own existence, and that there is no better tomorrow. Like Sartre and Camus, Charles

Wright understands that the "authentic" existential hero, or antihero, must be presented in a state of unconditional sin, a sin with no socially or culturally or politically mitigating circumstances. It is to Wright's credit as artist and thinker that he chooses to ground Charles in circumstances that would lead him so convincingly to a state of Otherness.

Until the existential nature of Charles Stevenson is understood, until his character is solved in terms I believe Wright intended, and until we understand how codified American and African American critical practices, as regimes of power/knowledge, repress and misrepresent Charles Stevenson and the project of *The Messenger*, along with other existential texts by African Americans—such as Ralph Ellison's *Invisible Man* (1952), Richard Wright's *The Outsider* and *Native Son*, Cyrus Colter's *The Beach Umbrella* (1970) and *Hippodrome* (1973), John Edgar Wideman's *A Glance Away* (1967) and *Hurry Home* (1970), Henry Van Dyke's *Blood of Strawberries* (1968), William Demby's *Beetlecreek* (1967), Robert Boles's *The People One Knows* (1964) and *Curling* (1968), and Bill Gunn's *All the Rest Have Died* (1964)—*The Messenger* will continue to be, if not misunderstood or repressed, at least not fully celebrated for all that it offers. And until American, African American, and existential critics acknowledge that within African America there is a "limited population" under some "limited set of conditions" who understands and identifies experientally and cognitively with existentialism, *The Messenger* and the other existential texts written by African Americans will never have contingent value. Until this acknowledgment or acceptance happens or is forced to happen, *The Messenger* will never have cultural capital and, therefore, will remain out of print.

CHAPTER SEVEN

THE BLUES IDIOM LIFESTYLE, COUNTER-HEGEMONY, AND CLARENCE MAJOR'S *DIRTY BIRD BLUES*

The blues idiom as an expressive musical form and as a way of life has been a part of African American life since the times of slavery. It represents a definition of life that is different from that of mainstream, middle-class, Christian American life. In this polycentric representation of African American literature, it becomes another vantage point to view the African American. Thus, it functions counter-hegemonically within society, defining the African American (male) outside the features, characteristics, and definitions of the white/black binary that dominates social reality in the United States. Clarence Major's *Dirty Bird Blues* embodies this counter-hegemonically blues tradition.

Most experts agree that the blues as a musical form probably began to take shape in the mid to late nineteenth century after emancipation, Reconstruction, and segregation. But the spirit and mood of the blues, argues James H. Cone in *The Spirituals and the Blues,* have roots stretching back to slavery (109). "The blues was conceived," writes LeRoi Jones in *Blues People,* "by freedmen and ex-slaves—if not as a result of a personal or intellectual experience, at least as an emotional confirmation of, and reaction to, the way in which most Negroes were still forced to exist in the United States" (142). The blues invites African Americans to embrace the reality and truth of black life. It expresses the "laments of [subaltern] African Americans over hard luck, careless or unrequited love, broken family life, or general disappointment and dissatisfaction with a cold and trouble-filled world" (Cone 110). The blues artist, according to Daphne Harrison in *Black Pearls,* speaks directly of and to the people who have suffered pain, and assures them that they are not alone, that someone understands (6).

147

In addition, the blues is philosophically secular. From a theological perspective, the blues is closely related to the "slave seculars," music that was nonreligious, occasionally antireligious, and was often called "devil songs" by Christians. Blues people/subaltern African Americans—the field slave, the convict, the migrant, the roustabout, the pimp, the prostitute, the working and lower working class, and the urban or rural illiterate outsider—were almost completely beyond the pale of Christianity. Given the choice between whether they should accept with meekness the cross they must bear in this world and join the church with the promise of "Eternal Peace in the Promised Land" or whether they should attempt to meet the present world on their own terms, blues people chose the latter. They sought freedom and meaning through the blues. "As the poetic voice of a people distinctively victimized by the whole gamut of the repressive forces of bourgeois/Christian civilization (economic exploitation, political disenfranchisement, racism, etc.)," argues Paul Garon in *Blues and the Poetic Spirit,* "the blues long ago found itself in the service of human emancipation by virtue of the particular manner in which it deals with such repression" (2).

In the twentieth century, the blues, according to Paul Oliver in *The Meaning of the Blues,* continued to thrive during the migratory movements and social advancements of millions of people (24). It followed the migration of African Americans from rural to urban centers and was part of the development of African American urban communities at the turn of the century in Atlanta, New Orleans, Birmingham, Cleveland, Chicago, Detriot, and New York City. As "boogie woogie," the blues found a home in the Chicago of the 1920s, and by the 1930s the urban blues of Harlem and the Chicago south side had emerged.

The blues as a musical form, portraying a blues way of life, was popularized from the 1920s through the 1950s by such great blues musicians as Mamie Smith, Ma Rainey, Robert Johnson, Bessie Smith, Blind Lemon Jefferson, Son House, Sonny Boy Williamson, Big Bill Broonzy, Howlin' Wolf, Muddy Waters, Big Mama Thornton, and others. In these blues were to be found the major catastrophes, both personal and national, the triumphs, and the miseries that were shared by all, yet remained private to one. In the blues were reflected the family disputes, the upheavals, dislocation, and alienation caused by poverty and migration, as well as the violence and bitterness, the tears and the happiness. In the blues, argues Oliver, an unsettled, unwanted people during periods of social unrest and dislocation "found the security, the unity and the strength that [they] so desperately desired" (32).

For blues people/subaltern African Americans, the blues is counter-hegemonic. It resists and challenges a hegemonic, middle-class, Christian definition of life. In *Marxism and Literature,* Raymond Williams defines a "lived hegemony" as:

> always a process. . . . It is a realized complex of experiences, relationships, and
> activities, with specific and changing pressures and limits. In practice, that is,
> hegemony can never be singular. . . . [I]t does not just passively exist as a form

of dominance. It has continually to be renewed, recreated, defended, and modified. It is also continually resisted, limited, altered, challenged by pressures not at all its own. (112)

The reality of any hegemony is that, while by definition it is always dominant, it is never either total or exclusive. Forms of alternative cultures exist as significant elements in the society and become counter-hegemonic. They resist, limit, and modify the hegemonic culture. The blues, which is an alternative culture within American and African American societies, is counter-hegemonic because it affirms blues people's essential worth, even as the dominant, Christian, middle-class American society defines them as devalued Other. The blues tells us about individuals who refuse to accept society's negative representation of them. These individuals affirm through blues music that they are human beings/subjects.

The blues idiom as a lifestyle, as an extension of a blues philosophy, and as a dramatic enactment of a blues definition of the human condition, entered African American literature as early as the mid-nineteenth century. We discern traces of this blues definition of the human condition in the margins of many "canonical" African American texts such as Frederick Douglass's *Narrative*, Paul Laurence Dunbar's *The Sport of the Gods*, Nella Larsen's *Quicksand*, Langston Hughes's *Not Without Laughter*, Rudolph Fisher's *The Walls of Jericho*, Zora Neale Hurston's *Their Eyes Were Watching God*, Ann Petry's *The Street*, Ralph Ellison's *Invisible Man*, Toni Morrison's *Sula*, and Bonnie Greer's *hanging by her teeth*. But the blues as a way of life moves from the margin to the center in Wallace Thurman's *The Blacker the Berry*, George Wylie Henderson's *Jule*, Langston Hughes's *The Weary Blues* and *Fine Clothes to the Jew*, James Baldwin's "Sonny's Blues" in *Dark Symphony*, Evan Hunter's *Street of Gold* and *Second Ending*, John Clellon Holmes's *The Horn*, William Melvin Kelley's *A Drop of Patience*, James Alan McPherson's "Papa Doc" in *Hue and Cry*, LeRoi Jones's "Going Down Slow" in *Tales*, Herbert Simmons's *Man Walking on Eggshells*, John A. Williams's *Night Song*, Kristin Hunter's *God Bless the Child*, and Jane Phillips's *Mojo Hand*. More recently, blues-centered narratives include Gayl Jones's *Corregidora*; James Edgar Wideman's *Sent for You Yesterday* and "The Song of Reba Love Jackson" in *Damballah*; Albert Murray's *Train Whistle Guitar*, *The Spyglass Tree*, and *The Seven League Boots*; Xam Cartier's *Muse-Echo Blues*; John McCluskey's *Look What They Done to My Song*; Toni Cade Bambara's "Blues Ain't No Mockin' Bird" in *Gorilla, My Love*, and "Witchbird" in *The Sea Birds are Still Alive*; Michael Ondaatje's *Coming Through Slaughter*; Arthur Flowers's *De Mojo Blues* and *Another Good Loving Blues*; August Wilson's *Seven Guitars*; Bart Schneider's *Blue Bossa*; Walter Mosley's *R L's Dream*; Rafi Zabor's *The Bear Comes Home*; and Clarence Major's *Dirty Bird Blues*. This blues tradition in American/African American literaure is basically ignored and repressed by the canon of African American literature.

I want to do a reading of Clarence Major's *Dirty Bird Blues*, showing how it provides a dramatic enactment of a blues definition of the human condition, examining how it disrupts the white/black binary of signification that defines whites as normative and superior and represents blacks as victim, as devalued Other, or as inferior. The blues knows that to be represented as a victim of racial oppression is to be defined exclusively and negatively by someone else's discourse. Rather, the blues represents the African American as a blues figure who is affirmative, existential, individual, vibrant, and different.

Dirty Bird Blues is the story of Manfred Banks, the text's protagonist, and his struggle to become a successful blues man, especially as he negotiates the responsibility of providing for his wife Cleo and his daughter Katrina. Initially, Manfred wanders from Atlanta to New Orleans to Chicago and finally to Omaha, Nebraska, looking for a place where he can play his blues. Manfred, who comes from the African American subaltern, meets up with the middle-class, Christian Cleo in Chicago and marries her. But the marriage is in trouble because, in addition to his "general disappointment and dissatisfaction with a cold and trouble-filled world" (Cone 110), his devotion to his music and alcohol cause him to neglect his responsibilities to his family. Therefore, Cleo leaves him for another man, exacerbating his blues. He hopes to began anew in Omaha, where Cleo and Katrina later join him. *Dirty Bird Blues* concerns the working through of Manfred's two loves. Ultimately, *Dirty Bird Blues* is about Manfred's ability to face and hug the darkness within himself, something he has been pushing away and denying all his life.

At the end of *Dirty Bird Blues*, after confronting successfully the complexities inherent in the human condition, Manfred has a revelation and is able finally to maintain "equilibrium despite precarious circumstances" (Murray, *Stomping* 251). He becomes the embodiment of a blues definition of life. This transformation occurs after Manfred reaches a moment in his life in which he has abandoned the "slave" (job); lost his best friend Solly, who is unable to control his passion for women and wine, becomes a failed blues man; and given up Old Crow, which he has used to cope with and escape from the troubles of life. Walking up Twenty-fourth Street in Omaha, he smiles to himself and thinks:

> Life was funny. It was hard to imagine not being friends with Solly any longer. And yet here he was, friendless, sober, west of the wide Missouri, jobless, saxophoneless, but strangely with a lot still to feel good about. If he only could. Got Cleo. She ain't gone nowhere. Got things going nice at the Palace. No craving. Ain't raving. Doing mo than hanging on. Any day now something. Don't know what but something could give. Time. Just gots to take yo time. Own sweet time. He could hear the rhythm of his footfalls, a music: slap do blap, slap do blap, slap do blap, slap do blap. Time. All it takes is time. Something could give. Something big. Something real. Things be changing all the time. Never can tell what gon come round the corner and step on yo toes, or kiss you between the eyes, shake yo hand, and lead you on. (276)

Manfred has confronted, acknowledged, and contended with what Murray in *Omni-Americans* calls "the infernal absurdities and ever-impending frustration inherent in the nature of all existence by playing with the possibilities that are also there" (89–90). He has faced and hugged the darkness within himself and persevered in life's troubles. Therefore, he is prepared to live a self-directed life, which is a major tenet of the blues philosophy. He has become a man who expects the best but is always prepared, at least emotionally, for the worst.

But more important, at the end of the text and after his revelation, Manfred seems open and able and willing to swing. "Improvisation is the ultimate human . . . endowment . . . even as flexibility or the ability to swing (or to perform with grace under pressure) is the key to that unique competence which generates the self-reliance and thus the charisma of the hero" (Murray, *Hero* 107). Having reached this functional equilibrium, Manfred is now able to swing life, to be at home with his sometimes tolerable but never quite certain condition of not being at home in the world. Also, he can now regard his obstacles and frustrations as well as his achievements in terms of adventure and romance.

But the process of reaching this "equilibrium despite precarious circumstances" and of "achieving elegance in the very process of coping with the rudiments of subsistence" (Murray, *Stomping* 251) is what forms the stories of *Dirty Bird Blues*. If a blues life means a life fraught with troubles, which are inherent in the human condition, Manfred Banks has always lived a blues life. But he has not always accepted a blues life, which includes accepting all the facts of life. He encounters his first blues experience and has the "blues for the first time" in Atlanta when he is four or five years old, and his uncle Aloysius, his aunt Effie, their two daughters, and a son come to visit. Uncle Aloysius hurts Manfred's feelings by telling Quincy, Manfred's father, that "that young'en [Manfred] that is justa about the ugliest, blackest little monkey I ever seed" (245). Manfred does not fully understand what his uncle has said, but he detects from his mother's and his father's reaction that his uncle has said "something mean about him. So he start[s] crying" (245). Supposedly consoling him but really compounding his hurt, aunt Effie picks him up and calls him "a nice looking boy" as she laughs sarcastically. Manfred wiggles and struggles to get out of his aunt's arms. When he succeeds, "wanting to hide his shame and pain," he runs "out of the house, and down the back steps, and [hides] himself under the back porch, sobbing and holding his stomach, tears dropping in the dust at his naked feet" (245–46). Manfred is hurt because adults know—they are authority figures—and two have told him that he is "ugly and black" (246).

Later in his youth, no one, especially his father, thought that Manfred would "mount to nothing." His father "laid into [his] ass all the time. Got so everybody down on [him], teachers, the other kids" (208). For most of his life, nobody thinks anything of him; therefore, Manfred decides to think nothing of himself: "I cut up a lot, beat up other kids, threw erasers at the teacher when his back was turnt. . . . Guess I bought they picture of me. And that's why I got into music, you know. I been trying to get myself out of being like that, the way they made me be" (208–09). Thus, his early life was a series of disappointments and dissatisfactions. He bought a negative image of himself and had to spend some of his life "trying to get [him]self out of being like that." Manfred's struggle is one of finding the strength to survive, to face the darkness within, to endure, and to maintain his self-worth and self-respect in the midst of a trouble-filled world.

This blues attitude of affirming the self, of constructing one's identity so that one is not defined as a victim or devalued Other, is partially shaped for Manfred by his aunt Ida, who ran an elevator in a big building up on Piedmont Street in Atlanta. He lives with her and uncle Sam between the ages of ten and twelve, a period when he and his father did not get along. Aunt Ida is the first person to tell him that she loves him, and she teaches Manfred to love and respect himself and not to allow anyone to disparage him. She also talks "straight with him about sex" and tells him "to be good to his wife" (22). When Manfred encounters a bully at school, he beats him up. Later, aunt Ida advises him, that "when somebody mistreat you, Man, you got a right to be sad. Sing about it, boy. It's like turning the other cheek. That's the Lord's way. But you disnounce violence. You hear me?" (19). Accepting life as possessing sadness is one of the common tenets of the blues, and singing about that sadness is the essence of blues music. But affirming one's self is also a part of the blues idiom.

Manfred's blues education continues into his teenage years. Unable to get along with his father ("Daddy wasn't so bad. Man just didn't want anybody always telling him what to do" [62]), Manfred leaves home at fifteen for the streets of Atlanta and later New Orleans, where he is indoctrinated/socialized into the blues music and the "sporting life." Decatur and Butler were streets in Atlanta where the blues:

> could live and be appreciated. . . . He hung out [on Decatur and Peidmont], picking up the sounds, shooting craps, playing the numbers with the older boys in the barbershop, the shoeshine parlor. Fellow in the shoeshine parlor could make his rag talk like a musical instrument . . . [these were places] where everybody come out in their best, strutting and jiving when they got some money in their pockets. (58)

Manfred procures his own place in Madam Gazella Bellamy's rooming house, a kind of gambling house on Butler Street. In her house, he is further indoctrinated/socialized into the values and ways of life on the streets. He becomes sexually active. He begins to sing the blues. But he cannot find work singing the blues in Atlanta. Disappointed and dissatisfied, he leaves Atlanta for New Orleans because everyone tells him New Orleans is where he can get work singing.

But New Orleans turns out to be as disappointing and dissatisfying as Atlanta in terms of finding employment. In New Orleans, Manfred continues to live the "sporting life" and becomes a hobo. He is hungry during most of his stay there, standing in soup lines and going to charity stations for food. He sleeps on the streets or in flophouses, "playing his harmonica in the French Quarter for handouts" (63). His father dies while he is in New Orleans, and his family cannot get in touch with him. Finally, because everyone keeps saying "Chicago is where it happening. . . . N' Orleans [is] a thing of the past" (37), he moves to Chicago.

In witnessing Manfred's journey from Atlanta to New Orleans to Chicago, the reader can discern the dislocation, disappointment, dissatisfaction, and alienation caused by poverty and migration. But the wandering challenges Manfred. It tests his endurance. It prepares him to encounter and overcome obstacles, such as surviving hunger, finding shelter, and finding his way on the streets, thereby bringing out the best in him. Surviving and overcoming the obstacles, according to Murray in *The Hero and the Blues*, "make it possible for him to make something of himself" (38).

It is in Chicago that Manfred attempts to "make something of himself," to use the blues to make himself somebody, to ferret out a blues identity or blues life in the midst of joy, frustration, and personal troubles. Discovering Solly playing the guitar in the park, he finds a friend, a soul mate. The two become fast friends. Also in Chicago, during the summer of 1947, Manfred meets Cleo, who is twenty years old, strong willed, and independent. Cleo grew up in New Orleans in and about her parents' restaurant, a popular Creole and soul food place called "Cafe LeRoi." Cleo has a "calm at the center of her face, even when she [is] full of fire. A calm-like inside her. No matter how upset or mad she got, it seemed to be always there. That was one of the things about this woman that attracted [Manfred] in the first place" (43). They are married three months later, and Katrina, their daughter, is born in September of the following year.

What is established for Manfred in Chicago is a tension between his desire to be free to play his blues and the obligations he has to his wife and family. In a blues world, where people possess little that is their own, human relationships are placed at a high premium. The love between a man and a woman becomes immediate and real. Manfred lives in this kind of world. At first, Manfred and Cleo have "some happy times" together. They have a great sex life. When they go to the Loop, he feels a little out of place among white people, but he is happy being with Cleo. Both of them like the Tivoli. They also "went to the Regal or the Met on Forty-seventh. First movie they saw together that summer was *The Best Years of Our Lives*. Double feature with *Song of the South*" (42). And when they are not going to movies, they are walking in Jackson Park. During this time, Manfred is working at Chicago Steel and playing the blues at "clubs on Sixty Third [Street] mostly, three of them right along the strip" (43). But hard times come during the winter of 1948. People everywhere "were bitching about the economy and because things were so bad President Truman just barely got enough votes to be reelected" (43). The hard times put pressure on their relationship, and the birth of Katrina interferes with "that great-God-Almighty feeling of peace and the pleasure" Manfred once had with Cleo (47).

Manfred and Cleo are quite different, and the difference becomes a source of tension. They come from different classes and different backgrounds. Cleo grew up happy in the security of her family in New Orleans. She is Christian, middle class, and romantic. She believes in the Protestant work ethic, and after they were married, "she kept right on going to that screaming-and-shouting church" (13). She also "wanted to just stay home and read these thrilling romance stories about heartbreaking love and that kind of carrying on" (42). She listens to Johnny Mathis "whining one of them ballads" and to Brenda Lee "singing one of them light fluffy things that made her famous" (43). Manfred, who comes from the African American subaltern, a nontraditional family, and an oral tradition, never did have any patience for reading. He does not believe in the Protestant work ethic. He never intends to give his life to a "slave" (job). His "favorite type of entertainment was to have a drink in his hand in a bar with a lot a happy people and good music. That was heaven for him next to making the music himself. But Cleo didn't care for bars and the people in them" (42).

When *Dirty Bird Blues* opens, Manfred, in Chicago, is in a blues funk because, after a dispute, his wife has left him for another man. He finds himself on Christmas eve "feeling so goddamned sick and drunk and mad at Cleo" (2). Cleo has left Manfred because he has failed in his family responsibilities: he has not provided the necessities such as food for the family and diapers for the baby. Now Manfred clearly has the blues. The night Cleo left, he "sat up all night, . . . on [his] bed and sang to himself, humming and singing, blew a little harmonica" (46). He is hurt and disappointed, and he feels the confusion and isolation of human love. He has the lament, the grief, and the disillusionment that are endemic to the blues: "You can have the Chicago Monkey Man Blues and still be all right. You can be down and out like a yellow dog at the end of the Yazoo Mississippi line and still feel like shouting, Jelly, jelly, mama, roll me some of yo good biscuits, let me hoe in yo cabbage patch. Took a lot to get a good man down" (2).

When he goes to Reverend Bedford's apartment for Cleo, Bedford shoots him. When Manfred goes to the hospital, the nurse "look[s] at him like he [is] a door or a wall. Nobody knows the shit [he] done seen" (5). After he is treated at the hospital for gunshot wounds and released, Manfred is manhandled by two African American policemen, Lizard and Bullfrog, who have reputations for beating other African Americans. Manfred is "sick, not from the buckshots, but from the pain of the punching, from tiredness and hunger, from no sleep, and the whiskey [is] wearing off and he [has] a bad headache and a raw stomach. He [is] fit to die" (10). Back at home, playing the sax, he feels "alive for the first time since way back there before he jumped from the ground in the alley, grabbing that fire escape, lifting himself up, feeling nothing but this siren in his head" (16). With his sax, he plays a little number he "wrote by himself . . . just a little sad sweet thing he liked to play when he was kind of down like this and needed a liftup, a thing with no name, but with words he heard in his head" (17). Playing the blues does not allow Manfred to deny "the existence of the ugly dimensions" of his life, but to encounter the "full, sharp, and inescapable awareness of them" (Murray, *Omni-Americans* 88). It allows him to renew himself for living and being.

Upon further reflection, Manfred realizes that his life is in an upheaval because he has not been able to establish a balance between his two loves and one need: his wife/family, his music, and alcohol. Devoting too much attention to his music, he failed to notice the signs that his wife was unhappy. Before Cleo left him, Manfred remembers her "going to church more and more" (14). But for Manfred, Cleo's going to church "gave him more time by himself. Didn't have to hear her nagging him about drinking. Could practice his singing, play his harmonica, or fool around with the sax. Sit in the chair and blow. Or go out to Jackson Park and blow to the sky. Blow up a breeze. Walk around and blow" (14). He now asks "Why he hadn't seen the signs" (13). Cleo wanted him to put her and the baby "at least on a level with [his] music" and to lay off the bottle; she "never thought he had any kind of right to just do his music and not work a slave [job] for a living" (27). But Manfred thinks he needs drinking for his music. It makes him "mellow. It [is] inspiritualration for [his] music" (45).

Now, separated from his wife and unable to find work singing the blues in Chicago, Manfred wants to go to Omaha "where [he] can be a big fish in a small pond" (37). He feels if he stays in Chicago there is "no telling when [he] might go off again and head over there [to the Reverend Bedford's house]" (28). He also realizes that he has many reasons to leave Chicago: "You know, it hit me: I coulda lost my life last night" (37). But he is reluctant to leave his wife and child. After two months of separation, Cleo comes to visit, and again they discuss the relationship, his drinking, and his putting his music first every time. Cleo encourages his move to Omaha, stating that "it might be just what you need right now. A different city. A smaller town might be the right place" (47)."

The Omaha that Manfred finds is a typical, pre–civil rights, midwestern American town of the early 1950s. It has social, residential, and occupational segregation. Most of the blacks in Omaha came "out on the trains, working as porters and in the sleeping cars back in the 1890s" (55). In the 1950s, blacks are still being lynched by white mobs in Nebraska, and young black males are routinely stopped by the police. Driving in the downtown area of Omaha, blacks are watched "something terrible" (53). Twenty-fourth Street is the African American community's main thoroughfare. In this non–middle-class community, reason and rationality have not penetrated completely all of the social spaces; it is a place where "everything happens." Black-owned businesses line Twenty-fourth Street, and the community has two black newspapers, the *Messenger* and the *Monitor*. Blacks live in the "rows and rows of square dull-looking wooden houses, poor shotgun houses, the kind he'd seen in Atlanta's black section" (55)," another blues community. Omaha has:

> the same kind of easygoing feeling Atlanta had. . . . Boys hanging out front at the local poolroom down the street. Jivers sitting on the curb talking shit. Fat daddies cruising by in their big new Cadillacs and Lincolns. Secondhand stores, greasy spoons. If my folks ain't bragging they complaining. It's the way of the world. You hear babble in the rabble. Vendor on the corner, head sticking out of his booth, calling, "World-Herald!" Man thought, This just might be my kinda place. A place where the blues could live and be appreciated, a place where his own life might become a song. (57)

Although Manfred tells himself that deep down he hopes Cleo will "come out so they could start over again," simultaneously he also tells himself, in a typical blues fashion, that he has "to keep on keeping on right now, not live in the past" (52). He comes to Omaha thinking about his music first with a job on the side. But later, after he settles in with his sister Debbie, he realizes that "since leaving Chicago he hadn't stopped thinking about, brooding on, his wife" (62). To get Cleo to Omaha, Manfred is willing reluctantly to consider putting a job first with his music on the side.

On his first night in Omaha, he accompanies Beverly, a friend of Debbie's, out on the town where he is introduced to blues in Omaha. She takes him to the Palace, which immediately puts him in his blues element. When Beverly and Jorena, the owner of the Palace, convince him to sit in with Greg Wakely and his band, Manfred comes home to the blues in Omaha:

> The audience went wild as he walked over, taking his third glass of whiskey with him, and hopped up on stage. He was feeling damned good, suddenly popping his fingers along the way, dancing a little bit too. . . . People were on the floor cutting up. Everybody having a good time, a rocking good time. . . . Now, this the way to live. . . . He had a feeling right then the rest of the night was going to be all right. If he had trouble in mind, it was going to sleep for a while. He was riding high, feeling mellow, in spirit with good-time people. He was feeling so good he could have turned himself into a little red rooster or a big black kingsnake. He was feeling that good. High and mighty. Felt so good just to be breaking new ground. Like sudden Freedom. . . . In other words, he felt about as good as liquor could make a poor miserable young man feel on a winter night in a new town. (71–73)

But in Omaha, despite finding his blues element, Manfred is still unable to reach Murray's "equilibrium despite precarious circumstances" that is required to live a blues life. First, he is still lonely. The love of his life is still in Chicago. Second, despite the fact that he wants to find a job singing the blues full time, he ends up working as a janitor at Lomax Steel, where again he has a boss (another father) telling him what to do. However, Jorena does offer him a weekend job singing the blues at the Palace. Third, he is afraid of the darkness within him and so still needs his whiskey to help him deal with life's trials and tribulations, the horrors of human existence, its ugliness and meanness. Omaha, thus, becomes a real test for Manfred. Does he have, in Ellison's words, the "ability to deal with chaos" (257)? Can he confront and acknowledge life in all its dimensions and absurdities? Can he face and hug the darkness within himself? Can he achieve what Murray calls "elegance in the very process of coping with the rudiments of subsistence"? Can he become the blues song described by Ortiz Walton, "where both [his] joys and pains are synthesized and resolved into an emotional-spiritual unity that helps make possible life's continuance" (29)?

With his two jobs, Manfred sets about solving part of his problem: he works on getting Cleo to come to Omaha. And when Cleo arrives, Manfred thinks that the meaning of life has revealed itself to him and he will not have the blues again: "That night Man sat out on the front porch with his harmonica. Cleo beside him. The baby upstairs sleeping. He felt devilishly happy, happy as a hoodoo doctor in a slip-in, joyful as an all-night kicker in a dance joint" (99). In this moment of ecstasy, he can only see "in the beginning of their new life" (99), having forgotten the tension that existed between his devotion to Cleo and Katrina and his love for his music. The tension has something to say about the nature of the blues.

The blues is highly personal in nature. "The blues," states Garon, "is indeed a self-centered music, highly personalized, wherein the effects of everyday life are recounted in terms of the singers' reactions" (9–10). For Sippi Wallace, a blues singer and songwriter, the blues is a part of her total being and a source of solace: "I sing the blues to comfort me on. . . . Most all my [blues] is about myself" (qtd. in Harrison 6). Manfred writes most of his blues songs, and they are the stories of what has happened to him. For example, when the nurse who is "wrapping bandages around his chest" asks him where he is going, Manfred sings "the natural story of what happened to him" (6). When he hits the numbers and wins, he writes "Policy Number Blues" (26). When Solly introduces Manfred to his mistress Estelle, Manfred looks at her and begins "writing himself a song about her" (30). When he has to tell Beverly that Cleo is coming to Omaha and, therefore, he cannot see her anymore, he starts "doing what he did lots of time, composing in his head. Hearing the beat and the words to the beat, that offbeat" (84).

When Manfred sings the blues, he is free and happy. "The sense of well-being that always goes with swinging blues is generated," argues Murray, "not by obscuring or denying the existence of the ugly dimensions of human nature, circumstances, and conduct, but rather through the full, sharp and inescapable awareness of them" (Murray, *Omni-Americans* 88–89). "Singing was his way of talking out [this] furious, crazy thing in him that made him glide, leap, holler, and scream as if over treetops without even moving" (13). Manfred uses the harmonica or the saxophone to make himself fully aware of his feelings and troubles. The sax is saying what he is thinking, and in the process of blowing or riffing on his troubles, he transcends them. What the song says basically is "that he's not going to let his troubles kill him. He is not going to let them take [him] down to that ice cold lake" (24). Singing the blues puts Manfred in a state of mind that affirms his self-worth and sustains his humanity.

And when Manfred sings the blues at the Palace, he assists others in working through their trials and tribulations, their pain and suffering and joy; he assists them in affirming their own humanity. Studying the crowd when he and Solly perform the first time at the Palace, Manfred sees a:

> hard-drinking Friday night crowd and they were loud, tired, and blue, but somehow they seemed to hear and appreciate what was happening on the stage. When he finished, again there was loud clapping and shouting and

whistling and foot stomping. By now folks were doing the Hully Gully, talking all at the same time, drinking fast, spilling liquor, giggling, strutting, sassing and jiving, wooh-wee-ing, waving dime notes, tapping their daisy-beaters and spoons, their fingers, the flat palms of their hands on tabletops. (153)

When Manfred sings before an audience at the Palace, his singing "allows people a certain distance from their immediate trouble and allows them to see and feel it artistically, thereby offering them a certain liberating catharsis" (Cone 125). The blues aesthetic disguise, or artistic form, which maintains the distance necessary for mastery, operates in such a way that painful emotions can be recalled and mastered when listening. On the other hand, the listener gains "pleasure by identifying with an artist who is singing" about the pleasure of both the unpleasant and the happy things in life. The unpleasant in art is experienced as pleasurable because the aesthetic illusion, or the blues idiom, acts as a protective device (Garon 16–17). Thus, through listening and identifying, the members of the audience are able to rid themselves of tension and unhappiness. "The Blues idiom dance music," argues Murray in *The Hero and the Blues*, "challenges and affirms [the listener's] personal equilibrium, sustains his humanity, and enables him to maintain his highest aspirations in spite of the fact that human existence is so often mostly a lowdown dirty shame" (37).

In addition to listening to and playing the blues, Manfred has a storehouse of folklore and wisdom, established by the elders, that he can call on for blues guidance. When Louis Irving at Lomax asks him, "how's [your] pecker hanging," Manfred plays the dozens and replies: "Ask your mama." When he is challenged by Louis and a fight between the two becomes a possibility, Manfred remembers the blues wisdom of his mother: "Glad he hadn't exploded and gone up against the peckerwood. Remembered his mama's words: When you goes down the street, try to be nice and neat, watch yo step long the way, and be careful what you say" (87). Later, in an argument with Cleo about her wanting to get a job, Manfred reminds Cleo that he "ain't likes other mens. If I was I be dead by now," then quotes an old folk saying to reinforce his position: "Like the old folks used to say, heap of good cotton stalks gets chopped down from just being mongst the weeds. I stay way from weeds" (118). When he thinks about getting old and ponders how to deal with it, he turns again to the elders for knowledge and guidance: "like the great old blues singers always say, everybody got to come to this party and do the jitterbug. And he remembered what old folks used to say: You gots to walk that lonesome valley by yoself" (133). Finally, in his altercation with Eliot about picking up scrap metal, he becomes "pissed. Then suddenly he felt released from anger, if only for a moment, because he knew what was coming—if not today, soon. . . . And he knew, from what old folks used to say, a tin plate don't mind dropping on the floor" (164). For the up-and-coming blues man, knowledge and wisdom do not come from books or university education. They come from the wisdom distilled from the African American historical experience, the myths and folklore produced by that collective history. Finally, the folklore, like the music, reformulates and reinforces the blues life in the text.

Just as Manfred's music and the folk wisdom from the ancestors generate the dominant blues theme in *Dirty Bird Blues*, the music heard on the jukeboxes in the taverns and palaces and on the car radios also reformulates and reinforces the text's blues idiom. After he is shot by Reverend Bedford and is headed for the emergency room at Booker T. Washington Memorial, Manfred hits Sixty-third Street, where he "heard the jukebox music coming from the Red Tiger and Ducky Wucky's, one stomping a Trixie Smith-type freight train beat, the other laying into a cool daddy jazz sound. Jazz was all right but he couldn't feel it like he could him some blues" (3). On his first visit to Miss Etta's Tavern, Miss Etta calls out to Niggerdemos to put some quarters in the jukebox and "play something good, something lowdown and lawless. . . . Niggerdemos dropped some quarters in the jukebox. The first song to come up was somebody singing Bessie Smith's *Careless Love Blues*. Ah, shit he [Manfred] thought. One of his favorites" (132, 134). Finally, after he is fired from Lomax, Manfred sits at the bar in the Palace "with a double shot of Old Crow on the rocks . . . listening to Billie Holiday singing *Good Morning Heartache*" (180). These blues songs are indices or messages that function to give order, coherence, meaning, and understanding to Manfred's blues life as he tries to survive amid the "infernal absurdities . . . inherent in the nature of all existence" (Murray, *Omni-Americans* 89–90).

As a blues man who fits neither into the conventions of the white/black binary that defines reality for him as victim nor into the normative, middle-class conventions and values of the upper half of the binary that would make him the Same, Manfred is still defined as Other by both blacks and whites. The cops in Chicago call him "one of them backwoodsy niggers fresh outta the sticks" (10). Being a blues man "made him look like a bad nigger to white folks. He knew that. Mercy, mercy. And it made colored folks worry about him or laugh at him. Double Mercy. It was why his wife left him" (13). But Manfred does not allow others to define him. He defines himself and his self-worth according to the blues tradition, which is challenging and subversive, not only to the stereotype of the African American as a pathological victim but also to the middle-class, American Christian norm.

He defines himself as different from other men. He is a person with feelings: "[He] got a powerful feeling to be more than just a working man, slaving way his life. [He] gots something fine in [him]" (45). We have in Manfred a man who rejects the dominant society's language and image and who constitutes himself in a language and a music form that is excluded by the dominant society. He is making the self. Manfred has traveled extensively, has lived on the streets of Atlanta and New Orleans, has been a hobo, has suffered and endured pain, has been shot and beaten up by the police, has enjoyed a wonderful musical friendship with Solly, has experienced immense love with Cleo, and has lived the "sporting life." Although these varied experiences are sanctioned neither by middle-class blacks nor by the dominant society, they make Manfred an interesting person. They make him a potential blues person.

But being a blues man means you love yourself and, therefore, do not allow anyone to disrespect or belittle you. Manfred is offended when he goes to visit Beverly and her visiting father inquires who is at the door and she says, "Nobody." Even after Beverly has gone to Los Angeles and returned, Manfred still cannot forget that she acted "like he was nobody" (106). Earlier, his feelings are hurt when he learns that Shawn, Cleo's sister, thinks Cleo picked "up some common nigger in the park" when she met him (105). The blues man has to love self before he can love anyone else.

Also, he does not establish a social hierarchy in which he normalizes self and Otherizes others. He accepts differences. He critiques those institutions and individuals whose rigidity forces them to repress desires and needs, to pass judgment on others, or to not feel free. His objection to the church is that it is repressive. In Atlanta, when his sister Debbie makes him take her sons to Big Bethal A M & E Church, he remembers:

> feeling all kinds of mixed-up feelings about going into that church with his sister. . . . That church always scared him anyway, what he heard tell of it, saved folks and sinners marching down the aisle together and all those hundreds of women and men singing in there together like voices down from heaven *passing judgment on everybody.*" (61; emphasis added)

The blues represents basic instincts, desires, and needs; the church moves to control those desires and needs. "Religion has always been an agency of repression, concerning itself chiefly with the inhibition of aggression and desire, and the maintenance of guilt" (Garon 144). Whereas Cleo seeks freedom and spiritual nourishment through the church, Manfred seeks freedom and spiritual nourishment through the blues. The church never made:

> him as happy as sin. God's dangers weren't as much fun. But he figured if there was a God he didn't have to go to any church to sing for him. Folks talk about the blues being sinful, but in his judgment, any God in his right mind was going to like the blues much as he liked the spirituals. Blues done saved as many lives as church songs. (52)

Manfred does not judge other people. Although his sister Debbie and brother-in-law Lyle strive for middle-class Christian respectability, Manfred does not pass judgment on them. Debbie, who picks him up at the train station in her new "1950 lemon yellow Cadillac," owns her own business, a beauty parlor. She attends church every Sunday, and when she thinks of singing, she means the church choir. She raises her sons, Wade and Marvin, to be middle class and not to act like "some old lazy niggers [from] down South" (61). They have chores and they have to dress a certain way. (There is some indication that Debbie once played the blues on the piano, but she has repressed that part of her life/past.)

Lyle works at a steel company, Lomax Steel, and he has just been promoted to crew boss. In a few years he will become a partner/owner of Lomax Steel. "He is a good family man. No riffraff" (181). Neither Debbie nor Lyle patronizes the Palace. Both Debbie and Lyle are successfully pursuing the American dream. Yet, Manfred does not pass judgment on them for the way they live their lives.

But Manfred does identify and empathize with individuals who are marginal or who have suffered yet continue to do what they have to do to live. He relates empathetically to those who have been tested, who live and feel free. His response to the gossip about Jorena Jones's being a lesbian is "who cares? Not everybody needed to dance to a robinson or call hay bop-a-re-bop to a hairy chest. So what if some women, like men, liked the tickle of a Josephine Baker feather, the glow of a turquoise headdress, the touch of a flashing body covered with blue sequins and emeralds?" (68). Jorena understands Manfred, and he often asks why Cleo doesn't or cannot understand him the way Jorena does. For example, Cleo is not as understanding about music as Jorena.

But Jorena understands Manfred because she is a blues figure. Against her father's wishes, she left Creighton University once her troubles led her to drinking. But she overcomes adversity and ostracism to accept her lesbianism:

> I'm the lesbian in the community. The bull dyke. At first I had a lot of trouble accepting that role. In fact the role was assigned me long before I ever knew who I was sexually, before I had a sexual identity, back when I was just a girl in elementary school. It followed me everywhere. Even the white kids at Creighton whispered about me. I'm not sure if I was born attracted to women or the whispering caused me to feel the way I feel. (208)

Manfred defines his landlady, Sofia Sweenzy, as a fellow blues traveler. Sofia has this repressed hatred of African Americans. When she becomes inebriated, she rants about the "Niggers over me, niggers all around me!" (108) Sofia spends nights in her apartment "throwing and breaking things and cussing" (139). But Manfred identifies with her suffering: "It was strange but stronger than this black-and-white race shit. He knew her suffering. He knew sure as death they were down there in the same ocean of clouds together unable to stop the storm. He didn't know about her, but he knew he could learn better how to read the weather forecast" (137).

Likewise, Manfred understands and empathizes with Poppa Leon, who is a numbers runner. Poppa Leon has a handicap: he lost his legs in World War I. Legless, Poppa Leon's "torso [is] fitted into a square wooden box with low sides," and he gets around Omaha by "scooting along on eight skate wheels, two in each corner," using his "hands, pressing his palms against the sidewalk, propelling himself forward at a fast speed" (57). In the box, Poppa Leon wheels "himself along, to a riffing rhythm, like he was in a hard-driving boogie, with his long chimpanzee arms, a big grin on his wide black face, white cigarette stuck between his purple lips" (130). When Manfred sees Poppa Leon getting on with

his life, despite the handicap, he feels ashamed, for Poppa Leon has a good attitude toward life. Manfred realizes that Poppa Leon's good attitude is due to the
fact that he has been tested. "That made him appreciate life more than somebody who ain't never been tested. Been tested, arrested, and invested" (197).
Looking at Poppa Leon, Manfred thinks, "he cain't boogie but he ain't nobody's
monkey man either, he be his own man, and got a good attitude about it too"
(130). For Manfred, Poppa Leon is heroic in character. His life is fraught with
frustration and personal troubles. Yet, he confronts life openly: he deals with it
in all its dimensions, possibilities, potentialities, and aburdities.

Seeing Poppa Leon "coming along the street in his box . . . with a cigarette
in his mouth, grinning," Manfred eventually wonders "where he get[s] his feel-
good spirit?" (97). Poppa Leon, thinks Manfred, keeps on keeping on because
of "some strong hoodoo so deep it be in the bone marrow. And cheerful too.
Just scooting along and joyful like a morning finch. Put all the rest of us to
shame" (197). Freedom, maturity, and the ability to maintain "equilibrium despite precarious circumstances" cannot be achieved until someone has been up
against the edge of life, experiencing the hurt and pain of existence, and facing
the fear of the darkness within the self. A person cannot appreciate the feel and
touch of life until he has "been tested, arrested, and invested." He has to come
to acknowledge and accept that pain and suffering are a part of life. Jorena and
Poppa Leon have achieved this freedom, this equilibrium. They have confronted
their fear of the darkness. They accept and endure life's stress, strain, and hard-
ship, and they proceed with life despite its troubles. They have achieved a "functional equilibrium in terms of the blues tradition of antagonistic cooperation"
(Murray, Hero 102). But Manfred is still striving for this freedom, this equilibrium. He is still trying to get and sustain the "feel-good spirit."

The Manfred Banks who loves himself, who refuses to allow anyone to disrespect his person, has to resist becoming a victim of racism. He has to define
racism as just another obstacle to be overcome. To become angry, or to express
despair or black rage at racism, is to direct an indictment "against indifference,
injustice, or brutality, rather than [providing] an example of the obstacles which
beset all quests for manhood, or rather personhood, selfhood, the just society
and everything else" (Murray, Hero 45). As a blues hero, Manfred cannot become angry or bitter, or pity himself; anger and bitterness are clear signs that
one cannot face/accept life. With anger, one loses control; protesting the injustice defines one as a victim. Anger "ain't eating nobody's insides but yo own"
(172). It drains from your "head, face, and shoulders, down into [your] stomach
and formed there like a tight fist" (180). The blues hero has to assume that every
obstacle is to be overcome.

At Lomax, which is a site of racial oppression, Manfred is severely tested as
to whether he can keep racism as just another obstacle to overcome. He encounters daily racism from his white workmates. They represent him as a nobody, negatively and stereotypically. Ralph talks to him like he is a dog. Oliver
Fergus offends him by wanting to know whether when he is promoted to

welder, he will go out and buy a Cadillac. Amos Mozella disrespects him when he asks if he "got any last night." Mark Harvey, another welder, is always asking, "Hi, hotshot. How's your peter hanging? You get your ashes hauled this weekend? How are them little colored gals out there on North Twenty-fourth Street?" (85). Louis Irving, another welder, wants to know if Manfred brought "some watermelon for lunch today" (85). The jokers on his job give him trouble. And the dilemma he faces is how does he maintain his own self-worth and self-respect in this kind of dehumanizing, racist, oppressive environment.

He copes in a number of ways. One way he copes is to escape in his dreams: "In his dreams he sometimes pulled a Bat Masterson on them, mowing them all down, sometimes whipping a Nat Turner on them. But big as he was he was strapped as though to a public torture rack, like a black man in a circus booth sitting on a stool over a bucket of water with a sign over his head: HIT THE BULL'S-EYE, KNOCK THE NIGGER IN THE WATER" (85). Other times he escapes the humiliation by thinking about Cleo. When his boss, Eliot Selby, chastises him for not cleaning the locker room to his satisfaction, Manfred cleans up the "lunchroom and the locker room, did it all like he was walking on air, doing Cow Cow Boogie at Jamboree time, his mind on Cleo. Let the good times roll. Unsung feelings now came to the surface and kept him grinning" (86). And when he is finally promoted to the position of welder, and receives resentment and hostility from his white workmates, "[h]e knew what he had to do. Words didn't hurt him. So he told himself. Far as he was concerned, they were just a bunch of ignorant redneck Okies and hillbillies. He did his job and stood his ground, making them walk around him, get out of his way much as possible" (85–86). The racism at Lomax and all of the obstacles test Manfred's heroism. The "difficulties and vicissitudes which beset" Manfred "not only threaten his existence and jeopardize his prospects," they also function to "bring out the best in him." They put on display his integrity and self-respect. They make it possible for Manfred "to make something of himself" (Murray, *Hero* 38).

After Cleo arrives and Eliot promotes him to welder, Manfred begins to lose control of himself and his life. Cleo, who now wants to work, complains about his coming home from work and drinking. She tells him she is unhappy, that all she is asking for is for them "to do things together sometimes, go places" (116). Coming home from work after receiving his promotion, Manfred encounters an angry Cleo who is about to "go nuts in this place" (116). The arrival of Solly from Chicago puts additional pressure and tension on his job and his marriage.

In addition, compounding his troubles, Manfred's boss has it in for him. Eliot has seen Manfred in a car with a white woman, and although the unidentified white woman was just giving Manfred a ride from the racetrack back into town, Eliot disapproves. Therefore, he decides to make Manfred's life at work a living hell. He moves Manfred from third-level welding to drilling, and then refuses to accept the quality of the work he is doing. When Manfred asks Eliot if the union approves of Eliot's having him work a job in which he has not been trained, Eliot calls him a boy and tells him basically that he makes the rules. Manfred refuses to become angry and keeps his cool.

After Ralph gives him hell all day, shouting and cussing him, even putting his life in danger, Manfred goes home with the blues. Cleo again does not understand or sympathize with his troubles. When he explains to her the hellish day he has had, Cleo blames him: "Fred, maybe it's you. Maybe you're the one being too touchy. You're not trying to find some excuse to quit, are you?" (129) Showing weakness, Manfred becomes angry, "angry enough to smash something. He gazed at Cleo. He'd never hit her and was determined to keep it that way. He would not become his father. If he did nothing else in life, he meant to rise above that shit his father was. None of that low-life, dull, stupid shit. He would never stoop that low, hitting a woman" (129).

Therefore, rather than hit his wife and become like his father, who obviously cannot maintain "equilibrium despite precarious circumstances," rather than betray the lesson of his aunt Ida to be "good to his wife," Manfred leaves, thinking, "This ain't living. Fuck naw, this ain't living. Do a man got to just take the life he been dealt? Couldn't he change things. Lift himself up. Do something different. If you stand still long enough people throw dirt on you" (129). Although he is a blues man, Manfred still has not confronted and acknowledged the fact that "people throw dirt on you," that pain and suffering and problems with his wife and work are not aberrations but a part of life, and, therefore, must be contended with. He still fears the darkness within himself. He still has not learned how to proceed despite ugly situations. Rather than confront and acknowledge the facts of life, he escapes the troubles of life by getting drunk. "He just wanted to get halfway drunk. Not have to think too much. Not wanting to be too far out of control, he wanted to just get mellow" (130).

Because he is restless, he walks. His search for meaning, resolution, and equilibrium causes him to wander the streets of Omaha. On the streets he encounters Poppa Leon again and admires "him because he's his own man," which leads him to think of traveling, wandering, "just saying fuck it, hit the road, catch a train, going anywhere: train, train, running fast, cain't see nothing but the land go past" (130–31). "The Blues," argues Cone, "express[es] a belief that one day things will not be like what they are today. This is why buses, railways, and trains are important images in the Blues. Each symbolizes motion and the possibility of leaving the harsh realities of an oppressive environment" (139). But the obstacle to Manfred's impulse to leave, to escape, is his love for Cleo and his desire to be with her and Katrina. Entering Etta's Tavern, he encounters the young drunk and the prostitutes, and he sees the bottom. Faced with debilitating despair, he does not want to go there. For Manfred, the people, "the drunks and cheap whores" (131), in Etta's Tavern are too low for him. They seem not to have any dignity and self-respect. They are nobodies. They do not have an affirmative attitude toward life; they have not learned to deal with a perpetual environment of despair, estrangement, alienation, disappointment, change, and fragmentation. They do not possess the heroism to endure stress and strain, or the magnitude and complexity to overcome obstacles. Despair, lamentation, and protestation prevent what Murray calls "heroic endeavor." Referring to the young drunk, Manfred states: "True, a black man's life ain't shit in the eyes of most peoples but you a piss-po excuse for a human being if you got to join them in thinking of yoself like that. Man shook his head in disgust" (131). He tells a joke about the "nigger" and God, concluding that God doesn't help the falling "nigger" because he "ain't lived a good clean life" (130). A blues man cannot compromise his integrity and self-respect. He cannot accept other people's negative definition of him.

But Manfred also realizes that a place like Etta's Tavern—where a "bunch of drunks and cheap whores hung out," a place of weekend stabbing but also a place "known for great blues on the jukebox"—"is a place of unprettified truth, and the bare truth is healing. Here, every tub sets on its own bottom" (131). After he pays for, but then rejects, the prostitute, Manfred leaves, thinking, "Got me a woman with a light round her shimmering but just cain't seem to get along with her. Maybe if I groom slick, wear zoot suits, act like one of them black juice stealing preachers everything would be all right. Naw. That ain't the way. I know I got something. A new front door ain't the answer" (137). Then Manfred has the realization that "he himself [is] his own worst problem. Got a good wife. A good kid. A great future. Just got to change my mind. I am changing my mind" (137).

When Manfred returns to work on the last Friday in June, he knows this day will present the ultimate test, that it will be the catalyst for him to change his mind. "Getting through this day was going to be like swimming upstream in a river full of alligator shit" (158). When Eliot asks him to drill, something he is not trained to do, he feels trapped again. He cannot drill holes to satisfy Eliot, and his coworkers laugh at him. He pleads with Eliot to stop disrespecting him and to get off his back. Eliot reminds Manfred that he is the boss. Manfred wants to quit, but he keeps thinking of Cleo and the baby. When Eliot tells him to stop drilling and "pick up scrap metal," he becomes angry, but he also feels "released from anger, if only for a moment, because he knew what was coming—if not today, soon. . . . [H]e knew what he had to" (164–65). Again, he thinks about escape options—joining Poppa Leon and running numbers. But he realizes that Cleo will not accept that lifestyle. After lunch, he returns to thoughts of traveling, of not going "back at all, just keep on going by the gate, on up Sherwood Avenue. Find the first liquor store, buy a half-pint and get nice and mellow. Forget about all this shit and worry" (166).

As he enters the gate to return to work, he again thinks of leaving, hitching a ride to California. Back at work, Manfred then asks Eliot why he is treating him this way: what did he do to piss him off? Eliot grins and says, "You haven't done anything to me personally. But I'll tell you, you're halfway out of the door, boy, already. If you want to work at Lomax you gonna do as I tell you" (167). Rather than quit, Manfred decides to make Eliot fire him so he can draw unemployment benefits. He provokes Eliot by asking him for an apology. Eliot spits on him, and Manfred hits him (only later does he learn from Bernie, one of his black co-workers, that Eliot has been riding him because he had seen Manfred with a white woman). Fired from Lomax, the first thing Manfred wants is a drink. Unlike the successful blues man, who acknowledges and confronts the ugliness and meanness in the world, Manfred still needs to escape the world's troubles through drinking.

Realizing that because he is a blues man who has difficulties adjusting to the social norm, Manfred tries to figure out how he can use his music to escape being trapped in jobs like the one at Lomax: "He was crossing the railway tracks when he thought how much nicer it would be if he could just make himself some dough-re-me playing and singing and not have to put up with any old monkey-time job or broken dick white mens—or tricky niggers, for that matter. Just make some bread doing what he loved" (172). But the job is just one of his problems. He still has a tense relationship with Cleo, the woman he loves, and he still needs his Old Crow to escape the ugliness of life.

After he loses control once more, raising his hand to hit Cleo after she tells him she is going to church and he thinks she is lying, he begins his descent to the bottom. There is still something about Manfred's life that is not allowing him to confront and acknowledge his problems, then proceed with life despite his troubles—to live by a blues philosophy. He explains his dilemma to Jorena, and she tells him, "You're a good man. You're not like most men. You have a gift, and you have a soul" (206). She also tells him that he sings "straight up from [your] guts. It comes out of everything that you are. . . . [T]here is nothing wrong with whiskey. . . . Some people can handle it, others can't. You're one of the ones who can't, Fred. Sometimes it takes a long time to know that" (206). Hearing this, Manfred "suddenly felt naked, completely exposed before her" (206).

Manfred Banks, who is now working with Percy at Sears, hits rock bottom one night when he goes to work drunk. He develops a stomachache, causing him to leave work early. When he arrives home, Cleo is away, and he panics, thinking that she has left him, again. He drinks more, and as he wanders throughout the city, he hits rock bottom and tastes death. When Manfred hits rock bottom and is "down in the crisscrossed darkness of himself," he comes "up hard against his own flesh, up against his limitations," and sees "the watered-down end of himself. Yeah. What'd they call it in the Bible? A revelation. He had had himself a revelation. Saw his own naked fear and had himself a scared-shitters revelation. From the depths of his own self-disgust he'd looked up, somehow, if blindly, and sensed, with fear, what he was doing to himself" (237). He decides that he wants to live and "the way to do that is stop drinking" (237).

As a blues person, Manfred has based his life in the folk–blues wisdom of the people. The movement toward self-acceptance is long and hard. But Manfred finds answers within himself, relying on his own internal resources to arrive at an acceptance of himself. Reaching "equilibrium despite precarious circumstances" comes at great costs. Who can determine the value of the rootlessness, homelessness, alienation, deprivation of education, dislocation, social oppression, and family degradation that have been the cost of Manfred's blues survival and equilibrium?

Hitting rock bottom and having a revelation, Manfred confronts and acknowledges the pain and suffering; he faces and hugs the darkness within himself, which he has used Old Crow to deny, even if it brings tears to his eyes. He faces his fear of "being alone, lost and alone." In acknowledging the "darkness of himself," he confronts his limitations and accepts life in all of its dimensions ("Things are changing all the time" [276]) and aspects. He can now proceed with life "in spite of, and even in terms of, the ugliness and meanness inherent in the human condition" (Murray, *Hero* 36). He has accepted the "facts of life" and has made the best of a bad situation. He has learned to persevere. With his revelation, Manfred, like a good blues man, becomes resilient. He can now acknowledge chance, possibilities, and probabilities ("Never can tell what gon come round the corner and stop on yo toes" [276]). He is now able to swing life, to improvise/experiment/riff or play with life's possibilities. He is able to "acknowledge essentially the tenuous nature of all human existence" (Murray, *Omni-Americans* 89). He is able to be at home with his sometimes tolerable but never quite certain condition of not being at home in the world: "Any day now something. Don't know what but something could give. Time. Just gots to take yo time. . . . Never can tell what gon come round the corner and step on yo toes, or kiss you between the eyes" (276).

Now that he has learned to confront, acknowledge, and proceed with life in all its dimensions and absurdities, the crucial questions are, Can he make peace with Cleo? Can he exist in a relationship with Cleo and remain true to his blues? As I have discussed, the most salient differences between Cleo and Manfred are religion and class. She is middle class, independent, and Christian, and he is a blues man from the subaltern, who has at times patriarchal tendencies. The blues man is typically proud and arrogant, sure of himself, and relatively immune to middle-class conventions. He is a free agent, indifferent and even hostile to the Protestant work ethic and the repressive myths of "responsibility." In many ways, Manfred is a typical blues man. The differences between the two cause tension and friction. But when he plays the patriarchal role, he sometimes critiques himself.

After an argument with Cleo, Manfred assesses critically: "He knows it is a line of defense [and] he dislikes the pettiness of his own position. He want[s] to be a bigger and better man than this" (12). Cleo is willing to accept Manfred's non–middle-class, non–Christian blues life if he is willing to take responsibility for the family, to stop drinking, and to put her and Katrina at least on equal footing with his music. After Manfred has begun working with Percy at Sears, he thinks, "If he could make Cleo happy he'd have the answer to the sixty-four-thousand-dollar question" (191). When Cleo responds to the question of what she wants, she says that "all I really want out of life is a good life for our daughter. . . . That and a good church" (192). The two accept the fact that they are in love, but that they are different and that there is no need to make the other over into the Same. Thus, they seem to tolerate and accept each other's differences and shortcomings.

By the text's end, Cleo is working at Debbie's shop and going to church. Manfred has quit drinking, is drawing unemployment, and is "packing em in [at the Palace] like never before" (272). He no longer has a need to drink to "mellow" out. Not drinking and no longer losing control alleviate at least one of the sources of tension between him and Cleo. Now that he can make a living playing his music, he can take responsibility financially for his family. He can also become his "song." His mind and body can be doing the same thing. In Manfred's final dream when his name is added to the list of the "real blues singers" such as Son House and Charlie Patton, who were from the "cotton fields," he reconnects and reaffirms that earlier, rural blues tradition that begins during, and continued after, slavery. In Manfred's dream, we see freedom, the satisfaction of desires, and new possibilities of an unrepressed life.

Having slain his dragons and accepted a blues life philosophy does not mean Manfred lives a utopian life. He can now accept differences. He can accept the spectrum of life in all its trials, tribulations, and troubles. He can acknowledge and proceed with the world despite all its problems. He can acknowledge the fact that human existence is almost always a matter of endeavor and, hence, also a matter of action. But he knows that life is never certain and secure: "Life is life. You try to make things happen but when they don't you still got to just go along, dry-long-so. I have to do a lot of shit I don't want to do" (117). The successful blues man is a humanist. He "affirms that which is upstanding in human nature, that which stands out against the overwhelming odds of the non-human and anti-human elements in the universe" (Murray, *Hero* 43). He has a blues "attitude toward life." In developing a blues way of life, Manfred achieves "elegance in the very process of coping with the rudiments of subsistence" (Murray, *Stomping* 251). He becomes the blues song, "where joys and pains are synthesized and resolved into an emotional-spiritual unity that helps make possible life's continuance" (Walton 29).

Clarence Major in *Dirty Bird Blues* uses the blues idiom and its image of the African American (male) as someone who defines self and existence as different from normative, middle-class American definitions and values to challenge, resist, and show the limitations of the dominant society's white/black binary's representation of the African American as victim, as inferior, or as devalued Other. The "blues singer rejects and even ridicules the repressive norms of the white [and black] bourgeoisie, negating bourgeois ideology by the mere act of non-acceptance" (Garon 54). He is perceived, according to Jon Spencer in *Blues and Evil*, by the norm "as causing anarchy rather than as functioning to open up social and psychological boundaries, to enlarge the scope of the human, and to turn repressive dead-ends into liberative crossroads" (12).

While the image of the African American as victim, or as devalued Other, in the white/black binary allows the binary to reproduce itself, the blues idiom as a reason of the Other produces a blues representation of the African American that is affirmative, existential, individual, vibrant, and different. It has its own logic, agency, and subjectivity. It offers the reader a different definition of the admired actions and desirable attributes of the hero/protagonist, thereby challenging the normative way the white/black binary maintains itself and the African American. *Dirty Bird Blues* constructs in Manfred Banks a dramatic enactment of a blues definition of the human condition. Manfred is an African American male who performs a disruptive, revolutionary act. Manfred, the blues man, defines himself as an "undeciphered enigma on the American landscape, a lonely wanderer chanting a disturbing litany of past regrets and current complaints. He is a symbol of freedom, the outsider who says 'no' to the system" (Finn 192). In this instance, the blues man escapes the victimization, the self-hatred, and the double-consciousness that accompany being defined by the white/black binary.

This blues representation of the African American constitutes a whole series of sites of individuation, identity, social definition, and politics that cannot be comprehended either by the white/black binary regime or by elite/middle-class organizations and concepts such as the African American sociopolitical mission of racial uplift, the canon of African American literature, the NAACP, the National Urban League, Marcus Garvey's United Negro Improvement Association, the Council of Negro Women, and the Southern Christian Leadership Council.

Because these cultural apparatuses and political organizations and movements embrace many of the values and definitions of mainstream American society, their silence on, or ignorance of, the counter-hegemonic blues definition of life functions to maintain and control it. In the 1970s/1980s reinvented canon of African American literature, blues-centered novels are excluded and repressed. They are neither mentioned nor discussed in Houston A. Baker Jr.'s *Long Black Song* and *Singers of Daybreak*, Robert Stepto's *From Behind the Veil*, Henry Louis Gates Jr.'s *Figures in Black* and *The Signifying Monkey*, and Valerie Smith's *Self-Discovery and Authority in Afro-American Narrative*. Obviously, these blues-centered texts cannot be read into a critical narrative about a mythic African American past or into a critical narrative about the quest for the journey of the African American to the values of the mainstream society. More important, salvation with the blues comes from a source within, rather than from some external, collective African American narrative. The reality is that there is a limited population of Americans/African Americans who believe in, and live by, the blues idiom lifestyle. There is also an American/African American blues tradition in American/African American literature. Until mainstream American/African American critics who have cultural capital acknowledge this lifestyle and literary tradition, Major's *Dirty Bird Blues* and other blues-centered texts will continue to be ignored and repressed. They will not be invested with cultural capital or contingent value. However, with my blues chapter on Albert Murray in *Discourse and the Other*, Houston A. Baker's *Blues, Ideology, and Afro-American Literature*, Hazel Carby's work of black women writers and the blues,

A. Yemisi Jimoh's *Spiritual, Blues, and Jazz People in African American Fiction: Living in Paradox,* Patricia Liggins Hill's forthcoming work on the blues and black women novelists, and others, we are beginning to see some critical attention given to this important repressed tradition in African American literature. We are beginning to discern and appreciate how the blues definition of life is just another representation of the African American.

CHAPTER EIGHT

NAMING THE SUBALTERN

THE SWINGING LIFE AND NATHAN HEARD'S *HOWARD STREET*

When Dial Press published the hardback edition of Nathan Heard's *Howard Street* in 1968, there was no advanced publicity, and unlike racial uplift novels/autobiographies such as James Weldon Johnson's *The Autobiography of an Ex-Coloured Man* and Richard Wright's *Black Boy*, it did not carry laudatory blurbs by America's most prestigious writers. Heard did not embark on a book tour, and *Howard Street* was ignored by the book clubs. It was not even promoted on its front and back covers, though the front cover of the 1970 Signet paperback edition of *Howard Street* shows a picture of a black prostitute and a blurb from a *San Francisco-Sun* reporter stating: "a tremendous new Black novelist has written the raw shocker of the year." *Howard Street* did eventually become a success, selling more than five hundred thousand copies. But, it never reached the classic status of *Black Boy*. So, how is a text that is set in, and deals with, African American life in urban American communities received and interpreted by the American literary establishment? Why was *Howard Street* defined as a "raw schocker"?

First, I want to examine the reception of *Howard Street* and then do a reading of the text to show how it represents a regime of power/knowledge rooted in subaltern African America, one that is different from the middle-class, Freudian, Christian regime of truth and power that has been sanctioned and naturalized by mainstream African American and American critics and reviewers. I want to show how it represents a repressed and excluded literary tradition in African American literature. *Howard Street* does not generate or reaffirm the dominant African American journey from the subaltern to the values of mainstream American society, which has been defined by elite/middle-class critics as the African American experience or the "black experience." Instead, it speaks from the periphery and its critique departs from the exteriority of the African American subaltern. It gives us the African American subaltern in terms of its own logic or distinction.

Mainstream American intellectuals, writers, and critics define Harlem, or the African American subaltern, not as a culture or community that is different but equal but as a place that is Other than reason, that is negative, that is different and less. To them, Harlem is, to use the terms of anthropologist Quetzil Castañeda, a "zero-degree culture." It does not have its own beliefs, subjectivities, rituals, and culture that are as complex as the middle-class norm. It has been erased from the "ethnographic mappae mundi through which anthropology [and other social sciences] plots its contesting classifications of sociocultural forms to their proper space-time localities via the operations of theory building" with the result that Harlem represents a "scandal" (39).

I want to give a reading of *Howard Street* that interprets it not as representing the middle-class Christian American but as defining a regime of power/knowledge that is actually antithetical to that middle-class Christian norm. I will read *Howard Street* as representing a swinging life in which individuals flow with desires and wants. I will read it as representing a definition of life that is non-middle class, non-Christian, non-Protestant work ethic, and nonhumanist. I want to read it as a subaltern text within the American colonizer/colonized binary.

When Heard, in an interview in *Library Journal*, states that *Howard Street* "is about a way of life which challenges America" ("Review" 3586), he is referring to a way of life that has a different social organization and a different cosmology than middle-class, Christian American life. He is referring to a swinging (subaltern) life. Finding the subaltern in African American life and literature is an easy task. The African American subaltern is the main focus in William Wells Brown's *My Southern Home*; Charles Chesnutt's "The Goophered Grapevine" in *Dark Symphony* and *The Conjure Woman* (which deal almost exclusively with African American folk culture); James Weldon Johnson's *God's Trombones*; Claude McKay's *Home to Harlem* and *Banjo*; Rudolph Fisher's *The Walls of Jericho*; Arna Bontemps's *God Sends Sunday*; Sterling Brown's *Southern Road*; Zora Neale Hurston's *Jonah Gourd Vine* and *Mules and Men*; George Wylie Henderson's *Ollie Miss*; Iceberg Slim's *Pimp*, *Trick Baby*, *The Long White Con*, and *Doom Fox*; Vern E. Smith's *The Jones's Men* (1974); and Robert Deane Pharr's *Giveadamn Brown*. The African American subaltern exists as the field workers in the margins of the middle-class Christian slave autobiographies such as Frederick Douglass's *Narrative*, as the peasants and low-life urban dwellers in W. E. B. DuBois's *The Souls of Black Folk*, James Weldon Johnson's *The Autobiography*, Jean Toomer's *Cane*, and Wallace Thurman's *The Blacker the Berry*. The African American subaltern exists in Tea Cake and the muck in Zora Neale Hurston's *Their Eyes Were Watching God* and in Mrs. Hedges and Boots Smith in Ann Petry's *The Street*. It also exists in the Bottom in Toni Morrison's *Sula*. But with the exception of Morrison and Hurston, these canonical African American writers write from the top, defining, according to Renato Rosaldo in *Culture and Truth*, "those most down and out" as lacking "culture" (200). They cover over the African American subaltern as the Same as the elite/middle-class African American, or define it completely negatively.

But unlike sanctioned and canonized African American writers and intellectuals who patronize and speak for subaltern African Americans, Heard in *Howard Street* develops a different relationship with it. He takes an African American social milieu that has been defined as having a "zero-degree culture," and he reinscribes and recharts it until it becomes simply a different cultural/social milieu. He enters, to use the words of Gayatri Spivak, "into a responsibility structure with the subaltern [African American], with responses flowing both ways: learning to learn without this quick-fix frenzy of doing good with an implicit assumption of cultural supremacy which is legitimized by unexamined romanticization" (qtd. in Landry and MacLean 78). It is difficult for the subaltern to enter into organic intellectuality, and Heard, who once belonged to the subaltern but who has since become an organic intellectual/writer, serves as a namer of subaltern African Americans. He represents and analyzes and describes them, but he is not claiming to give them a voice. He is writing their texts to be read. Heard gives us a representation of subaltern African Americans, the Howard Streeters, that is not "laid down by the official institutional structures of representation" (Landry and MacLean 306) and that does not cover over the African American subaltern into the Same as the elite/middle-class African American norm. And in presenting the Howard Streeters as what Julia Kristeva calls "irrecuperable foreigners," he provides a "sort of separate vigilance that keeps" mainstream American and African American societies "from closing up, from becoming homogenous and so oppressive" (qtd. in Guberman 45). Thus, Heard defines the role of the African American subaltern as a "sort of vigilance, a strangeness, as always to be on guard and contestatory" (Kristeva qtd. in Guberman 45). But despite its contestatory intention, *Howard Street*'s language still appropriates certain references and comparisons that are definable in normative American systems.

In *Howard Street*, if we look at American society in colonial terms, middle-class white Americans are the colonizers; elite/middle-class African Americans are the "indigenous elite"; and the Howard Streeters are the Other/subaltern. Within modern American society, the Howard Streeters are marginalized. They represent what Tzvetan Todorov calls the "something capable of being not merely an imperfect state" of the colonizer (43) and what Spivak calls a "space of difference" (qtd. in Landry and MacLean 293). They belong to that "space that is cut off from the lines of mobility," below the "vectors of upward, downward, sideward, [and] backward mobility" (288). And because they are outside the lines of mobility, when they make an "effort to the death to speak," they are "not able to be heard" because "speaking and hearing complete the speech act" (292), and the various entities on the lines of mobility refuse to hear them.

I want to begin my discussion of *Howard Street* with the character Harry Conrad. After Heard has given us life on Howard Street, he introduces at the beginning of part 2 of the text a character, Harry Conrad, who embodies and represents the privileged half of the white/black, colonizer/colonized oppositions. Conrad is a representative of the eastern, educated, upper-middle-class, progressive liberal establishment. Representing Conrad as a colonizer, as the upper half of the white/black binary, Heard writes:

> Harry was typically white upper middle class. He had a healthy respect for parents and family; he had a care for what his neighbors thought of him. He cared what happened to himself; he liked people generally and cared what happened to them also. He was idealistic and was glad to admit it. But it was only last year that he, at the age of twenty-two, had become aware of the plight of black people in America. Being white, when he thought of America and Americans he thought of white people. It bothered him tremendously that he'd never thought of blacks as Americans, too. (146)

And in representing the people of Howard Street as Other than reason, Conrad states:

> It's still a matter of education. . . . I don't mean the three R's, but rather an education to give them a sense of *correct* values, moral, spiritual, and otherwise— a sense of fair play, if you will. These people must obviously be explained in terms of their environment. Their values are *wrong*, so naturally their application to the mainstream of this country's values will be *wrong* also. It's not so much that they like doing *wrong*, it's that they don't know any better. . . . A person can go through his entire life doing the wrong things in the wrong manner; if he's not shown a better way he'll probably keep doing wrong. (148–49; emphasis added)

Usually, we think of the Other as the enemy—someone we can welcome only on conditions of delegitimating and annulling the Other. But, as Kristeva points out, when we encounter the Other in a community "we try to help one another, all." In *Howard Street*, Conrad does not define the Howard Streeters as enemies because he defines them as being a part of his community and, therefore, is able to hear them as "tracked by some pathology, by some anomaly." Because he does define them "as weak, . . . as potentially sick" (Kristeva qtd. in Guberman 41), his objective is to cure them, to make them well. This becomes the basis for his form of morality.

To Conrad, the Howard Streeters are Other than reason. Therefore, he defines them negatively. Conrad wants the Howard Streeters to be like him and like middle-class white Americans. He is an assimilationist in an unconscious and naive fashion; his sympathy for the Howard Streeters is, again, to use the words of Todorov, "naturally translated into the desire to see them adopt his own customs" (43). According to Conrad, the Howard Streeters are being "deprived of all cultural property: they are characterized, in a sense, by the absence of customs, rites, religion" (Todorov 35). "As a structure of alterity," argues Peter Mason in *Deconstructing America*, "assimilation is a process by which the otherness of the other is eliminated and the other is reduced to self" (163).

And although Conrad can recognize the injustice and the racism inflicted on African Americans, or he can see clearly that on one level white supremacy was/is essentially privileged and normalized, Conrad cannot conclude that white supremacy, on another level, has to be deconstructed before African Americans, particularly subaltern African Americans, can be seen as equal and different. Because he defines his I with the "universe—in the conviction that the world is one" (Todorov 43), he cannot acknowledge the Howard Streeters, the subaltern, as *resisting* middle-class Christian American society.

Conrad is not the only American on the lines of mobility who has the power to not hear the Howard Streeters when they speak, who cannot admit that the Howard Streeters are subjects who have the same rights as himself, but different. They are also not heard by Myers, the attorney who makes his money by "getting people off by payoffs to his downtown connections" (172). He considers himself an authority on blacks in general. Yet, he defines them as devalued Other. He cannot respect blacks, "mainly . . . for 'acting like niggers' " (173). He defines them as "the criminal and hustling element" (173). Furthermore, the Howard Streeters are not heard by the elite/middle-class Christian African Americans, represented in the text by those middle- and upper-middle-class blacks "who've convinced themselves that they're white" (151).

Nor are the Howard Streeters heard by those African Americans who live on or near Howard Street and have middle-class aspirations, those who are on Spivak's "vectors of upward and downward mobility" in "the official institutional structures of representation." Jackie Brown has "an attitude so vastly different from their own." Having fallen from a scholarship athlete at Rutgers to Howard Street, he has "come to Howard Street with the intention of trying to do something to help the Streeters find a path into the mainstream of American life. . . . He couldn't, or wouldn't, understand why, with the knowledge of a better way of life, the Streeters chose the life they did" (51, 52–53).

When Franchot, who aspires to upward middle-class mobility, visits Hip's apartment with Gypsy Pearl, he "looked at Hip with a pity and contempt that almost overwhelmed him. Hip looked like a bum" (77). Franchot constantly asks Hip, "When you gon' get yourself together, Lonnie?" (78). Franchot does not hear Hip; he only wants Hip to be like him, to embrace the same values as he. Although Sue uses the Howard Streeters to climb the economic ladder of the community, she also does not hear Hip. Sue likes Hip "but he was a junkie and she didn't mess with them under any circumstances" (117). Gypsy Pearl's mother, whose "main concerns [are] Church and discipline" (80), refuses to even walk on Howard Street. Finally, when Hip explodes and speaks to Rosemary, who believes in "Christian ethics and law and order," telling her who he is and what he thinks, she only "heard him talkin' crazy stuff" (188). Harry

Conrad, Myers, and all the middle-class and aspiring middle-class African Americans cover over the Howard Streeters, representing them as different and Other than reason. In this instance, the Howard Streeters as Others are both domesticated and at the same time distanced from them. The taming of strangeness that occurs in the identification of the Howard Streeters suggests a more general process through which they can be narratively smoothed over and repressed.

If Howard Street is not exactly a "harrowed hell," as I seem to be arguing, what is Heard's subaltern? What is the way of life on Howard Street? What are its belief systems? What is the reason of this Other? The otherness of the Other? What is its regime of power/knowledge and how does it differ from normative American life? I want to begin the discussion of the way of life on Howard Street by first discussing Sigmund Freud's pleasure principle, one of the main tenets of middle-class life in the West. In *Beyond the Pleasure Principle*, Freud writes:

> In the theory of psychoanalysis we have no hesitation in assuming that the course taken by mental events is automatically regulated by the pleasure we believe, that is to say, that the course of those events is invariably set in motion by an unpleasurable tension, and that it takes a direction such that its final outcome coincides with a lowering of that tension—that is, with an avoidance of unpleasure or a production of pleasure. (3).

The sole function of the id is to provide for the immediate discharge of those quantities of excitation (energy or tension) that are released in the organism by internal or external stimulation. The function of the id fulfills the primordial or initial principle of life that Freud called the pleasure principle. The aim of the pleasure principle is to rid the person of tension or to reduce the amount of tension to a low level and to keep it as constant as possible. Tension is experienced as pain or discomfort, whereas relief from tension is experienced as pleasure or satisfaction. The aim of the pleasure principle may be said, then, to consist of avoiding pain and finding pleasure.

Yet, to create a better society and better people, Freud believed in the application of psychological principles to reeducate members of society. "If one were to yield to a first impression," writes Freud in *Civilization and Its Discontents*, "one would say that sublimation is a vicissitude which has been forced upon the instincts entirely by civilization. . . . [I]t is impossible to overlook the extent to which civilization is built upon a renunciation of instinct" (51–52). For the good of society, members are asked to delay gratification. Sexual instincts and irrational drives are shaped and transformed to accommodate, in this instance, a society that believes in sex within marriage, the Protestant work ethic, and middle-class respectability and mores.

Class, race, and culture are key factors in the existence and marginalization of the inhabitants of Howard Street. Legal and *de facto* racism has denied African American subalternity legitimate access to the fruits of mainstream society's institutions and apparatuses, despite the fact that African Americans have been exposed to, and have had knowledge of, the rewards of these institutions. Racism precludes them from having "dreams of becoming something in the professions or business" (*Howard Street* 27). Class and cultural differences cause middle-class African Americans to segregate themselves from their "lesser" brethren. Thus, race, class, and cultural segregation provide the condition of possibility (or the prohibitions) for the heterogeneous subaltern swing life on Howard Street. But it is only after the Howard Streeters culturally, physically, and cosmologically have found a place—notably when they have detached themselves from the racial-victim weight of the mainstream society or when they have succeeded in arranging a lighter, freer relationship to middle-class Christian American society—that they can play with the norms and values of mainstream American society or that they can devise their own culture.

Howard Street has an interesting and distinctive composition. Physically, Howard Street is a segregated, oppressed, and marginalized community in Newark, New Jersey.

> Two blocks bisected by Howard Street are bordered by Court, Broome, and West Streets, and Springfield Avenue. Dark little Mercer Street crosses Howard between Court Street and Springfield Avenue. . . . The short block between Mercer Street and Springfield Avenue is something so different as to be *classed almost as another world*. While laborers and domestics—poor but respectable people—live on the long block, the short one is as wild and as rowdy as Dodge City or Tombstone ever was, with no Hickock or Earp in evidence. It also has the strange, but familiar and inevitable, combination of religion mixed in with every conceivable vice. (23; emphasis added)

Howard Street has evolved as the Other of productive rationality, epistemic propriety, and political power. It constitutes a cultural residue or byproduct, and its position is clearly subaltern.

In addition, Howard Street is a community outside the law. "Assault and murder on Howard Street was seldom prosecuted except by the unwritten law of the lye can, switchblade, and sometimes, the gun" (20). There are "teenage gangs who roamed about mugging and rolling drunks, and it was they who painted on the side of buildings: *Tricks and Lames, Beware* in glaring white letters" (20). The gangs roam the streets, preying on the weak, robbing, and mugging, but the "real threat lay with the adults" (20). Of course, Howard Street "could not function so efficiently without the complicity of the authorities" (99). Pimps pay off the police to protect their prostitutes. And when prostitutes are arrested, lawyers with connections downtown get them out. Thus, chances of an arrest are slim if it happens at all on Howard Street.

The Howard Streeters, as subalterns, are affected remotely by socialized capital. "It's just that in the subaltern's subject production," argues Spivak, "the process is remote. Especially today, when one talks about colonial historiography and the financialized globe, . . . it would be hard to find a group that is not affected by socialized capital" (qtd. in Landry and MacLean 292). There is money on Howard Street, but success is not defined by a college education, a prestigious job, and a wife and children. Actually, with the absence of rational, middle-class, Protestant work ethic pressures, the men on Howard Street have never bought into the quasi-Freudian psychology in which real manhood or success is defined as holding a job, being married, and supporting your wife and children.

Howard Street has its own hierarchy and its own definition of success. To be successful on Howard Street, one "would wind up being a pimp, or opening a tavern, or making it big in the numbers racket, fronting for a syndicate" (27). Success carries with it a flamboyant attitude toward life, cars, fast living, and fast friends. There is the ease of handling money, women, and gambling. There is no delayed gratification. Unlike Freudian-constructed subjects, individuals on Howard Street seek pleasure according to the dictates of their instincts and de- sires. As a reaction to external and internal stimulations, the Howard Streeters' id provides for the immediate discharge of quantities of excitation. Success means entry into Sue's place, designated for Howard Street's elite:

> The crap games were expensive, as were the drinks and the women. To go to Sue's was a sign of affluence, one was really "into something" if he could hang out there. . . . Around the table were concentrated the elite of Howard Street's fast life: Hammerhead Willie, Bill Grumsley, Fish-Man Floyd, Joe Magic, Red Shirt Charlie, and Cowboy, among others. These were the people who made the most of the vices of Howard Street; much of what they made found its way into the pockets of the big-time white gangsters and cops, lawyers and politi- cians. Even so, what they managed to keep for themselves made them rich, or, as Third Ward people said, "nigger-rich." (115, 118)

Socially and culturally, Howard Street is very heterogeneous. It is com- posed of an unstable, but equal, collection of people and discourses. That col- lection comprises prostitutes, pimps, tricks, squares, homosexuals, junkies, the "nigger-rich," winos, civil rights workers, working-class laborers and domestics, Father Divine and his followers, and failed athletes. The community has a "masseur's bathhouse next to [a] tavern" (23). There are residential apartment buildings next to religious institutions and bars:

> In the same block as Mann's Manor and the Howard Bar, but on the opposite side of the street, are a few of the establishments belonging to Father Divine and his followers. . . . The M & M Bar is on the same side of the street as the Divine establishments and caters mostly to homosexual trade, mostly female. However, everyone goes there as much as to the other two bars. (35)

And next to a "restaurant specializing in fried fish" is:

> an alley which serves as a shooting gallery for addicts, a place to turn tricks for whores . . . , a cover for muggers to mug or rapists to knock off a quick piece, a place to cop a fast blow job from a fag, and an escape route for everybody—

leading to Springfield Avenue or Broome Street—when the cops are out to make a bust. (23–24)

The people on Howard Street are not encoded with middle-class pride, ego respectability, or the fear of pain. They have their own culture and belief systems, their own regime of power and knowledge. They possess a peripheral consciousness. They do not believe in Enlightenment ideas and progress. They are not humanists. The word *humanism* was invented in the nineteenth century to describe the ideas of European Renaissance scholars that drew on a knowledge of classical antiquity, but with an emphasis on its moral and practical rather than its aesthetic values. Humanism is a social philosophy of justice, values, and morals. It assumes the dignity and centrality of European man in the universe and insists on the primacy of reason, considered a distinctively human factor as opposed to the instinctual or nonrational dimensions of man, in ordering human life. European Renaissance humanists were pious Christians who incorporated the concepts and ideals inherited from classical antiquity into the frame of the Christian creed. Humanism is the moral philosophy that has anchored the political and social systems of Western society since the Enlightenment, and thus it is the political imaginary that grounds all Western science, from physics and comparative literature to Marxism. What the Howard Streeters share is not so much a contempt for a humanistic, middle-class life as a sure knowledge that middle-class values are completely irrelevant to their lives. They believe that the official American ideology of self-reliance, the Protestant work ethic, and happy families is obsolete or irrelevant because it does not reflect their own experience. Since few of the Streeters had ever been to high school, they have circumvented one of the main carriers of modern, secularized consciousness and humanist indoctrination.

Instead, the Howard Streeters operate out of a cosmology/social philosophy that insists on the primacy of the instinctual or nonrational dimension of man. One accepts death, pleasure, joy, laughter, pain, and suffering all together. The Streeters deal with them by becoming indifferent to them. In fact, they look on everything with the same indifference. Unlike Western societies in general, and mainstream American society in particular, which accept a secularized, evolutionary concept of 'time' (in which time accomplishes or brings about things in the course of evolution), the Howard Streeters have adopted what Johannes Fabian calls "archaic timelessness" (41). Their time is circular, rather than linear and evolutionary. They are "indifferent to time passin', life stagnatin'" (150). Describing Howard Streeters and their circular concept of time on her release from jail, Gypsy Pearl states:

> Howard Streeters didn't really need time. Days swung into nights and back again, and nothing ever changed for them but the seasons. They did the same things day in and day out with little variation—hard drinking, fighting, tears, laughter; hard fucking, hating, and praying; hard, hard living, all passion, no love, not for each other and not for themselves. (186)

They are also indifferent to each other. They do not care about, or take responsibility for, each other. They "blow the whistle on each other an' still stay tight, like ain't nothin' happened" (37). Pimps take each other's prostitutes. Dope dealers sell their known customers "bad" drugs. Gamblers cheat their friends at the gambling table. Prostitutes rob their johns. At the news of Tricky Dick's overdose, the prostitutes didn't bat a "false eyelash. . . . They didn't feel nothin' because he didn't buy no pussy off 'em"; Emma Dee, who used to be his woman, "didn't even flinch at the news. . . . She don't give a sentimental fuck— not even for old time's sake" (157). The Howard Streeters live by the credo: "A man can't fool with the Golden Rule in a crowd that don't play fair. . . . When you've got a fool on your hands, you're supposed to use him" (149, 150). As Jackie explains philosophically, you cannot make it on the "street until you learn to say, I don't want to hear that shit." There are no norms in a place that thrives on chance and street smarts. The Streeters are shrewd, rugged individuals who can con, manipulate, and live it up without regard for expense and consequence. The Streeters are "a mankind whose solidarity is founded on the consciousness of its unconscious—desiring, destructive, fearful, empty, impossible. Here, we are far removed from a call to brotherhood, about which one has already ironically pointed out its debt to paternal and divine authority" (K. Oliver 290). To have brothers, there must be a father, and there are no fathers on Howard Street.

Further, Howard Streeters have a style. On Howard Street, you cannot admit to being scared; you have to be tough. You cannot be a weakling; only the strong survived. "For in a black slum . . . one is loud-mouthed and aggressive" (27). There are no conventional expressions of feeling and there is no love. They do not fret over an "uncool dilemma. A down person didn't hang out problematic laundry like Blue Monday wash for everyone to dig: people peeped your hole card then, knew where you were at and saw that you weren't such-a-much after all" (175).

The people of Howard Street flummox the dominant value system that lectures about meritocracy and individual responsibility and values. They do not believe in the Protestant work ethic. The Streeters response to work is: "Yeah, man. I know where you at—but that gig ain't sayin' nuthin'. Like, it's a drag, man. That white man don't wanna get up off no bread [money] at all. I c'n make more'n that in a good day's hustlin', man" (52). The Streeters do not believe that we live in a meritocracy—where even the most damaging circumstances can be overcome if you really try because if you reach out someone will help you. They do not believe in the Protestant work ethic and self-reliance because neither reflects their own experience.

Father Divine and his church also coexist with the people on Howard Street:

> The streeters don't bother the Divine followers. They don't steal from them or try to con them of anything. The followers in turn don't try to beat their religion over anyone's head or even attempt to proselytize. It seems a mutual

agreement, a tacit understanding with toleration on the part of the followers and respect on the part of even the most disrespectful of the fast-lifers. (35)

Father Divine and his church have saved many of the Howard Streeters from starvation. When he visits Howard Street, "the street was sometimes entirely blocked by big, beautiful cars belonging to him and his followers" (112). People left Divine's meetings with "looks of pure joy on their faces; they came away from the meetings broker, but filled with righteousness and good food. The streeters really admired Father Divine and called him a Master Player; he had, they said, a heavy game" (112).

Within the bars on Howard Street, away from the dominant American society, forms of gender and sex are also organized differently—so differently that they subvert the dominant society's normative categories. In *Howard Street,* Heard shows how compulsive heterosexuality, which is pervasive in mainstream society, loses its effectiveness when sexuality and gender are removed from a social context that underwrites heterosexuality. Discussing compulsory heterosexuality and sex and gender performativity in *Gender Trouble,* Judith Butler argues that compulsory heterosexuality is characterized as a:

> hegemonic discursive/epistemic model of gender intelligibility that assumes that for bodies to cohere and make sense there must be a stable sex expressed through a stable gender (masculine expresses male, feminine expresses female) that is oppositionally and hierarchically defined through the compulsory practice of heterosexuality. (151).

In this power/knowledge regime, a rigid natural order is posited that assumes a causality that proceeds from a bipolar sexed subject (male or female), to gender bipolarity (man and woman), and to a hetero-normative sexuality. In a deconstructive move, Butler in *Gender Trouble* aims to trouble/disturb this power/knowledge regime by suggesting that this presumed order of nature is a contingent, politically enacted social order. Compulsory heterosexuality is a naturalized construct of the Western patriarchy. Butler concludes that "gender is culturally constructed: hence gender is neither the casual result of sex nor as seemingly fixed as sex" (6). She also concludes that sex is culturally constructed: "If the immutable character of sex is contested, perhaps this construct called 'sex' is as culturally constructed as gender; indeed, perhaps it was always already gender, with the consequence that the distinction between sex and gender turns out to be no distinction at all" (7).

Thus, within the bars on Howard Street, where compulsory heterosexuality and the bourgeois nuclear family are attentuated, a whole series of sites of sexual desire, individuation, identity, pleasure, social definition, and politics multiply and proliferate. Sex, gender, and identity become performative. In the bars, as "the whiskey flowed, the music swung, [and] the money flew fast across the bar" (217), female homosexuals, fags, and drag queens mingle socially and sexually with pimps, whores, and squares (straights). Everyone "lets the good times roll." On one night at the M&M, "about five male couples were in the place—queens with their 'husbands'—talking in high, shrill tones, and laughing loudly in lavish efforts to attract attention. There were only two mixed couples among the customers" (47). Heard continues with the description:

> Next to Franchot were a fag and a Puerto Rican, who obviously thought the fag was a real woman. . . . It wasn't hard for Franchot to see why the man had mistaken the fag for a woman: he looked very female indeed. He looked about twenty years old, with a fragile, girlish face, smooth and unmarked by the inconvenience of having to shave. If he hadn't had such exaggerated vocal inflections, Franchot would've been fooled into thinking he was a woman, too—especially in this bar—and he'd been sitting next to him for a half hour. (48)

On another night at the M&M bar, "the door was open and the music splashed out into the street along with billows of smoke and laughter. The dance floor was covered with women—some who could easily have been mistaken for men—clutching possessively at each other" (114). As described earlier, there were also men "who could easily be mistaken" for women. Here, men are performing the sex and gender of women, and women are performing the sex and gender of men. For example, the drag queen, Lillie, picks up the straight or "square" Jorge who does not know that Lillie is a man. Lillie introduces Jorge to Hip with: "Hip, dahling! Come meet mother's new husband" (114). There is also "Miss Curtis, the queen of interpretive dancers, who was so beautifully womanlike that he modeled female clothes and appeared in fashion magazines" (215). As drag queens, Lillie and Miss Curtis challenge and disturb the sex/gender/sexuality system that underwrites heterosexuality by exhibiting the performative character of sex and gender and their fluid relation to sexuality. In showing how drag disturbs this system, Heard exposes the heterosexual/homosexual regime of power/knowledge as social and political.

On Howard Street, even "straight" Hip flows with the sexuality/sexual difference, expressing sexual desires, individuation, and identities not comprehended by the heterosexual/homosexual regime. He sleeps with both Gypsy Pearl and Lillie, and he does not appear to be oppressed by the system of compulsive heterosexuality. When he enters the M&M and encounters Lillie, Lillie says, " 'I want you to know that I thought you were simply mahvelous Thursday night. Oh, child did you ever perform! Let mother feel your lovely muscles.' Hip grinned shyly as Jorge morosely eyed Lillie's hand caressing Hip's arm" (114). Thus, within the bars on Howard Street, the differences between heterosexuality and homosexuality lose their significance, and sexual boundaries become fuzzier. The need and desire to label behavior and people disappear. The end result of this erosion of sexual difference is the demise of distinct homosexual and heterosexual orientations and identities.

Furthermore, what Heard presents in the bars on Howard Street are carnivals that express energies suppressed in modernized everyday life and that also undermine the dominant society's normative categories. Peter Stallybrass and Allon White, in their chapter "Bourgeois Hysteria and the Carnivalesque," appropriate and generalize the Bakhtinian notion of "carnival" into their notion of transgression, which involves a violation of the rules of hierarchies in any of a number of different areas, including literary genres and conventions, psychic forms, the human body, geographical space, and social order. Carnivals have always been a loose amalgam of procession, festing, competition, games, and spectacle. But in the modern era, carnival is "sublimated." It becomes spectacularized, the object of a large audience's remote and sentimental gaze (284). Carnivalesque rituals reinflect the grotesque and the disgusting into a stylized, comic form. They become ways of enacting terror.

In *Howard Street*, Heard gives us two stylized, ritualized carnival scenes. The first is the fight between Big Frieda and Bunny Scotia, two of Bill Grumsley's whores at the M&M bar. The two women hate each other and have had a couple of fights that are famous in the neighborhood. Bill usually stops them before one of them gets really hurt. "They argued or fought only when he was around, at other times they left each other alone" (38). This particular fight begins when "the band came down for intermission [and] someone turned the jukebox down." Frieda and Bunny begin to create a spectacle where they belittle and put each other down, thereby releasing tension and anger. Frieda tells Bunny to "git your yaller ass outta that seat!" and Bunny reaches into her bosom and pulls out a fifty-dollar bill. "Can you do that, bitch?" she asks contemptuously. As Big Frieda throws Bunny's barstool to the floor, Bunny's dress flies up around her waist. Bunny wears no underwear. Big Frieda starts for her, and when Bill turns and grabs her by the hair, her wig comes off in this hand. Within the ritualized spectacle, Big Frieda and Bunny are able to enact their hatred/dislike of each other. Calling each other names and pulling each other's clothing and hair become stylized ways of releasing suppressed energies. And the audience defines it for what it is: carnivalesque. "The crowd in the bar roared with laughter as the banter and wisecracks flew between the two women" (39). Bill informs the two to stop, the musicians return to the stand, and "the crowd turned immediately back to their conversations, drinking, and propositionings as the band swung into 'Sister Sadie'" (40).

The second carnival scene comes during a "loud-talk session" between Tal and Irene, also at the M&M bar. This is an indoctrination/initiation of Irene into the hip life. Tal's "reputation depended upon his performance. The whole phenomenon had a double meaning for pimps and whores: an exhibition of freedom and virility for the man, and proof for the woman, through the subjugation of her will to his, that she belonged to someone" (218). So, Tal proceeds to humiliate Irene, demanding that she light his cigar or telling the crowd what he did to her last night.

Derisive laughter broke out. It was a poor pimp whose loud-talk backfired on him; he wasn't so hot after all. . . . Tal cursed Irene with the nastiest words he could think of. He kicked her several times as she hugged the floor. . . . Fat Mose . . . grabbed Tal roughly, lifting him completely off his feet like a toy, and flung him into the arms of the crowd. Then he called Angel Pope and had her take Irene to the ladies' room. . . . The show was over. Everyone had been well entertained, and they had something to talk about for another few hours. Tal would go home and change, then he and Irene would make up in some other bar. That was the way it usually went. (220)

For Tal, ridiculing Irene, cursing her with the "nastiest words," kicking her several times as she hugged the floor became an exhibition of freedom. The acts release energies suppressed in modernized everyday life. They reinflect the grotesque and the disgusting into a stylized, comic form. And, again, the audience understands the ritual.

Finally, in the absence of Christianity, middle-class respectability, and the bourgeois nuclear family, interesting family arrangements and different structures of domestic life emerge on Howard Street. The most poignant one is Two-Day Sheik and his eight women. All of his women live in the same apartment building. He pays their keep and regularly spends two consecutive days with each of them. His clothes are distributed evenly in each apartment, and he does not object if the women date other men, as long as the men are not around during his two-day occupation. This arrangement, which is a site of social definition absent of jealousy and the desire for possession, differs from the middle-class, nuclear family.

Thus, within the bars and in the community of Howard Street, we encounter a whole series of sites of individuation, identity, sexual desire, pleasure, social definition, and politics that are quite different from, and not comprehended by, mainstream society's heterosexual matrix and middle-class norm. These sites provide a social space in which selves can fashion bodies, gender identities, and sexualities without the normative constraints of compulsive heterosexuality and bipolar gender norms. Their existence/presence exposes this mainstream regime/system as social and political.

But although its inhabitants all share the swing life, I should make it very clear that philosophically and cosmologically Howard Street is truly heterogeneous. Many of the people on Howard Street do not live fully by the philosophy of the street. Irene and Gypsy Pearl become victims of the street. Jimmy and Jackie end up on Howard Street because they failed at success in mainstream society, and both, along with Gypsy Pearl, end up internalizing, in addition to the philosophy of Howard Street, the ideology of the American dream and the concept of middle-class respectability. Franchot also practices the values of the American dream. It is Hip, more than any other developed character in the novel, who comes to embody the street's philosophy. He lives a totally honest life, seeking self-gratification and immediate pleasure at everyone's expense.

Within *Howard Street*, Heard juxtaposes the lives of these two brothers, Franchot and Hip, who represent the values of mainstream society and Howard Street, respectively. But unlike the other novels and autobiographies mentioned at the beginning of this chapter, *Howard Street* does not Otherize the Howard Streeters. They are not covered over and represented as the Same. Instead, Heard gives us in the Howard Streeter the reason of the Other. And Heard makes them speak as subalternity not in the "official institutional structures of representation" (Landry and MacLean 306). As a result, the reader gets Franchot and Hip speaking from and representing their respective spaces without having their voices and textual positions represented hierarchically.

When Franchot was growing up on Broome Street, everyone predicted that he would wind "up in jail for life, or die by the hand of a policeman or the executioner at state prison" (27). People felt that he was "criminally inclined" because of his "sullen attitude and his persistent—often insulting—silence. For in a black slum if one is not loudmouthed and aggressive, then one is mean, a square or a punk; and Franchot was not a punk in any sense of the word" (27).

In contrast, Hip had been predicted to go far, "which in the Third Ward of Newark—'the Hill' as they called it—could mean that he would wind up being a pimp, or opening a tavern, or making it big in the numbers racket" (27). The people in the neighborhood saw something special in Hip: "The women could actually picture him as their personal doctor attending to their sickbeds, because he was so good-looking and spoke to them so politely. The men could see him as an eloquent power in the courtroom, winning their compensation suits, because he was, by their standards, an articulate extrovert" (27). They thought Hip capable of being successful, of moving up the ladder of the "official institutional structures of representation."

But Franchot is the one who buys into the values and definitions of the mainstream American society. He is ambitious. He becomes hard-working and responsible. He believes in the Protestant work ethic, progress, the patriarchy, family, and love. He "usually felt pretty good after a hard day's work" (28). After their parents' deaths—"of heart attacks one month apart"—he supports his brother Hip. He works in a toy factory and attends classes at the Boys' Vocational and Technical High School. He is currently a brick mason, and he has a "good chance of making foreman on his job next year, and eventually perhaps even forming his own construction company, which was his ultimate dream" (127). He tries unsuccessfully to get and keep Hip in steady employment. He wants to send Hip to business school, as "he'd already done with a number of other young men whom he considered good potential salesmen, ambitious and personable" (30). Franchot is poised to become the American success story.

Hip, or Ronnie Ritchwood, at twenty-six, is Franchot's complete opposite. After Hip wins The Golden Gloves, he quits school and begins to hang around the gym on Market Street. "He roam[s] the streets with his cronies, talking slick, and his bouncy, one-shoulder-hunched walk soon earn[s] him the name Hippy-dip, which [is] shortened to Hippy, and finally to Hip" (29). He becomes the epitome of cool. In his first venture onto Howard Street, he takes money from johns. Franchot's attempts to get him interested in something constructive fail. Responding to the idea of a job, Hip retorts: "damn if he was going to work on some rich bastard's job, slaving for just enough to live on. That wasn't his idea of a good living" (222). Franchot eventually accepts the fact that Hip will "accept no responsibility for anything" (29).

Hip embodies the culture, values, and wisdom of Howard Street. He thumbs his nose at everything—marriage, job, progress, materialism, Christianity, morality—that comprises and drives twentieth-century Western society. He lives outside the law in quiet, passive rebellion against the rest of society. He has "only one standard—self-preservation" (235). He is only concerned with the "course [of action that] would be the most beneficial for him" (171). He lives a totally honest, selfish life, seeking immediate gratification at everyone's expense. He is very quick, agile, and intelligent; he can read the nuances in any situation. He does not play fair and he uses all fools, including his brother Franchot. (However, he does respect smarts.) Anything that is not relevant to his present situation, he shuts it out. This means that Hip lives in the here and now, eschewing any historical tradition or any notion of historical continuity. Gypsy Pearl's sole function to him is to finance his drug habit:

> Aware that she was special, being without a woman at the time, he acted on the premise that if he could put her on Howard Street he'd clean up. She'd easily be a ten-dollar chick and he'd be through worrying about where his next fix was coming from. He could stop throwing so many bricks at the jailhouse and lie back in the shade, cooling it. (82–83).

He sees Gypsy Pearl as "a damned good meal ticket, and a status symbol with high prestige for him" (84). He rules/controls Gypsy Pearl by force and fear. "An independent whore was unmanageable—a man couldn't tell her anything" (167). He calls her "bitch," gives her "hostile" looks, and threatens her with physical violence: "On your ass if you don't shut up" (78). And although he controls Gypsy Pearl because she is the source of his livelihood, he is not possessive of women. He, like Two-Day Sheik, believes that you should "dig her action and . . . let somebody else dig [it], too."

Hip's life, as with other Howard Streeters, is not one of middle-class respectability and materialism. His daily routine consists of eating, sleeping, and either shooting heroin or looking for it. Neither he nor Gypsy Pearl works legitimately, that is, in a respectable establishment. Nor do they hold any aspirations to attain any of the material things that accompany a good job, such as a home, responsibility, taxes, or an ordered, conventional lifestyle. Instead, he trades middle-class respectability, which he obviously defines as stifling to his freedom, for a single room, the laws of the street, and the freedom to do as he wishes, when he wishes.

Of course, Hip is aware that he has options and choices, that he can become middle class and respectable. On several occasions, he thinks of "kicking the habit, getting a job and settling down" (89). But he, like the other Streeters, also knows that given his economic position in society, he can only be exploited as cheap labor. A job also means giving up his freedom to live in the here and now, to seek immediate gratification and pleasure. A job will prevent him from living according to the "hip" values of Howard Street.

Hip's philosophy of life is summed up in a conversation he has with Franchot's girlfriend, Rosemary. Hip and Gypsy Pearl are living with Franchot on the condition that Hip will stop taking drugs, clean up his life, and get a job in Franchot's construction business. When Franchot goes to get Gypsy Pearl out of jail, Hip finds himself alone with Rosemary, who aspires to the African American middle class and believes in the values of mainstream society. In response to Rosemary's question of why he uses drugs, Hip answers: "Sure, I got a million reasons. Take a look at the things that go on, like the way people act to each other, and you'll see plenty reasons. Every time I shoot up I'm sayin' to them: 'Fuck you and your system, lames!'" (177) When Rosemary says that his attitude is wrong, Hip explodes:

> Shit, your attitude's wrong, not mine. You talk that passive junk and you don't get nowhere, not against aggressive and exploitin' people. You gotta rebel and fight! That's what junkies is doin': fightin' against hypocrisy like yours. They see how y'all "good" citizens say one thing and do the exact opposite. Every time a junkie takes off he's rubbin' your face right in your own hyprocritical shit. That what y'all don't like about dope fiends—they take the freedom that y'all is scared to take. You keep on bein' passive and your behind'll be more familiar with shoe leather than your feet." (177–78)

And when Rosemary responds with: "I ain't passive, but I do believe in Christian ethics and law and order" (178), Hip again explodes:

> I ain't botherin' nobody. I ain't no cop and I ain't no soldier. I don't build no bombs and I don't fly no planes nowhere to drop none. I ain't no red-blooded American tryin' my damnedest to spill the red blood of other countries, and I ain't responsible for none of the mess in the world. I'm just a dope fiend. Why they persecute me? I ain't looking for nothin' but peace. Why they pick on me and call me one of the worst things in the world when they killin' people by the thousands—and gettin' ready to kill 'em by the millions? I ain't done nothin' to nobody. All I do is shoot good dope in my arm. Sure, I make an illegal dollar here and there and I don't follow no Christian ethic—but then, I don't claim none, neither. Y'all hypocrites can't say as much, can you? (178).

Finally, when Rosemary asks him if he thinks "prostitution is good, somethin' to be proud of," Hip says:

Right? Good? Where you at, woman?—in the first century somewhere? If a woman wanna sell some and a man wanna buy it, what the hell is your phony morals gotta do with it? Yes, I not only think it's good and right, I know it is. A man is a natural pimp and a woman is a natural whore, anyway, regardless to what the law say. I dig natural law. Dig this. . . . Why you think a man shows off his wife to his boss? Why you think them politicians play up the fact that they are married? And why you think the dumb bastards in this country won't vote for a bachelor for president? Lemme hip you, girl—it's because he ain't got no whore to show. That's pimpin' Christian style, this showin' of wives! So if you git right down to the nitty gritty, the man is livin' off the woman. Just think: all this shit we go through for a crack hung up between some legs! That's where it's at, baby. (180)

Reinforcing this point, poet Nikki Giovanni, in her review of *Howard Street*, writes:

When Gypsy Pearl goes out for Hip, she's doing what every school teacher or social worker does for her husband/man—working to help them both meet another day. It's so easy to condemn a prostitute for selling her body, but who doesn't? What is it but prostitution when we sit somewhere for eight hours a day and make the proper responses to people and things that have no meaning for us? We are placing ourselves at the hands of the same whoremonger as she; only she has the whoremonger's disdain while we have his praise. And of the two, we are the most likely to contract his social diseases. (72-73)

Hip uses "smack [heroin] in order to live" (175). It gives him immediate pleasure and gratification. It gives him a "heavenly peace," a "comatose relaxation" that casts "all other feelings and thoughts away upon the garbage heap of another time. . . . Nothing in the sober world of reality was as good as this; only a fool couldn't dig it" (169, 170). Hip allows the White Lady [heroin] to:

have her way with him. She subdued his body's tremble and gave his weary soul rest. She sent him soaring like a celestial body. He was God, making the world in his own image, peopled by nothing but down souls bursting with all the happiness he could dispense to them. Not a worry anywhere in his world; not a wrinkle on one soul's brow. This was where it was at. This was where it had to be. (182)

And since he is indifferent to death, pain, and suffering, and since he does not believe in progress or a tomorrow, there is no context to talk about Hip destroying his body with drugs, or getting his life together, or preparing for the future. His present is the future.

Hip defines shooting heroin as a form of fighting and rebelling against a system that practices hypocrisy. The system publicly advocates Christian ethics and humanism, but it practices clandestinely and hypocritically the free flow of desires and instinct, "say[ing] one thing and do[ing] the exact opposite" (177). Junkies are honest about their desires and wants. The system has these Thomas Moore utopian ideals of fair play and reason, and the Freudian notion of delayed gratification for the sake of a better society. But what good is a reasonable, ordered utopia if it is populated by a society of stiff-necked, restrained people interested only in doing what falls within the bounds of reason? In taking the illegal step of acting on desires and instincts that are repressed by the system, in taking the illegal move of shooting heroin, Hip becomes an outlaw, a criminal. And it is as an outlaw or a criminal that he achieves freedom. It is also as a criminal that Hip launches an attack on Western culture. He practices honestly the freedom that "good" citizens are afraid to practice. In no longer allowing the system to define him, Hip violates the rules and disrupts the system. More important, he sheds the label of victim, or devalued Other, that the system heaps on him. In renouncing order and reason, and the conventions and values of middle-class Christian society, Hip has chosen a form of radical individualism, which entails the pursuit of happiness—or rather, self-gratification—in order to attain/achieve every possible amount of pleasure out of a drab and tragic existence.

Unlike Johnson's *The Autobiography*, which ends with the ex-coloured man passing for white, seeking the American dream, and embracing the values of middle-class America, Heard's *Howard Street* ends by affirming and validating the swinging life or the non-middle class, nonhumanist, non-Freudian, and non-Protestant work ethic regime of truth and power of the Howard Streeters. After Gypsy Pearl is arrested and Franchot bails her out, Gypsy Pearl and Hip move in with Franchot. Gypsy Pearl returns to prostitution, and Hip, who again has promised Franchot that he will accept a job that Franchot has found for him, disappears. In reaction to Franchot's demand, Hip makes it very clear that he will always live a swing life: "if he didn't want a job that was his business. Didn't nobody own him. If he wanted a swinging life instead of squaring up, who was to say he couldn't have it? Not a damned soul! He didn't owe anybody anything" (223).

When Hip does return to Franchot's apartment, he invites junkies over, and when the narcotics officers bust Franchot's apartment and Gypsy Pearl puts Hip's drugs in her body, the question becomes who will take the weight and go to jail. In letting the narcotics officers know that the apartment does not belong to him, Hip is willing to let Franchot go to jail. He also deduces that Franchot is in love with Gypsy Pearl. Franchot believes that "all she [Gypsy Pearl] needed was to be treated like a woman instead of a whore; to be guided away from Howard Street and the life, or nonlife, it offered. She could be rescued. Her condition was not her fault but his brother's. . . . She was not bad or stupid, she was only afraid" (237). Thus, the dilemma is not who will go to jail, but who/what will Gypsy Pearl choose. Will she choose freedom or prison? Franchot or Hip? She chooses Hip. She "can't send Hip to jail" (238). Seizing on this situation and thinking only about his own self-preservation, Hip ponders:

> If he offered to take the weight for Franchot before she made a choice, chances were that she'd still be his woman after this was over, and Franchot

would still be in his corner. He knew that Franchot wouldn't want a woman who couldn't make up her mind whether she wanted to save him or another man from jail, or sacrifice herself and their chance at happiness by going to jail herself when she didn't have to. With Franchot most things had to be 100 percent or nothing. (240)

Hip also knows that Gypsy Pearl is a whore and will always be one: "The bitch understood that, that's why it was so hard for her to make a decision. She had dreamed for a little while and thought she'd like to be a houswife; that was all right, it was normal. All whores did that now and then, it was expected. But it wasn't for real" (241).

In the end, with the offer of probation from Myers, Hip takes "the weight for the possession" (237). He defines the decision as a "sound investment in his future." Hip then goes through his perfunctory ritual of telling Franchot that when he gets out, he will find a job and get his life together. The difference this time is that Franchot has had a relevation. He has finally realized that Hip has no desire to change. Therefore, he says no to Myers's offer to get Hip out on bond, and he says no again to Myers's proposal to offer Hip probation. This move by Franchot is not expected by Hip, and perhaps for the first time, Hip becomes the fool of someone else's game. Someone outsmarts him. In taking the weight, Hip still has Gypsy Pearl as his woman because Franchot does not want a woman who cannot make up her mind. But Franchot is no longer "in his corner." Thus, Hip, who has no desire to give up the swinging life, to become middle class and respectable, will do his time in jail before returning to Howard Street.

Gypsy Pearl also finally reconciles herself to being a Howard Streeter. She begins to:

fully realize that [Franchot had] meant what he had said, that there was no for-giveness for her, and, strangely enough, with the realization came resolution and acceptance of his decision. She couldn't do otherwise. He had his values and she had hers. She had tried to measure up to his, and through trying, even though failing, she could understand them. She couldn't live his life, but she could appreciate it, perhaps even more than he himself. (245)

As she travels with Franchot in a taxi up Springfield Avenue, Gypsy Pearl reaches a new calm: she knows where home is. When the taxi approaches Howard Street, she tells Franchot to "tell him [the taxi driver] to let [her] out at Howard Street, please." And in offering Franchot a "reduced rate," blowing him a kiss, and walking "beautifully into the bar," Gypsy Pearl accepts the swinging life on Howard Street and accepts the non–middle-class, non–Freudian, non–Christian regime of power and knowledge that characterizes it.

Howard Street ends openly. It ends with a continuation of life on the street. Gypsy Pearl has been released from jail and is returning to Howard Street. Hip is in jail, but after serving his time, he will return to Howard Street, and business will continue as usual. Heard makes no attempt to draw any conclusion about the people of Howard Street. Instead, he seems to simply show the flow of the swing life on the street.

What Heard in *Howard Street* offers is not the romanticized notion that the Howard Streeters, the subaltern/Other, are simply the revolutionary mirror-image of the Western self, that they represent a coherent and unitary subject–position that speaks with the clear and transparent "voice of the oppressed." He also rejects the idea that there is "zero-degree culture" in *Howard Street*. Rather, Heard's *Howard Street* offers a way of life that is different from normative American society. It offers a regime of truth and power that organizes social relations, cultural practices, sexuality, and power relations differently. It offers different definitions of the admired actions and desirable attributes of its characters. The breaking with the rules of normative society and the presentation of a different regime of power and truth can be seen as Spivak's subaltern insurgency: "the cultural constructions that are allowed to exist within subalternity . . . are changed into militancy. In other words, every moment that is noticed as a case of subalternity is undermined" (qtd. in Landry and MacLean 289). *Howard Street* presents a small community that has collectively (and perhaps unknowingly) managed to thumb its nose at everything that comprises and drives twentieth-century industrial American society.

Previously, I discussed how Conrad, through a violent process of assimilation, reduced the Howard Streeters to self. But assimilation works in both directions. Responses flow both ways. Just as normative society defines the Howard Streeters as the Other, the Howard Streeters also define normative society as the Other. The hypocrisy, the social and sexual repression, the rationalism, the Protestant work ethic, and the idea of delayed gratification shared by aspiring and elite/middle-class Americans serve the "internal negative self-definition" of a Howard Streeter like Hip. What is made clear by a subaltern African American such as Hip is that the Other, elite/middle-class America, is not the self.

Although Heard in *Howard Street* uses a swinging life and radical individualism, where immediate self-gratification and the free flow of desires are the norm, to counter a middle-class Christian society, he does not escape completely all the values and definitions of mainstream society. There are certain references to social, economic, and racial hierarchies, notions of beauty, and comparisons such as pimp/whore or husband/wife that suggest a classification of discourses in terms of precisely definable Western/American systems and subsystems.

Like Western societies, as well as many African and Third World societies, the different world presented in *Howard Street* is patriarchal. Because Gypsy Pearl is constructed by all the men in her life, she, to use Luce Irigaray's words, "does not have access to language," and therefore cannot represent herself, except through recourse to "masculine" representation (85). After graduating from high school, her first job is in Red Shirt Charlie's restaurant where she becomes his woman. She is "dazzled by his flamboyant attitude toward life, his new car, fast friends, and the ease with which he handled money and women" (82). But after the fight between Hip and Red Shirt Charlie, Gypsy Pearl becomes Hip's woman, and Hip becomes "responsible for whatever she was" (46).

There are several moments when Gypsy Pearl, certainly a subaltern, tries to speak, to represent herself outside what Irigaray calls the "models that remain foreign to her" or the "'masculine' systems of representation which disappropriate her from her relation to herself and to other women" (85). First, the fact that she uses a "sponge" with her johns indicates that she is trying to save her body, "trying to make it [as] easy as she can" (16). Second, the reader—but none of the men in her life—hears her voice as she rebels against the denial of her "specificity" when Hip asks if she is marrying Red Shirt Charlie and she says, "But what you don't seem to know is that maybe *I don't wanna marry him*" (83; emphasis added). Finally, Gypsy Pearl's attraction to Franchot emanates from an obvious fantasy she has of wanting to be a wife. But she ultimately does not see a way out of prostitution into a "way of living a decent life . . . with someone like Franchot."

Once she enters the life of Howard Street as a prostitute, Gypsy Pearl is constructed as the ultimate sexual object. She is a prop for the enactment of man's fantasies and sexual pleasures. "'Masculine' systems of representation" impose an "identity" on her "according to models that remain foreign to her" (Irigaray, 85). At Red Shirt Charlie's restaurant, where Gypsy Pearl worked, "male patronage increased. . . . She was beautiful and they spent money to watch her walk and hear her talk" (82). At another bar, "one man moving around the bar behind her seemed to rub against her more than was necessary" (25). Even when she was with her pimp, Hip, at the bars, "the men greatly enjoyed looking at her hips in the tight skirt she wore" (112). At Mann's Manor, when Gypsy Pearl enters, Franchot stares "at her in fascination. . . . She moved like a graceful dancer, and a tight green skirt showed the full and ungirdled curve of her hips" (41). And near the end of the text, when Franchot bails Gypsy Pearl out of jail for the last time and she gets off the elevator with Myers and Kaplan, Franchot again constructs her as a caged sexual object: "she stood between the two men like a captured angel. Her shapely legs and round buttocks, her thin waist and the proud set of her shoulders and head, spoke their familiar language to him" (184). But because she is an object of a male transaction, her sexual needs are never met. "She'd never had an orgasm before, not even with Hip or Red Shirt Charlie" (45). Certainly, none of her johns ever touched "her in order to make her really feel it" (45). That Gypsy Pearl may find pleasure in the role of a prostitute is possible. But such pleasure is never more than a masochistic prostitution of her body to a desire that is not her own, and it leaves her in a familiar state of depending on men.

Other women in *Howard Street* are trapped in the patriarchy. Although Rosemary Baker, Franchot's girlfriend, considers herself better than, and/or morally superior to, Gypsy Pearl, Heard in *Howard Street* places her in a predicament similar to Gypsy Pearl's. She will service Franchot's needs, and although the middle-class, Christian, Freudian-socialized reader will view Franchot as more respectable than Hip, Franchot still wants from Rosemary what Hip gets from Gypsy Pearl: someone to help him survive. He wants a wife/woman to "rub [him] down when the working day [is] over, to give [him] a good, hot supper and equally hot loving at night" (28). Both Gypsy Pearl and Rosemary are "working to help [their men] meet another day."

Even in the two carnival scenes, the patriarchy rules. As Mary Russo points out, carnivals have often been sites not of emancipation for women but of brutal violence directed against women:

> Making a spectacle out of oneself seemed a specifically feminine danger. The danger was of an exposure. . . . For a woman, making a spectacle out of herself had more to do with a kind of inadvertency and loss of boundaries: the possessors of large, aging, and dimpled thighs displayed at the public beach, of overly rouged cheeks, of a voice shrill in laughter, or of a sliding bra strap— a loose dingy bra strap especially—were at once caught out by fate and blameworthy. (53)

In the first scene, as Big Frieda and Bunny humiliate and put each other down while they fight over Bill, Bill Grumsley "was in his glory: the unquestionable lord and master. The last time the two women had fought he'd smacked them both, asserting his masculine sovereignty. Now he was playing cool, posing for the crowd" (39). When Bunny's dress flies up around her waist and she is not wearing underwear, a spectacle is made of her because of her "exposure" and "loss of [personal] boundaries" (Russo 53). In the second carnival scene, the "loud-talk session" and the initiation of Irene into the "hip" life serve as "an exhibition of freedom and virility" for Tal and as "the subjugation of [her] will to his, that [she] belonged to" him (218).

Even Sue, who is the most economically successful woman on Howard Street, depends on men for survival. Sue is a capitalist entrepreneur on Howard Street. She owns a house of prostitution, and she has a gambling house where all the affluent gamblers and hustlers congregate. Also, she is defined as the black Third Ward success. Upon visiting Sue's house of gambling, Hip marvels "at the cleanliness of everything, at the richness of the surroundings and the soft, polished appearance here that contrasted so sharply with the upstairs part of the house, and Howard Street in general" (116). But to protect her businesses, Sue has to pay off Detective Slim McNair, who "knew things that happened on the Street even before many of the streeters themselves did" (99).

Howard Street also practices racial discrimination. Brady Torrence's fighting ability is common knowledge on the street; he has had to "dump quite a few guys to establish his position." But because he is white, Brady "wasn't respected as a black man who'd only accomplished half as much as he. Like a black man among whites, he was discriminated against, though not to the same degree, and his reaction was similar: he took what they threw at him, grumbled sometimes, but bore it" (220–21).

Finally, as in any social formation or definition of existence, *Howard Street* has its excesses, paradoxes, prohibitions, and human tragedies. Of course, the most visible and chilling prohibition in *Howard Street* is when Brother Butch,

Jimmy, and Sy rape Sy's mother. Out to rape a prostitute, the three grab the first "unescorted woman coming in their direction," then blindfold and rape her. But the "unescorted woman" is Sy's mother and mothers are revered on Howard Street: they are authority figures. When Jimmy, who loves his mother, is arrested, he is "glad he didn't have to face his mother yet; he didn't want to go through that. He could hear her already: 'Why did you do it, why did you do it?'" (65). Still, when Jimmy does think about his situation in jail, he hopes "his mother [will] soon come and bring him some money" (72). Reflecting on the rape, Jimmy "could only think of his own mother and what he would have done if it had been her that they raped" (74). Earlier, Sy was late because "his mother didn't want [him] to go outta the house, so [he] had to sneak" (63). He later tells the others that he "can't stay out too late. . . . My mother'll have a goddam fit on me if she finds out I split," adding with Brother, "you know how mother is" (65). Sy commits suicide by jumping out of the window at Martland Medical Center.

Thus, Heard's *Howard Street*, unlike Johnson's *The Autobiography*, does not end up reinforcing and reaffirming the middle-class American norm. Instead, it offers a different regime of power and truth that shows/exposes the middle-class norm as a construct. It gives us a subaltern site/location to represent the African American male. It takes certain American social references or cultural signs and recodes them. And despite the fact that *Howard Street* reproduces certain references and comparisons that suggest discourses/classifications that are definable in normative American systems, it also gives us "irrecuperable foreigners" who provide a "sort of separate vigilance" that keeps normative American and African American societies "from closing up, from becoming homogenous and so oppressive" (Kristeva qtd. in Guberman 45). Finally, in recoding certain social and economic references, and in offering a different regime of power and knowledge, it exposes, resists, and contests the middle-class Christian norm as being absolute and total.

Because it does not reaffirm the middle-class American norm, mainstream American reviewers and critics have had difficulties assessing the text. They fail to impute it with cultural capital. Like the aspiring middle-class characters in the novel, most of the mainstream reviewers and critics could not define *Howard Street* as an Other with its own belief system and culture. Instead, they defined it against their middle-class values. They moved to control or transform or even incorporate it. Writing in the *New York Times Book Review*, Alan Cheuse assesses *Howard Street*: "[Heard's] first novel reveals enough news about the criminal class of Newark's black Third Ward. . . . His simple characters thrive not by virtue of their relative purity but because of their natural talents for vice" (9). Using his own middle-class value system, Cheuse defines the Howard Streeters not as African American subalterns who have their own reason, who are different but equal to middle-class Americans, but as "simple characters" who are the "criminal class of Newark's black Third Ward." He interprets their clearly defined "hip" culture and philosophy as "vice." The reviewer for *Publishers' Weekly* describes *Howard Street* thusly: "Howard Street is the heart of the jungle: a street of doomed (but vivid and defiant) souls—whores, junkies, pushers, winos, thieves, corrupt cops—in the smouldering ghetto of Newark" ("Fiction" 70). But despite the move to limit, transform, or control it, *Howard Street*, to use Raymond Williams's terms, is "at least in part [a] significant break beyond them" (114).

Some mainstream reviewers and critics spoke favorably about *Howard Street*. Although they did not define it as radically and gloriously Other to the American middle-class regime, they either recognized its difference or acknowledged certain artistic qualities. Robert Gross in *Newsweek* explains that *Howard Street* "explores a world devoid of middle-class illusions—the vice center of Newark's black ghetto, where junkies, prostitutes, winos and muggers survive by their wits according to their own special amorality. . . . Heard doesn't ask us to pity or to convert the denizens of Howard Street" (97). Gross even discusses *Howard Street* in the context of universal literature. He thinks that "the underlying themes— the search for identity and alternate values—are all integral parts" (97) of *Howard Street*. Echoing a similar recognition of *Howard Street* as a different social organization, Christopher Lehmann-Haupt in the *New York Times* writes: "[*Howard Street*] is a milieu remote from and inaccessible to the Great White Way, and Nathan C. Heard obviously knows it stone cold. He has filled his story with representative vignettes, realistic dialogue, accurate (to me) characterizations, and potentially shocking scenes" (45). Even the reviewer for *Publishers' Weekly* recognizes that "each of Mr. Heard's fully realized characters is individual and distinct. What they all share is not so much a contempt for middle-class life as a sure knowledge that middle-class values are completely irrelevant to their lives" ("Fiction" 70). These reviewers and critics recognized *Howard Street* as possessing a different social milieu, as the product of a peripheral consciousness. But Gross, Lehmann-Haupt, and the reviewer for *Publishers' Weekly* were not willing to accept the Howard Streeters as existing as an Otherness of the same ontological status as the middle-class American norm, without there being mounted an immediate effort at their appropriation.

Among the 1970s/1980s reinventors of the African American literary canon, Heard's *Howard Street* is ignored. It is excluded from Houston A. Baker Jr.'s, *Long Black Song* and *Singers at Daybreak*, Robert Stepto's *From Behind the Veil*, Henry Louis Gates Jr.'s, *Figures in Black* and *The Signifying Monkey*, George Kent's *blackness and the adventure of western culture*, Michael G. Cooke's *Afro-American Literature in the Twentieth Century*, and Valerie Smith's *Self-Discovery and Authority in Afro-American Narrative*. And Heard and *Howard Street* are completely repressed in the recent magnum corpus, *Norton Anthology of African American Literature*, edited by Henry Louis Gates, Nellie McKay, and others. Through their silence, we see how the American/African American literary canons produce and limit their own forms of counterculture. However, Heard's *Howard Street* is mentioned briefly in two major surveys of African American literature. Bernard Bell, in *The Afro-American Novel and Its Tradition*, lumps *Howard Street* into a list of 1960s "first novels" that are about the "appeal of several types of traditional realism. . . . Some are graphic, naturalistic accounts of the sporting life of hustlers, whores and addicts" (245). Likewise, Addison Gayle, in *The Way of the New World*, lists Heard as one of many African American novelists whose fiction "borders . . . upon the naturalism of Richard Wright" (302). Sherley Anne Williams in *Give Birth to Brightness* also places Heard's *Howard Street* in the naturalistic tradition of Richard Wright (85).

But the swinging life—the non-Freudian, non-middle-class, non-Christian, nonhumanist, and non-Protestant work ethic tradition—that informs *Howard Street*, along with the other subaltern African American texts I have mentioned, puts it outside of the aesthetic, political, and literary expectations of most American and African American scholars and critics—scholars and critics who very much operate intellectually within the Western, middle-class, humanistic tradition. When Bell, Gayle, and Williams define Heard's *Howard Street* within the naturalistic tradition of Richard Wright, they are repressing that which is innovative and original about the text and are appropriating it into mainstream American and African American literary norms and aesthetic values.

Perhaps the most interesting and insightful response by an African American to *Howard Street* comes from poet Nikki Giovanni. In a review essay, Giovanni defines *Howard Street* as a:

> masterpiece. For a single work we would compare it to [Carlene Polite's] *The Flagellants*, which we compared to [Ronald L. Fair's] *Many Thousand Gone*, which we link to [Ralph Ellison's] *Invisible Man*, and on into classic Black literature, for just the sheer technical skill and Black understanding he brings us in the book. Nathan Heard not only knows but also loves every one of his characters, and he doesn't waste himself or our time trying to justify it. (71–72)

Giovanni is aware of the class and cosmological differences between the subaltern Howard Streeters and elite/middle-class Americanm and African American critics and readers. She knows that such critics judge that which is different from them as being inferior or less: "Perhaps we mention this [potential class bias] because our middle-class approximations require that he [Heard] indeed should judge them and justify his love. . . . Heard simply says we are—take it or leave it" (72).

Giovanni advocates/warns readers not to Otherize or cover over the Howard Streeters as the Same, but to accept them as Other on their own terms:

> But it doesn't matter what the white man thinks or what we think or even what Nathan Heard thinks about Hip, Gypsy Pearl or Franchot because the only reality is how they feel and how they relate to that feeling—and we can look or not, like or not; it has essentially nothing to do with their lives anyway. Amoral? We would simply think a new [or different] morality. How could any of us dare to judge Hip . . . on the old terms? (72).

Thus, the swinging life in Heard's *Howard Street*, which has its own hierarchies, is not necessarily better or worse than middle-class, Christian American life. However, it is different, and it does contest a representation of the African

American subaltern as pathological and deviant, as possessing "zero-degree culture," as is found in the margins of canonical African American texts such as James Weldon Johnson's *The Autobiography of an Ex-Coloured Man*. Instead, it represents the African American subaltern as possessing distinct subjectivities and agency, as being rich, diverse, and simply different. In *Howard Street*, Heard has simply given us a narrative that cannot be compared socially and culturally to other European humanistic or sociopolitical models. And its difference causes *Howard Street* not to have cultural capital or use-value among those practitioners of European humanism, including elite/middle-class African American literary critics. Until American and African American critics realize that there is a large, but limited, population of African Americans under some set of conditions who live the swing life and who define the world differently than the middle-class, humanist norm, *Howard Street*, which is currently out of print, and an entire tradition of American/African American literature will never be imputed with contingent value, will never be cited, recited, and discussed.

CHAPTER NINE

IDENTITY POLITICS, SEXUAL FLUIDITY, AND JAMES EARL HARDY'S *B-BOY BLUES*

James Earl Hardy's *B-Boy Blues,* published in 1994, is linked politically to what Steven Seidman calls a "politics of interest" or "identity politics" (116–18), or to what Gayatri Spivak calls "identity claim" (qtd. in Landry and MacLean 294). This refers to a politics organized around narrowly defined grievances and goals—the claims for rights and social, cultural, and political representation by a particular racial, sexual, or gendered group. For Spivak "identity claim" is "political manipulation of people who seem to share one characteristic," and in this instance it is the homosexual experience (qtd. in Landry and MacLean 294). According to gay-identity politics, one's sexuality is all-important. It is constructed as a separate, exclusive identity and behavior and is, therefore, comprehensible only to gays. It sets one apart from the mainstream. Gay-identity politics' main focus is on equality within the social framework that heterosexuals have already established. Gay-identity activists, according to John D'Emilio, want to "emancipate themselves from the laws, the public policies, and the attitudes that have consigned them to an inferior position in society" (1). Thus, gays seek freedom by becoming the Same as mainstream, middle-class, straight society.

But gay identity politics and its vision of homosexuality exist in a heterosexual/homosexual binary that otherizes homosexuality and represses sexual fluidity. Sexuality fluidity is the idea that sexuality is plural and fluid, freeing individuals from the constraints of a sex/gender system that locks them in mutually exclusive heterosexual/homosexual and feminine/masculine roles. The first-person narrator and the main protagonist in *B-Boy Blues*, Mitchell Crawford, is the embodiment of gay-identity politics. Although Hardy through Mitchell humanizes the homosexual African American by defining him as the

Same as the heterosexual African American and, therefore, worthy of acceptance, he still reproduces the heterosexual/homosexual binary that defines heterosexuality as normative, timeless, universal, and natural; and homosexuality as
deviant, as sin, as unnatural, as marginal, as ugly, or as devalued Other. But there
also exists in *B-Boy Blues* an element—the b-boys—that undermines gay-identity politics and points toward/signifies sexual fluidity. The b-boys define homosexuality not as Other but as normal.

    B-Boy Blues makes central (homo)sexual themes and experiences that al-
ready exist in the margins of African American literary texts—such as Claude
McKay's *Home to Harlem*; Wallace Thurman's *The Blacker the Berry* and *Infants of
the Spring*; James Baldwin's *Go Tell It on the Mountain*; Gayl Jones's *Corregidora*,
Eva's Man, and "The Women" and "Persona" in *White Rat*; Alice Walker's *The
Color Purple*, John Edgar Wideman's "The Statue of Liberty" in *Fever: Twelve Stories*; Darryl Pickney's *High Cotton*; Ntozake Shange's *Sassafrass, Cypress, and Indigo*; and Jacqueline Woodson's *The Autobiography of a Family Photo*—and that
exist centrally in Alice Dunbar Nelson's "A Carnival Jungle"; Bruce Nugent's
short story "Smoke, Lilies and Jade" and his poetry; Langston Hughes's "Cafe: 3
A.M."; James Baldwin's *Giovanni's Room* and *Just Above My Head*; Ann Shock-
ley's *Loving Her* and *Say Jesus and Come to Me*; Rosa Guy's *Ruby*; Audre Lorde's
Zami and her poetry; Pat Parker's poetry; Jewelle Gomez's *The Gilda Stories, Oral
Tradition*, and *Don't Explain*; Samuel Delany's *The Mad Man*; Gloria Naylor's
"The Two" in *The Women of Brewster Place*; Randall Kenan's *A Visitation of Spirits* and *Let the Dead Bury the Dead*; Sapphire's *Push*; and April Sinclair's *Coffee Will
Make You Black* and *Ain't Gonna Be the Same Fool Twice*. This homosexual liter-
ary tradition in African American literature has been repressed by the sociopolitical mission of racial uplift, the canon of African American literature, and the
Black Aesthetic movement in African American literature. Hardy's *B-Boy Blues*
challenges and exposes this exclusion.

    From at least the early 1950s through the mid-1970s, the idea was wide-
spread in American society that what was called "gay" was "a phenomenon with
a uniform essential meaning across histories" (Seidman 116). Both mainstream
Americans and mainstream gays and lesbians assumed that homosexuality marks
"out a common human identity, which is fixed, non-problematic, and non-ne-
gotiable" (116). Since the mid-1970s, lesbian and gay activists have fought to
build national gay communities and cultures. They formed more than one thousand organizations that directed their energy outward, exerting pressure on leg-
islatures, schools, the media, churches, and the professions (D'Emilio 2).

    Today, a fully elaborated and institutionalized gay community dots the so-
cial landscape of virtually all major cities in the United States. A pivotal part of
this social development was the creation of a national, public lesbian and gay political and cultural apparatus that includes political organizations, liberation
movements, newspapers, periodicals, gay national presses, health clinics,
churches, multipurpose social centers, specialized businesses, and artistic and literary associations. This range of institutions implied the existence of a separate,

cohesive gay community. By the mid-1980s, a national gay and lesbian culture existed for the first time in the United States (Seidman 120). Thus, since the 1960s, a vision of homosexuality as defined by gay-identity politics and culture has been distilled. Gay-identity politics is an ideological construction that reproduces a value system based on the ethnic minority model—that gender preference defines sexual orientation and that homosexuality is defined as a site of identity. I use the term *gay* to identify the ideological construction of this vision of homosexuality.

This national gay and lesbian culture has an African American counterpart/component. Like its national, mostly white, mainstream counterpart, African American gays and lesbians initiated a similar move toward Africentric gay and lesbian community building. And a pivotal moment in their social development was the creation of a national, public black gay and lesbian cultural apparatus that now includes newspapers, monthlies, and quarterlies such as *VENUS, SBC: A Monthly for the Africentric Homosexual, The Malebox, Black Lines,* and *KICKS*; anthologies such as *The Road Before Us: 100 Gay Black Poets* (edited by Assoto Saint), *Brother to Brother: New Writings by Black Gay Men* (edited by Essex Hemphill), *In the Life: A Black Gay Anthology* (edited by Joseph Beam), *Ceremonies* by Essex Hemphill, Audre Lorde's *Sister Outside,* Barbara Smith's *Some of Us Are Brave* and *Home Girls: A Black Feminist Anthology, Shade: An Anthology of Fiction by Gay Men of African Descent* (edited by Bruce Morrow and Charles H. Rowell), and *Go the Way Your Blood Beats* (edited and with an introduction by Shawn Stewart Ruff); movies/documentaries by Marlon Riggs (*Tongues Untied* and *This Is Black . . . This Ain't Black*) and Isaac Julian (*Looking for Langston*); and associations such as The Black Gay and Lesbian Leadership Forum or national conferences such as The National Gay and Lesbian Task Force. This Africentric gay and lesbian cultural apparatus also includes, according to Stanley Bennett Clay:

> a number of small black publishing houses such as GrapeVine Press, Ishai Books, Redbone Press, Moyo Books, Mountain Top Publishing, International Writers and Artists, [and] ProCord Book. . . .[that] turn out dozens of books, fiction and non-fiction, on the lives, loves, the struggles and the triumphs of African American hetero- and homosexuals. (8)

With this cultural apparatus came the emergence of literary texts by African American gay males such as *Invisible Life, Here I Am, This Too Shall Pass, Abide With Me,* and *Not a Day Goes By* by E. Lynn Harris; *B-Boy Blues, 2nd Time Around, If Only for One Nite,* and *The Day Eazy-E Died* by James Earl Hardy; *Like Breathing* by Ricc Rollins; *Gym Rats* by Eric Saunders; *Detached* by Lorenzo C. Robertson; *The Best Man* by Dwayne Carter; and *Low-Hanging Fruit* by G. B. Mann. As does the national, mostly white, mainstream Gay and Lesbian movement, this Africentric Gay and Lesbian cultural and political movement—brilliantly represented in all its passion, ideology, affirmations, conflicts, limitations, and contradictions by

Hardy's *B-Boy Blues*—exists within a naturalized heterosexual/homosexual binary. Within this binary, the two terms *heterosexuality* and *homosexuality*, form an interdependent, hierarchical relation of signification, according to the logic of boundary defining that necessarily produces a subordinated Other.

But homosexuality is both historically created and the result of interpretation. If we acknowledge that sexuality is fluid, negotiable, contextualized, and slippery; that it embodies multiple, competing passions, and that it includes the complex histories of special but nevertheless overlapping and interconnected sexual experiences—straights who have sexual encounters with gays, gays and lesbians who are fathers and mothers, someone with a gay identity who has heterosexual passion, men who could love women as though they (the men) were women, women who could love men as though they (the women) were men, bisexuals, and so on—there is no particular intellectual reason to define it simply as Other than reason, for these features belong to both halves of the binary.

Heterosexuality is also a particular historical way of perceiving, categorizing, and imagining the social relations of the sexes. It was invented in the late nineteenth century to identify "the norm." It is an ideological construct, concealing its signifying practice, masquerading as the normative sexual practice, and occupying a privileged position. All other sexualities must define themselves in relation to it (J. Katz 7). Heterosexuality encompasses the gender difference and the balancing between two essentially different beings: man and woman, strong and weak, hard and soft, rational and emotional. Drawing on the works of Monique Wittig, Michel Foucault, and Adrienne Rich, Judith Butler in *Gender Trouble* defines the heterosexual matrix as:

> that grid of cultural intelligibility through which bodies, genders, and desires are naturalized. . . . [It is] a hegemonic discursive/epistemic model of gender intelligibility that assumes that for bodies to cohere and make sense there must be a stable sex expressed through a stable gender (masculine expresses male, feminine expresses female) that is oppositionally and hierarchically defined through the compulsory practice of heterosexuality. (151n)

Compulsory heterosexuality is a construct that denies sexual fluidity.

Even Freud's theory of infantile sexuality exposes heterosexuality as socially constructed. According to Freud's theory, we are all born in possession of undifferentiated sexual desire. In *Three Essays on the Theory of Sexuality* and in *An Autobiographical Study*, Freud promotes the idea that individuals could share a capacity for both heterosexual and homosexual feelings. He argues that everyone is born with a " 'constitutional bisexuality,' . . . [and] that before the Oedipal complex, erotic desires are initially pluralistic and diverse, without differentiation between attraction to male or female" (qtd. in Tatchell 41). Socialization, rather than biologically innate preference, is the pivotal force in the formation of sexuality. Thus, within the terms of Freud's theory of infantile sexuality, heterosexuality—the differentiation of desire according to sexual difference—is not an innate condition but rather something that is compulsorily imposed through the patriarchy and the Oedipus complex.

The construction of heterosexuality, particularly masculinity, in our society is built on the equation of homosexuality with women's effeminacy and the repudiation of both. Gayle Rubin writes, for instance, that "the suppression of the homosexual component of human sexuality, and by corollary, the oppression of homosexuals, is . . . a product of the same system whose rules and relations oppress women" (qtd. in Sedgwick 3). Within the construction of heterosexuality, traits associated with women and male homosexuals include passivity, subordination, weakness, and wimpiness. Their male opposites are aggression, dominance, strength, and stoicism. It is with the notion I have just discussed of sexual fluidity and against identity politics, or this heterosexual/homosexual regime of power/knowledge and the hierarchies it establishes, that I want to discuss Hardy's *B-Boy Blues*.

In reacting against the unnatural and stereotypical representations of gay African Americans by both elite/middle-class, Christian African American communities and mainstream American communities, Hardy's *B-Boy Blues* produces another vantage point to represent the African American male. It not only effectively humanizes the demonized and Otherized African American homosexual, but through the b-boys also challenges the heterosexual/homosexual regime of power/knowledge. This regime is at the core of Western civilization and serves as a master framework for constructing self, sexual knowledge, and social institutions. It not only defines homosexual experiences as (sexual) Other but also reduces the notion of "the sexual" since it leaves out of consideration any explicit concern with the body, sensual stimulation, and sex acts and relations other than in terms of gender preference.

Hardy's *B-Boy Blues* is told in the first person by Mitchell Crawford, an avowed, middle-class, college-educated, Africentric homosexual African American who works as an editor for *Your World,* "known as the *Time* magazine for teens" (40). As Hardy points out in an interview, the novel is written from Mitchell's point of view, where his wants, desires, interests, politics, class, and aims construct the world of the text (Travis 13). The text explores the joys, pains, and problems of Mitchell and his friends as they live openly gay–identified lives in New York City in the 1990s. More specifically, *B-Boy Blues* concerns the love story between the middle–class Mitchell and the b–boy Raheim Rivers.

Mitchell defines/represents gays as seen through the lens of identity politics. It is a politics that demands equality for gays and lesbians. In short, it is a politics that defines gays as the Same as the dominant society. It comprises a value system based on the ethnic minority model. Arguing for an issue of *Your World* to be devoted completely to gays, "a group of people who are so misunderstood," Mitchell states:

> Lesbians and gays are coming out of the closet more and more, and gaining
> mainstream prominence. The issue will talk about the struggle to be viewed as

> a minority group; legal issues surrounding gay-rights bills and protection from
> discrimination in housing, employment, and adopting and raising children; fa-
> mous homosexuals in history; the controversy surrounding whether to "teach"
> young people about it in school; and how the homosexual community is very
> diverse, racially, culturally, and sexually. (114)

Family and friends are much of the reason why Mitchell accepts his homosexuality. Since his mother, who accepts him "with no strings," and his aunt
Ruth had acquiesced to the silence "surrounding [their brother Russ's] invisible
life and death," they "promised that that would not happen to [Mitchell]," and
when he told his mother that he was gay, she said she already knew and was "just
happy that [he] finally decided to tell her" (166). Mitchell's aunt Ruth had also
"been there for [him], learning as [he] learn[s], discovering as [he] discover[s].
[He] think[s his] Aunt Ruth has read more about homosexuals and homosexuality than [he has]; sometimes she'll come up with something [he has] never
heard of" (167). Mitchell also receives acceptance and positive affirmation/sup-
port from his uncle Russ, who tells him on his deathbed as he dies of AIDS,
"Don't ever be ashamed of who you are, Mitch, no matter what family says, no
matter what friends say, no matter what the world says" (166).

In addition to his family, Mitchell has a group of close friends in Eugene
"Gene" Roberts, Barry "BD" Daniels, and Courtney Lyons, who is known as
"Babyface." They are also middle-class, college-educated, young urban professionals who provide him with social validation and emotional support. Gene is
vice president of public relations at Simply Dope Records, which specializes in
producing rap acts. Babyface is a New York assistant district attorney. BD, the
classic pretty boy, had a career as a dancer with Alvin Ailey before he started his
own "gay-identified" company, NIA, which means "purpose" in Swahili. As a
group, they give each other a social network and positive reinforcement to re-
buff and counter negative representations of homosexuality. They care for, love,
and support each other. They spend Gay Pride Week together, and when one
member of the group has a problem, they call a "Brothers Brunch" to give each
other company and support. They counsel each other after racist and homophobic incidents/encounters.

Also, like many of their Eurocentric brothers, Mitchell, Gene, BD, and
Babyface are (Africentric) humanists who believe in the idea of progress, the
Protestant work ethic, monogamous homosexual marriage, sentimental love,
and a certain purity in values. More important, they have learned to desire from
within the heterosexual norms and gendered structures of mainstream society.
Their vision includes the homosexual as a part of the American norm.

With reinforcement and affirmation from family and friends, Mitchell is able
to become an active, aggressive, and healthy homosexual African American in the
workplace and in society. Being gay becomes a matter of pride. At work, he displays on his desk pictures of beautiful black men. His coworkers at *Your World*
know that he is gay, and he receives love, support, and understanding from several

of them. In staff meetings, he is aggressive, agile, forceful, confident, intelligent, and rational, especially in the way he refutes his coworker, Elias's proposals. But more important, Mitchell's healthy sense of himself as a gay African American male and the recognition of his marginal status allow him to develop a heterogeneous vision of the world that challenges those closed structures, myths, and social constructs that Otherize, objectify, repress, and exclude other people, especially the homosexual African American. He rejects the work of Robert Mapplethorpe and is disturbed by the S & M works of Tom of Finland because they objectify black men. He critiques the bourgeois nuclear family because it marginalizes and belittles "the lives of a majority of the American public," and redefines and expands the definition of family with: "I say we celebrate the family, yes, but not just one type. No matter what type of unit you come from, you can succeed" (117). *Kenan*

Second, Mitchell's sense of himself (and his ambition to view the homosexual African American as the Same as the normative society) allows him to critique other institutions and social constructs that exclude and repress homosexuality. He exposes the African American cultural narrative that says African Americans cannot "be homosexuals because it is not part of [their] culture" (114). He attacks rap lyrics that are antigay. He chastises the black church on its hypocritical stand toward gays.

Finally, in continuing his critique of those modern social structures that exclude and Otherize, or that establish hierachies, Mitchell deconstructs mainstream white gays and lesbians—or a white, middle-class, unitary gay-identity construction—for reproducing the white/black regime of power and truth, which represents itself as normative and superior, because it excludes and marginalizes lesbian and gay-identified people of color. He states:

> I've worked, mostly on a volunteer basis, for a half dozen lesbian and gay groups, and every single time I've come up against this [patronizing, paternalistic attitude.] Whenever I said something sensible . . . you'd think I'd farted. Folks would frown, surprised that I could not only think but express my thoughts. . . . White homosexuals can be just as. . . . racist as their heterosexual cohorts, and the non-relations between the races and the segregation in the Vill[age] are proof. (79–80)

And in a move that causes him to disrupt/challenge the historical representation of the white gay/black gay regime, in which white gays are subjects and black gays are objects, Mitchell chooses to love black men.

Other African American gay writers—such as Melvin Dixon (*Vanishing Room* and *Trouble in the Water*), Larry Duplechan (*Eight Days a Week, Blackbird, Captain Swing,* and *Tangled Up in Blue*), Canaan Parker (*The Color of Trees* and *Sky Daddy*), Steven Corbin (*Fragments That Remain* and *A Hundred Days from Now*), Darieck Scott (*Traitor to the Race*), and Randy Boyd (*Uprising* and *Bridge Across the Ocean*)—who focus on interracial gay relationships become entrapped in the white/black gay regime even as they protest its inequality. But Hardy, along with E. Lynn Harris, Eric Saunders, and Ricc Rollins—in presenting relationships between African Americans that show black men loving black men—contests, debunks, and disrupts the stereotype/myth that black men prefer white men where white gays are defined as the locus/focus of lust and desire, and black gays are represented as intellectually inferior, as the exotic sexual Other.[1]

Therefore, in his love of "color au natural," Mitchell liberates himself from being victimized by this regime and commits what he thinks is a revolutionary act. Discussing why he prefers loving black men, Mitchell states:

> I am not an equal-opportunity lover. When I look into another man's eyes, I want those eyes, his total reflection, to complement mine—physically, emotionally, historically, and spiritually. I don't want to spend my days and nights being a spokesperson for all Black folks, educating my lover about me, about us, constantly challenging his arrogance, correcting his ignorance, and justifying my existence. (202)

Of course, there is something terribly reductive in this description of black men loving black men, for it assumes that all black men who sleep with other black men "complement" each other "physically, emotionally, historically, and spiritually." Mitchell also assumes that all white men are arrogant and ignorant of black life and culture. But despite his rigid conception of white/black gay relationships and his generalization about relationships between black men, Mitchell does understand clearly how the media and other visual institutions have produced this particular white/black gay representation.

But in choosing to love other black men, Mitchell develops a fantasy and a lust not for other middle-class, college-educated gay African Americans but for b-boys who belong to the African American urban subaltern. Because he has "always been a softie, a sensitive, sensuous guy who cries at the drop of a hat," he is jealous of b-boys' "in-yo'-face, gruff-and-grandiose air," and he comes to find this quality about them "sexy" (28). In addition to daydreaming "about having a B-boy," Mitchell has a "curiosity [that] boiled to the point of deep-seated desire," fantasizing about being "picked up in a bar by one homie, agree to go to his house to have some fun, and [they] are joined by two of his buddies. They pass [him] around like a '40,' taking turns sipping and gulping [him] down" (29). When he meets Raheim, he has encountered "the fantasy in full-bodied flesh" (30).

There is a distinct class difference between Mitchell and his friends and the b-boys. Gene recognizes this difference. He thinks that Mitchell's "craving for B-boys [is] due to [his] dealing with so many [middle-class] 'soft' men in the past" (33). Gene is against Mitchell's dating Raheim because "it makes things easier if you're with someone whose income or [social] status is equal to yours" (48). Mitchell also recognizes this difference. He is aware that "most [b-boys] don't want to be bothered with folks who aren't like them" (33). Yet, he pursues them anyway.

But in dealing with b-boys, Mitchell reproduces in his self/other relationship with them the white/black gay regime he criticizes earlier. For the middle-class, college-educated, Africentric Mitchell and his friends, b-boys are appropriated otherness. Mitchell, in his dealing with b-boys, deprives them "precisely of the very alterity by which" they are b-boys (Levinas 33). But like white homosexual racists who Otherize black male sexuality, Mitchell and his friends also Otherize the b-boys by projecting onto them their own lurid sexual fantasies. Gene admits, "their [b-boys'] aura screams sex-lusty, animalistic, ravenous sex" (28). Mitchell wants a b-boy who "could bring out the freak in [him]" (39). To use Julia Kristeva's concept of the Other as the subject's unconscious, the b-boys become Mitchell's unconscious (41). Whatever he recognizes is not doing well in himself—his animalism, his hard exterior, his uncontrollable drive, his eroticism, his bizarreness, his masculinity, his aggressiveness, his outlawness, his heterosexuality, his bisexuality, all of these uncoded marginalities that are not recognized by his constructed gay-identified male subject—Mitchell projects to the exterior and onto the b-boys.

B-boys are Others, or "something else entirely, absolutely other" (Levinas 33), because they reject what bell hooks calls the "masculine ideal rooted in a notion of patriarchal rule requiring a man to marry and care for the material well-being of women and children and an increasing embrace of a phallocentric 'playboy' ideal" (*black looks* 95). They eschew any serious notion of middle-class respectability or the Protestant work ethic, and with time on their hands, they break the law:

> They are the boyz who move to a rhythm of their own—the swagger in their step, the hulking strut that jerks their bodies to and fro, front to back, side to side, as if they are about to fall. Their arms sway to their own beat. . . . They are boyz who . . . are always clutching their crotches. . . . They are the boyz who just don't give a fuck. They are the boyz who are the true hip-hopsters, the gangstas, the menaces 2 and of society, the troublemakers, the troubleseekers, the hoods, the hoodlums, the hood-rocks . . . the rugged hard-rocks. . . . (*B-Boys* 25, 26)

Mitchell's story is about his love relationship with b-boy Raheim. It is also about the clashing of two regimes of power/knowledge and Mitchell's move to appropriate a b-boy into his middle-class narrative.

Raheim Rivers is a b-boy. He often has the "classic B-boy profile: arms folded against his chest, head cocked down, and eyes raised" (121). Like other b-boys, he has a hard exterior and defines himself as a virile heterosexual man. He has had a girlfriend, Crystal, and he has a son. Yet, he has also had a series of male lovers. He has come to terms with his homosexual desires and feelings, and in public he adopts a b-boy stance. Raheim, as Hardy indicates in an interview, "does not identify [himself] as gay or bisexual. He is trying to deal with the fact that he is in love with another man," so he "separates the sex act—or sex itself—from who" he is: "He is just a man who happens to be in love with another man." He cannot see himself as a "homosexual given all that he has been conditioned to believe about homosexuals" (Travis 13).

Given, on the one hand, Mitchell's fantasy of meeting a b-boy who is the exotic Other and, on the other hand, Raheim's qualified openness to his own homosexuality, the stage is set for the inevitable clash between the two. Coming from two different classes, or regimes of power/knowledge, both Mitchell and Raheim define relationships differently. For the middle-class Mitchell, a proponent of gay-identity politics, legitimate homosexual sex should be embedded in a long-term, intimate, committed relationship. He believes in romantic love and gay marriage. For Raheim, who lives for the moment, homosexual sex is more diffused. It is body centered, motivated by carnal pleasure, casual, and involved with role-playing. He looks straight, acts straight, and even thinks that he is straight. He just likes "to fuck other men" (28). Raheim has overlapping and interconnected sexual experiences; he is "self-centered and self-absorbed." The crucial question is, How will two people from different regimes of power and truth, from two different cultural and class milieus, develop a relationship?

Since Mitchell is telling the story, the relationship will be defined within the terms of his gay-identity politics. Immediately, the heterosexual matrix, which is a feature of gay-identity politics and which "assumes that for bodies to cohere and make sense there must be a stable sex expressed through a stable gender that is oppositionally and hierarchically defined" (Butler 151n), defines the relationship between the two. Raheim takes on the role of the stereotypical man, or the active, aggressive partner, the counterpart to his mother in her heterosexual marriage to Anderson ("We both have men in our lives who are younger than us—and they deliver" [164]). Mitchell takes on the role of the stereotypical woman, or the passive, submissive partner. He is the subordinate Other, and his homosexuality takes on the equivalency of women's effeminacy. "He [Raheim] had become my life. . . . My whole world revolved around him" (107). Mitchell sets up house, cleans, cooks, and nurtures, and Raheim becomes the authoritarian/patriarch. Raheim gives the orders and determines the tenor of the relationship. As Mitchell holds the fort, Raheim goes and comes as he please. Raheim desires, and Mitchell is desired. Mitchell becomes the sexual object that Raheim pats on the behind.

Mitchell's gay friends also define themselves within patriarchal, heterosexual terms. They construct themselves as the female/woman in heterosexual-modeled relationships. They practice compulsory homosexuality. Mitchell refers to Gene as Tina Turner's "soul sister" at the beginning of the text. Gene calls Mitchell "Miss Thang." When Raheim hits Mitchell and his friends come to comfort him, they announce upon their arrival that "your sisters are here" (195). In other words, none of the gay-identified characters in the text are willing to give up their egos, their rigid sexual and gender identities, to draw in the being and presence of others, thereby saying there is no (sexual) space others inhabit that cannot be a space they can connect with (hooks, *Outlaw* 219). When Gene and Mitchell are discussing why African American gay males are not coupling—coupling on the heterosexual model being a privileged space in the text—they define bisexuality or fluidity in sexuality as confusion: "They [bisexuals] are confused . . . don't know whether they are gay, straight, bi, or otherwise" (200)

And when the members of his family define Mitchell's relationship with Raheim, it is only defined as the heterosexual Same, thereby keeping in place the heterosexual matrix. Both Mitchell's brother Adam and his mother Annie define/respond to Mitchell as the passive, weak partner who has to be protected. When Adam learns that Raheim hit Mitchell, he wants " to fuck Raheim up" (233). They also respond to Raheim in terms of his manliness. For Adam, Raheim is his "kind of man" (159). When Annie discusses Raheim with Mitchell on the telephone and learns Raheim's name, she retorts: "Raheim . . . how manly" (163). Later, she refers to him as her son-in-law. Both Adam and Annie define this relationship in patriarchal, heterosexual terms, with Mitchell playing the role of the passive, unmanly woman.

But more important, the best confirmation that the relationship between Mitchell and Raheim repeats the heterosexual matrix is the fact that Raheim penetrates Mitchell, which is an obvious sign of the mythic power of men. Raheim's being on top during the sexual act signifies domination. The hetero-eroticism of the relationship, and Raheim's dominant position in it, generates for Raheim a sense of superiority over Mitchell. Conflict arises in the relationship when Mitchell challenges Raheim's dominant position. Further conflict occurs when Raheim reluctantly brings his homeboys to visit Mitchell and they use the word *nigga* loosely in their conversation. When the middle-class, politically correct, Africentric Mitchell objects to the use of the word, Raheim "no longer acknowledged [him] with a smile or squeeze or pinch" (105). Later, Raheim inquires as to why he "had to dis [his] boy" (105). After challenging Raheim for the first time, Mitchell becomes afraid of him.

Another conflict occurs when Mitchell confronts Raheim about not spending the weekend with Junior, his son. When Raheim uses the word *faggot* and Mitchell states that Raheim, too, is a faggot since he has been sleeping with Mitchell for two months, Raheim hits him. In this particular instance, Mitchell, in his move to force Raheim to live by his definitions, has not only challenged Raheim's authority in the relationship but also has attempted to assume a superior male position as well. To reassert his superiority, his dominance, and his masculinity, Raheim uses physical force. The most "masculine" thing a man can do is use violence to show his power.

Mitchell has allowed this relationship with Raheim to repress his aggressive, manly side. Later, Mitchell reflects on whether he "purposely [fell] into a 'feminine' role thinking that would not threaten Raheim's masculinity, so he'd stick around" (259). If we examine some of Mitchell's dealings/affairs and relationships prior to Raheim, we do find a Mitchell who is much less feminine and passive. For example, when he is dating the b-boy Ricky, Mitchell leads. He teaches Ricky how to make love, how to kiss, and how to do foreplay. He also begs Ricky to let him penetrate him.

His awareness of playing the "feminine" role in the relationship gives Mitchell the impetus and desire to reconfigure himself. Therefore, when Mitchell and Raheim reconcile after their fight and express their love for each other, Mitchell gets Raheim to understand that being with another man does not make him a "punk, a pussy . . . or, more to the point, a faggot" (272). It is only after this understanding that Raheim is able to express his love for Mitchell, to become emotional and cry, as Mitchell counsels him: "Half the battle is already over. You know how you feel. Now all you have to do is not be afraid or ashamed of it. . . . And you can't be afraid or ashamed of who you are" (272).

Thus, for a moment after the second conflict, Mitchell and Raheim disrupt the heterosexual model in which they have constructed their relationship. In their first intimate and sustained sexual encounter after these revelations, the reader witnesses further a disruption and transformation of this heterosexual/homosexual, man/woman matrix. Hardy draws a picture of Mitchell and Raheim that is sexually equal with mutual desire. When Mitchell becomes aggressive and penetrates Raheim, who becomes emotional and cries, for a moment Raheim is taken beyond his traditional heterosexual male identity, both formulaic and prescriptive, and Mitchell is taken beyond his traditional submissive homosexual identity. This experience signifies a radically different concept of 'masculinity' and 'sexuality.' It signifies a radically different world. In this moment, Mitchell and Raheim come to represent new definitions of (African American) (homo)sexuality and manhood, ones that eschew an antiquated, patriarchal, heterosexist concept of 'manhood' and ones that engage in what Ron Simmons calls "introspection without fear. To not have to wear a mask of utter invincibility and to realize that identity, and notions of liberation, are intrinsically fluid and require a constant ongoing reflective analysis of self and of society" (141). Hardy, in this moment with Mitchell and Raheim, exhumes from the trenches sexual identities and notions of masculinity and sexuality that exist outside the gay-identified heterosexual matrix.

But this brief, disruptive moment exists only as a rupture and is soon lost in a larger move by Mitchell to not arrive at some fluid concept of manhood and sexuality in the relationship but to get "under that street-tough image" (99) and to appropriate Raheim into his middle-class, gay-identified Africentric narrative. I have already discussed how Mitchell and his friends define the b-boys as different and, therefore, less. But rather than accepting Raheim as "something else entirely, absolutely other" (Levinas 33), Mitchell moves to make Raheim the Same. Discussing theoretically how the Other becomes the Same through comparison, François Hartog in *The Mirror of Herodotus* writes: "Comparison, which is part of the fabric of the world in which things are recounted, enables one to see how things are, either directly . . . or analogically. As an operator of translation, it filters what is 'Other' into what is the 'Same' " (230).

The process of appropriation, of making Raheim the Same, begins when Mitchell identifies those features and values of Raheim, such as the Protestant work ethic and middle-class respectability, that make Raheim the Same as he.

Mitchell points out to a doubtful Gene that Raheim is a BMW—Black Man Working—and he is "making an honest living. It is very easy for a guy his age to be doing something illegal" (48). Earlier, Mitchell makes the point that Raheim, unlike other b-boys "who ain't exactly known for being giving," serves him sexually (62). Later, refuting the stereotype of the b-boys as being dumb, Mitchell argues that Raheim "may be rugged, but [he] has such a great mind. He is not a hoodlum" (97). He points out that Raheim loves to read: he "turned out to be a serious page-turner. He must have studied at Brotha Hakim's School of Speed Reading" (97). Raheim has read two books, *In the Life* and *Brother to Brother*, both African American gay anthologies, "from cover to cover: he was reciting verses from poems and lines from the essays as if he had the books opened in front of him. And, he expounded on what he read, looking to me for guidance in case he misinterpreted or misunderstood something" (97–98). Watching the television program *Jeopardy*, Mitchell is surprised that Raheim offers questions to answers easily: "You'd think he was Encyclopedia Brown" (98). Mitchell's objective is to compare Raheim analogically to his normative definitions and values, to "filter" the Other, Raheim, into the Same.

In his reconfiguration of Raheim as the Same, Mitchell also imposes gay-identity sexuality on him. Early on, Mitchell shows Raheim as coexisting and cohabiting within both homosexuality and heterosexuality. But Mitchell, in his appropriation of Raheim, represses this sexual fluidity by imposing compulsory homosexuality. For example, we are aware that Raheim's sexuality has a heterosexual dimension. He has a son, Junior, and he has been in a relationship with Crystal, Junior's mother. But Mitchell has Raheim dismiss/reject his heterosexuality by saying that Junior was conceived when he "was clockin' most pussy. But that was befor' I found out wha' makes my shit really jump" (126).

Thus, the attempted transformation and appropriation of Raheim by Mitchell into his middle-class world—which also is an attempt by Mitchell to fight the uncoded marginalities in his own unconscious—is accomplished as a result of all kinds of exclusions and repressions. With Mitchell's counsel, Raheim gives up the tough guy, b-boy exterior and learns to cry and be emotional. He becomes less self-centered and self-absorbed and more responsible. He apologizes for hitting Mitchell: "I'm sorry. I neva shoulda hit you. . . . I ain't neva gonna do it again, Baby" (270). He accepts being penetrated sexually by Mitchell. Also, when Mitchell counsels Raheim that he should not be "ashamed of who [he is]," Mitchell is talking about not being ashamed of being a gay-identified person. And because he loves Mitchell, Raheim is expected to stop using the language of his world. He will not call Mitchell a "bitch," "ho," or a "nigga." He will reject the world he comes from where homosexual sex is more diffused.

In Mitchell's attempted transformation of Raheim and the b-boys into the Same, the reader sees how Mitchell covers over their alterity and represses differences. He sees how Mitchell does not allow b-boys to speak, how he patronizes and speaks for all subaltern African American homosexuals. The reader sees how Mitchell determines what the subaltern African American's interests ought to be. The reader also sees what kind of construction of the African American homosexual is taking place. What readings of African American homosexuals are being subordinated and repressed. But more important, the reader discerns the class position and interest from which Mitchell speaks, and how Mitchell's middle-class, college-educated values become the values for all African American men who sleep with other African American men.

Mitchell's narrative in *B-Boy Blues* effectively humanizes homosexual African American males by defining them as the Same as the heterosexual, middle-class norm, by exposing hierachical binaries, and by contesting stereotypical notions of men loving men. For Mitchell, being gay is a matter of pride, not pathology; of resistance, not self-effacement. Although for only a moment, he also signifies a radically different and more fluid concept of manhood and (homo)sexuality. Still, he does not challenge his class position or his Christian morality. He does not challenge structurally and completely the heterosexual/homosexual regime of power/knowledge. The Mitchell/Raheim relationship not only defines homosexual experiences as Other but also reduces the notion of the sexual. It leaves out of consideration any explicit concern with the body, sensual stimulation, and sex acts and relations other than in terms of gender preference. Mitchell's narrative does not dismantle the whole conceptual schema that categorizes homosexuals as deviants. For example, for a book to speak so brilliantly about a vision of the world that does not Otherize or objectify, that "really stand[s] for the rights of all people to be protected against all forms of oppression" as Hardy advocates in an interview (qtd. in Travis 16), that does not force individuals to repress desires, and that does not establish a hierarchy that privileges certain races and definitions of family, gender, and sexual roles, while it still preserves the heterosexual model, Mitchell Crawford's narrative in *B-Boy Blues* becomes a paradox.

First, like the narrators in the popular fiction of Terry McMillan (*Disappearing Acts* and *Waiting to Exhale*)—fiction that is enmeshed in mass culture—Hardy's narrator in *B-Boy Blues*, on the one hand, critiques the objectification of African American males and, on the other hand, participates in and reinforces that objectification. Mitchell rejects the works of Robert Mapplethorpe because of their objectification of black men. He critiques some white gay males because they reduce black men to such stereotypes as studs or Mandingos. Yet, in most of his descriptions of potential African American lovers and sexual partners, Mitchell resorts to a similar kind of objectification. His descriptions of Raheim are all sexual. When Raheim walks into the bar, Mitchell describes him thus: "He looked like he'd stepped out of a Cross Colours ad. A green cap was on his head. His nipples poked out of his long-sleeve blue-block green-striped shirt, which nicely draped his protruding chest. . . . [H]e was at least six feet tall, maybe two hundred pounds, had pretty Hershey's Kiss chocolate-drop skin" (16). In the bar, when Gene goes to get the scoop on Raheim, he brings back to Mitchell the size of Raheim's penis. Later, when Raheim delivers photos to

Your World, Mitchell again describes him solely in physical and sexual terms: "He stood up and, as I took him in, from head to toe, I gagged. It was Raheim. He was wearing a white tank and black Spandex, both hugging him so well they seemed to be holding his physique hostage" (44). And when he describes their first night together, Mitchell describes Raheim thus:

> While his physique was as solid as a rock, it was also as smooth as a baby's bottom. His clear skin didn't have a bruise, a blemish, or a blotch anywhere—not even on his big pretty feet. And the only cuts to be found were those that defined his manly muscle legs, manly muscle thighs, manly muscle arms, manly muscle hands, manly muscle abs, manly muscle chest, and manly muscle back. Uh-huh, a brick . . . *howse.* (59)

In these detailed sexual and physical descriptions, Mitchell objectifies Raheim into his vision of the idealized man. He is attracted to Raheim for his manly qualities: his physique, his height, and his sensuality and sexuality. And these graphic erotic descriptions seduce the reader to project himself/herself into this relationship.

A second paradox in Mitchell's narrative concerns his definition of gay marriage. Despite his professed Africentricity and advocacy for expressed individual desires, Mitchell's narrative and his gay-identity politics become entrapped in a Judeo–Christian, heterosexual, repressive, monogamous definition of marriage. My aim is not to establish an argument against homosexual marriage. In a society in which marriage has become very much a secular institution, any two individuals who want to get married should be able to apply for a license and get married. Marriage per se is not my concern here. My concern is whether homosexual marriages, as they are represented by Mitchell's narrative in *B-Boy Blues,* challenge or transform the heterosexual/homosexual regime of power/knowledge. We first encounter the concept of marriage in *B-Boy Blues* when Gene argues against a relationship with a b-boy and Mitchell concludes that "for people like me [Mitchell], who are looking forward to being 'married' someday, a b-boy is not exactly husband material" (28). Also, during the weekend when Raheim and his son visit Mitchell, and Mitchell prepares dinner for the two, Mitchell, as he washes the dishes, "wishes that he could have Pooguie's [Raheim's] baby" (133). After BD and Babyface decide to get married, Mitchell refers to BD as Babyface's "soon-to-be-wife" (254). Thus far, this idea of marriage and togetherness seems very much modeled on the Judeo–Christian, middle-class, heterosexual definition of marriage where it is monogamous and its main function is procreation.

The nature of Mitchell's conception of 'marriage' is further clarified when we examine Babyface and BD's engagement and planned wedding. Before getting married, Babyface and BD agree to have their one last fling. With BD's permission, Babyface will have an affair with Mitchell because he, BD, knows how much Babyface has "wanted" Mitchell. BD will have his fling with Vincent Alloway, or the Muslim salesman. Then the two will settle into a monogamous marriage. At the end of *B-Boy Blues*, Gene, the "certified synic (sic) . . . who has been burnt very badly," comes around, falls in love with Carl, and considers a monogamous relationship/marriage. Of course, as Pat Califia points out, this monogamous institution of marriage will force Gene, Babyface, and BD to repress individual desires and wants. Thus, Mitchell in *B-Boy Blues* ignores "the entire assumption about human nature that lies behind the concept of marriage" (Califia 61). Just as Babyface, Gene, and BD have desires for others before their marriage, they will have desires for others during their marriage. But as Califia points out, "very few people who get married, let alone homosexuals, remain monogamous" (61). And Babyface and BD do not have children and property to force them to stay together. Therefore, when their repressed desires eventually manifest themselves in extramartial affairs, the repressive institution of monogamous marriage will not be critiqued, only the expression of those repressed desires. Neither Babyface nor BD will ask questions about the institution of the family and its linchpin, marriage—which are based on inequality and coercion—as problematic constructions whose basic structure and unconscious sexual dynamics are at odds with a relationship between two modern democratic men. You would think that Mitchell could have come up with a new social form or ritual of togetherness that reflects, rather than represses, these desires. Instead, he reproduces in gay relationships the repressive, heterosexual, middle-class, Christian monogamous notion of marriage.

There is a third way that Mitchell's middle-class, gay-identified narrative in *B-Boy Blues* becomes a paradox. Although Mitchell successfully deconstructs other naturalized and hierarchical structures or regimes of power/knowledge such as mainstream white gays and lesbians, the black church, and the bourgeois nuclear family, he establishes his own hierarchies. In his quest for political correctness, he represses and marginalizes other African Americans, particularly those African Americans who do not practice his "correct" form of homosexuality. Although Mitchell argues against an exclusionary model of the family that we all should follow to be an American family, he ends up arguing for a correct model for black men loving black men.

Mitchell has this incredible need to define everybody according to rigid sexual labels such as *gay* and *straight*. His stepfather and Adam are straight. When Raheim meets Mitchell's brother, Adam, and jokingly says, "I'm gonna hafta try botha ya'll out befo' I make up my mind," Mitchell says, "He's straight. But I ain't" (56). When Raheim introduces Mitchell to his son, Mitchell's first question is:

> [S]ince he has a son, does this mean that he is not gay? Of course, there are a lot of gay men who have children. . . . In order to do that heterosexual "life style" thang right, they court women, which can naturally result in their producing children. . . . And if he turned out not to be gay—something I assumed was so—that would certainly change things. I had dated (unknowingly) so-called straight and bisexual men before, and it's nothing but heartaches (123).

Mitchell's "gaydar" also tells him that Elias is gay and that his cousin Alvin is gay (123).

Despite the fact that the majority of men who sleep with men also sleep with women, Mitchell will only accept a model of (homo)sexuality in which men sleep with men exclusively. He belittles the lives of the majority of African American men who sleep with both men and women. He puts down his ex-lover Edward Rochester II, a Morehouse man with "matinee-idol looks and class for days" (84), who is married. He cannot imagine and accept a world and a sexuality in which multiple, competing passions exist, in which his coworker Phillip Cooper can sleep with men, be "flamboyantly heterosexual and also [be] engaged to a Spelman beauty queen" (114). And this project to deny sexually fluid individuals, bisexuals, and b-boys their voice and to constitute them as Others who have to be covered over as the Same is to demand "the repression and denial of whatever [is] within [African Americans who practice sexual fluidity] and each other [that] doesn't fit that paradigm" (Simmons and Riggs 140). This project to deny the voice of sexual fluidity is what Spivak calls epistemic violence ("Can the Subaltern Speak?" 280). Thus, we see Mitchell practicing and perpetuating a violence similar to the one that Riggs refers to in his discussion of all African American males being forced to accept a rigid image of masculinity.

Mitchell also applies his rigid definition of the middle class to the b-boys. In his attraction to b-boys, he knows that they define the world differently than he, that they do not believe in middle-class respectability and the Protestant work ethic, and that they use words such as *ho*, *bitch*, and *nigga*. Yet, he refuses to accept them as different and equal. For example, Mitchell cannot accept the b-boys' use of the word *nigga*. Raheim—trying desperately to speak, to make Mitchell hear him—explains his world to Mitchell. "That is just the way he talks. . . . Yo, I can tell you ain't down wit it. You jus' don' undastan'. But ev'rybody don' think like you, a'right? . . . It's where he comes from. If you ain't a part of it, you not" (105). This move by Raheim can be interpreted as counterinsurgency. It is his effort to involve himself in representation that is not according to the middle-class American norm. But his move does not catch, and therefore, he cannot speak. Yet, Mitchell, who critiques his editor in chief, Steve Goldberg, for "being ignorant as the rest of the white men at *Your World* about anything and anybody that doesn't fall into the realm of their white male world," refuses to accept anybody "that doesn't fall into the realm" of his middle-class, gay-identified world. Mitchell argues that "there is only one way to take that word [*nigga*]," and he cannot accept, as Raheim argues, that DC has "taken a term that thousands of [African Americans] have been killed with . . . doing a little spelling change, and using it as a term of endearment when addressing 'brothers'" (106). Rather, Mitchell wants them to accept his middle-class values and his middle-class belief system, and when they refuse, he defines them negatively. More important, Mitchell cannot imagine the kind of power and desire that inhabit the b-boys, for everything he says and does is caught within the debate of the constitution of the middle-class homosexual subject, in which homosexuality and a concept of the middle class are sites of identity.

Mitchell is complicit in the persistent constitution of b-boys as the self's shadow. He simply refuses to tolerate any other organization of homosexual African American life that is not gay identified, mainstream driven, and middle class.

For Mitchell, Gene, BD, and others, as Peter Tatchell argues, gay identity and middle-class status have become sexual and class security blankets that they clutch tightly at all times. These concepts define their whole being. Providing more than a mere sexual orientation, their gay identity offers a complete, ready-made alternative lifestyle. Uncomplicated and unchallenging, their gay identity offers a mental refuge from the unpredictable sexual ambiguities and vagaries of the social world where heterosexual and homosexual desires so often coincide and intermingle. The loss of that identity will undermine the core of their being. They cling tenaciously to a sense of gayness and to a notion of the middle class, with all of their connotations of invariable sexual and class orientation, certainty, and exclusivity. Anything that clouds the distinctions between straight/gay and middle class/subaltern is considered suspect and dangerous. Hence, their hostility to class difference and sexual fluidity, bisexuality and bisexuals. Their identities as middle-class gays give them the security of a stable, fixed, nonnegotiable, unchanging class and sexual orientation (Tatchell 46).

Mitchell's straight family is also caught up in equally narrow and repressive class and sexual structures. Regardless of how much Annie, Anderson, Ruth, and Adam say they love and accept Mitchell, Mitchell has this gay identity, a (homo)sexuality that is Other, alien, or different and, therefore, less to them. To them, homosexuality is not normal. Annie, Ruth, Anderson, and Adam take unconscious pleasure in the security of their naturalized heterosexuality. They have what Slavoj Žižek in the introduction to *The Metastases of Enjoyment* calls "enjoyment as a political factor" (1). Žižek , who is from Bosnia, uses the example of coming to the United States to lecture on Alfred Hitchcock at an American university campus to illustrate this type of enjoyment. During his lecture, a member of the audience asks him immediately:

> "How can you talk about such a trifling subject [as Hitchcock] when your ex-country is dying in flames?" [He answers] "How is it that you in the USA can talk about Hitchcock? There is nothing traumatic in me behaving as befits a victim. . . . [S]uch behavior cannot arouse compassion and a false feeling of guilt that is the negative of a narcissistic satisfaction—that is, of my awareness that they are all right while things are going badly for me. . . . This experience of mine tells us a lot about what is really unbearable to the Western gaze in the present Balkan conflict. . . . The unbearable is not the difference. The unbearable is the fact that in a sense there is no difference: there are no exotic bloodthirsty 'Balkanians' in Sarajevo, just normal citizens like us. The moment we take full note of this fact, the frontier that separates 'us' from 'them' is exposed in all its arbitrariness, and we are forced to renounce the safe distance of external observers . . . so that it is no longer possible to draw a clear and unambiguous line of separation between us who live in a 'true' peace and the residents of Sarajevo who pretend as far as possible that they are living in

peace—we are forced to admit that in a sense we also imitate peace, live in the fiction of peace. Sarajevo is not an island, an exception within the sea of normality; on the contrary, this alleged normality is itself an island of fictions within the common warfare. This is what we try to elude by stigmatizing the victim." (1–2)

Žižek is explaining how we establish false security to attain enjoyment and pleasure, and how we subsequently repress differences by naturalizing and homogenizing and totalizing our own space, and Otherizing and devaluing others.

I want to use Žižek's frame to deconstruct the heterosexual/homosexual binary that Mitchell and his friends and family use to construct naturalized and Otherized notions of identity and sexuality. In this analogy, Mitchell and homosexuality become the victim/Other. Ruth, Anderson, Annie, and Adam define Mitchell as a victim, and they relate to and identify him only in terms of his homosexuality/gayness, which, within the binary, is different and less. But in their secure naturalized heterosexuality, there is Žižek's "narcissistic satisfaction." Annie, Ruth, Anderson, and Adam are all right while things are tenuous for Mitchell. But, as Žižek warns the Americans, and the warning is appropriate for Annie and the rest, "the unbearable is not the [homosexual] difference. The unbearable is the fact that in a sense there is no difference": that homosexuals are not some mysterious, abnormal Others, but just normal citizens like heterosexuals, and that homosexuality is not something that is (sexually) Other or a burden that ten percent of the population unfortunately possesses, but a part of everyone. There is no frontier that separates the straight Annie, Ruth, Anderson, and Adam from the gay Mitchell, Gene, BD, and Babyface.

There is no (homo)sexual Other or frontier that separates straights from gays because everyone is both heterosexual and homosexual, regardless of whether she/he acts on both. Heterosexuality and homosexuality are not watertight, mutually contradictory, and irreconcilable sexual orientations. Sexuality is fluid; it is a continuum of desires and behaviors, ranging from exclusive heterosexuality to exclusive homosexuality. Besides Sigmund Freud and Judith Butler, others such as Hélène Cixous, Julia Kristeva, and Gilles Deleuze and Felix Guattari define a pre-Oedipal and non-Oedipal sexuality that is fluid. In *The Anti-Oedipus*, Deleuze and Guattari define this fluid sexuality as bisexuality. They write:

> [E]veryone is bisexual, everyone has two sexes, but partitioned, noncommunicating; the man is merely the one in whom the male part, and the woman the one in whom the female part, dominates statistically. So that at the level of elementary combinations, at least two men and two women must be made to intervene to constitute the multiplicity in which transverse communications are established—connections of partial objects and flows: the male part of a man can communicate with the female part of a woman, but also with the male part of a woman, or with the female part of another man, or yet again with the male part of the other man, etc. (69)

Hélène Cixous uses:

> the qualifiers of sexual difference, in order to avoid the confusion man/mascu-
> line, woman/feminine. . . . Bisexuality . . . is . . . the location within oneself of
> the presence of both sexes, evident and insistent in different ways according to
> the individual, the non-exclusion of difference or of a sex, and starting with
> this "permission" one gives oneself, the multiplication of the effects of desire's
> inscription on every part of the body and the other body" (from "Sorties" qtd.
> in Sellers 41).

Finally, Julia Kristeva in *Desire in Language* defines this fluid sexuality as "semiotic." The semiotic process relates to the chora, a term meaning "receptable,"
which she borrows from Plato, who describes it as "an invisible and formless
being which receives all things" (6). It is also anterior to any (sexual) space.

When Annie, Ruth, Adam, Anderson, Gene, BD, Babyface, and Mitchell,
as well as others, realize that the straight/gay binary is arbitrary and that everyone has located within them two sexes or bisexuality, they will be "forced to re-
nounce the safe distance of external observers, so that it is no longer possible to
draw a clear and unambiguous line of separation" (Žižek 2) between straights
who pretend to live in a naturalized, safe heterosexual world and gays such as
Mitchell, Babyface, Gene, and BD who pretend as far as possible that they are
living in a secure homosexual world. With sexual fluidity or bisexuality or semiotic, all are forced to admit that in a sense they are imitating safety, that they all
live in the fiction of safety. To use Žižek's words, homosexuality is not "an island,
an exception within a sea of normality." On the contrary, this alleged heterosexual "normality is itself an island of fictions" within sexual fluidity (2). A concept of 'sexuality' that *normalizes* homosexuality is what Annie, Ruth, Anderson,
Adam, and other straights are trying to elude to by Otherizing/stigmatizing homosexuality and the homosexual victim. Unfortunately, Mitchell also eludes to
sexual fluidity. He does not normalize homosexuality. In defining homosexuality outside the (hetero)sexual norm, he reaffirms the heterosexual/homosexual
binary and the representation of the homosexual as deviant or devalued Other.
Neither Annie, Ruth, Anderson, and the other "heterosexuals," nor Mitchell,
Gene, BD, and the other gay-identified "homosexuals" understand the language
of sexual fluidity. Therefore, they continue to define self-identity and sexuality
according to the language of the heterosexual/homosexual binary, which defines heterosexuality as natural and normative and homosexuality as deviant, unnatural, and Other.

Obviously, I am not arguing that people do not *practice* exclusive homosexuality and exclusive heterosexuality. Nor do I want to privilege sexual fluidity as
an essentialized alternative. However, I am arguing that neither homosexuality
nor heterosexuality is natural or essential. Both are fictions/constructions. I am
also arguing that sexuality is fluid, formless, and amorphous, that it is a continuum of desires and behaviors, and that we can only know it through the various
forms, fictions, and discourses in which it manifests itself. Everyone's liberation is

irrevocably bound up with the dissolution of separate, mutually exclusive, rival orientations and identities. Once everyone accepts the fact that she/he is both homosexual and heterosexual, (sexual) Otherizing and stigmatizing disappear.

Finally, there is a fourth way that Mitchell's narrative in *B-Boy Blues* becomes a paradox. There is an indication of "a discussion on Africentrism" (86). Mitchell considers Raheim as "being Africentric" (104) because he espouses occasionally black nationalist rhetoric. But the only thing Africentric about Mitchell's vision is the language. In *B-Boy Blues*, Mitchell and, to some extent, Hardy go the distance in critiquing a white male-centered gay-identity politics. But when you examine Mitchell's politics, he in many ways has reproduced those white male-centered gay-identity values and definitions in an African American site. Mitchell and his middle-class, college-educated, urban professional, gay-identified friends believe in the idea of progress, the Protestant work ethic, monogamous homosexual marriages, sentimental love, and a certain purity in values. Thus, despite the fact that Mitchell refers to his vision as Africentric, his values are staunchly middle class, Christian, and Protestant work ethic. The appropriation of an Africentric vision, which purports to be something other than mainstream white America, becomes a way that Mitchell shows how he needs the Other, the non-middle-class African American, in the construction of his narrative as different without acknowledging that Other as Other.

Thus, Mitchell in *B-Boy Blues* does not disrupt but reinforces the heterosexual/homosexual regime as a master category of sexual and self-identity. His compulsory homosexuality or gay identity becomes a mirror opposite of the compulsory heterosexual model whose tyranny it disputes. It becomes as exclusivist, limited, provincial, and discriminatory in its suppressions and repressions as the heterosexual regime. "An intentionally oppositional gay identity, by its very coherence," argues Leo Bersani in *Homos*, "only repeats the restrictive and immobilizing analyses it set out to resist" (3). Mitchell's gay-identity politics or compulsory homosexuality is oppositional. It erects rigid psychological and social boundaries that are self-limiting and socially controlling, and that inevitably give rise to systems of dominance and hierarchy—certain feelings, desires, acts, identities, and social formations are excluded, marginalized, and made inferior. It stigmatizes the experiences of those individuals for whom sexual object-choice does not adequately describe their sexual and intimate lives. In short, in my critique of Mitchell's gay identity, I am arguing against the very question of identity, which can be oppressive. When you fight for something, as many gays (and straights) do, you begin to believe that you are what you are fighting for. I want to clear a space from which to create a perspective on sexuality that is a self-separating project and that is against territorial occupation, but that need not bring in questions of identity and voice.

Mitchell in *B-Boy Blues* is assuming that homosexuality is a phenomenon with a "uniform essential meaning across histories" (Seidman 116), that homosexuality is fundamentally integral, coherent, separate, and, therefore, comprehensible only to homosexuals. The difficulty with theories of essentialism and exclusiveness, or with barriers and sides, is that they give rise to polarizations that absolve and forgive ignorance and demagogy more than they enable knowledge. The danger with compulsory homosexuality and the whole movement of identity politics is that resistance can harden into dogma. A strain of fascism and conservatism runs through Mitchell's sex-based-identity politics—revealed by the shrillness with which its name and symbol are debated and the vehemence with which its boundaries are policed. However, due to the traditional location of gay rights within leftist politics, Mitchell's fascist streak, inherent in demanding such a fixed identity, is obscured. Mitchell's representation of homosexuality in B-Boy Blues, no matter how sincerely it speaks in the name of liberation, cannot escape the suspicion that it exhibits particular social interests and entails definite political effects. All images of homosexuality have power and knowledge effects or are perceived as a production of social hierarchies. In essentializing compulsory homosexuality, Mitchell's narrative in B-Boy Blues fails to keep community before coercion, criticism before mere solidarity, and vigilance ahead of assent.

Furthermore, in this essentializing, oppositional effort, the heterosexual/ homosexual regime of power and truth that defines the heterosexual as natural, timeless, and normative and represents the homosexual as Other, psychologically abnormal, morally inferior, and socially deviant remains in place. It remains a master framework for constructing self, sexual knowledge, and social institutions. And in leaving in place this regime, Mitchell does not challenge a social regime that perpetuates the production of the homosexual subject and of social worlds that still represent the homosexual as Other. With its focus on, and privileging of, homosexuals as a common human identity, monogamous marriage, middle-class respectability, and Protestant work ethic, Mitchell's narrative in B-Boy Blues resignifies the dominant culture, but in ways that could only fortify that culture's dominance. He also surrenders to what Seidman calls current, popular, and fashionable liberal gay politics to a single interest group politics of assimilation. Mitchell's advocacy of gay rights alone, without any deeper commitment to the transformation of sexuality, to use the words of Tatchell, is "concerned only with removing homophobic discrimination"; he wants "to reform society, not fundamentally change it" (47). But, homophobia is an integral part of the heterosexual/homosexual regime.

And although Mitchell does everything within his power to deliver gay-identity politics as the appropriate way to define black men sleeping with black men, and to appropriate b-boys and Raheim into the Same, he does not succeed completely. Despite the ending in which Raheim accepts his homosexuality, accepts the fact that to love another man is not to be defined as a "punk" or "faggot," he never comes out—the signature acceptance of gay-identity politics. Raheim (and the b-boys), unlike Mitchell, Gene, Babyface, and BD, never practices "identity politics" or makes Spivak's "identity claim." His sexuality does not set him apart from mainstream society. He "separates the sex act—or sex itself— from who he is. He is just a man who happens to be in love with another man" (qtd. in Travis 13). He is open to (homo)sexuality without organizing his identity around it. In an interview, in response to the comment, "I notice you didn't get him [Raheim] to come out. I think most people were expecting that given *B-Boy Blues'* ending," Hardy states: "I know most people were expecting that . . . but it's not going to happen" (qtd. in Travis 15). Raheim never organizes his identity around narrowly defined grievances and goals—the claims for rights and social, cultural, and political representation by a homosexual subject.

Thus, in the margins of Mitchell's narrative, where b-boys are repressed, appropriated, and subordinated, Hardy constructs a more fluid concept of 'manhood/masculinity/sexuality.' The b-boys not only defy an iconic and mainstream definition of African American manhood/sexuality, but also destabilize the heterosexual/homosexual regime by refusing to define (homo)sexuality as unnatural, as a sin, or as deviant. Hardy constructs a representation of manhood and sexuality in the b-boys that flaunts traditional masculine/sexuality facades. He gives us b-boys who have come to terms with the possibility of homosexual feelings, desires, and yearnings not only in themselves but also in their friends and homies. Hardy assesses:

> Here are "men" who throw their masculinity around for the entire world to not only see but swallow. . . . Of course, it is a rather . . . exaggerated take on manhood. . . . Banjeeness has become a boyz2men rite-of-life for many pre-teen/teenage post-teen males in the so-called inner city. And the vibe these fellas give off is an overtly "straight" one. But B-boys do come in all ages, . . . persuasions, . . . mutations, . . . and orientations. (27)

With the b-boys, heterosexual and homosexual desires coincide and intermingle.

Hardy disrupts/challenges this regime further by having "heterosexual" b-boys not only coexist but also cohabit with homosexuality. Through the b-boys, Hardy brings "masculinity into perilously close contact with that which must always be disavowed: homosexuality" (Simpson 5). In this disruption, Hardy undermines and challenges traditional categories of masculinity and heterosexuality and, thus, opens the space for different forms of masculinity/sexuality to emerge. As I have stated, b-boys inhabit both the heterosexual and homosexual spaces. For them, having sex with another man does not make them less of a man or less valuable. They see it as liberating, as inhabiting all the possible spaces available to them. Through the early Raheim, before he is unsuccessfully appropriated, and the other b-boys in *B-Boy Blues,* Hardy again disrupts and challenges this heterosexual/homosexual regime by asserting the right to sexual fluidity, by normalizing, rather than Otherizing, homosexuality. In accepting their homosexuality as normal (even without the public's permission), the b-boys ultimately transcend homosexuality.

Furthermore, in transcending homosexuality, the b-boys represent a broader sexuality, one that expands erotic boundaries in sex-positive directions. They undermine the heterosexual hegemony and by doing so they contribute to the diminution of all erotic guilt and repression, heterosexual and homosexual. They represent an extension of sexual freedom that ultimately benefits everyone. The b-boys' assertion of the right to sexual fluidity creates the conditions for the dissolution of homophobia and the evolution of a new eroticism that transgresses the boundaries of the heterosexual/homosexual regime/binary. In normalizing homosexuality, the b-boys establish the precondition for the abolition of the heterosexual/homosexual regime. They erode the heterosexism that is the ideological cement of the heterosexual/homosexual division. They dismantle the whole conceptual sexual schema that categorizes homosexuals as deviants. Within the b-boys, sexual differentiation has broken down, distinct orientations have become blurred, and the labels of *straight* and *gay* have lost their meaning and relevancy.

Although Mitchell claims to hold the only definition of Africentric homosexuality—or of black men sleeping with other black men—the individuals in *B-Boy Blues* who most closely represent the self-identified, politically active, sexually predatory gay black man, the typical or mainstream African American homosexual (if typical or mainstream means majority) are probably Raheim, who has a son, Junior, by Crystal with whom he had a relationship; DC, who has a three-year-old daughter named Precious and a girlfriend named Latricia; and Angel, who has a four-year-old daughter, Anjelica, and who lives with a woman. They are guys who have wives or girlfriends and a child/children and who also hang out with their boys, go to gay bars and b-boy bashes once a week on Fridays, and warn their wives/girlfriends not to ask what they are doing on their night out with the boys. They are in the army, in the gyms, and living at home with their parents, acting straight all day with friends held from high school, but getting on gay phone-sex lines, the Internet, or visiting their male lovers at night.

Of course, my intention is not to romanticize b-boys and establish another binary. Although b-boys in Hardy's text effectively disrupt the heterosexual/homosexual binary and the middle-class notion of manhood, they do not escape the patriarchy completely. Although Angel and DC have come to terms with sexual fluidity and practice a different concept of manhood, they are sexist. They still think in terms of dominant/weak and subject/object. They refer to women as "hos" and "bitches." Also, they define gay-identified males as weak, passive, and Other. When both respond to the relationship between Raheim and Mitchell, they define Raheim as the dominant/subject half of the binary and Mitchell as the weak/object half. Outside their practice of sexual fluidity, the two remain patriarchs. The crucial question is, could Angel and DC recognize and accept a relationship between two dominant, aggressive men? Could they accept a relationship between equal b-boys in which both inhabit heterosexuality and homosexuality? Can they accept the brief moment when Mitchell and Raheim step outside their prescribed roles? The ending of *B-Boy Blues* might indicate that Raheim, in no longer defining Mitchell as the passive, submissive partner, has disrupted even this dominant/weak binary. Of course, this ending also has much to do with Mitchell's need to appropriate Raheim into his middle-class narrative. Thus, although Hardy in *B-Boy Blues* shows a different representation of manhood/sexuality in the b-boys, he represses and subordinates it for the middle-class, college-educated narrative of Mitchell Crawford.

Raheim and the b-boys who practice sexual fluidity are much more in tune historically with (homo)sexuality as it has been practiced and documented in black communities than with Mitchell and his gay-identity politics. Many prominent African American figures have practiced a (homo)sexuality that is more diffused. They have had complex histories of overlapping and interconnected sexual experiences and have practiced a fluid sexuality that embodies multiple, competing passions.

Although she was married to Will "Pa" Rainey, Ma Rainey, the first vaudeville entertainer to incorporate the blues into her performance who has justifiably become known as the "Mother of the Blues," was known to take women as lovers. Bessie Smith, the "Queen of the Blues," was also known for her bisexuality. Claude McKay, a writer associated with the Harlem Renaissance though he spent most of the 1920s in Europe, was active in Parisian gay circles and pursued relationships with both sexes (Garber 326, 337). Countee Cullen, also a poet of the Harlem Renaissance, was a husband and a homosexual. In 1928, at a highly publicized ceremony attended by several thousand, Countee Cullen married Nina Yolande DuBois, the daughter of W. E. B. DuBois. Months later, he was rumored to have sailed off to Europe with Harold Jackman, his best man at the wedding. Divorcing Yolande in 1930, Cullen in 1940 married Ida Mae Roberson, sister of the singer Orlando Roberson (Garber 337). Although playwright Lorraine Hansberry was married for most of her adult life, states Elise Harris, she somehow found time between writing *Raisin in the Sun* and drinking bourbon with James Baldwin to have passionate affairs with highly eligible bachelorettes (97).

This tradition of signifying on sexual fluidity among prominent African Americans continued after the 1960s. With the rise of the gay-identity movement in the 1960s, Samuel R. Delany, the noted African American novelist, in an interview with Joseph Beam, quotes Bruce Nugent, who was born in 1905 and was a Harlem Renaissance artist–writer, on the movement: "I just don't see why everyone has to be labeled. I just don't think words like homosexual—or gay—do anything for anybody" (Delany and Beam 204). Even in describing his own experiences and history, Delany represents his life in terms of difference: "As a black man, I tended to straddle worlds: white and black. As a gay man, I straddled them too: straight and gay. I'd been leading a pretty active gay sexual life from the time I was seventeen. But on my second or third heterosexual experience, I found myself on my way to being a father. So, at nineteen I got married" (186).

James Baldwin, in an interview, echoes a similar resistance to gay-identity politics. In response to Richard Goldstein's question, "Do you feel like a stranger in gay America?" Baldwin responds:

The word "gay" has always rubbed me the wrong way. I never understood exactly what is meant by it. . . . I simply feel it's a world [the gay world] that has
very little to do with me, with where I did my growing up. I was never at
home in it. Even in my early years in the Village, what I saw of that world absolutely frightened me, bewildered me. I didn't understand the necessity of all
the role playing. And in a way I still don't. (qtd. in Goldstein 174).

Later, in response to the question of what he thought about gay men being parents, Baldwin, who spent most of his life practicing exclusive homosexuality, retorts, "Look, men have been sleeping with men for thousands of years—and
raising tribes" (182). Echoing sexual fluidity and stating the normality of homosexuality, Baldwin, in response to the question of whether homosexuality is
universal, says, "Of course there's nothing in me that is not in everybody else,
and nothing in everybody else that is not in me" (182).

The poet Audre Lorde was a wife, mother, and lesbian. Finally, the noted
African American dancer, Bill T. Jones, who was bisexual in college and who
had an eighteen-year homosexual relationship with Arnie Zane, also questions
the rigidity of gay-identity politics. He states: "I think that sometimes as gay
people we're too uptight about, 'Are you gay? Are you straight?' . . . I think
we're a little too tight. . . . Particularly gay men. . . . I think a lot of it is in men's
heads though" (qtd. in A. Jones 37). Yet, ironically, Hardy in *B-Boy Blues*, who
professes an Africentric vision, is much more in the tradition of mainstream,
middle-class white gays and lesbians than in this historical African American
homosexual tradition.

Writing in the introduction to *In the Life*, Joseph Beam argues that homosexual African Americans "have always existed in the black community" (16). In
this chapter, I have shown that there is a long, diverse, and rich homosexual
African American literary tradition. Yet, this tradition has been ignored, repressed, and excluded not only by the 1970s/1980s reinventors of the African
American literary canon but also by all the previous inventors, reconfigurators,
and reinventors of that canon. Even the magnum opus, *Norton Anthology of
African American Literature*, edited by Nellie McKay, Henry Louis Gates Jr., and
others, represses and excludes this tradition. But through anthologies, critical
studies, journals, newspapers, and quarterlies, African American writers, scholars, and intellectuals are creating a gay/sexual fluid site/location to represent the
African American.

VOODOO, A DIFFERENT AFRICAN AMERICAN EXPERIENCE, AND DON BELTON'S *ALMOST MIDNIGHT*

In 1986, when William Morrow published Don Belton's *Almost Midnight*, African American literature was in the midst of a renaissance, especially among black women writers. In 1982, Alice Walker received the Pulitzer Prize for fiction for *The Color Purple*, which sold more than four million copies and was adapted into a movie. In 1983, Paule Marshall's *Praisesong for the Widow* had high visibility. Also in 1983, Gloria Naylor's *The Women of Brewster Place* sold well in hardback and paperback. It won a 1983 American Book Award and was later the basis for a television movie. In 1988, Toni Morrison's *Beloved* won the Pulitzer Prize for fiction. In 1989, Terry McMillan's *Disappearing Acts*, which sold thirty thousand copies in hardcover, was auctioned off to a paperback reprinter for more than $180,000. McMillan's *Waiting to Exhale,* published in 1993, was even more successful commercially. It remained for months on the *New York Times* bestseller's list and was auctioned off to a paperback reprinter for more than one million dollars. In 1990, Charles Johnson received the National Book Award for *Middle Passage,* and in 1993 Ernest J. Gaines greeted a Pulitzer Prize for fiction for *A Lesson Before Dying.* Later, in 1997, Morrison's *Song of Solomon* and Gaines's *A Lesson Before Dying* would become bestsellers again as a result of the *Oprah Winfrey Show*'s book club. And in 1993, for the first time, three African American women writers—Morrison (*Jazz*), Walker (*Possessing the Secret of Joy*), and McMillan (*Waiting to Exhale*)—were simultaneously on the *New York Times* bestseller's list. Finally, in 1994, Morrison became the first black woman and first African American to receive the Nobel Prize for literature. But in the midst of this renaissance in African American literature, Belton's *Almost Midnight* was un-heralded and went quietly out of print.

With the women-focused renaissance in African American literature as a result of the Feminist movement and the reconfiguration of the African American literary canon in the 1970s/1980s,[1] a repression took place within African American fiction, especially among post-1960s black male writers. Despite the fact that the 1970s/1980s was a period of growth in African American fiction, the selected texts that were privileged by African American critics were few. Many earlier novels by African American males—such as Chester Himes's *If He Hollers Let Him Go*, Nathan Heard's *Howard Street*, William Melvin Kelley's *A Different Drummer*, Willard Motley's *Knock on Any Door*, John O. Killens's *And Then We Heard the Thunder*, Charles Wright's *The Messenger*, John A. Williams's *The Man Who Cried I Am,* and others that were popular and critically successful before the 1970s/1980s reconfiguration of the canon—were also lost from the literary histories of African American literature. Likewise, many novels by black male writers that were published after the women-focused renaissance, the Black Aesthetic movement, and the canon reconfiguration but that did not meet the aesthetic, political, and ideological criteria of either were also excluded, re-pressed, marginalized, or simply ignored. Richard Perry's *Montgomery's Children* and *No Other Tale to Tell,* Jake Lamar's *Bourgeois Blues* and *The Last Integrationist*, Darryl Pinckney's *High Cotton*, and John Holman's *Squabble and Other Stories* come to mind. Belton's *Almost Midnight* is also one of these "invisible others." Why was Belton's novel published and then simply ignored?

The history of the critical reaction to, reception of, and subsequent repression of *Almost Midnight* is complicated and varied. But it is accurate to say that it has been reviewed, represented, and interpreted by mainstream American and African American critics and reviewers as an anomaly, as an Other than reason. Belton's *Almost Midnight* is informed by Voodoo, and *Almost Midnight*, and the heterogeneous Voodoo regime of truth and power that informs it, is defined by mainstream critics as something alien, otherworldly, and mysterious. But it is its Voodoo belief system and vision that allows the text to construct/textualize an African American life and to present a protagonist outside the white/black bi-nary. *Almost Midnight* and Voodoo constitute another, different site/location to represent of African American life and literature. Because of its Otherness, *Almost Midnight* does not have any sanctioned, mainstream literary capital. But, its Oth-erness, its Voodoo representation of African American life effectively disrupts the white/black binary, challenges the position of the African American as inferior and as devalued Other, and supports the argument for African American differ-ences. Therefore, I want to observe and reevaluate *Almost Midnight* because I be-lieve it has contingent value for a "limited [American and African American] population" under some "limited set of conditions" (B. H. Smith 94).

I want to read Belton's *Almost Midnight* as a minor text. In a thought-pro-voking chapter entitled "What Is a Minor Literature?" Gilles Deleuze and Felix Guattari define the literatures written by oppressed minorities in a major language as minor: "A minor literature doesn't come from a minor language; it is rather that which a minority constructs within a major language" (*Kafka* 16). For Deleuze and Guattari, the minor is an intensive, often vernacular use of a language or form that disrupts its official or institutional functions. The minor has no desire "to assume a major function in language, to offer its service as a sort of state language, an official language" (16).

Deleuze and Guattari delineate three major features of a minor literature. First, in a minor literature, "language is affected with high coefficient deterritorialization" (16), which is largely the effect of a decoding of the major language. The minor comes into play precisely because it is innocent of any passion for the code of the majority language—a language that has denied the minority its own validity, its own existence. Therefore, the minor literature moves to expose the very mishmash that the code of the majority language seeks to exorcise.

A second characteristic of a minor literature, state Deleuze and Guattari, is that "everything in [it] is political" (17). In major literatures, the individual concern joins with other individual concerns. The history and the social are a given. The major literature assumes everyone knows them. But the history, culture, and social milieu for a minority in a major language are never a given, because the majority language has a tendency to exclude, repress, or subordinate such aspects of minorities. Therefore, in a minor literature, the individual concern becomes all the "more necessary, indispensable, magnified, because a whole other story is vibrating within it" (17). "A minor literature's cramped space," argue Deleuze and Guattari, its constant efforts to write itself into existence, to validate its existence, "forces each individual intrigue to connect immediately to politics" (17).

A third and final feature of a minor literature, according to Deleuze and Guattari, is "that in it everything takes on a collective value. . . . What each [minority] author says individually already constitutes a common action, and what he or she says or does is necessarily political, even if others aren't in agreement" (17). The collective nature of a minor literature is derived from the fact that "minority individuals are always treated and forced to experience themselves generically" (17)

Belton's *Almost Midnight* is a minor text constructed in the majority language. It has no desire "to assume a major function in [the majority] language, to offer its service as a sort of state language, an official language." It has no passion for the code of the majority language. Rather, it wants to ruin, exceed, or decode the majority, middle-class Christian language. It wants to give history, validity, and existence to Voodoo as a way of life that has been excluded, repressed, or subordinated by the majority language. It wants to present a world not defined by white injustice, or the white/black binary, but one defined in its own system of referentiality or its own code of communication—in other words, in its own language. (Belton and *Almost Midnight* face an even more difficult task in that the very language or philosophical discourse he must necessarily use to depict the specific world he wants to depict is one that is debased by mainstream society.)

Therefore, *Almost Midnight* moves to expose the very mishmash that the code of the majority language seeks to exorcise. In opposing the oppressive quality of the majority language, *Almost Midnight* restores, to use Hal Foster's concept, the "conflictual complexity of productive modes and sign-systems that is written out of the causal history" of mainstream American/African American culture and contests the majority code as "an absolute sign system" (178).

Almost Midnight's Voodoo philosophical countertradition and minority status put it outside all of the critical and aesthetic expectations and preconceptions of various mainstream reviewers. Because *Almost Midnight* represents a countertradition that is non-middle class, non-Freudian, nonconventional Christian, nonhumanist, and non-Protestant work ethic and because it gives a different representation of the African American, it comes under considerable repression when it appears before the tribunal of the bourgeois, humanistic morality of mainstream critics and reviewers who have the power to impute texts with literary/cultural capital. Reviewing *Almost Midnight* for *Booklist,* Mary Ellen Quinn writes: "Perhaps because our encounters with him [Daddy Poole] are mostly secondhand, it's never clear why Daddy was able to exert such a powerful influence throughout his long life" (1181). In her review in *Essence,* Paula Giddings relegates the text to the status of the Other:

> the story unfolds with the language and razored sensibility of the ghetto, but, although there are flashes of skillful writing, the author's inadequate use of dialogue to reveal characters' inner workings keeps them from ever rising above stereotype. Nevertheless, those who enjoy this type of social realism will find it worth reading. (28)

Reviewing *Almost Midnight* in the *New York Times Book Review,* Claudia Tate writes: "Without a doubt, this novel presents an assortment of unusual characters, but the power to make the reader share the force of their lives is not sustained. Telling an interesting story and making readers feel its intensity, ultimately moving them to understand the author's commitment to it, are different activities. Don Belton's first novel is absorbing. The next one may wield memorable power" (24).

To understand the negative critical reception of *Almost Midnight,* one has to understand the structural limitations of mainstream American and African American critics. One has to understand the liberal, middle-class, humanist Christian tradition within which they write and how *Almost Midnight* and its Voodoo belief system threaten them. When mainstream critics such as Tate, Quinn, and Giddings cannot rewrite a text into the institutionalized norms of the African American literary canon, the Black Aesthetic movement, or black feminist literary inquiry, when they cannot appropriate a certain literary text to serve their cultural, political, and ideological agendas, or mainstream aesthetic and humanistic conventions, they simply ignore it or define it negatively as the Other.

Therefore, since neither Giddings nor Tate can accept *Almost Midnight* as a narrative text presenting a normalizing human/literary experience, they Otherize it by defining it as different and, therefore, less. For them, *Almost Midnight* becomes "this type of social realism" as Giddings condescendingly defines it and an "assortment of unusual characters" as Tate labels it, indicating that the characters are out of the norm or are Others. Of course, neither Giddings, Quinn, nor Tate mention Voodoo in their reviews of Belton's novel. To interpret the novel in a different heterological critical site in which it receives positive affirmation, in which the Other is defined by its own logic, distinction, reason, and rules, one has to define and interpret it within a Voodoo philosophical tradition.

In a blurb inside the front jacket of the book, Madison Smartt Bell alludes to this philosophical countertradition, this difference, that informs *Almost Midnight*.

> It came at a good time, just when I was beginning to think that almost all contemporary fiction has turned deathly dull. This book is a rare thing: a really comprehending treatment of people who are usually either ignored or noticed in all the wrong ways. And Belton has seized hold of a living language and brought it to magical intensity.

A second blurb by Nicholas Delbanco inside the front jacket of the novel also refers to and accepts the text's difference from mainsteam texts. Delbanco writes: "There's dark power here, the brooding nighttime presence of Daddy Poole and his stable of women—those dying generations at their chant. Much vivid language, many lightning-lit tableaux: a first-rate novel and gift." Finally, reviewing *Almost Midnight* for the *San Francisco Chronicle*, Bonnie Nadell writes that "Belton . . . produces voices that have the power of a gospel meeting in full swing. . . . Don Belton has written a tale of characters and a city that readers won't forget for a long time" (4).

But just what is the Voodoo philosophical countertradition that informs *Almost Midnight*? Who are the people that are ignored or noticed in all the wrong ways? How is their existence defined? How do they challenge the representation of the African American as victim or as Other than reason? In Belton's *Almost Midnight*, the people who, as Bell notes, "are usually ignored," or who are "noticed in all the wrong ways," are whorehouse madams, prostitutes, pimps, Voodoo priests and priestesses, numbers runners, hit men, illiterate urban peasants, the working poor, homosexuals, and drug sellers, all of whom are different from and, therefore, are denied voice, power, and representation within traditional middle-class, Freudian, Christian society. These people are joined by lawyers, doctors, politicians, and other professionals whose spiritual needs and desires are not being satisfied by traditional Western religions. In *Almost Midnight*, Voodoo "brought deliverance to [these] captive people, made saints of thieves and prostitutes, [and] healed the sick" (47).

In *Almost Midnight*, the architect of this Voodoo philosophical countertradition is Daddy Poole. *Almost Midnight* tells the story of Daddy Poole, who was born to Mozelle, a madam and Voodoo queen in New Orleans, and was raised there by his middle-class, Christian Creole grandfather Dominick Sylva, and later in Newark, New Jersey, by his mother. He becomes a Christian minister very early, but that ministry ends in failure. It is only after his mother teaches him the works of Voodoo that he is able to build a philosophy, a life, a congregation, and a following that exist outside and, therefore, challenge organized Western religion. As a new Christ, Daddy Poole ushers his flock into life after death, into a world of multiple, free-flowing desires. He devises a church that allows him and others to satisfy their own desires, regardless of race, class, or spiritual needs. Daddy Poole is a radical individualist whose "game" it is to use everyone and everything to achieve and maintain power.

When the novel opens, Daddy Poole, now an old man, lies dying at the rear of 28 Prince Street in Newark. He has been living at 28 Prince Street for many years, but no one sees him go and come. There is a calm about him as he prepares for death, communicating with his dead mother Mozelle. He has lived a life in which he acted on his desires and attained power. This action has allowed him to take control of his destiny, to build his Metaphysical Church of the Divine Investigation. And taking control of his destiny has allowed him to live a rich and fulfilling life, teaching and helping others to act on their own desires and to better their own lives. He has passed the family's Voodoo tradition on to his daughter Martha, and he now awaits the end.

Like his church, Daddy Poole exists as multiple entities, as a series of signifiers. He has a series of names (Sam, Gabriel, Daddy Poole) and a series of identities. The reader hears Daddy Poole's voice only briefly. He is defined, constructed, and represented almost completely through the language/narrative of various female narrators who take turns telling their stories and the story of Daddy Poole. Each narrator projects a personal meaning onto Daddy Poole. In telling her own story, she takes from Daddy Poole what she needs. But Belton is effective in showing that each narrator's story is a discourse that permits and excludes certain information, for in the telling, each narrator's story supports and undermines the other stories. This means that truth exists only in narrative/discourse (and it is a contingent truth).

Peanut's and Savannah's stories, or their representations of Daddy Poole, are perhaps the most modern. Their stories are rigid and repressive. They are weighed down with all the mores, prejudices, values, taboos, and conventions of Enlightenment ideas and Judeo–Christian beliefs. Both women have clearly defined notions of right and wrong, good and bad. They believe that there is a Christian God who will punish those who behave badly, that there is retribution for those who practice what their narratives define as evil and wickedness. In short, they are completely ignorant of the intricacies of Daddy Poole's Voodoo game.

The tone of Peanut's narrative is one of bitterness and anger. Peanut has spent all of her life in Daddy Poole's shadow, and she thinks he is wicked and evil. Her mother Mattie works for Daddy Poole during the Depression when Savannah Spark is his main woman. Peanut grows up around Daddy Poole's game in Newark, which consists of his church, a stable of whores, an illegal gambling business, magic powders and potions, and a drug business. She is aware of his political power in Newark: he is a ward boss, and he has the commissioner, the police, and the mayor on his payroll. She believes he has "the gifts of visions." According to Peanut, Daddy Poole is a larger-than-life figure for anybody growing up in Newark. "Daddy turned himself into a dream in this here city and entered the minds—in one way or another—of every man, woman and child" (47).

Also, Daddy Poole turns Peanut out. When Daddy Poole dismisses Leavima because she refuses to stop doing drugs, Peanut becomes one of Daddy Poole's main whores. "All I knew was I was having a ball. I felt like I was rich or a movie star. I was wearing them fancy form-fitting gowns with the padded bra and padded ass. . . . You couldn't tell me I wasn't into something" (161). Peanut tricks for Daddy Poole for five years, until one morning she "just woke up and aint fe[lt] nothing no more for him" (162).

Convinced that she knows the truth about Daddy Poole and that he has to "answer for the things he made us do" (16), Peanut, discussing him with Martha, Daddy Poole's youngest daughter, defines Daddy Poole from a Judeo–Christian, logocentric perspective, in which notions of sin and good and evil are paramount. She condemns him for having babies all over Newark. She says that he fucked "many young girls" and put them out "on the street and left [them] dried up and crawling with the rails" (16). She says that he brought dope "into these streets, . . . [e]ver since the heroin came to town, we been living in our last days" (24). She points out that Daddy Poole had a stable of whores who were in love with him and he "used to fuck every one of [them] at least one or two times a month" (149).

Peanut also recounts how Daddy Poole controlled and physically abused his prostitutes, especially Leavima, whom he had turning tricks in the bathroom, and Blanche, whom Peanut thinks he physically abused after she birthed a daughter, Martha, rather than a son. Blanche, according to Peanut, lived with Peanut for several months before she disappeared. "How the hell he [Daddy Poole] think he going to drag hisself into Heaven with one foot in Christianity and the other in sin? Your father aint never cared about nothing but money and keeping his pecker stuck in some sister's gash. Nobody don't know what all he done to get all that power and money, a half-black man in 1904. Or what he had" (166). She believes that he has to pay for his sins.

Peanut blames Daddy Poole for the downfall of many women. She says to Martha, "A whole lot of women been messed up with your father. Not only colored women, but white ones too, all kinds. Not just here in Newark, but all over. One thing about all of them: Once Daddy marked them, they never got free. That include me. . . . Your Daddy got to pay for the shit he dealt women" (27, 28).

Peanut is telling her story "because somebody's got to tell it. Because it's got to be told" (25). When Martha asks why she is dwelling on the past, Peanut retorts that the past is "the days what made today and made every day to come"

(25). She is bitter and angry and wants revenge, and the bitterness informs her narrative. She also believes in the Enlightenment idea of progress. She thinks that by telling Martha her story of Daddy Poole's ruinous behavior, she can save Martha. Peanut lectures: "I'm drumming it [her story] into you same as my mother drummed it into me. The biggest problem with niggers is they don't know they own history. And you got to know your history, else you just going up against a beast . . . like Little David without a sling" (25). Peanut believes stories can save people. Her mother's story about Daddy Poole stopped her "from wanting to be [Daddy's] whore when [she] was a kitty. . . . [I]t saved [her] from ever being Daddy's fool" (150, 151).

Peanut believes that Martha is the last link in a chain that has denied women freedom from Daddy Poole. She defines Martha as being a "part of something [that] started long before [she] was born," as the "last link on the chain of [her] father's women. [She is] the link what could break and set [them] all free" (26). Peanut envisions Martha "walking . . . clean and free. Walking for [herself] and for all the women [who] came before [her]. Women what could have walked. Free women what couldn't claim they freedom" (26). Therefore, she wants Martha to abandon Daddy Poole and to "get [herself] a man and give [her] baby a father" (13). Peanut thinks that if Martha learns the truth about Daddy Poole, she can give herself "a chance to be somebody" (16).

Despite its persistent, consistent, and bitter condemnation of Daddy Poole, Peanut's narrative undermines itself in a number of ways. First, Peanut problematizes her narrative early when she states to Martha: "Nobody knows how your father ran his churches and all his business. . . . Some people said it was a kind of hoodoo the way your daddy did his business" (44–45). She knows nothing about Daddy Poole's *modus operandi*. Second, Peanut makes it clear that Daddy Poole never brainwashed her and that she became one of his prostitutes on her own free will: "And you can say whatever you want about me, but Daddy aint never had me brainwashed" (149). This means that her mother's admonishing story about Daddy did not stop her from becoming one of Daddy's whores. Also, Daddy Poole did not force Peanut to become/remain one of his whores. When she meets Jake, she gets "a pad over on Peshine Avenue. No more tricks" (44). Thus, Peanut's action contradicts her earlier statement that "once Daddy marked them [women], they never got free."

Third, despite her condemnation of Daddy Poole, Peanut praises him for making "the whole city swing" (42). Peanut's definition of the good life comes from the life Daddy Poole has created in Newark. The ease with which she moves from turning tricks for Daddy to being Jake's woman is a result of the kind of non-middle-class, non–Christian Voodoo blues community produced by Daddy Poole and his church on the Hill. Also, the ease with which she moves from having sex with men to having sex with Martha is made possible by the new social space created by Daddy's game on the Hill. Thus, although Peanut, on her mother's advice, believes that there is "nothing in the streets," she spends her entire life enjoying the freedom, the immediate gratification, and the free flow of desire of the streets. She likes to dance. In fact, as the section of her narration ends, she calls into work sick and heads to Brooklyn to party.

Fourth, there are times when Peanut simply does not have the facts about Daddy Poole and, therefore, comes to the wrong conclusion. For example, Savannah Sparks says she heard Daddy's "first sermon in Newark and [she] heard his last" (36). But Peanut argues that Savannah "never once set foot in one of Daddy's churches for nothing" (154–55). In another instance, Peanut believes that Daddy killed Miss Blanche, but Martha refutes that statement by saying Daddy "wouldn't kill nobody. He love life—all of it" (74). In addition, Sarah Anderson would disagree with Peanut on her conjecture that once Daddy Poole marked her, she "never got free."

Finally, it is problematic whether Peanut knows Mozelle. She thinks that Mozelle was "a spirit sitting up in a chair at [Daddy's] church" (87). But Martha informs Peanut that "Mozelle was before your time. Before your mother's time" (87). Later, Peanut admits that her mother came to Newark not "long after 1927" and that she had heard "about this near-white madam . . . who had a cathouse supposed to be so great on Avon Avenue," but she had never heard "nothing about this landlady being the mother of Daddy Poole" (87). Thus, it is very clear that Peanut's narrative is a product of a socialization that intermingles the nonrational, non–middle-class, Voodoo-blues street life with conventionally Christian, Enlightenment ideas. But she never conceptualizes the Voodoo aspect of this street life. She simply lives out the contradictions.

Savannah Sparks, like Peanut, was one of Daddy Poole's whores. She remembers "when he used to set up tents in the empty lots and preach" and admits that he "could preach awhile. . . . Preached that he would never die" (36). She witnesses him heal people, how he would break "those crutches, and the people would go off walking and praising God" (36). But now Savannah has forgotten all of Daddy's teachings. After ending her relationship with Daddy, becoming a Christian, and looking back in hindsight, she believes he was/is "wicked and corrupt." She believes that he "showed how foolish people are. How in the world he going to be God himself, and then God's ambassador and doing his business like any other man with a wildness dangling in between his legs" (36–37).

Obviously, the modern, logocentric Christian narrative that Savannah uses to represent Daddy Poole cannot engage his contradictions and inconsistencies, his free flow of desires, his Voodoo definition of existence. It cannot reconcile his wanting to be God, or God's ambassador, and simultaneously his wanting to express his sexual desires freely. Unable to accept Daddy Poole as a bundle of contradictions or as a play of differences, to accept Daddy Poole on his own metaphysical terms, Savannah simply thinks that what he represents and believes in is "nonsense" (37). Therefore, Savannah thinks he must pay for his wickedness.

Of course, despite the fact that they lived lives contrary to their beliefs, Peanut's and Savannah's Judeo–Christian, logocentric narratives cannot tolerate difference. They want Daddy Poole to embrace and practice their own Judeo–

Christian values. But Belton in *Almost Midnight* undermines their Judeo–Christian, logocentric narratives by implicating both women in Daddy Poole's game or life. *Almost Midnight* makes it salient that both Savannah and Peanut became Daddy Poole's whores by choice. They were never forced, and they left whenever they wanted to.

Sarah Anderson, the daughter of Savannah Sparks, was born before Savannah became Daddy's woman. She is raised in Georgia but returns to Newark/Hillside Place after Savannah leaves Daddy. Sarah Anderson is the consummate bourgeoisie. She is extremely conscious of African Americans who are darker in skin color than she. She takes great pride in the fact that she moved to Prince Street when she and Daddy were the only black residents. She complains constantly about other people's children's noise: "I'm moving off this street full of niggers" (19). She does not allow her daughters "to play with any of the children on the block" (19).

Because she is a weak woman, Sarah goes to men for help. She tells herself stories in which glamorous men give her furs and earrings. Every action requires a man's assistance: "If she was to come to God, she would need a man to carry her the distance. Daddy Poole was Sarah's man" (181). She encounters Daddy on a Sunday in 1945 in Harlem when her man has just left her and taken her mink coat and her two hundred dollars. Sarah had fought with her young husband, Jimmy Anderson, and run away, ending up in Harlem with another man she did not know but had met in a bar. When he abandons her, "Daddy's voice save[s] her" (178). Later, his sermon seduces her: "She could not feel anything until she heard the preacher's voice from downstairs. His voice lapped at her feet. She had dressed herself under the power of the sermon" (178–79).

For nine years, Daddy is Sarah's man. With him, she travels all over the world where "she was the ornament of Daddy's organization" (186). She is with Daddy Poole in Harlem, Paris, Spain, and Milan where he "introduced her to prosciutto and melon" (187). She is with him in Zanzibar and Niger "while Daddy established his African missions" (187). Sarah ends her relationship with Daddy Poole when he "wanted to take away her sexuality. He wanted her to practice celibacy while he had sex with other women. She refused. She went back to Jimmy Anderson and [to] maintaining a home" (190). She leaves his church in 1956.

But unlike her mother, Sarah Anderson is a true believer in Daddy Poole. She represents Daddy Poole in a way that is the total opposite of Peanut's and Savannah's constructions. Her representation of Daddy is personal and spiritual. For Sarah, Daddy Poole is her Prince Charming who introduces her to the rich life:

> All I know is what he did for me. He never showed me anything but a digni-
> fied gentleman with a Big Daddy heart with room for everybody. All I know
> is the wonders he did—not only in Newark but in Europe, Africa, Japan and
> South America. I saw what he meant to people. What other man do you know
> . . . to rise up and be the king Daddy was for people—rise up out of these

streets? I won't let anyone talk him down before me. Whatever he was, he was a good man, an old spirit. (37)

Daddy protects her. Sarah's criticism of Daddy is that he wouldn't let "no one love [him] good as [he] loved himself" (30). She believes that he is a great man, but a selfish one.

Unlike Peanut and Savannah, Sarah, a Voodoo faithful, refuses to represent Daddy Poole in terms of good and evil. To her he "was a blessing to this entire neighborhood. Daddy Poole was a blessing to the world. Was a time didn't a summer pass he didn't take all the neighborhood kids to the shore for an outing. In the winter he had such parties in that house" (21–22). He led "parades down Springfield Avenue" (33). He possessed great wisdom. She remembers those days after Red Bobby had finished massaging him and Mrs. Lyon had not completed dinner, when Daddy Poole would "just talk—over the radio and all the evening sounds on Prince Street. He would only be talking about life, the nature of people, of things, but those soft evening talks by Daddy up in that room would be like seminars of the magnitude that people travel day and night and pay money to attend" (31–32). But in taking a personal approach to the meaning of Daddy Poole, Sarah becomes blind to some of his violence.

Finally, Martha, Daddy Poole's youngest daughter and last child, has an equally different representation/construction/interpretation of Daddy Poole. She inherits the Voodoo tradition. Martha is "old past her years, generations and wars older than the perilous seventeen years she called a girlhood" (23). She possesses "the hard, river-cold eyes of a survivor" (23). Martha defines Daddy Poole as someone who exists outside the conventions, values, and definitions of a middle-class, Judeo–Christian, Freudian, logocentric rational society. Unlike Peanut and Sarah, Martha did not know Daddy in his glorious days. She was born when Daddy was in his eighties, at a time when his game had declined and he had returned to 28 Prince Street in Newark to die. She never saw the bodyguards, the big cars, the cathedrals, the healing, the women, the whoring, the gambling, and the twenty-two-room house in Chatham, New Jersey. She never knew her mother.

But Martha knows that her father came to "Newark in 1927 with one suitcase" and that he became a "celebrated negro millionaire" (14). She also knows about her father's churches, knows that "they had probably always been fronts for prostitution and the numbers game. She knew Daddy fucked his whores in Newark and overran the city with bastards" (15). Finally, she knows that his followers rose up and forced him from the pulpit in 1964.

But unlike Peanut and Savannah, and like Sarah, Martha does not define her father as an "ordinary man." He was godlike. He is the "true Christ, Ethiopian Jesus, a prophet under the law of love" (77). He could "heal himself over and over with roots and herbs and sometimes with nothing but words" because he was "from God and could lay down life and take it up when he want[ed]" (76–77). According to Martha, the religion she received from Daddy Poole "is real. It has nothing to do with good or bad, being in the world or being in the church" (83). Martha believes that "good and evil give out and break right down where her father begin[s]" (83). More important, Martha does not believe Daddy will die.

Therefore, she does not define her father's having sex with her as something evil—certainly something that would be defined as evil by all of the modern Western narratives. Rather, Martha defines her father's having sex with her within the context of a religion, a religion that she receives "when [she] was eleven years old . . . laying up in [her] father's bed" (83). "What business he had grinding in me, doing the nasty and kissing me with his tongue when I wasn't barely old enough to know what the hell he was doing? What I know what business he had? Or why he did it. He did it because he did it, that's all" (75). In having sex with her, he was "trying to teach her about divine love" (89). As she makes clear, it is only after she enters school, one of the carriers of modern Western consciousness, that she is able to view her experience with her father differently and morally. "It was through finding out they [the other girls at school] were virgins and hearing them talk that I began to really understand I was ruined by my father" (90). But even after she receives this knowledge from mainstream society, what Martha refuses to do is use it to reinterpret and define negatively her relationship with her father.

As for Peanut's thinking Daddy Poole is evil for turning women into whores, Martha interprets it differently. Martha informs Peanut that Daddy Poole "got using women the way he did from his own mother," Mozelle, who:

> was one of the biggest whorehouse queens on the East Coast . . . and who helped [Daddy Poole] set up his churches here, helped him get hooked up with her rumrunner boyfriend. . . . So, it came to him natural, and that's why he made it a part of his vision. You can say it was a demon vision or a vision from God, but the thing is it was a vision with power. It was a vision my daddy was big enough, bad enough and man enough to act on. (85, 86, 88)

But Belton, through Peanut, undermines/problematizes Martha's narrative. While Martha believes that her mother "walked free," Peanut argues that Daddy Poole had her beaten up and killed, that he had begun mistreating her when she had failed to birth him a male heir. Martha's credibility is further undermined because of her belief that Daddy will never die, but he does die.

It is from these dispersed and contradictory narratives, along with the materials provided by an omniscient narrator who recounts Daddy Poole's life in New Orleans, that the reader gets a glimpse of Daddy Poole, the Voodoo *hungan* (priest) in Newark. So, who is Daddy Poole? How did he come to be the person he is? Daddy Poole, who in his early years was known as Gabriel/Sam, was the offspring of Mozelle, a reigning madam in New Orleans, and maybe Poule, a "blond, muscular Frenchman, [who was] passing through the gambling rooms one night on Bourbon Street" (127). Abandoned by Mozelle, Sam was retrieved from an orphanage and raised by Dominick Sylva, Mozelle's father and the richest colored man in New Orleans (he made his fortune in real estate and slaves), and the second Mrs. Sylva, Mother Elodie. Sylva is seen as a "man of refinement [who] can make something out of him [Sam]" (108), a member of the "finest of the black Creole families left in New Orleans since the war" (113).

Under Sylva's tutelage, Sam is indoctrinated/socialized into middle-class Christian American society. Sylva has internalized the values and definitions of the white/black binary. He wants to be the Same as the dominant white society. Sylva tells Sam: "My people were bred for luxury, bred to be as good as the white man, with his own blood. Our women are the most beautiful women in the South, exotic plants produced in a force bed, produced only for love." (116). Sam also learns about racial hierarchy. Sylva tells Sam that he is better than other darker-skinned blacks: "The blood of the pure blacks will never be equal to ours. . . . We are no Africans, descended from an unknown black beast. A nigger, boy, is the worst thing in the world. Never let anyone put you in their class" (115, 116). Sam's place is to be among the Creole elite, among Sylva's people. And with Sylva ruling "the enchanted kingdom of [Sam's] childhood," Sam knows nothing about his mother (112). He first encounters her at Sylva's funeral. Later, when he is nine years old, Zozo, the help, tells him about his mother, whom he comes to associate with the swamp, a place that is "full, fragrant and cool" (110). He dreams of Mozelle, often—as mother, sister, and bride, thereby further destabilizing or ignoring the Freudian mother–son relationship.

Gabriel/Sam becomes a preacher because he is obsessed with salvation—"salvation not only from sin but from the mysterious evil of Mozelle" (124). While other boys became interested in sports, girls, careers, and wives, "he grew more and more hungry for God. He hungered for a world of piety and justification" (124). Gabriel/Sam's first church is Sylva's church, the traditional Holy Love Methodist Church, but his words there fail "to fuse the spirit of the congregation" (121). Holy Love was founded in 1851 and had always restricted membership to only those African Americans who had money and "long pedigrees." At Holy Love, Sam is a pet, indulged for his physical beauty and the music of his voice, as well as out of deferrence to Dominick Sylva's memory.

But there are two key moments in Gabriel/Sam's early life that force him to question Sylva's teachings, to question/assess Western binaries such as white/black, haves/have-nots, good/evil, Baptists/Catholics—binaries that are at the foundation of Western civilization and that have always relegated the subaltern African American to the lesser half, to the position of the victim or devalued Other. The first epiphanic moment comes when he realizes the contradiction in the class distinctions he has been taught by Sylva. Gabriel/Sam has been raised by Sylva, whose father was white, to believe that "a nigger . . . is the worst thing in the world" (116), that "his own blood . . . was different from the blood of common Negroes" (115). But at Sylva's funeral, when he looks at the "black, bovine, God-moaning woman," who was an ex-slave, "standing before Mother Elodie and the colored Creoles in the parlor" and singing a spiritual, he fails:

to see an inferior, a descendant of a beast. What he saw, setting in the spell of her song, though he could not have called her this, was a mystical mother–father, the human–god–beast in one, singing with the same cello-rich authority Sylva used when he spoke. He saw a power equal to the majesty and peace and dignity his beloved Sylva had had. (116)

With this observation, the light-skin/dark-skin, upper-class/lower-class binaries for Gabriel/Sam are undermined and exposed.

The second epiphany, which leads Sam/Daddy Poole to reject Sylva's teachings and the Holy Love Methodist Church, and to organize his eclectic and heterogeneous Metaphysical Church of the Divine Investigation, comes when Daddy Poole is very early in his ministry at Holy Love. One night he is preaching when a "nigger came running and bleeding with terror—fraught shouts down Love Street, chased by a mob of white men. . . . That nigger . . . was a black man just nineteen and too full of his manhood, who staggered his way drunk into the white men's barroom on the corner and demanded service" (122). When the black man is chased, he begins:

> to run through night-empty Love Street, screaming for help. . . . When he came to Holy Love's doors and pounded the smooth wood where the stains of his blood had now soaked in, the hearts of those saints knew his cry but could not grasp it. They were silent except for the out–in breathing of listening and waiting while a mob came up on their steps and dragged the nigger away, lynched him, burned him and left his charred body hanging on gibbets in front of the Mississippi River. (122)

Gabriel/Sam is affected by this happening, and he makes a covenant with God: "Lord, if you raise me up, I will draw all men—black, yellow, red and white—unto You. Not for form or fashion, Lord, but for the eternal magnification of Your name" (123).

Unlike the other eleven light-skinned, middle-class members of the congregation who define the world in terms of the values of mainstream American society, Sam cannot define the running "nigger" as Other and, therefore, worthy of this treatment. He feels empathy with, and connection to, the scared, beatened man. He could imagine himself in the nineteen-year-old black man's place. Sam's response to this racism, this victimization of a black man by a white mob, is: " 'Sweet Jesus. . . . We have to help him' " (124).

Sam's transcendence of the congregation has a twofold meaning. First, he is making quite poignant the limitations of the modern, traditional church and denominational religions. Their rigidity prevents them from dealing effectively with racial and class divisions and separations. Denominational religions do not undermine or challenge the white/black, rich/poor binaries that define white/rich as normative and superior and represent black/poor as devalued Other. Second, he becomes aware that even those elite/middle-class blacks and Creoles who emulate white society and who have the need to destroy/crush subaltern African Americans are also oppressed victims. "They barely survived the war and Reconstruction, and now Jim Crow [is] sweeping them away forever" (124). He changes; he is transformed, and he pledges/promises a new kind of church and religion. But as he speaks to the congregation, Mother Elodie and the rest of the congregation walk out, rejecting his transformation and new vision.

Sam now begins his quest to find a religion/church that can be effective and applicable to all people, regardless of race, economic class, social status, or religious denomination. Although he has the voice, charm, and looks to be an effective/successful preacher, Gabriel/Sam still has not found a way to ignite the spirit of a congregation. A second church in New Orleans, the Free Church of the Living God, goes under when "Big Muddy rose up" and it "got washed out down there," where he "was pastoring to a poor, black fold" (129). It is only after Mozelle teaches him Voodoo and he has some experience at living that he is able to become a hungan, that he is able to develop "a vision with power," and that he becomes big enough, bad enough and man enough to act on.

In Voodoo, a *mambo* (priestess) or hungan is the head of an autonomous sect or religious group, rather than a member of a clerical hierarchy. She only has authority over those who voluntarily offer themselves as servants of the spirits worshiped in her sanctuary. If a servant wishes to get a hearing from the spirits, it is better for her/him to have recourse to the skills of a mambo or a hungan. Some mambos or hungans "enjoy a reputation which goes no further than the limit of their district and others attract crowds of clients and are known all over the country" (Metraux 62–63). Voodoo priests/priestesses:

> use the word "knowledge" to describe what we would define as "supernatural insight and the power which is derived therefrom. . . . In addition to this power, which depends more or less on supernatural gifts, hungan and mambo must also acquire a more technical kind of education: they must know the names of the spirits, their attributes, their emblems, their various special tastes and the liturgies appropriate to the different kinds of ceremony. Only those who have mastered this lore deserve the title hungans or mambos. To do so requires perseverance, a good memory, musical aptitude and a long experience of ritual. (64)

Most of those who choose the profession of hungan or mambo do so at the impulse of a motive in which faith, ambition, love of power, and sheer cupidity are all inextricably mixed.

Mozelle is a mambo who attracts "crowds of clients" and is "known all over the country." At the age of thirteen, she runs away from her father, Old Sylva, "to lay up with gamblers and murderers" (120). She moves up north and returns "ten years later to the French Quarter where she dances naked with the Voodoo on Congo Square" (106). "One of the crime-rich Italian men had her, covering her down with jewels like a zombie doll. [He] moved her into a tumbling big house on St. Peter Street" (121). Her clients come from the oppressed and the marginalized. Black servants and some whites visit her. "Say she stronger than God, gets her power from the Devil himself, say: She give spells and charms to do evil and good. They calls her the 'Mother of Whores,' 'Queen of Queens,' 'Consort to Snakes and Crocodiles'" (121). Later, in Newark, Mozelle continues to be a mambo. She serves a multipurpose role: "They come to me. It is the will of the spirit. In one door they come for love and diversion. In another door they come, the disconsolate, for Mozelle—help with illness and crossed conditions. I become a god for them and tell them the tidings of the spirit" (129). Mozelle also "was one of the biggest whorehouse queens on the East Coast. She was making big money and skimming off the top to pay the police for protection. She didn't deal in nothing but fine, almost white girls, and she had plenty of them in service at her house on Avon" (85).

Thus, after Sam/Gabriel goes to Mozelle and asks to learn how to "give spells to people to perform good or evil," Mozelle outlines for him a new gospel:

> It is all right to wish to be a preacher and bring Light. It is well. But men were finding God before there was a Bible to read. But you must read the scripture of your own heart. You must go hand in hand with the spirit and learn this world for yourself. You must go down in the wilderness where nobody pray. Where the fangs of beasts glitter, snapping for your soul. Through living, you will get God. You must come through the gate. The gate is hunger. The gate is lust and sorrow. The gate is fear. You must come through. Then when you speak no one will traverse your authority. They will not sit like dead stones. Your words will pour out fire on them. They will have to move. (135)

Later, Mozelle takes Gabriel/Sam into her room and initiates him by taking him through the various Voodoo rites of which serpent worship, sacrifice, and the drinking of blood are just a few. She places a large emerald in his hand. "Here is emerald, the egg, the mystery. It will give the power to understand the particular and open the stream of the mind. Let your mind be clear so you can realize your potential. Let your heart and mind be in the same place" (137). Next, Mozelle has him drink pigeon's blood. Then, as he stares at the snake, he watches Mozelle sing. "Her song was a sweet wordless cry spilling out the narrow space between morning and night, and he knew she had become . . . the oracle of the snake. He received the song. It was as though a thunderbolt or the sun or some supreme light had entered him and was spreading its illumination to the world from his heart" (137). The snake is one of the most popular of the Voodoo gods. The snake, who in Voodoo is revered as a symbol of fecundity and wisdom, as life giver, is also held to be the reincarnation of the dead and the living spirit of the ancestors: "The Voodoo—that is to say the snake—will not give its power or make known its will, except through a priest and priestess, known as 'king and queen, master or mistress or even papa or mama.' In them we recognize the *hungan* and the *mambo*, 'leaders of great Voodoo family,' which must pay them unlimited respect." As a queen, Mozelle decides whether the snake approves the admission of her son Gabriel/Sam to the society. She sets out his duties, the tasks he must fulfill (Metraux 36).

Finally, Mozelle teaches Gabriel/Sam about power. From her, he learns that it is only power that is important, not good or evil. "What I do is not for good or evil. It is like electricity in the air, not evil or good, only power. Man makes his evil or good" (129). To those of European heritage, things are defined in terms of binaries such as white/black or good/evil. But in the African belief that has been passed down through Voodoo, "good and evil are but two sides of the same coin"; Voodoo is a "world view that emphasizes relativity, not absolutes" (Haskins 85). In Voodoo, something is good or evil depending on the circumstances.

After being initiated my Mozelle, Gabriel/Sam performs the miracles of healing and incorporates Voodoo into his antichurch. During his first three years in Newark, Gabriel/Sam has opened a series of storefront churches. All of them have failed because he does not have the experience to galvanize a congregation. Then, Gabriel/Sam develops a ministry in Hartar, Mississippi, "where his congregation turned him out for preaching a double ministry and trying to bring the Devil into the pulpit with Christ" (140). Gabriel/Sam escapes Hartar, Mississippi, with a new name, Daddy Poole, and returns to Newark after a two-year absence just as Mozelle is realizing her mortality. He had changed. "He believed it was so, but now seeing how Mozelle looked at him with reverence, he knew he was, at last as if by some final and absolute evolution, perfected" (143).

In Newark, Daddy Poole is able to build his church initially out of the non-middle-class community on the Hill. It consists of pimps, prostitutes, homosexuals, dope dealers, and users. As in Heard's *Howard Street,* which is also set in Newark, the bars on the Hill are the center of the community social life, places where normative gender and sexual categories blur. Peanut narrates:

> The faggots was effeminate, but they was big. They could dress up in all the women's clothes they please and stick fake hair under they long veils and be scratching up them bar floors with high heels and pricking the air with perfume—but them faggots could all fight and would throw down in a minute. The bars was wild, and in that day, the Hill was a wide-open district. Almost every corner had a bar and every bar had a back room. Them rough-party negroes raised the devil every day on this hill from midnight to noon, but they pitched a real mess on Friday night. . . . That was the night all the rackets had they payday. (41)

But in the 1950s, Daddy Poole is a successful, internationally known hungan. He uses his power to reach his potential. He can do "a new thing in the spirit," can now speak and "no one will traverse [his] authority"; his "words . . . pour out fire on" his congregation and "they have to move" (135). "A good *hungan,*" argues Alfred Metraux:

is at one and the same time priest, healer, soothsayer, exorcizer, organizer of
public entertainments and choirmaster. His functions are by no means limited
to the domain of the sacred. He is an influential political guide, an electoral
agent for whose co-operation senators and deputies are prepared to pay hand-
somely. Frequently his intelligence and reputation make him the accepted
counsellor of the community. Those who frequent his humfo bring their troubles to him and discuss with him their private affairs and work. He combines
in his person the functions of *cure,* mayor and notary. Material profit is not the
only attraction of his profession: the social position which goes with it is such
as to interest all who feel they have enough talent and application to raise
themselves above manual labor. To become a hungan or mambo is to climb the
social ladder and be guaranteed a place in the public eye. (64)

Daddy Poole climbs the social ladder. As a ward boss who pays off the commissioner, the police, and the mayor, he becomes an "influential political guide."
With his church, he fulfills his promise to God to "draw all men—black, yellow,
red and white—unto" God (123). His church is one that undermines and challenges racial, social, denominational, and economic hierarchies and binaries. His
seat, crown, and stick, where the spirit dwells, are the source of his power, and
"only Daddy Poole knew the significance of the seat" (173).

Thus, Daddy Poole uses power rather than morality to organize and
make sense out of the world. Daddy Poole uses power not for the salvation of
the soul, but to release the self from the bondage of modern social, economic,
racial, and religious structures that enslave. He uses power to "understand the
particular and [to] open the stream of the mind," to let his "mind be clear so
[he] can realize his potential" (137). In a world organized by power, rather
than by morality, conventional, modern Christian and Freudian taboos against
such behavior as gambling, prostitution, incest, the numbers racket, and illegal
drugs gain legitimacy. And the focus on power relatively, rather than on some
totalized moral narrative, to give people's life meaning, is at the core of Daddy
Poole's regime of power and truth. Daddy Poole's church gives back to its
members that power that they have been made to fear: the power of desire.
Desire is not moral; it is not a contained object representative of a moral supernatural. Rather, it is an impersonal, indifferent multiplicity that by its very
nature cannot point to a hierarchy of gods, beliefs, or behavioral systems. In
Voodoo, one's power resides instead in an object. For Daddy Poole, his power
is in "a pure gold staff, a hoodoo stick from Egypt. The stick was invisible to
anyone but Daddy Poole" (175). And it is from this vantage point that we
begin to understand Daddy Poole's role as savior in the antichurch. Daddy
Poole, as a new Christ, ushers his flock into life after death, into a vibrant existence from the stagnancy and self-delusion of modern, rigid narratives. Like
his mother Mozelle, Daddy Poole realizes that people are dreamers, and so he
decides to take advantage of them, to use them to acquire power and move toward the acquisition of his own immortality. He is willing to use violence to
maintain his power.

Perhaps a deeper understanding of Voodoo can explain the tenets of Daddy Poole's church and give us some further insight into this philosophical counter-tradition that animates the text. First, Voodoo is the ancient African vision of man's relationship to the mystery. The origins of Voodoo lie in the African past, in the quasi-universal belief in *ophiolatry* (serpent worship), which held that the founder of the race originally sprang from a serpent. For this, the serpent is revered as a symbol of fecundity and wisdom, and as a life giver. Others honored include the god of war, the great spirit of the waters, and the goddess of fertility (Finn 9). Voodoo has no argument with any other theology. It has a place in its system for any way of perceiving man's relations with the unknown. It is flamboyantly undogmatic. Discussing Voodoo as an eclectic approach to life, Ishmael Reed, in an interview with Robert Gover, states:

> Voodoo is eclectic. Always has been eclectic. It picks up whatever ideas are around. It's always contemporary. . . . Voodoo doesn't compartmentalize the mind. The mind is open-end. There are always new experiences that can be added, "real" or unreal. . . . Voodoo is a method of healing, both psychic and physical. And dance—we're still doing those dances, but we don't even know it. (13)

Daddy Poole's church has an eclectic foundation. It comprises many sources.

> He made his church out of the scraps and broken furniture hanging out in the back of his mind. His church had a lot of the same things the other ones have (Jesus, the Bible, a choir, testifying, baptism—they sang the old Christian hymns, but there wasn't no Christmas or Easter celebrations), but everybody knew Daddy's church had something no other church had. It was all his, and nobody understood it but him. (45)

Daddy Poole's church also borrows elements from other religions and rituals from around the world. He borrows from the Bible, Pentacostal rituals, Catholic saints, and spirits inside candles. From these diverse religions, Daddy Poole is able to create his own religion that, like Mozelle's, has relative and multiple purposes for his members. "Voodoo gives its adepts," argues Metraux, "an escape from reality which is too often sordid. Within the framework of a Western-type civilization, it is a many-sided institution suited to various uses—but an institution, above all, in which a man can participate with his whole being" (364–65). Daddy did not have many rules in his church. "All you had to do was tithe and receive his word. You could pay to have private lessons with him, and there was a time he sold cures and spells for everything from TB to love trouble. In the thirties and forties he sold magic powders and potions" (47).

Daddy's church, the Metaphysical Church of the Divine Investigation, is an antichurch. It operates on several levels. On one level, it allows Daddy Poole to be a completely selfish dictator/sovereigner who rules his church alone and as he pleases, allowing him to use everyone and everything to achieve and maintain power. On another level, it serves as a vehicle to assist disillusioned and weak individuals who have not received any support or reinforcement from the mainstream institutions and apparatuses, people from all walks of life and from all racial, religious, social, and economic levels, in finding hope, personal meaning, and inspiration.

It is a church/religion that is multiple and heterogeneous. "Catholics belonged to his church; Baptists and Pentacostals. It wasn't denominational. Faggots was in there, whores, numbers runners, hit men—everything in 'the life.' Forty-eight-thousand-dollars-a-year lawyers was in there. So was doctors and, on occasion, in the dignitary section, different politicians and entertainers" (46). Discussing the relativity of Daddy Poole's Metaphysical Church, Peanut narrates:

> People loved that church maybe because you didn't have to understand it. People just took from it what they did. For some it was a healing. For others it was financial blessing. Or it might have been victory over an enemy or victory over they own low nature. Or it was just being in the glittery large building on Sundays and Tuesday nights with all those people reeling and rocking to his voice and then dancing with the choir-dancing yourself out your miserable bones and flesh—dancing youself clean one more week. . . . People came to his church just as they was. They worshipped there at all different levels of understanding and for different reasons. Some people gave up everything to follow him. Others dragged in every now and then. (45–46)

It is a church where members can "hide in [their] day of trouble, a tabernacle where [they] could offer sacrifices of joy, singing praises to God" (55).

Voodoo and Daddy Poole's church provide the masses, the disenfranchised, the poor, and the forlorn and alienated with security, psychic and physical healing, blessings, and spiritual salvation in a way that traditional Christianity has failed to do. "From a strictly economic point of view," argues Metraux, "it is undeniable that Voodoo heavily burdens the resources of the peasant [subaltern] population. . . . But the inner man himself also needs security; it is precisely because he is poor and always in danger of want or illness that the peasant is strongly attached to Voodoo" (363). Daddy Poole's Metaphysical Church decenters our traditional concept of the Christian church in the West. In the Metaphysical Church, there is not one signified—the word of God. Instead, the Metaphysical Church has no signified, but many signifiers. There are as many meanings to his sermons as there are individuals. And each individual receives from the church the meaning he or she desires. The success of Daddy Poole's Metaphysical Church is contingent on its ability to maintain and sustain multipurpose functions, to cater to people's individual needs, wants, and desires.

In addition, Daddy Poole also uses his church to peddle spiritual healing. Within the church, members come for healings and blessings: "In the thirties and forties . . . he sold magic powders and potions with names like Lucky Jazz, Get Away and Easy Life. He even sold a hair pomade called Wonder Fix what straightened our kind of hair better than anything on the market. He sold incense sticks for controlling and drawing spirits, love oils and sacred sands" (47).

According to Sister Sarah, when members of Daddy's church receive the power, they did a dance: "The people would jerk and tremble. They leaped against the walls and rolled along the floor. They hollered and retched and some fell out in a dead faint. It was a whirling, sanctifying dance, and after that dance they walked with God in conversion, married to the Holy Ghost" (201). In Voodoo, possession is closely linked with dancing. When the loa/spirit is possessing a body, the person appears to lose "control of [his] motor system. Shaken by spasmodic convulsions, [he pitches] forward, as though projected by a spring, turn[s] frantically round and round, stiffen[s] and stay[s] still with body bent forward, sway[s], stagger[s], save[s himself], again lose[s] balance, only to fall finally in a state of semi-consciousness" (Metraux 121). People dance themselves clean.

Of course, in becoming a successful, internationally known hungan, Daddy Poole does not simply use people, especially women. In her review of *Almost Midnight,* Claudia Tate argues that "the women are unsuccessful in untangling the meaning of their own lives. Hence they cannot separate themselves from their memories of him. He is the fixed point around which they revolve. He marks the beginning and the ending of their stories, and they are doomed to repeat them" (24). Tate's assessment seems to indict Daddy Poole as a despot. It assumes that he is using people to his own ends. But can a despot exist in a world where there are no rules, no morality? Daddy Poole is not forcing people to submit to him; they submit to him willingly. Therefore, the term *despot* cannot be applied here, for where there are no laws, there are no victims and no abusers. Daddy Poole, in gaining wealth and prestige by the work of others, is merely fulfilling his desire. Others have the right to leave anytime they want, and some do.

Thus, within the context of Voodoo, we can now understand why Daddy Poole uses his church for multiple purposes. Within his Voodoo organized worldview, power is the only operative term. There is no good and evil. Thus, within a Voodoo worldview, there is nothing wrong with Daddy Poole's using his church to front "for prostitution and the numbers game" (15), or using his church to front "for narcotics and running bitches" (48). If power is the only operative term, and not Western Judeo–Christian morality, then we can understand why Daddy Poole had sex with "his whores in Newark and overran the city with bastards" (15), and why he would have sex with his eleven-year-old daughter. "The prohibition of incest," argue Deleuze and Guattari, "would therefore imply an oedipal representation" (*Anti-Oedipus* 172), and Voodoo is not Oedipal. It is the constrictions of the Oedipal, Judeo–Christian philosophy that would prohibit these actions. But according to Daddy Poole's worldview, good and evil are human constructed. Laws against prostitution, gambling, drugs, and incest are man-made. They are the consequence of human-made narratives.

But Daddy Poole's Metaphysical Church begins to decline when his members and other sectors of society no longer use the church to define their own relative meanings but instead make judgments; then start to construct notions of good and evil and impose them on Daddy Poole and his church. His church cannot withstand the onslaught or the challenge. Other movements and religious establishments emerge and begin to organize people's lives according to absolute, totalized narratives that have one meaning. Elijah Muhammad and the black Muslims set up binaries of good and evil, "regulations for his people and women was (sic) separated from men in everything but making babies and couldn't straighten their hair or wear wigs—had to go natural and stay covered in white sheets" (48). Malcolm X "was making real what the Prophet Elijah was teaching. . . . Martin Luther King . . . was getting through to middle-class negroes and the churchgoers" (48). These emerging, middle-class, moral religious organizations and individuals, which were modeled on Western notions of progress and which defined things in terms of binaries and hierarchies, make Daddy Poole's Metaphysical Church "look more like a holdback than a headway," especially as these organizations with a very clear moral sense of good and evil begin to hear the rumors "about how [Daddy Poole's] big churches . . . was fronts for narcotics and running bitches—which they was and always had been" (48).

In addition, pressure for change begins within Daddy Poole's congregation. Church members such as Jake and the Operation ADVANCE "started organizing to see what they could do about changing the reputation the church was getting on the street" (48). Jake "didn't know about the dope and whores [Daddy Poole] was peddling right along with the gifts of visions, trances and healing at them church services" (44). Of course, Daddy Poole is furious at the challenge to his power, and he defines their action as "opportunity-happy." He is furious because Jake and the group are undermining his mission by attempting to bring back a morality that suppresses individual desire. Daddy Poole has his first stroke, and people begin to stay away from his church. As the members of his congregation begin to internalize the values and virtues of mainstream America and become more moral and rational and middle class, as they begin to believe that their salvation/hope lie in mainstream American society, "most people agreed [that Daddy Poole] had run a beautiful game, but his time was dead" (53). People begin to defect, rebel, and splinter away. "A lot of them young brothers working with Jake . . . broke off from Daddy's church . . . and was carrying on they plans on they own" (53). They wanted to clean up the slums of Newark. One of the boys had already been killed trying to work with the police to bust a "dope supplier out on Long Island" (53). Others thought of instigating a takeover of Daddy's church from within.

After Daddy Poole recovers from his stroke, realizing that his power has been challenged by human-made notions of good and evil and realizing that members of the congregation have forfeited/reneged on the church's initial mission, Daddy ends his Metaphysical Church. Members of the congregation had gotten "to the place where [they thought they didn't] need [him], where [they were] restless and felt like [they could] do better" (55). He retreats to Montmartre, France, to reorganize "his game," with someone in Europe backing him. When he returns to Newark at the age of seventy-five, he again has power and is in full control of his destiny. Although he returns in a long white limousine, escorted by two police cars, his concern or focus is still not money and material wealth, but power. Surrounded by an army of bodyguards, Daddy Poole continues to run his illegal empire. He continues to trade in prostitution, including putting his new woman, Miss Blanche, out on the street to turn tricks. Daddy Poole wants power to attain immortality. "It was like he had a mojo hand against time. Daddy had the power to freeze his time like no other living man" (57). This need to defy death and become immortal is also echoed in Savannah's observation of Daddy Poole. She remembers his early sermons when he "preached that he would never die" (36).

But as the novel opens, Daddy Poole, dying at the rear of 28 Prince Street, is dreaming:

> His mother [Mozelle] was in the room. Her breasts were heavy with milk though she was fifty years dead. As she approached him, her nipples hardened and forced at the hell-red cloth of her dress. At the bed she uncovered one of her breasts and guided it into the hungry old mouth of Daddy Poole. Her breast milk was cool and sweet. As he sucked, she disappeared. (10).

"Spirits are apt to communicate with the faithful," states Metraux,

> by means of dreams. . . . In this respect priests and priestesses are particularly favoured. Spirits constantly come and give them advice . . . , or talk over with them some new rite which they hope to see introduced. . . . Supernatural beings seen in dreams usually have a human form. They readily assume the appearance of a friend or relation. (143)

Perhaps, in this opening scene, Mozelle is present in Daddy's dream, appearing in "human form," to remind/advise him not to fear the afterlife. Later, when Martha cleans Daddy Poole and changes his bed clothing, she whispers in his ear "Don't be afraid" and he responds with: "Baby, your daddy ain't hardly 'fraid' " (11).

Despite Martha's ignorance, Daddy is ready to die. In his 1945 sermon in Queens, New York, he preaches about the midnight hour when God is going to "dispel heartaches, vanquish sickness and sorrow. . . . At midnight we can shout our trouble over, for the King of Kings and the Lord of Lords is going to come back and carry us home" (175–76). In his last dream, "his window turn[s] into the indigo-tinted mirror in Mozelle's old apartment on the Place du Tertre in Montmartre" (196). Because he only has two more days in Paris, Daddy begs her not to go out. But Mozelle does go out, promising him to be back by midnight. Now, in the dream, she is returning at midnight. Finally, even as Martha tries everything to keep her father alive, he tells her that he wants "to die at home in his own bed" (191). Thus, as midnight approaches, he tells Martha to "wind up the clock on the night table," he asks her what time it is, and he asks her where is Mozelle. He is clearly ready and prepared to die. When Sarah Anderson arrives, he asks her "What is truth?" which is the appropriate "greeting of the Voodoo priestess by the *hungan*-priest" (209).

In Voodoo, there is an interesting relationship between the Voodoo hungan and his devotees. Metraux discusses this relationship: "Initiation serves to create a mystic bond between loa and devotee, making the spirit a mait-tete for the human being. Later, other spirits may possess the initiate, but the one who first made him his 'horse' remains his particular patron and protector" (244). When Daddy Poole initiates Sarah and Jimmy Anderson and Savannah Sparks, he creates a "mystic bond" between them and himself. Therefore, as midnight and his death approach, this bond brings them to his deathbed. After sixteen years of not communicating with Daddy Poole, Sister Sarah crosses the street and rings the doorbell at 28 Prince Street. Despite the fact that she is now possessed by another spirit, Christianity, Savannah Sparks is "sitting in the back of a yellow cab parked in front of 28. Her head was inclined toward the house" (209). Daddy Poole's anointing was in Jimmy's bones and in his clothes. Daddy Poole had chosen Jimmy and "it was the mystery of that choosing that had Jimmy Anderson stopped in the frame of his [Daddy's] door" (210). Had Mary Ellen Quinn understood the relationship between the Voodoo hungan and his devotees, she would have known "why Daddy Poole was able to exert such a powerful influence throughout his long life" (181). Had Claudia Tate understood Voodoo, she would know why "the women [and the men] are unsuccessful in untangling the meaning of their own lines" (24).

Martha is the inheritor of Daddy Poole's and Mozelle's Voodoo tradition. Despite the fact that Daddy Poole has taught her about power, the mysteries, and the foundation, Martha has not learned them correctly. She has not been initiated, and she is not possessed. This explains her failure with the chicken. In Voodoo, the *passer poule* brings luck. If the priest knows that among the faithful before her there are some who are ill, she will touch them with the chickens on whatever part of their bodies that are afflicted. "This action suggests [that she] intends to permeate the patient with the effluvia which earlier ceremonies have accumulated in the sacrificial victims" (Metraux 172). As her father "smelled death each day," Martha tries "everything, and everything had failed," including the killing of the chicken and the arrival of the charlatan, Reverend Lewis. She does not believe that Daddy will die. "The judgment on her father was death. Martha did not care what people said. Her father was God. That was all she knew" (191).

But after Daddy Poole dies—something that all of his disciples such as Sarah, Savannah, and Jimmy know will happen—Martha, who "can't remember the last time [she] danced or heard something to make [her] feel like [she wants] to dance" (168), enters Mr. Wonderful's Bar and Lounge and there is music everywhere:

> The band played a slow blues. The baritone sax anchored Silk's alto sax. The song took on a rough majesty under the flourishes of the double saxophones. Silk stepped into a lavender spotlight and muscled a tight solo, relaying the song's colorful figures with dreamy twists and turns. . . . The music exploded

inside Martha. She opened herself to the music, her arms dangling, her gross
mouth slack. . . . The music weaved through blues, gospel, ragtime, jazz and
funk. . . . [Then, Martha begins to dance.] Martha's truncated amazon's body
became fused. Her mind snapped free. She clapped her hands, straining
against the fabric of her maid uniform. Martha moved her hips, fucking the
bitter night. She began to dance. The music piled up crescendo after
crescendo. Her body quickened and jerked. She twisted and snaked out in the
center of the dance floor, performing small, dervish spins and body-popping
turns. . . . She could no longer see the room before her. She lost the rhythm
of the music. Martha fainted. She saw her father resting on a throne chair in
a white pavilion, coming down from God. His eyelids trembling, his eyes
turned inward, he ripped from his chest the moving, bleeding heart. When
she came to, she was sitting at a table by the door. Martha felt hot and good.
She felt clean. . . . She went outside and walked back to Prince Street under
her father's shadow. (212–13)

Martha is possessed. In Voodoo, possession is closely linked with dancing.
Metraux argues that "music and dance are so closely woven into the [religions]
that one could almost speak of 'dance religions.' Dance is itself linked with divine possession—the normal mechanism by which a divinity communicates
with the faithful" (29). In ripping "from his chest the moving, bleeding heart,"
Daddy Poole passes on to Martha his and Mozelle's tradition. And in being
taken by the music and dancing, Martha communicates with the spirits. And just
as Mozelle passed the tradition to Daddy, Martha will pass it on to her son, Man.

Of course, there is a pattern to the way this Voodoo tradition is passed from
one generation to another. Mozelle and Daddy Poole break out of middle-class,
stifling family situations and reinvent themselves. She has "no future and no
past" and Daddy Poole "slithered out of a crack of lighting one day" (55). Both
create a game or life in which they control their own destiny, where they find a
way out of the "maze of the streets." They become outlaws, rejecting all notions
of traditional family, middle-class respectability, Christian morality, and the
Freudian Oedipus complex. They, to use Emmanuel Levinas's terms, become
"something else entirely, absolutely other" (33). As Daddy Poole was to do,
Mozelle runs away from Sylva "to lay up with gamblers and murderers" in New
Orleans. She is "pleasuring herself like the carnal night had no morning" (120).
As Daddy Poole was to do, she births many babies and leaves them with their fathers or for others to take care of, thereby eschewing the middle-class notion of
motherhood. Both have plenty of sexual partners and money. Yet, they are not
into material possessions. Finally, both Mozelle and Daddy Poole pay off the police and city hall in order to maintain their illegal businesses. Just as Mozelle assists Daddy Poole in finding "a way out of this maze of the streets," Martha will
lead her son, Man, out.

With the Voodoo theoretical conception of 'life' represented in *Almost Midnight*, Belton has given another representation of the African American. It shows
that the middle-class, Christian representation is just one of many constructions

of the African American. In presenting characters such as Mozelle and Daddy Poole, who define themselves differently, outside the conventional values and definitions of mainstream society, Belton gives us sites of individuation and identity that cannot be comprehended by the white/black binary. He gives us characters who are different but equal, who are Others, and who live by their own logic.

In giving us a Voodoo way of existence, which is far from and alien to the middle-class, Christian American norm, *Almost Midnight* uses a form or language that disrupts the majority culture's official or institutional functions. It finds points of nonculture and underdevelopment in mainstream culture. It presents a non-hierarchical vision that accepts differences. It presents different ways of organizing spirituality, family, power, sexuality, and desires. It constructs different ways of being a son, mother, or father. And it connects with the contemporary African American cultural practices or Rastafarians, or the singer D'Angelo's musical CD, *Voodoo*, and with other past and contemporary Voodoo texts of Charles Chesnutt, Rudolph Fisher, Gloria Naylor, and Gayl Jones.

Almost Midnight decodes the majority language by exposing the very mishmash that its code seeks to exorcise: its class distinctions and hierarchies, its religious rigidity, its Freudian limitations, and its middle-class oppressive quality. The illumination of Voodoo and its nonsynchronous elements threatens to provoke the irruption of minor elements (contrary, revolutionary, emerging forces) in the present. Theoretically, such an irruption would not, to use Foster's terms, "play into the hands of the code, [but] would escape recuperation, precisely because these new and old signs would contest the code as an absolute sign-system" (178). The presence of *Almost Midnight* and other Voodoo-informed texts in the canon of American/African American literature allow the contradictory coexistence of different modes in one cultural present. This coexistence makes it impossible for any social movement or canon of literature to present itself as a total system. In short, the presence of Belton's *Almost Midnight* prevents the 1970s/1980s reinvented canon, the Black Aesthetic critics, and feminist critics from making the mistake of thinking themselves as absolute.

But because Belton's *Almost Midnight*, along with other Voodoo-informed texts—such as Charles Chesnutt's *The Conjure Woman*, Rudolph Fisher's *The Conjure Man Dies*, Ishmael Reed's *Mumbo Jumbo*, Steve Cannon's *Groove, Bang, and Jive Around*, Gloria Naylor's *Mama Day*, Jewell Parker Rhodes's *Voodoo Dreams*, Mary Monroe's *Upper Room*, Toni Cade Bambara's *The Salt Eaters*, Charles Johnson's *Faith and the Good Thing*, Ntzoke Shange's *Sassafrass, Cypress, and Indigo*, Darius James's *Negrophobia*, Gayl Jones's *Healing*, Carl Hancock Rux's *Pagan Operetta*, and Rainelle Burton's *The Root Worker*—affirms a non-middle-class, nonconventional Christian, non-Protestant work ethic and non-Freudian definition of life, it is excluded by the 1970s/1980s reinventors of the canon of African American literature. It is excluded or is lost from the literary histories of American and African American literatures. My intention here is to contest middle-class America and the African American sociopolitical mission of racial uplift and to present a different definition of African American life that has contingent value for a "limited [African American] population under some "limited set of conditions" (B. H. Smith 94). But this limited American/African American population who believes in the ideas and tenets of Voodoo does not have the cultural power to not only protect *Almost Midnight* from physical deterioration but also to have it frequently read or recited, translated, commented on—in short, to have it culturally reproduced. Therefore, it remains out of print. However, in terms of African American women writers and Voodoo, several African American critics have engaged this issue. Marjorie Pryse in *Conjuring: Black Women, Fiction, and Literary Tradition*, Houston A. Baker's *Workings of the Spirit*, Karla Holloway's *Moorings and Metaphors*, and Joyce Ann Joyce's *Warriors, Conjurers, and Priests* discuss the fiction of Zora Neale Hurston, Alice Walker, Ntzoke Shange, Gloria Naylor, Toni Morrison, and others in terms of Voodoo.

CHAPTER ELEVEN

CONCLUSION

As I have discussed in detail in the previous chapters, in the United States, until the 1960s, the white/black binary, the African American sociopolitical mission of racial uplift, the historical emancipatory African American narrative, and the canon of African American literature defined African American social reality. Because they are middle-class, Christian, and center-oriented, they repress and exclude African American differences. They reduce the polyvalent nature, the plurality and heterogeneity of American/African American history, literature, criticism, and life to sets of apprehensible units that can be ordered. In examining how mainstream Americans and elite/middle-class Christian African Americans—who have a monopoly on the construction of African American literary, cultural, and social reality—construct African American social reality, we can discern how it is modeled on the Western, Hegelian notions of linearity, closure, and progress. We can discern how it would be middle class and Christian.

This social reality renders secondary and marginal those African American differences—texts, individuals, and images—that deviate from their norm. It ignores other vital African American issues/lives and devalues desires, behaviors, and value systems that are different. This social reality is tainted at birth by its historical roots in the systematic inequalities of conquest, slavery, and exploitation.

I do not for a minute want to criticize anyone for engaging the issues of conquest, slavery, racism, and exploitation. In chapters 2 and 3, I discuss at length the brutal history of racial oppression, showing how even at the turn of the century structural discrimination and otherization still exist for all African Americans. The struggle by African Americans for full equality in America has been and continues to be a major priority for all sectors of African American life and for the liberal sector of mainstream American society. I am also willing to admit that the struggle for social equality is an important item on the agenda. But that struggle has become who we are. It has shaped/constructed our image/representation of the African American until the 1960s, and it is a narrow representation. Given the economic, social, and intellectual changes that have happened since the 1960s, I have to conclude that constructing African American life, history, criticism, and

253

literature according to social equality exclusively—according to the journey from the African American subaltern to the values of mainstream America, or according to some unified, mythic African past—ignores and represses much of that history, life, criticism, and literature. And within this repression, there are all kinds of violence.

In exposing the white/black binary as a construct, rather than a metaphysical certainty, and in taking a polycentric approach to African American literature, criticism, and history, thereby engaging differences in African American life, literature, criticism, and history, I have been able to disrupt, deconstruct, and de-territorialize the white/black binary system and re-territorialize and reconstitute a social space in which the positionality of the African American is one of differences. In my polycentric construction, I have repositioned the racial uplift literary tradition, of which James Weldon Johnson's *The Autobiography* is considered archetypal, and the sociopolitical mission of racial uplift in which they become two of many literary and historical vantage points for representing the African American, rather than centers/norms. If we recognize that the modern, working-class blues man Manfred Banks in Clarence Major's *Dirty Bird Blues*; the existential, sexually fluid, caring and giving, and racially mixed jazz man Charles Stevenson in Charles Wright's *The Messenger*; the urban, non-Christian subaltern, patriarchal Hip in Nathan Heard's *Howard Street*; the middle-class, compulsorily heterosexual, patriarchal, and Christian ex-coloured man in Johnson's *The Autobiography of an Ex-Coloured Man*; the gay-identified, middle-class Christian Mitchell Crawford and the sexually fluid, non-middle-class, non-Protestant work ethic, and non-Christian b-boys in James Earl Hardy's *B-Boy Blues*; the Voodoo, hungan, and capitalist Daddy Poole in Don Belton's *Almost Midnight*; the radical Thoreauvian, postcolonial, individualist Tucker Caliban in William Melvin Kelley's *A Different Drummer*, along with other images and representations of the African American that I have excluded, all represent limited populations of African American subjects under some limited sets of conditions, we have no other choice but to represent the African American and African American literature as ones of differences.

Each of these African American subjects and literature is a member of "shifting [American and African American] communities, each of which establishes, for each of its members, multiple social identities, multiple principles of identification with other people, and accordingly, a collage or grab bag of allegiances, beliefs, and sets of motives" (B. H. Smith 168). Manfred Banks belongs to the working class, the blues, the modern, and the Voodoo communities at different times in the text. Charles Stevenson, in being sexually fluid, existential, and a jazz man, has multiple identities. He belongs to numerous American and African American communities. Hip, urban subaltern, swinging with a survivalist philosophy and inspired by Voodoo, has multiple principles of identification. The representation of the African American in terms of these shifting communities, multiple identities, and multiple principles of identification not only proves that African American subjects and communities are not "totally homogeneous, that [their] boundaries and borders are never altogether self-evident" (182), but it also disrupts the white/black binary and the African American patriarchies because this particular, heterogeneous representation of the African American does not allow the binary, the patriarchy, or the African American sociopolitical mission of racial uplift to fix a single, stable representation/image of the African American that it can deem as inferior, as sexist, as victim, or as devalued Other.

In exposing the white/black binary as a construct, I have also reconstituted a space in which the positionality of the African American changes from the African American as Other-as-object, and thus as less, to the African American as Other-as-subject, as equal but different. I have constituted a space that strives toward a mode of reading, writing, and speaking nonexclusively of differences so that the Other is Other without being thought of in merely negative and positional terms. Finally, I have produced literary and historical spaces that acknowledge African American differences, that allow the mutual relations between the various African American communities, traditions, and lifestyles to be subject to the varying imperatives of their own internal development, rather than have them adjust unilaterally to some perceived norm or center. In my re-representation of the African American, along with African American criticism, history, and literature, despite the continued existence of racism, he is not defined as a victim, as an inferior, as a devalued Other, or as the Same. Rather, he is constructed as being plural, heterogeneous, always in flux with no clearly defined boundaries and borders.

Once defined as a unified Other, African American communities are now recognized as plural, multiple, and contradictory. A successful representation of the African American, along with the Native American, the Asian American, and the Hispanic, as different, plural, and multiple will eventually undermine, as Kelley's *A Different Drummer* attests, *whiteness* as a construction, thereby providing the social and cultural spaces for a reconfiguration and a rewriting of American culture in which hybridization and creolization and intermingling are a part of the hegemonic narrative—a narrative that would be much more in harmony with American social and cultural reality than the white/black binary. Of course, my objective is not to present this hybridization as an alternative utopia, for it is constantly changing and reconfiguring itself. The awareness of the constant changing prevents a single concept of American culture as hybrid from being conclusive and teleological.

NOTES

CHAPTER TWO:
HISTORY, THE WHITE/BLACK BINARY,
AND THE CONSTRUCTION OF
THE AFRICAN AMERICAN AS OTHER

1. It is highly likely that West Africans sailed across to the Americas before 1492. However, because there seem not to have been major mercantile-maritime port cities in West Africa—unlike in East Africa—it is not likely that transatlantic voyages before 1492 had a significant impact on Africa or on America. In the fifteenth century, much of the voyaging was across open ocean and much of it involved exploration.

2. Of course, with the establishment of a hegemonic European identity during the Renaissance and later, there were repressed and excluded internal European others who practiced different social, religious, and cultural practices. First, in the midst of the unified Christian Europe, Italy was still fractured into city–states. Protestant northern Europeans, who led the fight for the Europeanization/Christianization of Europe, demonized Catholic Spaniards and Italians. Also, there were England's darker corners—Ireland, Wales, Scotland: these people, along with Jews, Gypsies, Huguenots, Muslims, peasants, women, who, but for different reasons, were considered "savages." Later, during and after colonialism, these groups were to be joined by people of color from Africa, Asia, and the West Indies.

3. Muhammad and Islam practiced conquest and colonialism. The years 632–642 comprised the first decade of Muslim conquest. These Arab conquerors moved through the Near East, conquering Syria in 634 and Egypt in 639; and in 642 Persia rapidly succumbed to Arab conquerors. "The Arabs," argues Fernard Braudel, "found it harder to conquer North Africa, between the middle of the seventh and the beginning of the eighth centuries; but thereafter they overran Spain very rapidly in 711." Except for the mountains of Asia Minor, the Arab conquerors very quickly seized "the whole of the Near East, and then pushed beyond it towards the West" (44).

Likewise, the great empires of Africa—Ghana, Mali, and Songhai—also practiced conquest and colonialism. Under the African rulers of the Sessie dynasty, Ghana reached the height of its power as an empire. Tribes in Tichit in present Mauritania were brought under the control of the king of Ghana. In the south, Ghana's conquest "extended to the gold mines of the Falome and of the Bambuk whose yields supplied the coffers of the Sessie with the gold used in the trade with Moroccan caravans" (Franklin 12). Traditions speak of various founding dynasties, including nonblack northerners, doubtless a reflection both of Ghana's close contact with neighboring Berbers and of later attempts by West African Muslims to associate Sudanic states with Islamic and Arabic antecedents (July, 77).

257

The Mali empire conquered and colonized the people and the area throughout the whole bend of the Niger, the area of what is now French-speaking West Africa. In its rise to power, it brought small states—Susu, Diara, Galam—under its control. The Susu chieftaincy of Kaniaga moved to capture Ghana under the leadership of Sumanguru. After his victory over Ghana, Sumanguru subdued and colonized the Mandingan blacks who occupied the fertile land near the source of West Africa's gold supply (July, 79). Under the reign of Kankan Musa (1307–37), a number of merchants and educated people reached the banks of the Niger. Timbuktu then became an influential capital (Braudel, 128).

The Mali empire was conquered and colonized by the Songhai empire, with its capitals at Gao and Timbuktu. Beginning in the early eighth century at Gao, near the bend of the Niger, the Songhai empire had remained a small and relatively inconsequential kingdom for many years. By 1000 AD, through conquest and colonialism, it had expanded to include "other settlements on the Niger from Hukia to Timbuktu" (Franklin 16). When King Sunni Ali began his rule of the Songhai empire in 1464, most of West Africa was ripe for conquest. He conceived of a plan to conquer the entire Niger region by building a river navy that would seize control of both banks. By 1469, he had conquered Timbuktu and proceeded to capture Jenne and other cities, raiding deep into the homeland of the formidable Mossi, whose independent kingdoms in the Upper Volta basin had existed since the middle of the eleventh century. Finally, King Sunni Ali attacked the Kindgom of Mali and with its conquest the Songhai empire became the ruler of West Africa (17).

The empires of Asia also rose and fell as a result of conquest and colonialism. The Vedic "India" civilization passed through three or four main stages between 1400 BC and the seventh century AD. These two millennia were dominated by invasion and settlement by Aryan people from Turkestan, who entered India from the northwest and slowly spread across the plains of the Central Indus, then the Central Ganges (Braudel, 218). Between 1211 and 1279, in China, the northern Mongol's conquest and subjugation of the Sung dynasty in the south and the capture of its capital Hang-Chow are forms of imperialism and colonialism (190). Certainly, Japan's domination of China, Korea, the Phillippines, and Singapore, during different periods, was a form of colonialism/imperialism.

4. Universalism was a potential in all of these empires and states. However, ethnocentrism has been traditionally justified on cultural grounds, often religious in nature, and not on the idea that the other groups are inherently and biologically inferior. It was not until biological thinking began to displace religious thinking in the eighteenth century that racial distinctions in the modern sense could be made, and it was not until the nineteenth century that full-blown racial ideologies based on biological inferiority were developed. And until the development of classical European colonialism and capitalism in the nineteenth century, no society had succeeded in imposing itself and its values on a worldwide scale.

5. In *Black Athena*, Martin Bernal distinguishes between the "ancient model"— which simply assumed classical Greek civilization's deep indebtedness to both Africa (Egyptian and Etyiopian) and Semitic (Hebraic and Phonecean) civilizations—and the "Aryan model" which was developed in the wake of slavery, colonialism, and American racism. During the course of the nineteenth century, Greek civilization was redesigned. The Aryan model had to perform ingenious acrobatics to "purify" classical Greece of all African and Asian "contaminations": it had to explain away, for example, the innumer-

able Greek homages to Afro-Asiatic cultures, Homer's description of the "blameless Ethiopians," and the frequent references to the *kalo kagathos* (handsome and good) Africans in classical literature.

6. I am going to refrain from using the term *stripped of culture* for in almost every study of African American history and culture that I cite there are linkages to Africa.

7. Racism, although hardly unique to the West, and while not limited to the colonial situation (antisemitism being a case in point), has historically been both an ally and the partial product of colonialism. First, it should be emphasized that racism or racial ideologies are a modern phenomenon and do not predate the rise of classical European colonialism. When racial ideologies—and here I am talking about the shift from ethnocentrism, which believes in one group's superiority over another based on culture or religion, to racial ideologies, which argue for racial superiority of one group over another based on the idea that the other groups are inherently and biologically inferior—began to emerge in Europe in the eighteenth century, they were tied in all instances to the advancement of certain interests. There was usually the justification of privilege based on social inequality, but the protection of national interests also played a role. Much of the early race theorizing was not aimed at people of color, but at Europeans, although contacts with people of color influenced the general climate of opinion.

Racial ideologies became one way in which European aristocrats tried to fortify their class position in the face of radical challenges. These ideologies took the position that the aristocrats were descendents of the Germanic people who had overrun the old Roman empire. The common people, on the other hand, were depicted as descendants of other, inferior European stock, including the Romans. Thus, the aristocrats were the descendants of a race that had proved its superiority in the distant past and that had subsequently been responsible for the advance of Western civilization. By virtue of this inheritance, European aristocrats were ideally suited to rule and to maintain their class privileges. Later on, racist ideologies were transformed in Europe in order to serve the interests of nationalism, and France and Germany struggled for supremacy on the continent (Barrera, 198).

Today, in Europe, the most obvious victims of racism are those individuals whose identity was forged within the colonial cauldron: Africans, Asians, and the indigenous peoples of the Americas as well as those displaced by colonialism, such as Asians and West Africans in Great Britian and Arabs in France. Colonialist culture constructed a sense of ontological European superiority to "lesser breeds without the law." Racism is above all a social relation—"systematized hierarchization implicably pursued" (qtd. in Shohat and Stam 19) in Franz Fanon's words—anchored in material structures and embedded in historical configurations of power. It is a complex hierarchical system, a structured ensemble of social and institutional practices and discourses.

8. Matthew Frye Jacobson further argues that historically "whiteness," in addition to being a constant in American political and economic cultures since colonial times, has been subject to all kinds of contests and has gone through a series of "historical vecissitudes." He divides the history of the construction of whiteness in the United States into three epochs. First, the nation's first naturalization law of 1790 (limiting naturalized citizenship to "free white persons") demonstrates the convergence of race and "fitness for self-government." The law's wording denotes an unconflicted view of the

presumed character and unambiguous boundaries of whiteness. Second, fifty years later, beginning with the massive influx of highly undesirable but nonetheless white persons from Ireland, whiteness was subject to new interpretations. The period of mass European immigration, from the 1840s to the restrictive legislation of 1924, witnessed a reconfiguration of whiteness from a convergence of race and "fitness for self-government" to a hierarchy of "plural and scientifically determined white races." There was vigorous debate over which of these various European "races" was truly "fit for self-government in the good old Anglo-Saxon sense" (7–8). Thirdly and finally, in the 1920s and after, partly because the crisis of over-inclusive whiteness had been solved by restrictive legislation and partly in response to a new racial alchemy generated by African American migrations to the north and west, whiteness was reconsolidated: the late nineteenth century's white groups—which included the Irish, Germans, Italians, Poles, Rutherians, Slovenians, Magyars, Ukrainians, Lithuanians, Celts, Slavs, among others—were now remade and granted the scientific stamp of authenticity as the unitary Caucasian race (3).

9. In the massacre of 1622 in Virginia, Native American warriors slew every white they could find and spared every black. From that massacre until the end of the nineteenth century, there was active and constant cooperation between Native Americans and Africans/African Americans. There was an uprising of Africans and Native Americans in Hartford, Connecticut, in 1657. Thirty-three years later, in 1690, there was a panic in Newbury, Massachusetts, after Isaac Morrill was arrested on a charge of inciting insurrections among Africans and Native Americans. And there were the incidents in Queen's County, New York, in 1708, in New York City in 1712, in the Mohawk camp in the 1760s. And in terms of African/African American revolts and uprisings, there were Gabriel Prosser and Denmark Vasey, leaders of slave conspiracies; Nat Turner, leader of a slave revolt; Crispus Attucks, leader of the Boston Massacre; Harriet Tubman, one of the pioneers of the underground railroad; and many others who openly resisted slavery (Bennett 88–89, 135–138).

CHAPTER THREE:
THE WHITE/BLACK BINARY AND
THE AFRICAN AMERICAN SOCIOPOLITICAL
MISSION OF RACIAL UPLIFT

1. The notion of a unitary African American identity with an emphasis on cultural difference was fundamental to evolving African American communities. Elite/middle-class African Americans were supposed to articulate the "racial will" as though it were unitary, coherent, and whole. To protest a socially imposed categorization—that the African American is an inferior human being and, therefore, is deserving of his economic, social, political, and educational status—black educators and leaders organized and defined themselves politically around that category. Thus, they were organizing African Americans around narrowly defined grievances and goals: claims for the right to social, cultural, and political representation by the African American subject. Their dominant agenda was community building and the winning of civil rights and full equality. The assumption was that all who share the same racial oppression and discrimination based on skin color also share a common experience, outlook, and set of values and interests. The assumption also was that the common experience among African Americans marked out a common

human identity. This identity has become what today many call the "black experience." Therefore, at the height of the Jim Crow laws and legal segregation, elite/middle-class African American leaders and educators placed all people of African descent into a group they called "Negro." With the assistance of racial repression, they then built national African American communities and cultures. A pivotal part of this social development was the creation of a public cultural apparatus that included African American churches, schools, political conventions, newspapers, periodicals, specialized businesses, and debate, literary, and library societies, as well as artistic and literary associations.

Of course, as this ethnic identity model acquired cultural/political dominance in African American communities during post-Reconstruction, dissenting voices were muffled. Specifically, individuals whose experiences and interests were not represented in the dominant construction of racial uplift identity were excluded and repressed. Those African Americans who understood and believed in the immense sociohistorical diversity of meanings and social arrangements were also repressed.

2. The African American nationalist educators and leaders opposed the journey to the mainstream American values. In *The Condition of the Colored People*, Martin Delany criticizes black Christians for being too passive, for waiting too patiently for God to send them deliverance rather than working to free themselves. In the early twentieth century, one of the most zealous voices of black nationalism was Marcus Garvey, the West Indian leader of the United Negro Improvement Association. He had tremendous appeal for African Americans, winning thousands of ardent followers who saw in his program of separatism and his vision of a mass "return" to Africa their best hope for liberation and autonomy. Alexander Crummell was an early eloquent articulator of Ethiopianism, a literary–religious tradition common to English-speaking Africans. This tradition sprang from certain shared political and religious experiences. It found expression in the slave narratives, in the exhortations of conspiratorial slave preachers, and in the songs and folklore of the enslaved Africans of the Old and the New South. *The Golden Age of Black Nationalism 1850–1925* by Wilson Jeremiah Moses chronicles the history of nationalist thought and its movement among African/African American writers, educators, and political and cultural leaders, especially as they opposed the middle-class, Christian-driven African American sociopolitical mission of racial uplift. Nationalist thought reemerged in the 1960s and reached its peak in the 1970s with the Black Power movement.

3. Here I am using Gayatri Spivak's concept of the subaltern, which she defines as a "space of difference." These people belong to that "space that is cut off from the lines of mobility," below the "vectors of upward, downward, sideward, [and] backward mobility" (288). See interview with Spivak in Landry and MacLean (287–308).

4. Both DuBois and James Weldon Johnson were national leaders of the NAACP. Joseph Bass was head of the Grand United Order of Odd Fellows, a local branch of a national lodge, and Charles Alexander was a leader of the local Los Angeles branch of the NAACP. Noah Thompson became a leader of the Garvey movement in Los Angeles.

5. In the early days of the Civil Rights movement, the black press was a powerful and unifying force. During the 1930s and 1940s, many local black newspapers began to publish national editions, and by the late 1940s, sixty percent of their circulation crossed state lines. By 1955, there were more than two hundred black newspapers and magazines being published in the United States. These newspapers and magazines led the protest

against racial discrimination in the United States. When Emmitt Till was murdered in Mississippi in 1955, the *Chicago Defender* put the story on its front page and circulated it throughout the South. Also, these newspapers and magazines served as a vehicle for spreading the ideas of the African American sociopolitical mission of racial uplift. They showed how African Americans, if given equality, could become the Same as the normative American society. From beauty to entertainment to politics to education, these newspapers and magazines recorded African American "firsts." For more information on the black press, see *Eyes on the Prize* by Juan Williams.

6. Earlier American and African American critics who theorized about African American literary texts used mainstream aesthetics to determine the literature's worth and value. African American critics, prior to the 1960s, such as Benjamin Brawley (*The Negro in Literature and Art in the United States*), Nick Aaron Ford (*The Contemporary Negro Novel*), Sterling Brown (*The Negro in American Fiction*), J. Saunders Redding (*To Make a Poet Black*), Vernon Loggins (*The Negro Author in America*), Carl Milton Hughes (*The Negro Novelists 1940–1950*), Hugh M. Gloster (*Negro Voices in American Fiction*), Robert A. Bone (*The Negro Novel in America*), and David Littlejohn (*Black on White*) in varying degrees used mainstream aesthetic criteria to determine the value of African American literature. In all these constructions of African American literature by both American and African American critics before the 1960s, each critic, regardless of whether he thinks African American literature is distinct or indistinguishable from American literature, defines and judges African American literature aesthetically according to the standards, criteria, and themes of mainstream American literature. These early critics confronted African American literary texts with some external truth, and in most instances, when these texts did not measure up, they were defined as wanting. As a result, those African American texts that deal with middle-class and Christian themes and issues, that reflect the Protestant work ethic, and that are written in a particular literary language or literary style were privileged. Those texts that deal with other themes and issues such as the African American blues lifestyle, the African American urban subaltern, Voodoo, and the African American peasant farmers—all of which are not necessarily Christian and middle class—were repressed, subordinated, or ignored. In fact, in this exhaustive survey of African American criticism up to the 1960s, only Robert Bone in *The Negro Novel in America* and Carl Milton Hughes in *The Negro Novelists 1940–1950* even mention texts such as George Wylie Henderson's *Ollie Miss*, Arna Bontemps's *God Sends Sunday*, Zora Neale Hurston's *Jonah's Gourd Vine*, Claude McKay's *Home to Harlem*, and Rudolph Fisher's *The Walls of Jericho*, which deal with rural and urban subaltern African Americans. Bone and Hughes, however, mention these novels only in the context of African American folk culture. All of the other critics emphasize those African American texts which approximate aesthetically and thematically the institutionalized American norm. Thus, they end up basically defining African American literature negatively.

7. Although some African American critics might argue that they needed to select those African American texts that were similar aesthetically, experientially, and literarily to mainstream American texts, to have them accepted by the academy, they still have to take responsibility for the subsequent violence, exclusion, and repression that such a choice had for differences in African American literature.

8. In his book *blackness and the adventure of western culture*, George Kent, reacting against the normative critical fallacy that had dominated African American criticism be-

fore the 1960s, emphasizes the fact that he is not using traditional Western humanism to interpret African American literature. He states:

> The reader, I hope, will find no rigid allegiance to traditional high ground humanism. By high ground humanism, I mean the established values implicit in white writers . . . derived from Hebrew, Greek, and Roman traditions: the assumed triumph of the individual, the clarity of truth, the existence of transcendental beauty, the shining virtues of rationality, the glory of democratic freedom, and the range of Christian and Platonic assumptions that tend to form stubborn threads in the warp and woof of white tradition as a systematic and *abstract* universalism. (9)

As a critic, Kent promises to be flexible in his readings of black texts:

> to hang loose and follow. Which means that I'll follow him into high humanistic ground, if that's where he heads, and stand by holding a flashlight to see what rhythms he can make visible and throbbing. And I'll stand with him in the cool thickets in the low grounds of lonesome valleys where things go down dense and all definitions dissolve as they resolve or hold themselves together by dint of homemade existence-ism clubs. (10)

Kent wants to listen "for the voices of ancestors to enrich the resonance of contemporary black men. Voices sometimes cynical: sharp-edged. . . . In some, definitions provided by folk and cultural tradition, loosely defined, on which the writer can enforce as much signification as the definitions can be made to bear" (10). In some of the essays, Kent is "concerned about double-consciousness and about . . . the *sensibility* of the black writer" (13).

What is interesting about Kent's theory of literature is its purported openness to African American differences. He is willing to follow African American writers wherever they go. Kent does not subordinate those African American writers he examines to a mainstream American aesthetic, which is independent of and a priori to their existence. He engages these texts in terms of what Pierre Macherey calls "criticism-as-explanation":

> When we explain the work, we perceive its actual decentered-ness. We refuse the principle of an intrinsic analysis . . . which would artificially circumscribe the work, and deduce the image of a "totality" . . . from the fact that it is *entire*. . . . . What begs to be explained in the work is not that false simplicity which derives from the apparent unity of its meaning, but the presence of a relation, or an opposition. . . . To explain the work is to show that, contrary to appearances, it is not independent, but bears in its material substance the imprint of a determinate absence which is also the principle of its identity. (79–80)

But I wonder as I reexamine the African American writers that Kent chooses to follow, such as Claude McKay, Langston Hughes, Richard Wright, Gwendolyn Brooks, James Baldwin, and Ralph Ellison, just how far and in how many directions Kent would have to travel to follow them. After all, most are classical black writers. And although Kent, like Albert Memmi in *The Colonizer and the Colonized*, understands that the African American seeks freedom by embracing the values of the dominant white society and so has to crush and destroy that which is specifically African American, his respite from this double consciousness is to focus on the sensibility of the black writer. But what exactly does this mean? Does simply acknowledging that someone is a black writer remove him or her from white mythology? Are we to assume that having a black sensibility means that the black writer is outside Western values, definitions, and sensibilities? Does "massively absorbing his folk and

cultural traditions and forms" (Kent 11) mean putting the black writer, the black experience, outside of Western history and rationality? No, all of the issues and entities can be and
have been engaged within Western history and rationality and there is no sense in *blackness
and the adventure of western culture* that Kent escapes the West.

Sherley Anne Williams's *Give Birth to Brightness* constructs a Neo-Black theory of
contemporary black writers of the 1970s that "must, if it is to do this job without conde-
scension and at the same time preserve the uniqueness of this experience, use symbols
which have derived their meaning for Black people out of that experience" (19). In this
book, Williams is also reacting against pre-1960s African American criticism that measures
the worth of African American texts by showing how closely they approximate mainstream American literary standards and criteria. Her Neo-Black theory of literature allows
her to speak affirmatively about a diverse group of contemporary African American writers, such as Ernest J. Gaines, James Baldwin, Nathan Heard, and Amiri Baraka, who
turned "their attention [away from the definitions and values of mainstream society and]
inward seeking to identify the traditions of Black people, to explore their experiences, to
define themselves and their people in images which grow out of their individual quests
and group explorations" (17). Certainly, in approaching contemporary black writers as
producing work that includes the diverse symbols, black rituals, and cultural folkways of
African American—"themes and stories of the ghetto, ghetto English, the so-called
Negro dialect" (19), and jazz poetics—as well as work that has "many similarities and
sometimes identical characteristics" of mainstream American literature, Williams is signifying a theory of African American literature that celebrates African American differences.
Williams's Neo-Black theory of literature approaches post-1960s African American literature in terms of African American (male) differences. Unfortunately, we do not get a developed application of her Neo-Black theory, especially in terms of those differences.

But in discussing African American literature prior to the post-1960s Neo-Black
writers, Williams constructs a canon that is informed by the racial uplift narrative and by
1960s nationalist ideologies and sentiments, one that moves from the:

> great autobiographies of Frederick Douglass's *Life and Times* (1892), DuBois's *The Souls
> of Black Folk* (1903), Richard Wright's *Black Boy* (1945), Malcolm X's *The Autobiography
> of Malcolm X* (1965), and James Baldwin's *Notes of a Native Son* (1956), *Nobody Knows My
> Name* (1961), and *The Fire Next Time* (1964) to the novels of Richard Wright (*Native
> Son*, 1940) Ralph Ellison (*Invisible Man*, 1952), and Ann Petry (*The Street*, 1946). Some
> of the best literary works by Blacks are included in this list. (24)

In *Long Black Song*, Houston A. Baker Jr. defines a black American culture that is
both unique and different from white American culture: "There is a fundamental, qualitative difference between it [black culture] and white American culture" (15). Black culture is oral, collective, and repudiative. For Baker, jazz, folklore, classic black literature,
and the countless other facets of the entire body of intellectual and imaginative works
by African Americans reflect black American culture (16).

Arguing that black folklore, animal tales, trickster slave tales, spirituals, folk songs,
ballads, religious tales, and black music stand at the base of the black literary tradition,
Baker uses these African American cultural artifacts to selectively organize an African
American canon or a "black literary tradition as a whole" (16). In *Long Black Song*, Baker
traces the black folk base and the theme of repudiation as constants, or microsigns, in
black poetry from Paul Laurence Dunbar to Don L. Lee. He examines how these mi-

crosigns persist throughout contemporary black literature. To generate his folk-based African American literary tradition, Baker selects classic African American texts such as Frederick Douglass's *Narrative*, David Walker's *The Appeal*, Booker T. Washington's *Up from Slavery*, W. E. B. DuBois's *The Souls of Black Folk*, and Richard Wright's *Native Son*. Although Baker argues that African American culture is unique and different from white American culture, he does not allow for the fact that we know African American literature primarily through its various critical interpretations, and that most American and African American critical practices operate in the realm of normative criticism. Although he talks about using the symbols and artifacts of black culture—which he defines as separate and distinct from white culture and thereby with different values and a different cosmology—as tropes for interpreting and understanding black literature, he ultimately reads classic black texts as protest literature, which means reading them into the institutionalized American norm. Rather than interpreting Douglass's *Narrative* and Walker's *Appeal* (or, even more appropriate, African American narratives) as treatises for a different way of defining African American life, Baker reads them as protest against whites' denial of black humanity, as "indicting white Americans for their cruelty" (73), for being bad Christians. Both Douglass and Walker are middle-class Christians who are using African American folk-based culture not to define an alternative life, but to protest white rejection of their Sameness. They fit perfectly into Baker's canonical scheme that assumes "black Americans had little opportunity to participate in American dreams of rugged individualism or fantasies of individual advancement" (16), but that assumption is simply not true. To hold it, Baker has to ignore existentialist texts such as Charles Wright's *The Messenger*, which is readily defined as being about "fantasies of individual advancement" (16). And he has to repress blues-centered texts such as Albert Murray's *Train Whistle Guitar*, which is about the blues individual finding the source from within to seek freedom.

In *Singers of Daybreak*, published two years after *Long Black Song*, Baker continues to solidify the canonization of particular kinds of African American texts to the exclusion of others. He discusses many of the classical black texts mentioned earlier in an exploration of the writers, themes, and techniques that helped to illuminate the path for his newly canonical writers and their successors. James Weldon Johnson's *The Autobiography of an Ex-Coloured Man*, for example, is analyzed as a prototype for Ralph Ellison's *Invisible Man*. Baker also delineates parallels between the "careers of Dunbar and Brooks," adding that "it is perhaps enlightening to juxtapose Toomer's lyrical presentation of early-twentieth century black America with George Cain's [*Blueschild Baby*] portrayal of the contemporary black urban community" (x). What began for Baker as a way to define African American literature within an African American folk-culture-based aesthetic system, which has the potential for being subversive and for embracing all kinds of non-canonical African American texts, actually ends by affirming seven or eight classic black texts and the institutionalized American literary norm.

Using Northrop Fyre to posit that all cultures have "canonical stories," Robert Stepto in *From Behind the Veil* states that African American culture also has "canonical stories" or what he calls "pregeneric myths." These are:

> shared stories or myths that not only exist prior to literary form, but eventually shape the forms that comprise a given culture's literary canon. The primary pregeneric myth for Afro-America is the quest for freedom and literacy. The second is that once the pregeneric myth is set in motion in search of its literary forms, the historian of Afro-American literature must attempt to define and discuss the properties of genre. (ix–x)

In the first section of his book, Stepto delineates four types of slave narratives: the eclectic narrative, the integrated narrative, the generic narrative, and the authenticating narrative. In the first chapter, Stepto examines "the formal characteristics and narrative strategies" of Henry Bibb's *Narrative of the Life and Adventures of Henry Bibb, an American Slave*, Solomon Northrup's *Twelve Years a Slave*, Frederick Douglass's *Narrative*, and William Wells Brown's *Narrative of the Life and Escape of William Wells Brown* by way of making the point that the term "slave narrative" is really an "umbrella term for many types of narratives, and that while all slave narratives are personal histories of one sort or another, personal histories are not always autobiographies" (xi).

Using the slave narrative and the Afro-American pregeneric myth of the quest for freedom and literacy, Stepto builds on the African American canon already reinvented by Williams and Baker. Booker T. Washington's *Up from Slavery* and W. E. B. DuBois's *The Souls of Black Folk* "revise and revoice" (x) the generic and the authenticating slave narrative types. For Stepto's constructed canon, James Weldon Johnson's *The Autobiography of an Ex-Coloured Man* is:

> an intentionally aborted immersion narrative that revoices both *Up from Slavery* and *The Souls*—but especially *The Souls*; that Richard Wright's *Black Boy* is a narrative of ascent that revoices Frederick Douglass's *Narrative* of 1845; and . . . Ralph Ellison's *Invisible Man* is a narrative of hibernation that answers the call of both *The Souls* and the Douglass *Narrative*, while en route to discovering a new narrative form that bursts beyond those of ascent and immersion. (x)

Like Baker, Stepto reinforces the selected texts being used to reconfigure/reinvent a 1970s/1980s canon of African American literature. He, too, selects a subaltern African American trope, the call and response, which is found in black folk sermons, and appropriates it to read these selected African American texts into the institutionalized literary norm, where middle-class, Christian, Protestant work ethic values are emphasized.

In *Figures in Black*, *The Signifying Monkey*, and *"Race," Writing, and Difference*, Henry Louis Gates Jr., builds on the already reinvented 1970s/1980s canon of African American literature. He cites a letter that James Weldon Johnson sent to Carl Van Vechten in 1926, in which Johnson states: "I am coming to believe . . . that nothing can go farther to destroy race prejudice than the recognition of the Negro as a creator [of] and contributor to American civilization" (qtd. in Gates, *Figures in Black* xxiii). From the letter, Gates "gets the idea of the relationship between racial progress and art, between discrete demonstrations of Western civilization and the obliteration of race prejudice" (xxiii). In his letter, Johnson is espousing racial uplift ideology when he talks about proving the humanity and worth of the African American by showing white people that he can think, write, and reason the same as they. In *Figures in Black*, Gates locates the origins of this use of black literature in the European Enlightenment, although it was prefigured in the seventeenth century (xxiii).

After tracing the relationship between art and racial progress in seventeenth-century black literature, Gates concludes that African American writers judged their:

> own literature by a curious standard that derived from the social applications of the metaphors of the great chain of being, the idea of progress and the respectability of man, as well as the metaphor of capacity derived initially from eighteenth-century comparative studies of the anatomy of synian and human brains and then translated into a metaphor

for intelligence and the artistic potential of a "race". . . . This argument [in African American writings] persists from its origins in the seventeenth century at least through the New Negro Renaissance of the 1920s and even surfaces in recent writings by blacks. (xxxi)

In both *Figures in Black* and *The Signifying Monkey*, Gates examines classic African American authors and texts such as Phyllis Wheatley's poetry, Frederick Douglass's *Narrative*, Harriet E. Wilson's *Our Nig*, Jean Toomer's *Cane*, Zora Neale Hurston's *Their Eyes Were Watching God*, Sterling A. Brown's poetry, and Ishmael Reed's *Mumbo Jumbo*. Gates argues that "the relation of Reed's text to those of Ralph Ellison and Richard Wright, Jean Toomer and Sterling A. Brown, and Zora Neale Hurston is a 'signifyin(g) relation,' as the Afro-American tradition would have it" (*Signifying Monkey* xi). But in arguing that black writers signify upon each other, Gates totalizes African American literature. This idea of a "signifying relation" among black writers represses differences within African American literature.

Later, discussing the early slave autobiographies in the introduction to *"Race," Writing, and Difference*, Gates points out how, when the white American colonizers claimed that African Americans had no history and humanity because they did not measure up to the terms of the European Enlightenment, the slave autobiographers showed that they could become "equal to that splendid model" (Memmi 120) of the colonizer. They responded to:

> these serious allegations about their "nature" as directly as they could: they wrote books, poetry, autobiographical narratives. . . . Accused of lacking a formal and collective history, blacks published individual histories which, taken together, were intended to narrate in segments the larger yet fragmented history of blacks from Africa, now dispersed throughout a cold New World. The narrated, descriptive "eye" was put into service as a literary form to posit both the individual "I" of the black author as well as the collective "I" of the race. Text created author; and black authors, it was hoped, would create, or re-create, the image of the race in European discourse. The very *face* of the race was contingent upon the recording of the black *voice*. Voice presupposed a face, but also seems to have been thought to determine the very contours of the black face. (Gates, *"Race"* 11)

Establishing a critical practice that advocates the journey from the African American subaltern to the values of mainstream society as a way of refuting racism, obliterating race prejudice, and proving the African American worthy of social equality, Gates writes:

> The recording of an authentic black voice—a voice of deliverance from the deafening discursive silence within an enlightened Europe cited to prove the absence of the African's humanity—was the millennial instrument of transformation through which the African would become the European, the slave become the ex-slave, brute animal become the human being. So central was this idea to the birth of the black literary tradition in the eighteenth century that five of the earliest slave narratives draw upon the figure of the voice in the text—of the talking book—as crucial "scenes of instruction" in the development of the slave on the road to freedom. (11–12)

But Gates critiques this journey to the values of mainstream society when he asks:

> We are justified, however, in wondering aloud if the sort of subjectivity which these writers seek through the act of writing can be realized through a process which is so very ironic from the outset: how can the black subject posit a full and sufficient self in a language in

which blackness is a sign of absence? Can writing . . . mask the blackness of the black face that addresses the text of Western letters, in a voice that speaks English through an idiom which contains the irreducible element of cultural difference that will always separate the white voice from the black? Black people . . . have not been liberated from racism by our writings. (12)

The alternative that Gates offers is turning "to the black tradition itself to develop theories of criticism indigenous to our literatures" (13). But is Gates, like Kent, assuming that the theories that are "indigenous to our literatures" exist outside of Western language? Pointedly, neither Baker, Stepto, nor Gates selects texts informed by subaltern African American traditions that affirm values, beliefs, and theoretical conceptions of life and history that are not middle class and Christian.

As late as 1987 and long after certain black women critics had begun to question the male centeredness of this reinvented 1970s/1980s African American canon, Valerie Smith in *Self-Discovery and Authority in Afro-American Narrative* was focusing on the same classic black texts as Baker, Stepto, and Gates. Echoing and reinforcing other African American critics of the 1970s and 1980s, Smith begins her book with the statement that with: "Frederick Douglass's 1845 autobiography, *The Narrative of the Life of Frederick Douglass, an American Slave, Written by Himself*, has been the point of departure for numerous critical studies of Afro-American literature" (2). Smith also defines Douglass's *Narrative* as the referent to which dozens of later black narratives look back: "When he [Douglass] links the acquisition of literacy to the process of liberation, he [Douglass] forges a connection that resonates for subsequent generations of writers" (2). Smith argues that the slave narrators and the protagonist narrators of certain twentieth-century texts such as James Weldon Johnson's *The Autobiography*, Richard Wright's *Native Son* and *Black Boy*, Ralph Ellison's *Invisible Man*, and Toni Morrison's *Song of Solomon* affirm and "legitimize their psychological autonomy by telling the stories of their lives" (2). Of course, in her second book, *Not Just Race, Not Just Gender: Black Feminist Readings*, Smith moves away from the male-centered classics and the racial uplift narrative to a more diverse, feminist approach to reading African American narratives, films, class, social, and historical situations.

9. Obviously, Fishkin is aware that her reductionist, limited theory of literature has been critiqued. Yet, she remains at an impasse. In the footnote to her chapter, she acknowledges her exclusions of Asian Americans, Native Americans, and so on. Yet, four years later (2000) on a panel at the American Studies Association meeting in Montreal, she, in a talk entitled "Desegregating American Literary Studies," continued her white/black embedding argument. Also, although Fishkin uses Ralph Ellison and Toni Morrison as her forebears, neither Ellison nor Morrison reduce African American social reality to blacks and whites embedding each other. In *Invisible Man* and his essays, Ellison explores the diverse, hybrid, and multilayered American/African American social reality. Likewise, in her fiction, Morrison textualizes the complex, varied non-middle-class, non-Christian-African American life. Actually, in Morrison's fiction, despite what she says in *Playing in the Dark* and to the chagrin of mainstream American reviewers and critics, there is no white/black embedding. Morrison understands clearly that for most African American lives, whites' existence is marginal.

10. The seventh edition of *From Slavery to Freedom* by John Hope Franklin and Alfred A. Moss Jr., published in 1994, updates the struggle by elite/middle-class African Americans to become the Same as the mainstream white society. This updated edition

still does not address the African American subaltern and the African American working class who are not Christians. Likewise, in the sixth revised edition of *Before the Mayflower*, published in 1987, Lerone Bennett adds a section, "Landmarks and Milestones" (231 pages in length) that chronicles the struggle of elite/middle-class Christian African Americans to achieve parity with their white counterparts in the dominant American society. It comprises a chronology of African American "firsts."

CHAPTER 4:
FINDING FREEDOM IN SAMENESS:
JAMES WELDON JOHNSON'S
THE AUTOBIOGRAPHY OF
AN EX-COLOURED MAN

1. Although earlier African American critics ultimately defined *The Autobiography* as a major African American text, the pivotal placement of *The Autobiography* as an archetypal, canonical African American text did not happen until the 1970s and 1980s with the publication of George Kent's *blackness and the adventure of western culture*, Sherley Anne Williams's *Give Birth to Brightness*, Houston A. Baker Jr.'s *Long Black Song* and *Singers of Daybreak*, Robert Stepto's *From Behind the Veil*, Michael G. Cooke's *Afro-American Literature in the Twentieth Century*, Henry Louis Gates Jr.'s *The Signifying Monkey* and *Figures in Black*, Valerie Smith's *Self-Discovery and Authority in Afro-American Narrative*, and Bernard W. Bell's *The Afro-American Novel and Its Tradition*, which accompanied the reinvention of the African American literary canon. As I mentioned in chapter 3, all of these African American critics theorized about and canonized African American literature. All except Williams and Cooke focused on a select group of (mostly) African American male writers. In most, if not all, of these 1970s/1980s theories of a reinvented African American literature, Johnson's *The Autobiography* is reconfigured, repositioned, and, therefore, represented as pivotal.

Unlike Carl Van Vechten, Hugh M. Gloster, Carl Milton Hughes, and Robert Bone, who defined the text as a precursor to the Harlem Renaissance, Kent, Baker, Stepto, and Smith defined *The Autobiography* not only as a precursor both to the Harlem Renaissance and to contemporary African American fiction but also as the inheritor of a past tradition. Kent states:

> Because of its concentration upon the working out of the principle that character is fate, its low-key presentation of racial propaganda, and its varied portraits of black life, James Weldon Johnson's *The Autobiography* . . . is usually greatly emphasized as a precursor of the Renaissance. It also gives a more penetrating rendering of the psychology of the mulatto character who decides to pass than [the nineteenth-century African American writer, Charles] Chesnutt usually afforded. (18–19)

Baker in *Singers of Daybreak* represents *The Autobiography* as more pivotal to a canon of African American literature than Kent. Baker notes that *The Autobiography* "opens with a first-person narrator who belongs to the literary class known as 'tragic mulatto,'" and he compares Johnson's narrator to real-life historical figures such as William Wells Brown, Frederick Douglass, and W. E. B. DuBois. Baker concludes that "in a sense, *The Autobiography* . . . is a fictional rendering of *The Souls of Black Folk*, for Johnson's narrator stresses not only his bifurcated vision but also his intellectual genius" (22).

Perhaps the culmination of the drive to establish Johnson's *The Autobiography* as *the* archetypal, canonical African American text comes with Stepto: "*The Autobiography* identifies and collects from antedating texts—notably *Up from Slavery* and *The Souls of Black Folk*, but also the slave narratives—those key tropes which form the Afro-American literary tradition" (96). According to Stepto, *The Autobiography* borrows the "authenticating narrative initiated by certain slave narratives, and sophisticated almost singlehandedly by Washington's *Up From Slavery*" (97).

Finally, Stepto defines *The Autobiography* as a precursor to the Harlem Renaissance as well as to contemporary African American fiction. He attributes the:

> vivid portraits of Negro America's urban underbelly in the "renaissance" to the "Club" in Johnson's text. The significance of Johnson's invention [of the colored bohemia] becomes clear when we look forward in literary history to the literature fashioned by Jean Toomer, Langston Hughes, Claude McKay, and Sterling Brown. (123)

In the 1980s, African American critics such as Smith continued this pivotal positioning of *The Autobiography* as a major canonical African American text:

> James Weldon Johnson's *The Autobiography* . . . [is] a pivotal text in Afro-American letters. . . . A novel that foreshadows the tropes and the narrative situation of Ralph Ellison's *Invisible Man* and echoes and revises the structures not only of the former slaves' accounts but also of W. E. B. DuBois's book *The Souls of Black Folk*. Johnson's text, like all of these works, engages the interconnections of racial history and conditions with the life history of the individual. (44)

Furthermore, Johnson's *The Autobiography* is interpreted by African American critics, both prior to and after the 1960s, as reproducing hegemonic literary language, to use the words of John Guillory, "with its linguistic and generic constraints" (*Cultural Capital* 68). When Robert Bone refers to Johnson's "superior craftsmanship" and *The Autobiography*'s "form" that "demanded a discipline and restraint hitherto unknown to the Negro novel," he is reading *The Autobiography* into the institutional literary norm, associating the text with a form that is a part of the language of preserved texts. When Edward Margolies states that *The Autobiography*'s "principal strength . . . lies in Johnson's occasional lyric style and the thematic unity he gives to the episodic structure of the book" (26), he is recognizing what Guillory calls "literariness as *literary* language, as writing" (65). Johnson has written a novel "upon which literature appears as a particular kind of valorized language," whose text is "repositioned along a hierarchy of socially marked forms of speech" (Guillory 66).

2. I am working from the assumption that the sociopolitical mission of racial uplift, which dominated the worldview of elite/middle-class African Americans, informed Johnson's construction of the desires of the ex-coloured man.

CHAPTER 9:
IDENTITY POLITICS, SEXUAL FLUIDITY, AND
JAMES EARL HARDY'S *B-BOY BLUES*

1. Hardy, in an interview, discusses why the gay white press supports novels written by African American writers who deal with interracial gay themes rather than with black

men loving black men. He states: "It is very easy for a white editor, regardless of sexual orientation, to digest a story in which a Black character [who] is going through a trial or tribulation is caught up in some pathology and is naturally saved by some white person. And most of those books [novels dealing with interracial themes] fell into one of those categories." (qtd. in Travis 15). Therefore, to write a novel about black men loving black men or "where Black folks not only love each other, but themselves" is to "challenge the white gay status quo" (Travis 15).

Mitchell in *B-Boy Blues* echoes this same representation of white/black gay relationships. He feels that white gays are looking for "Mr. Mandingo," or a black "fetish or flavor of the night," and that white gays have a "patronizing, paternalistic attitude" that "spills over into the world of activism, be it political, social, or cultural" (79). What is always missing in this representation, he argues, is brothers loving brothers. In the white gay media, he:

> could count on one hand the number of images of brothers loving brothers. . . . We . . . are often depicted in some passionate embrace with a white man, particularly in safer-sex ads. The message is insidious, insulting, and very clear; we don't fuck each other. (201)

CHAPTER 10:
VOODOO, A DIFFERENT AFRICAN AMERICAN EXPERIENCE, AND DON BELTON'S *ALMOST MIDNIGHT*

1. Of course, this 1970s/1980s reconfigured canon was almost completely overshadowed by the emergence of a popular, African American romance, relationship-type fiction by such contemporary writers as Terry McMillan, Connie Briscoe, Benilde Little, Omar Tyree, E. Lynn Harris, Valerie Wilson Wesley, BeBe Moore Campbell, and others. But mainstream, academic American and African American critics have not rushed to impute these writers with cultural capital. However, many of them are enjoying commercial success brought on by a nontraditional and nonacademic reading public.

WORKS CITED

Abu-Lughod, Janet L. *Before European Hegemony: The World System A.D. 1250–1350.* New York: Oxford UP, 1989.

Adams, Charles. "Imagination and Community in W. M. Kelley's *A Different Drummer.*" *Critique* 26 (Fall 1984): 27–35.

Adelman, Lynn. "A Study of James Weldon Johnson." *Journal of Negro History* 52 (Apr. 1967): 128–45.

Afzal-Khan, Fawzia. *Cultural Imperialism and the Indo-English Novel: Genre and Ideology in R. K. Narayan, Anita Desai, Kamala Markandaya, and Salman Rushdie.* University Park: Pennsylvania State UP, 1993.

Albanese, Denise. "Making It New: Humanism, Colonialism, and the Gendered Body in Early Modern Culture." *Feminist Readings of Early Modern Culture: Emerging Subjects.* Ed. Valerie Truab, M. Lindsay Kaplan, and Mynpna Callaghan. Cambridge: Cambridge UP, 1996. 16–43.

Allen, Theodore W. *The Invention of the White Race: Racial Oppression and Social Control.* London: Verso, 1994.

Altieri, Charles. "An Idea and Ideal of a Literary Canon." *Canons.* Ed. Robert von Hallberg. Chicago: U of Chicago P, 1984. 41–64.

Amin, Samir. *Delinking: Towards a Polycentric World.* Trans. Michael Wolfers. London: Zed, 1990.

——. *Empire of Chaos.* Trans. W. H. Locke Anderson. New York: Monthly Review P, 1992.

Anderson, Jarvis. *Bayard Rustin: Troubles I've Seen.* New York: Harper, 1997.

Baker, Houston A. Jr., *Blues, Ideology, and Afro-American Literature: A Vernacular Theory.* Chicago: U of Chicago P, 1984.

——. *Long Black Song: Essays in Black American Literature and Culture.* Charlottesville: UP of Virginia, 1972.

——. *Singers of Daybreak: Studies in Black American Literature.* Washington, DC: Howard UP, 1974.

Balliett, Whitney. "Loner." *The New Yorker* 2 Nov. 1963: 206–09.

Barrera, Mario. *Race and Class in the Southwest: A Theory of Racial Inequality.* Notre Dame: U of Notre Dame P, 1979.

Barrett, William. "Reader's Choice." *The Atlantic Monthly* 212 (Aug. 1963): 120–24.

Bartlett, Robert. *The Making of Europe: Conquest, Colonization, and Cultural Change 950–1350.* Princeton: Princeton UP, 1993.

Beam, Joseph, ed. *In the Life: A Black Gay Anthology.* Boston: Alyson, 1986.

Beards, Richard. "Parody as Tribute: William Melvin Kelley's *A Different Drummer* and Faulkner." *Studies in Black Literature* 5 (Winter 1974): 25–28.

Bell, Bernard W. *The Afro-American Novel and Its Tradition.* Amherst: U of Massachusetts P, 1987.

273

Belton, Don. *Almost Midnight*. New York: Morrow, 1986.

Bennett, Lerone Jr. *Before the Mayflower: A History of the Negro in America 1619–1964*. Baltimore: Penguin, 1966.

———. *The Shaping of Black America: The Struggles and Triumphs of African-Americans, 1619–1990s*. New York: Penguin, 1993.

Bennett, Tony. "Really Useless 'Knowledge': A Political Critique of Aesthetics." *Thesis Eleven* 12 (1985): 33–44.

Bernal, Martin. *Black Athena: The Afroasiatic Roots of Classical Civilization*. Vol. I. New Brunswick: Rutgers UP 1987.

Bersani, Leo. *Homos*. Cambridge: Harvard UP, 1995.

bhabba, homi k. *the location of culture*. London: Routledge, 1994.

Birkerts, Sven. *American Energies: Essays on Fiction*. New York: Morrow, 1992.

Blauner, Robert. *Racial Oppression in America*. New York: Harper and Row, 1972.

Blaut, J. M. *The Colonizer's Model of the World: Geographical Diffusionism and Eurocentric History*. London: Guilford, 1993.

Bond, Jean Carey. "Book review." *Freedomway* 2 (Fall 1962): 503–04.

Bone, Robert. *The Negro Novel in America*. New Haven: Yale UP, 1958.

Bradley, David. Foreword. *A Different Drummer* by William Melvin Kelley. Garden City, NY: Anchor/Doubleday, 1989. xi–xxxii.

Braudel, Fernand. *A History of Civilizations*. Trans. Richard Mayne. New York: Penguin, 1993.

Burke, Peter. *The Renaissance Sense of the Past*. New York: St. Martin's, 1969.

Butler, Judith. *Gender Trouble: Feminism and the Subversion of Identity*. London: Routledge, 1990.

Byam, Milton. "Review of Wright's *The Messenger*." *Library Journal* (July 1963): 2730.

Byerman, Keith E. *Fingering the Jagged Grain: Tradition and Form in Recent Black Fiction*. Athens: U of Georgia P, 1986.

Byrd, James W. "Mythical Novel About the South." *Phylon* 24 (Spring 1963): 99–100.

Califia, Pat. "Polygamous Pat." *Ten Percent* 3 (May/June 1995): 61–62.

Campbell, Jane. *Mythic Black Fiction: The Transformation of History*. Knoxville: U of Tennessee P, 1986.

Canclini, Nestor Garcia. *Hybrid Cultures: Strategies for Entering and Leaving Modernity*. Trans. Christopher L. Chiappari and Silvia I. Lopez. Minneapolis: U of Minnesota P, 1995.

Castañeda, Quetzil E. *In the Museum of Maya Culture: Touring Chichen Itza*. Minneapolis: U of Minnesota P, 1996.

Cheuse, Alan. "Death and Blight on a Dunghill for Dreamers." *The New York Times Book Review* (19 Jan. 1969): 38.

Christian, Barbara. *Black Women Novelists: The Development of a Tradition, 1892–1976*. Westport, CT: Greenwood, 1980.

Clay, Stanley Bennett. "In Concept." *SBC: The Africentric Homosexual Magazine* 8 (Dec. 1999): 8.

Collier, Eugenia. "The Endless Journey of an Ex-Coloured Man." *Phylon* 32 (1971): 365–73.

Cone, James H. *The Spirituals and the Blues: An Interpretation*. New York: Seabury, 1972.

Cook, Bruce. *Listen to the Blues*. New York: Da Capo, 1995.

Cooke, Michael G. *Afro-American Literature in the Twentieth Century: The Achievement of Intimacy*. New Haven: Yale UP, 1984.

Cose, Ellis. *The Rage of a Privileged Class: Why are Middle-Class Blacks Angry? Why Should America Care?* New York: HarperCollins, 1993.

Cox, Oliver. *Caste, Class, and Race: A Study in Social Dynamics.* New York: Monthly Review, 1970.

Curley, Thomas. "City Sickness." *Commonweal* 78 (20 Sept. 1963): 566–67.

Davidson, Basil. "Columbus: The Bones and Blood of Racism." *Race and Class* 33 (Jan.–Mar. 1992): 17–25.

Davis, Arthur P. *From the Dark Tower: Afro-American Writers 1900–1960.* Washington, DC: Howard UP, 1981.

Davis, Charles E. "W. M. Kelley and H. D. Thoreau: The Music Within." *Obsidian II* 2 (Spring 1987): 2–13.

de Certeau, Michel. *Culture in the Plural.* Minneapolis: U of Minnesota P, 1997.

———. *Heterologies: Discourse on the Other.* Minneapolis: U of Minnesota P, 1986.

———. *The Writing of History.* Trans. Tom Conley. New York: Columbia UP, 1988.

Delany, Samuel R., and Joseph Beam. "Samual R. Delany: The Possibility of Possibilities." *In the Life: A Black Gay Anthology.* Ed. Joseph Beam. Boston: Alyson, 1986. 185–208.

Deleuze, Gilles, and Felix Guattari. *The Anti-Oedipus: Capitalism and Schizophrenia.* Minneapolis: U of Minnesota P, 1983.

———. *Kafka: Toward a Minor Literature.* Minneapolis: U of Minnesota P, 1986.

D'Emilio, John. *Sexual Politics, Sexual Communities: The Making of a Homosexual Minority in the United States 1940–1970.* Chicago: U of Chicago P, 1983.

Drake, St. Clair, and Horace C. Cayton. *Black Metropolis: A Study of Negro Life in a Northern City.* New York: Harcourt, Brace, 1945.

Dubey, Madhu. *Black Women Novelists and the Nationalist Aesthetic.* Bloomington: Indiana UP, 1994.

DuBois, W. E. B. "The Negro in Literature and Art." *Writings by W. E. B. DuBois in Periodicals.* Ed. Herbert Aptheker. Vol. 2. Millwood, NY: Kraus Thompson Organization, 1982. 88–91.

Dussel, Enrique. *The Invention of the Americas: Eclipse of "the Other" and the Myth of Modernity.* Trans. Michael D. Barber. New York: Continuum, 1995.

Ellison, Ralph. *Shadow and Act.* New York: Vintage, 1972.

Emanuel, James A. and Theodore L. Grass, eds. *Dark Symphony: Negro Literature in America.* New York: Free Press, 1968.

Fabian, Johannes. *Time and the Other: How Anthropology Makes Its Object.* New York: Columbia UP, 1983.

Fanon, Franz. *Black Skin, White Masks.* Trans. Charles L. Markmann. New York: Grove, 1967.

Fauset, Jessie. "What to Read." *The Crisis* 5 (Nov. 1912): 38.

"Fiction." *Kirkus* 30 (1 Apr. 1962): 340.

"Fiction." *Publishers' Weekly* 194 (16 Sept. 1968): 70.

Finn, Julio. *The Bluesman: The Musical Heritage of Black Men and Women in the Americas.* New York: Quartet, 1986.

Fishkin, Shelley Fisher. "Interrogating 'Whiteness,' Complicating 'Blackness.'" *Criticism and the Color Line: Segregating American Literary Studies.* Ed. Henry Wonham. New Brunswick, NJ: Rutgers UP, 1996. 251–90.

Fleming, Robert. "Irony as a Key to Johnson's *The Autobiography of an Ex-Coloured Man.*" *American Literature* 43 (1971): 83–96.

Foster, Hal. *Recodings: Art, Spectacle, Cultural Politics.* Port Townsend, WA: Bay, 1985.

Foucault, Michel. *The Archaeology of Knowledge.* Trans. A. M. Sheridan Smith. New York: Pantheon, 1972.

Franklin, John Hope. *From Slavery to Freedom: A History of Negro Americans.* 3rd ed. New York: Vintage, 1969.

Frazier, E. Franklin. *The Negro Family in the United States.* New York: Citadel, 1984.

Freud, Sigmund. *Beyond the Pleasure Principle.* New York: Norton, 1961.

————. *Civilization and Its Discontents.* New York: Norton, 1961.

Gaines, Kevin K. *Uplifting the Race: Black Leadership, Politics, and Culture in the Twentieth Century.* Chapel Hill: U of North Carolina P, 1966.

Garber, Eric. "A Spectacle in Color: The Lesbian and Gay Subculture of Jazz Age Harlem." *Hidden from History: Reclaiming the Gay and Lesbian Past.* Ed. Martin B. Duberman, Martha Vicinus, and George Chancey Jr. New York: New American Library, 1989. 318–31.

Garon, Paul. *Blues and the Poetic Spirit.* San Francisco: City Lights, 1996.

Garrett, Marvin P. "Early Recollections and Structural Irony in *The Autobiography of an Ex-Coloured Man.*" *Critique* 13 (1971): 5–14.

Gates, Henry Louis Jr. *Figures in Black: Words, Signs, and the "Racial" Self.* New York: Oxford UP, 1987.

————, ed. *"Race," Writing and Difference.* Chicago: U of Chicago P, 1986.

————. *The Signifying Monkey: A Theory of African American Literary Criticism.* New York: Oxford UP, 1988.

Gayle, Addison, ed. *The Black Aesthetic.* Garden City, NY: Anchor/Doubleday, 1972.

————. *The Way of the New World: The Black Novel in America.* Garden City, NY: Anchor/Doubleday, 1975.

Giddings, Paula. "Books." *Essence* (Oct. 1986): 28.

————. *When and Where I Enter: The Impact of Black Women on Race and Sex in America.* New York: Bantam, 1984.

Giovanni, Nikki. "Howard Street." *Negro Digest* (Feb. 1969): 71–73.

Godzich, Wlad. Foreword. *Heterologies: Discourse on the Other.* By Michel de Certeau. Minneapolis: U of Minnesota P, 1986. vii–xxi.

Goellnicht, Donald C. "Passing as Autobiography: James Weldon Johnson's *The Autobiography of an Ex-Coloured Man.*" *African American Review* 30 (Spring 1966): 17–33.

Goldstein, Richard. "'Go the Way Your Blood Beats': An Interview with James Baldwin." *James Baldwin: The Legacy.* Ed. Quincy Troupe. New York: Simon and Schuster/Touchstone, 1989. 173–85.

Gomez, Jewelle. "Representations of Black Lesbians." *The Harvard Gay and Lesbian Review* 6 (Summer 1999): 33.

Gonzalez Casanova, Pablo. "Internal Colonialism and National Development. *Studies in Comparative International Development* 1 (1965): 27–37.

Gossett, Thomas. *Race: The History of an Idea in America.* New York: Schocken, 1963.

Gover, Robert. "An Interview with Ishmael Reed." *Black American Literature Forum* 12 (Spring 1978): 12–19.

Graff, Gerald and James Phelan, eds. *William Shakespeare: The Tempest: A Case Study in Critical Controversy.* New York: St. Martin's, 2000.

Greenblatt, Stephen. *Marvelous Possessions: The Wonder of the New World.* Chicago: U of Chicago P, 1991.

Griggs, Sutton E. *Imperium in Imperio.* New York: Arno, 1969.

WORKS CITED 277

Gross, Robert. "The Black Novelist: Our Turn." *Newsweek* 73 (16 June 1969): 94–97.

Grumbach, Doris. "Fiction Shelf." *The Critic* (Aug.–Sept. 1963): 83.

Guberman, Ross Mitchell, ed. *Julia Kristeva: Interviews.* New York: Columbia UP, 1996.

Guillory, John. *Cultural Capital: The Problem of Literary Canon Formation.* Chicago: U of Chicago P, 1993.

———. "The Ideology of Canon Formation: T. S. Eliot and Cleanth Brooks." *Canons.* Ed. Robert von Hallberg. Chicago: U of Chicago P, 1984. 337–62.

Hajdu, David. *Lush Life: A Biography of Billy Strayhorn.* New York: North Point, 1997.

Hale, Grace Elizabeth. *Making Whiteness: The Culture of Segregation in the South, 1890–1940.* New York: Pantheon, 1998.

Hale, John. *The Civilization of Europe in the Renaissance.* New York: Atheneum, 1994.

Hall, Kim F. *Things of Darkness: Economies of Race and Gender in Early Modern England.* Ithaca: Cornell UP, 1995.

Hardy, James Earl. *B-Boy Blues: A Seriously Sexy, Fiercely Funny Black-on-Black Love Story.* Boston: Alyson, 1994.

Harris, Elise. "The Double Life of Lorraine Hansberry." *OUT* September 1999: 97.

Harrison, Daphne. *Black Pearls: Black Queens of the 1920s.* New Brunswick: Rutgers UP, 1988.

Hartog, François. *The Mirror of Herodotus: The Representation of the Other in the Writing of History.* Trans. Janet Lloyd. Berkeley: U of California P, 1988.

Haskins, James. *Voodoo and Hoodoo: The Craft as Revealed by Traditional Practitioners.* Lanham, MD: Scarborough, 1990.

Haweswood, William G. *One of the Children: Gay Black Men in Harlem.* Berkeley: U of California P, 1996.

Heard, Nathan. *Howard Street.* Los Angeles: Amok, 1968.

Hillard-Jones, Amy. "Diversity: A Global Success Strategy." *Fortune* 133 (15 Apr. 1996): 149–54.

Hine, Darlene Clark. "Reflections on Race and Gender Systems." *Historian and Race: Autobiography and the Writing of History.* Ed. Paul A. Cimbala and Robert Himmelberg. Bloomington: Indiana UP, 1996. 51–65.

hooks, bell. *black looks: race and representation.* Boston: South End, 1992.

———. "Black on Black Pain: Class Cruelty." *killing rage: ending racism.* New York: Holt, 1995: 163–171.

———. *Outlaw Culture: Resisting Representations.* New York: Routledge, 1994.

———. "Reconstructing Black Masculinity." *black looks: race and representation.* By bell hooks. Boston: South End, 1992. 87–113.

Hughes, Charles H. "An Organization of Colored Ertopaths." *Gay American History: Lesbians and Gay Men in the U.S.A.* Ed. Jonathan Katz. New York: Cornwell, 1976. 42–43.

Ingrasci, Hugh J. "Strategic Withdrawal or Retreat: Deliverance from Racial Oppression in Kelley's *A Different Drummer* and Faulkner's *Go Down Moses*." *Studies in Black Literature* 6 (1975): 1–6.

Irigaray, Luce. *This Sex Which Is Not One.* Trans. Catherine Porter with Carolyn Burke. Ithaca: Cornell UP, 1985.

Jackson, Katherine Gauss. "Books in Brief." *Harpers* 227 (Sept. 1963): 115–16.

Jacobson, Matthew Frye. *Whiteness of a Different Color: European Immigrants and the Alchemy of Race.* Cambridge: Harvard UP, 1998.

James, Etta with David Ritz. *Rage to Survive: The Etta James Story.* New York: Da Capo, 1995.

Johnson, James Weldon. *The Autobiography of an Ex-Coloured Man.* New York: Vintage, 1989.

———. *Black Manhattan.* New York: Atheneum, 1930.

Johnson, Mark S. "Interview with Ishmael Reed." *Conversations with Ishmael Reed.* Ed. Bruce Dick and Amritjit Singh. Jackson: UP of Mississippi, 1995. 51–58.

Jones, Anderson. "Still Here." *Venus* 4 (1998): 36–41.

Jones, Jim. "Voodoo is Trendy." *Knight Ridder Newspapers* 25 July 2001: 14. 27: 14. 16 October 2001 <http://www.voodooistrendy.com>.

Jones, LeRoi. *Blues People: Negro Music in White America.* New York: Morrow, 1963.

Jordan, Winthrop. *White over Black.* Chapel Hill: U of North Carolina P, 1968.

July, Robert W. *A History of the African People.* New York: Charles Scribner's Sons, 1974.

Kaiser, Charles. *The Gay Metropolis: A Landmark History of Gay Life in America since World War II.* New York: Harcourt Brace, 1997.

Katz, Jonathan, ed. *Gay American History: Lesbians and Gay Men in the U.S.A.* New York: Corwell, 1976.

———. "The Invention of Heterosexuality." *Socialist Review* 7 (Winter 1990): 7–39.

Katz, William Loren. *Black Indians: A Hidden Heritage.* New York: Aladdin Paperback, 1991.

Keil, Charles. *Urban Blues.* Chicago: U of Chicago P, 1966.

Kelley, Robin D. G. *Race Rebels: Culture, Politics, and the Black Working Class.* New York: Free, 1996.

Kelley, William Melvin. *A Different Drummer.* New York: Anchor Books/Doubleday, 1989.

Kent, George. *blackness and the adventure of western culture.* Chicago: Third World, 1972.

Kiely, Robert. "Exercises in Extremity." *The Nation* (29 June 1963): 549–50.

Kim, Jungwon. "Intersections." *A Magazine* (Feb./Mar. 1999): 39–43, 83.

Klinkowitz, Jerome. "The New Black Writer and the Old Black Art." *Fiction International* 1 (1973): 123–27.

Kluger, Richard. "Books." *New York Herald Tribune* (9 June 1963): 7.

Kristeller, Paul Oskar. "Renaissance Humanism and Its Significance." *Reconsidering the Renaissance.* Ed. Mario A. Di Cesare. Binghamton, NY: Center for Medieval and Early Renaissance Studies, 1994. 29–43.

Kristeva, Julia. *Desire in Language: A Semiotic Approach to Literature and Art.* New York: Columbia UP, 1980.

Landry, Donna, and Gerald MacLean, eds. *The Spivak Reader: Selected Works of Gayatri Chakrovorty Spivak.* New York: Routledge, 1996.

Laqueur, Walter. "The Schism." *Polycentrism: The New Factor in International Communism.* Ed. Walter Laqueur and Leopold Labedz. New York: Draeger, 1962. 1–8.

Lehmann-Haupt, Christopher. "Who Says What, and How?" *The New York Times.* (13 Dec. 1968): 45.

Lemann, Nicholas. *The Promised Land: The Great Migration and How It Changed America.* New York: Knopf, 1991.

Levinas, Emmanuel. *Totality and Infinity: An Essay on Exteriority.* Trans. Alphonso Lingis. Pittsburgh: Duquesne UP, 1969.

Levy, Eugene. "Ragtime and Race Pride: The Career of James Weldon Johnson." *Journal of Popular Culture* 1 (Spring 1968): 357–70.

Lewis, David Levering. *When Harlem Was in Vogue.* New York: Knopf, 1981.

Littlejohn, David. *Black on White: A Critical Survey of Writing by American Negroes.* New York: Viking, 1966.

Lyell, Frank H. "The Day the Negroes Left." *The New York Times Book Review* 67 (17 June 1962): 24–25.

Macherey, Pierre. *A Theory of Literary Production.* London: Routledge, 1978.

Major, Clarence. *Dirty Bird Blues.* San Francisco: Mercury, 1996.

Margolies, Edward. *Native Sons: A Critical Study of Twentieth Century Black American Authors.* Philadelphia: Lippincott, 1968.

Mason, Peter. *Deconstructing America: Representations of the Other.* London: Routledge, 1990.

McDowell, Deborah E. "Boundaries: Or Distant Relations and Close Kin." *Afro-American Literary Study in the 1990s.* Ed. Houston A. Baker Jr. and Patricia Redmond. Chicago: U of Chicago P, 1989. 51–77.

———. "New Directions for Black Feminist Criticism." *"The Changing Same": Black Women's Literature, Criticism, and Theory.* Bloomington: Indiana UP, 1995. 5–23.

Memmi, Albert. *The Colonizer and the Colonized.* New York: Orion, 1965.

Metraux, Alfred. *Voodoo in Haiti.* Trans. Hugo Charteris. New York: Schocken, 1972.

Mignolo, Walter. *The Darker Side of the Renaissance: Literary, Territoriality, and Colonization.* Ann Arbor: U of Michigan P, 1995.

Murray, Albert. *The Hero and the Blues.* New York: Vintage, 1973.

———. *The Omni-Americans: New Perspectives on Black Experience and American Culture.* New York: Avon, 1970.

———. *Stomping the Blues.* New York: Da Capo, 1976.

Myrdal, Gunnar. *An American Dilemma: The Negro Problem and Modern Democracy.* New York: Harper and Brothers, 1944.

Nadeau, Robert. "Black Jesus: A Study of Kelley's *A Different Drummer.*" *Studies in Black Literature* 2 (1971): 13–15.

Nadell, Bonnie. "Two Views of Paternal Love." *San Francisco Chronicle* 15 June 1986: 4.

Neilsen, Aldon Lynn. *Black Chant: Languages of African American Postmodernism.* New York: Cambridge UP, 1996.

Oliver, Kelly, ed. *The Portable Kristeva.* New York: Columbia UP, 1997.

Oliver, Paul. *The Meaning of the Blues.* New York: Collier, 1960.

O'Sullivan, Maurice J. Jr. "Of Souls and Pottage: James Weldon Johnson's *The Autobiography of an Ex-Coloured Man.*" *CLA Journal* 23 (Sept. 1979): 60–70.

Pagden, Anthony. *European Encounters with the New World: From Renaissance to Romanticism.* New Haven: Yale UP, 1993.

Patterson, Orlando. *Slavery and Social Death: A Comparative Study.* Cambridge: Harvard UP, 1982.

Percy, Walker. *The Moviegoer.* New York: Knopf, 1961.

———. *Signposts in a Strange Land.* New York: Farrar, Straus, and Giroux, 1991.

Powell, Timothy B. ed. *Beyond the Binary: Reconstructing Cultural Identity in a Multicultural Context.* New Brunswick, NJ: Rutgers UP, 1999.

Puckett, Newbell Niles. *Folk Beliefs of the Southern Negro.* New York: Negro Universities, 1968.

Quinn, Mary Ellen. "Adult Fiction." *Booklist* 28 (15 Apr. 1986): 1181.

Reed, Ishmael. "Some Questions and Answers on Biraciality." *Black Renaissance/Renaissance Noire* 2 (Fall/Winter 1998): 74–75.

"Reviews." *Library Journal* 87 (1 June 1962): 2157.

"Reviews." *Library Journal* 93 (1 Oct. 1968): 3585–86.

Robinson, Cedric. *Black Marxism: The Making of the Black Radical Tradition.* London: Zed, 1983.

Rogers, W. G. "Good New Reading for Summer." *New York Herald Tribune Book Review* 17 June 1962: 4.

Rosaldo, Renato. *Culture and Truth: The Remaking of Social Analysis.* Boston: Beacon, 1989.

———. Foreword. *Hybrid Cultures: Strategies for Entering and Leaving Modernity.* By Nestor Garcia Canclini. Trans. Christopher L. Chiappari and Silvia L. Lopez. Minneapolis: U of Minnesota P, 1995: xi–xvii.

Russo, Mary. *the female grotesque: risk, excess, and modernity.* New York: Routledge, 1994.

Said, Edward. *Culture and Imperialism.* London: Routledge, 1994.

———. *Representations of the Intellectual.* New York: Random House, 1994.

Sartre, Jean-Paul. "Existentialism Is a Humanism." *Existentialism from Dostoevsky to Sartre.* Ed. Walter Kaufman. New York: New American Library, 1956. 345–69.

———. *Nausea.* New York: New Directions, 1964.

———. "Self Deception." *Existentialism from Dostoevsky to Sartre.* Ed. Walter Kaufman. New York: New American Library, 1956. 299–328.

Schaufragel, Noel. *The Black American Novel: From Apology to Protest.* Deland, FL: Everett/Edwards, 1973.

Sedgwick, Eve. *Between Men: English Literature and Male Homosexual Desire.* New York: Columbia UP, 1985.

Seidman, Steven. "Deconstructing Queer Theory or the Under-theorization of the Social and the Ethical." *Social Postmodernism: Beyond Identity Politics.* Ed. Linda Nicholson and Steven Seidman. New York: Cambridge UP, 1995. 116–41.

Sellers, Susan, ed. *The Hélène Cixous Reader.* New York: Routledge, 1994.

Shohat, Ella, and Robert Stam. *Unthinking Eurocentrism: Multiculturalism and the Media.* London: Routledge, 1994.

Simmons, Ron and Marlon Riggs. "Sexuality, Television, and Death: A Black Gay Dialogue on Malcom X." *Malcom X: In Our Own Image.* Ed. Joe Wood. New York: St. Martin's, 1992.

Simpson, Mark. *Male Impersonator: Men Performing Masculinity.* London: Routledge, 1994.

Skerrett, Joseph. "Irony and Symbolic Action in James Weldon Johnson's *The Autobiography of an Ex-Coloured Man.*" *American Quarterly* 32 (1980): 540–58.

Smith, Barbara. *The Truth That Never Hurts: Writing on Race, Gender, and Freedom.* New Brunswick, NJ: Rutgers UP, 1998.

Smith, Barbara Herrnstein. *Contingencies of Value: Alternative Perspective for Critical Theory.* Cambridge: Harvard UP, 1988.

Smith, Charles Michael. "Bruce Nugent: Bohemian of the Harlem Renaissance." *In the Life: A Black Gay Anthology.* Ed. Joseph Beam. Boston: Alyson, 1986. 209–20.

Smith, Valerie. *Self-Discovery and Authority in Afro-American Narrative.* Cambridge: Harvard UP, 1987.

Spencer, Jon Michael. *Blues and Evil.* Knoxville: U of Tennessee P, 1993.

Spivak, Gayatri Chakrovorty. "Can the Subaltern Speak?" *Marxism and the Interpretation of Culture.* Ed. Cary Nelson and Lawrence Grossberg. Urbana: U of Illinois P, 1988. 271–313.

Stallybrass, Peter, and Allon White. *The Politics and Poetics of Transgression.* Ithaca: Cornell UP, 1986.

Stepto, Robert. *From Behind the Veil: A Study of Afro-American Narrative*. Urbana: U of Illinois P, 1979.

Tatchell, Peter. "It's Just a Phase: Why Homosexuality Is Doomed." *Anti-Gay*. Ed. Mark Simpson. New York: Freedom Editions, 1996. 35–54.

Tate, Claudia. "All the Preacher's Women." *The New York Times Book Review* 41 (17 Aug. 1986): 24.

————. *Psychoanalysis and Black Novels: Desire and the Protocols of Race*. New York: Oxford UP, 1998.

Thoreau, Henry David. *Walden and Civil Disobedience*. New York: Penguin, 1986.

Todorov, Tzvetan. *The Conquest of America: The Question of the Other*. Trans. Richard Howard. New York: HarperPerennial, 1984.

Togliatti, Palmiro. *On Gramsci and Other Writings*. London: Lawrence and Wishart, 1979.

Travis, Gregory Eugene. "The B–Boy Blues of Novelist James Earl Hardy." *SBC* 5 (Nov. 1996): 8–10.

Van Vechten, Carl. Introduction. *The Autobiography of an Ex-Coloured Man*. By James Weldon Johnson. 1927. New York: Vintage, 1989. xxxiii–xxxviii.

Walton, Ortiz M. *Music: Black, White, and Blue: A Sociological Survey of the Use and Misuse of Afro-American Music*. New York: Morrow, 1972.

Washington, Booker T. *Up from Slavery*. 1901. Rpt. in *Three Negro Classics*. New York: Avon, 1965.

Washington, Mary Helen, ed. *Black-Eyed Susans: Classic Stories By and About Black Women*. Garden City, NY: Anchor/Doubleday, 1975.

————. *Invented Lives: Narratives of Black Women 1890–1960*. Garden City, NY: Anchor/Doubleday, 1987.

Weyl, Donald M. "The Vision of Man in the Novels of William Melvin Kelley." *Critique* 15 (1975): 15–33.

White, Hayden. *Metahistory: The Historical Imagination in Nineteenth Century Europe*. Baltimore: Johns Hopkins UP, 1973.

Williams, Juan. *Eyes on the Prize: America's Civil Rights Years 1954–1965*. New York: Viking, 1987.

Williams, Raymond. *Marxism and Literature*. Oxford: Oxford UP, 1977.

Williams, Sherley Anne. *Give Birth to Brightness: A Thematic Study in Neo-Black Literature*. New York: Dial, 1972.

Willis, Ellen. "The Up and Up: On the Limits of Optimism." *Transition* 7 (1998): 44–61.

Wilson, William Julius. *The Truly Disadvantaged: The Inner City, the Underclass, and Public Policy*. Chicago: U of Chicago P, 1987.

Wolff, Geoffrey A. "After Their Fire, The Half-Baked." *New York Herald Tribune* 27 Mar. 1966: 3.

Wright, Charles. *Absolutely Nothing to Get Alarmed About: The Complete Novels of Charles Wright*. New York: HarperCollins, 1993.

Yarborough, Richard. "Race, Violence, and Manhood: The Masculine Ideal in Frederick Douglass's 'The Heroic Slave.'" *Frederick Douglass: New Literary and Historical Essays*. Ed. Eric Sundquist. New York: Cambridge UP, 1990. 166–88.

Žižek, Slavoj. *The Metastases of Enjoyment: Six Essays on Woman and Causality*. New York: Verso, 1994.

INDEX